IEW AND CONCISE HISTORY

ROCK AND R&B

ROUGH THE EARLY 1990s

A NEW AND CONCISE HISTORY OF ROCK AND R&B THROUGH THE EARLY 1990S

ERIC CHARRY

Wesleyan University Press   Middletown, Connecticut

Wesleyan University Press

Middletown, CT 06459

www.wesleyan.edu/wespress

© 2020 Eric Charry

All rights reserved

Manufactured in the United States of America

Designed by Mindy Basinger Hill

Typeset in 11/15pt Garamond Premier Pro

Library of Congress Cataloging-in-Publication Data

Names: Charry, Eric S., author.

Title: A new and concise history of rock and R&B through the early 1990s / Eric Charry.

Description: [First.] | Middletown : Wesleyan University Press, 2020. | Includes bibliographical references and index. | Summary: "This book about rock and R&B lays out key theoretical issues, covers the technical foundations of the music industry, and provides a capsule history of who did what when, with particular emphasis on the rapid emergence of distinct genres"— Provided by publisher.

Identifiers: LCCN 2019053822 (print) | LCCN 2019053823 (ebook) | ISBN 9780819578952 (trade paperback) | ISBN 9780819578969 (ebook)

Subjects: LCSH: Rock music—History and criticism. | Rhythm and blues music—History and criticism.

Classification: LCC ML3534 .C454 2020 (print) | LCC ML3534 (ebook) | DDC 781.6409—dc23

LC record available at https://lccn.loc.gov/2019053822

LC ebook record available at https://lccn.loc.gov/2019053823

5 4 3 2 1

I thank all the students who passed through my course MUSC 108 (History of Rock and R&B) at Wesleyan University, especially those who raised questions or were not shy about pointing out rookie errors. Their many hundreds of creative class projects (audio and video recordings and magazine articles) provided myself, themselves, and their peers I'm sure, with great entertainment and insight, with some song cover versions and rewrites surpassing the originals. Adult students in Wesleyan's Graduate Liberal Studies Program and at the Cheshire Correctional Institution also provided valuable feedback on versions of this manuscript. The latter students were especially open about questioning what they read, and I thank them for their candor and directness. I thank John Bergeron, Noah Baerman, and my teaching assistants for their help with MUSC 108.

My colleagues in the Music Department at Wesleyan University have provided a warm and inspiring environment, which has contributed greatly to my thinking about music. I thank Priya Charry for formatting all the figures; Suzanna Tamminen, director of Wesleyan University Press, for seeing this project through to completion; and the two anonymous peer reviewers, whose critical comments were invaluable in formulating revisions. I thank Dan for our many-decades-long conversation about the music covered here and, as always, Hannah, Priya, and Miriam for their support and for just being there.

This book offers a concise history of rock and R&B (rhythm and blues) through the early 1990s in three parts. Part 1 begins with a history of the music industry and then provides a capsule history of who did what when, with particular emphasis on the emergence of recognizable genres within relatively compact time spans. Part 2 contains the sixty-four figures that are referenced in part 1. They can be read on their own, as they tell a unique kind of story in a novel way. The focus in these two parts is a history illustrated with information-rich visually transparent figures. Part 3 explores key contemporary theoretical issues, with concrete examples that provide frames of reference for processing and interpreting the material in the first two parts. Throughout, I draw extensively on primary sources—the voices of musicians, writers, and consumers (using chart data) at the time.

This particular combination of approaches and methods offers a new perspective, and herein lies the uniqueness of this text. The sixty-four figures each tell a story, and the accompanying writing fleshes them out. The figures are intended to guide readers through a diverse, unwieldy, and seemingly anarchic field of musical expression. A crucial point to ponder with most of the figures is why these elements are put together on a single page. In other words, what do the artists, groups, genres, songs, albums, or record labels have in common? This gets to the heart of how a genre or style congeals.

With the increasing availability of quality online content, readers should be well prepared to move deeper into the stories; understand historical flows and ruptures; recognize innovations, overarching trends, and genre formations; critically evaluate an artist's or group's place within a genre; critique my own selection process; and, most important, listen. Most sections contain footnotes with specialized lists of additional print, film, and video resources.

A New and Concise History stops in the early 1990s for several reasons. It developed out of notes for an undergraduate course I have been teaching annually since 2002, and so it is keyed to what can reasonably be packed into a single college semester. As a text for a one-semester course, it already contains a dense amount of material for a sustained, intensive, and holistic experience. Those finishing this book should be well prepared to explore on their own more recent music, the reception and perception of which is in a greater state of flux. Furthermore, those born in the 1990s and later may have a more intimate and visceral relationship to music of the past several decades. Putting that music under a micro- (and macro-) scope, with a veneer of academic objectivity, runs a risk of diminishing returns. The historical distance with the subject matter in the following pages may help readers embrace a greater breadth of perspective on more recent music.

Throughout this book I adopt the spirit in which twenty-two-year-old Muhammad Ali referred to singer Sam Cooke as he made his way into the ring to congratulate Ali the night he won the world heavyweight boxing championship in February 1964. Cooke had been a star of the gospel music world before crossing over to the secular world of R&B, pop, and soul, a style that he personified—the previous year Cooke released an album titled *Mr. Soul*. Amid the celebration and a television interview, Ali called out, "This is Sam Cooke! Let Sam in. This is the world's greatest rock 'n' roll singer" (qtd. in Guralnick 2005: 558–59).[1] I often use the terms *rock and roll* and *rock* as shorthand to cover the fullest conglomeration of many loosely connected genres and subgenres. A narrower usage of the term *rock* in the popular press can refer to an aesthetic tied to the 1960s and 1970s, exemplified in a predominantly white, guitar, bass, and drums format.

Some prefatory notes will help the reader more quickly grasp the information presented. All song titles are in quotations marks; album titles are in italics. I often refer to *Billboard* magazine popularity chart positions (sales, radio airplay), and so it is crucial to understand their significance. Popularity does *not* necessarily equate with artistic merit. High chart positions primarily indicate that an artist or group is being widely heard (in homes on record, cassette, or CD players and on the radio) and most likely appreciated. (There is a valid argument that record labels and radio stations can collude, and have done so, to successfully push undeserving artists.) When the month and year of a record (and sometimes full date) is provided, it refers to its initial entry into a chart (unless otherwise noted). This marks its entry into the public consciousness, which could be right after its release or many months later. In cases where a record appeared in several charts with different entry dates, I occasionally opt (in the disco and electronic dance music sections) to indicate the month of entering the first chart and list the charts by chronological date of entry (e.g., entered charts October 1974: dance #1, pop #9, R&B #34). This enables the crossover path to be seen without too much clutter.

For the figures with timelines, the left-most horizontal alignment of the name of an artist, song, album, or record label marks the specific year or month. For artists

1 The full moment occasionally appears (and disappears) on YouTube.

the month indicates when they initially entered the charts, except for figures 19, 20, 29, 30, 32, and 58, which indicate the initial break into the Top 40 slots.

In the References section, I provide primary-source print citations for most magazine and newspaper articles to give readers a clearer sense of the historical context; many of these can be found online (e.g., those in *Billboard, New Yorker, Rolling Stone,* and *Village Voice*). For articles from less accessible magazines that have been reprinted on the subscription website Rock's Backpages (2019), I also provide that indication (as RBP). Citations can be found in one of three places: bibliography (print, online articles and websites, radio programs); discography (limited to certain vinyl or CD recordings) if -d is appended to the date (e.g., 1960-d); or the filmography/videography (documentaries, feature films, YouTube clips) if -v is appended to the date (e.g., 1960-v). I occasionally opt to bypass academic-style conventions in the interest of consistency and clarity, as in omitting hyphens when genre names are used as adjectives, such as "rock and roll era."

Given the expansiveness of the references (over 750 items) and the more than 1,000 songs, albums, and artists mentioned in the text and figures, one might note some irony in the use of *concise* in the book title. Think of each of the three parts as separate, somewhat independent, very different—and concise—takes on the same topic. They could be read in any order, even jumping around among them. I hope I have struck an appropriate balance with the stories they tell.[2]

---

2 Supplemental materials, including a historical timeline, playlists, and time stamps for the audio and video sources, are available on the book's website, www.wesleyan.edu/wespress/readers companions.

Rock and R&B are thoroughly enmeshed in a legal, economic, media, and technological network that is called the music industry. How did rock, or any kind of music for that matter, get commodified in the form of a sound recording and distributed in the first place? What legal and economic mechanisms were put in place so that musical artists would be able to reap the benefits of their creations—their intellectual property—and thereby devote their lives to making music? How did technological developments in sound recording and storage media transform the production, distribution, and consumption of rock? What role did radio, television, and print media have in the explosion and sustained presence of rock, making it an essential part of U.S. culture? And how were technological advances in musical instruments, including synthesizers and samplers, catalysts for new musical sounds, ideas, and styles? We will explore the answers to these questions and more in this chapter.

COPYRIGHT

The foundation of the U.S. music industry is based in copyright law, which gives the exclusive right to the composer and recording artist to reproduce and sell music; they may then assign that right to a publisher or record label in return for payment called royalties. Every sound recording has two sets of rights associated with it: (1) the musical composition (the abstract melody, chords, and lyrics) and (2) the recorded performance, that is, the sound captured in a vinyl single or album, cassette, compact disc, or other digital format (see figures 1 and 2).

If the Beatles record the Chuck Berry composition "Roll over Beethoven," then Chuck Berry should receive a royalty payment for each copy of the Beatles record that is sold (two cents until 1978; 9.1 cents in 2019). Berry, the composer, would typically split his royalty payment with his publishing company, the organization that registers his composition with the U.S. Copyright Office and looks after collecting the royalties. The Beatles version is called a *cover*. Chuck Berry does not have to give his permission—the Beatles can use a "compulsory license," which still requires that Berry receive royalty payments (called mechanical royalties).

If Jay-Z records his composition "Can I Live," consisting of him rapping over short looped excerpts (called samples) of Isaac Hayes's recording of "The Look of Love," then Jay-Z must get permission from Hayes (or more probably his record label) and negotiate payment, either a flat fee or a royalty per record sold. Hayes (or his label) has the right to refuse. (The owners of the rights to Beatles recordings—Sony/ATV, eventually reverting to Paul McCartney—do not allow samples.) Additionally, because Isaac Hayes's recording was a cover version of a composition by Burt Bacharach (composer) and Hal David (lyricist), Jay-Z must also share composer credits and royalties with them.

Bacharach and David registered "The Look of Love" with ASCAP (American Society of Composers, Authors and Publishers), one of the two major music performance rights organizations (the other is BMI [Broadcast Music, Inc.]), which licenses compositions for public performance, which is protected by copyright law. These performance rights organizations collect fees when works by their composers are played on the radio and TV, or at bars and other live music venues, and they distribute those fees as royalties to their artists. ASCAP lists four writers for "Can I Live" who would capture those royalties: Jay-Z (Shawn Carter); his producer, Irv Gotti (Irving Lorenzo); Burt Bacharach; and Hal David. ASCAP also lists three publishing companies, meaning that the various writers registered their songs ("The Look of Love" and "Can I Live") with different publishers to look after the benefits of copyright.[1] Separate from composer's royalties, record labels negotiate with their recording artists for the royalty percentage that they will earn as performers per recording sold, and they also control permissions to sample the recordings of their artists.

A musical arrangement—the style in which an abstract composition is rendered in performance by instrumentalists and vocalists—is not copyrightable. A federal court decision in May 1950 set the precedent for the rock and roll era, ruling that Evelyn Knight's nearly identical cover version of "A Little Bird Told Me" (on Decca Records) did not violate the copyright of the original version recorded by Paula Watson (on Supreme Records). The composer Harvey Brooks received the usual royalties from the cover version, but nothing else was due to him or anyone else involved in the original recording, including vocalist Watson, the arranger, or Supreme Records (*Billboard* 1950).

There is an important distinction between musicians reproducing or imitating a musical arrangement (or vocal style), on the one hand, and sampling a recording, on the other hand. (The original reference is to a process of digitally sampling an analog electronic signal.) The former (reproducing), as in the guitar introduction on the Beach Boys' "Fun, Fun, Fun," which was a close reproduction of Chuck Berry's introduction on "Johnny B. Goode," did not require permission or royalty payment; Berry's solo would be considered as part of the arrangement and not the composition. If reproducing a guitar solo were a matter of copyright, then Berry would in turn

---

1   Both ASCAP (2019) and BMI (2019) have online searchable databases.

owe something to Louis Jordan's guitarist Carl Hogan, whom Berry has credited as his influence (e.g., the introduction to Jordan's "Ain't That Just Like a Woman"). Sampling, on the other hand, requires explicit permission from the copyright holder of the recorded performance and negotiated payment.

Because composers (and their publishers) control the right to broadcast and publicly perform their music, and because they do not have the time or means to monitor such usage themselves, they register their compositions with ASCAP (formed in 1914) or BMI (formed in 1939). Typically, ASCAP and BMI would offer blanket licenses to the various businesses (radio stations, concert venues) so that the outlet would pay a single fee for the right to play music by any composer registered with ASCAP or BMI. Based on radio playlists and concert lists, ASCAP and BMI would distribute parts of their licensing fees to the various artist copyright holders.

Article 1, section 8, clause 8, of the U.S. Constitution (1789) gives Congress the power "to promote the progress of science and useful arts, by securing for limited times to authors and inventors the exclusive right to their respective writings and discoveries." The Copyright Act of 1790 was the first law of its kind enacted in the United States, granting protection to authors of books, maps, and charts for fourteen years, with the possibility of renewal for another fourteen years. The act has gone through many revisions to keep up with the times. The first general revision (1831) added printed sheet music and extended the protection period to twenty-eight years. The second general revision (1870) added artworks and centralized registration at the Library of Congress. Composers gained limited protection for the public performance of their music (primarily in music theater) in 1897. The third general revision (1909) extended the renewal period to twenty-eight years and added two provisions that would have a major impact on the industry: public performance for profit, which would become a major source of income for composers of copyrighted music; and compulsory licensing, which allowed anyone to make a new recording of a copyrighted composition (at two-cents royalty per item sold). Up until 1972 musical works had to be registered in the form of printed sheet music. In 1972 sound recordings became eligible for submission.[2]

See figure 1. Copyright in the United States
See figure 2. Copyright timeline

---

2 For more on copyright, see U.S. Copyright Office (2015, 2019a, 2019b, 2019c); for an in-depth history of U.S. copyright law and its implications see Vaidhyanathan (2001).

THE RECORDING INDUSTRY

All sound-recording devices are based on the principle of capturing sound waves. In the acoustic era (until 1925), sound traveled into the wide end of a horn and set a stretched membrane at the narrow end of the horn into motion, transmitting the vibrations to a small needle (called stylus) attached to it, which drew traces into a malleable form (at first tin foil, then wax coating on a cylinder or disc) in concentric circles. This is analog recording: a continuous direct trace of the sound waves. For playback the captured traces were tracked by the needle, which set the membrane in motion, which in turn sent out sound waves through the wide end of the horn. Initially, cylinders, and then discs (in the 1890s), were the storage media sold by record companies, which also sold the machines to play them back.

Before sound recording, music was sold as a material commodity in the form of sheet music (containing music notation and lyrics).[3] Consumers would purchase and play the music on their pianos at home, singing along. In the mid-nineteenth century hit songs by songwriter Stephen Foster were selling between 50,000 and 130,000 copies. By the late nineteenth century a hit could sell a million or more copies; Charles K. Harris's "After the Ball" (1892) sold over 5 million copies. Annual production of pianos and player pianos in the United States peaked in 1899 at 365,000 and averaged 300,000 per year in the first two decades of the twentieth century.[4]

The first device to record sound was a phonautograph, patented in France in 1857 by Édouard-Léon Scott de Martinville, which traced sound waves onto a sheet of paper blackened by soot (see figure 3). The traces were meant only to be seen and analyzed, as there was no means to play them back.[5] In 1877 Thomas Edison first demonstrated his phonograph, which recorded sound onto a rotating cylinder wrapped in tin foil, which could play back the sound. He received a patent the following year, and his investors formed the Edison Speaking Phonograph Company in 1878. The tin-foil recordings were not very durable, and the sound quality was poor, and so Edison

---

3 The standard text on the history of the music industry is Sanjek (1988, 1996), from which I draw extensively here.

4 Player pianos (or pianolas), dating to the 1870s, were automatically played when air pumped through perforations in a scrolling roll of paper caused piano keys to strike the strings. Coin-operated player pianos were introduced by the Wurlitzer Company in 1898. Figures cited are from Sanjek (1988, 2: 77, 296, 321–22).

5 Recently, computer analysis has allowed those traces to be heard (First Sounds 2008).

moved on to the incandescent bulb. In 1887 Charles Tainter and Chichester Bell (Alexander's cousin) demonstrated their graphophone (reversing *phon-o-graph*), which used more durable wax-coated cylinders, and the American Graphophone Company was formed. Edison responded and released his new gramophone later that year, and the Edison Phonograph Company was formed. Businessman Jesse Lippincott purchased interests in Edison's two phonograph companies and American Graphophone and formed the North American Phonograph Company to corner the market. Lippincott leased rights to sell the machines, and the Delaware, Maryland, and DC franchise would eventually become the first of the major record labels that we know today: Columbia Phonograph Company.

In 1889 recorded cylinders were used in coin-operated phonographs (activated for a nickel), the precursors to jukeboxes. By 1892 a downsized U.S. Marine Band had recorded over a hundred selections for Columbia, sold for two dollars a cylinder (prices would drop over the decade). The cylinder shape prohibited them from being mass produced, and so artists typically recorded in front of five to ten machines, each recording one cylinder. Additional machines could be connected to each of the master machines, and so a single two-minute recording session could yield up to fifty copies. Artists would have to perform the piece over and over again to produce more copies.

Emile Berliner's gramophone (patented in 1887) used a flat disc, which solved the problem of mass production. The wax master disc recording was electroplated and could then stamp out rubber (and later shellac) copies. In 1894 Berliner opened a factory in Baltimore and sold a thousand machines and twenty-five thousand records. With the help of inventor Eldridge Reeve Johnson, who developed an improved stable motor, the gramophone successfully competed with Edison's phonograph, and in 1901 Berliner and Johnson formed the Victor Talking Machine Company, the second of the major record labels that is still around (later RCA Victor, now RCA). In the first decade of the twentieth century, three major record companies dominated: Edison (cylinders), Victor (discs), and Columbia (cylinders and discs). Annual production of recordings increased tenfold: from 2.75 million in 1899 to 27.5 million in 1909. Cylinders outsold discs at the beginning of the decade by two to one; by 1914 discs outsold cylinders by nine to one.[6]

---

6   For more on the inventions of Edison and Berliner, see Library of Congress (2019a, 2019b) and UCSB Cylinder Archive (2019).

In 1902 Victor made a portable recording machine, allowing them to record music around the world. That year Enrico Caruso, star of Milan's opera house La Scala, made his debut recordings, the popularity of which prompted his move in 1903 to join the Metropolitan Opera Company in New York. Contracted to record exclusively with Victor from 1904 to 1920, he was initially paid $4,000 for the first ten sides and a royalty of forty cents for every disc sold. Caruso made over 250 recordings with Victor, earning several million dollars from them, making him one of the first international stars of the early recording industry. In 1903 the first royalty payments for performers were negotiated in a contract with Italian tenor Francesco Tamagno, at 20 percent of the retail price of each disc sold.

Until 1908 discs were recorded on just one side. Annual retail record sales peaked at $106.5 million in 1921. Retail record sales then dropped dramatically (in part because of the rise of commercial radio broadcasting in 1922); they began to recover after the advent of electrical recording (1926–29) and then sank to a low during the Depression of $6 million in 1933. Sales would not recover to its 1921 high until 1947 (Sanjek 1996: 62, 117, 120).

In the 1920s record companies discovered latent markets, including southern whites and African Americans, labeling the categories hillbilly (or folk) and race. The hillbilly market was later renamed country and western (or just country). The race category, which included spirituals, gospel, blues, and sermons, underwent many name changes: rhythm and blues (late 1940s), soul (1960s), black music (1960s–70s), and finally R&B. At first, race records were not impacted by declining sales in the 1920s: new releases went from about fifty (1922) to a high of five hundred (1929), at which point the bottom dropped out as the Depression kicked in (Dixon and Godrich 1970: 104–5). The new hillbilly category of records initially survived, on the back of Jimmie Rodgers, who was signed to Victor in 1927 and was tallying 350,000 copies sold for new releases between 1928 and 1930, but they eventually succumbed too.

The age of electrical recording began in 1925, using a microphone, vacuum tube amplifier, and electromagnetic recording and playback head and stylus. The recording studio then split into two distinct spaces: the studio itself, where the sounds of the musicians were picked up on microphones; and the control room, where the engineers ran the recording equipment that etched the electrical signals onto a master disc (later magnetic tape).[7] Victor's Orthophonic Victrola (1925) was the first

---

7   Zak (2001) and Horning (2013) offer rich explorations into the world of recording studios.

commercial phonograph to take advantage of the expanded fidelity. The difference between acoustic and electrical recording can be heard by comparing Bessie Smith's approximately seventy acoustic recordings made for Columbia between 1923 and January 1925 (e.g., "St. Louis Blues," recorded January 1925) with her first electrical recordings, which began in May 1925: "Cake Walking Babies" and "The Yellow Dog Blues" (B. Smith 1991-d).[8]

In 1929 Radio Corporation of America (RCA) purchased Victor, and Edison stopped manufacturing phonographs and recordings. Coin-operated jukeboxes expanded in the 1930s, reaching 150,000 by 1936, accounting for 40 percent of record sales. After World War II retail record sales surpassed the 1921 high, reaching $224 million in 1947. Independent record labels began expanding, breaking even with a record selling 10,000 copies, helped along with jukeboxes. Hit records in the R&B market in the early 1950s typically sold more than 150,000 copies. The new vinyl record technology gave a boost to sales in the early 1950s, and then sales exploded with the advent of rock and roll: from $277 million (1955) to $600 million (1960). The industry hit its high in retail sales of recordings in 1999 at $14.58 billion and then drastically declined because of internet file sharing to $8.48 billion by 2008.[9]

The Recording Industry Association of America (RIAA) was formed in 1951 to look after the interests of the record manufacturers. At the time about eight hundred record labels were officially registered, with fewer than forty-five of them doing annual business of more than $20,000. In 1958 the RIAA began certifying gold records (one million singles sold or one million dollars in wholesale album sales); in 1975 half a million albums sold earned a gold record and in 1976 platinum was introduced at one million for albums. In 1989 the new gold benchmark for singles was lowered to half a million copies sold (A. White 1990: viii, 3–4).

Recording-artist guarantees hit a turning point in 1967, after the Beatles renegotiated their contract with EMI. Some San Francisco bands, coming off of Monterey Pop Festival, got $250,000 to sign with a record label. A new high was set by Elton John when he renewed his contract with MCA in the 1970s, guaranteeing him over $8 million for six albums over a five-year period, including a $1.40 royalty on albums (selling for $6.98). The industry was expanding, reaching $2.2 billion in retail sales

---

8 Digital enhancement of the acoustic recordings may downplay the contrast.
9 Figures for 1947 and 1955–60 are from Gillett (1996: 492) and those from 1999 to 2008 are from Hutchinson, Macy, and Allen (2010: 43). Sanjek (1996: 285, 333) gives both $214.4 and $204 million for 1947.

in 1974. After receiving nine Grammy Awards and his six most recent albums selling over five hundred thousand copies each, Stevie Wonder received a seven-year contract from Motown worth $14 million, the highest up to that point, beginning with *Songs in the Key of Life* in 1976 (Sanjek 1996: 536–39).

The three earliest record companies, Edison, Columbia, and Victor, set the model for major labels, so-called because of their economic power and national distribution networks. Since the 1930s there have typically been four to six major record labels at any one point. Many smaller local independent record labels filled the voids, sometimes acting as farm teams, only to see their artists picked up by a major.[10]

───────

See figure 3. Growth of the recording industry in the United States to the 1930s

RADIO AND TELEVISION

The sudden explosion of nationally broadcast radio beginning in 1922 would have a major impact on the music industry and how people consume music. Musicians' unions, composers' rights organizations, record companies, and radio broadcasters were at odds with one another for decades, trying to figure out how to compensate artists from this new medium.

Radio transmission dates to Guglielmo Marconi transmitting Morse code signals several miles through the air via electromagnetic (radio) waves in 1896, building on Heinrich Hertz's earlier experiments (see figure 4).[11] In 1899 Marconi demonstrated his invention in the United States and established the Marconi Wireless Telegraph Company of America. By 1907 Lee De Forest, who was patenting versions of his audion, a vacuum tube that could amplify an electrical signal (a crucial step in radio broadcasting), was transmitting sound (music recordings) from the top floor of a building in New York City, and in 1910 a live broadcast of Caruso from the Metro-

───────

10 See the recent nine-part BBC radio series (Mason 2019) for an expansive history of the music industry and technology. For online histories of recording technology, see Beardsley and Leech-Wilkinson (2009) and Schoenherr (2005). For an online narrative of the record industry, see Medium (2014). For diverse studies of the music and recording industry, see Chapple and Garofalo (1977), Denisoff (1986), Goodman (1997), and Katz (2010).

11 The standard text on the history of broadcast radio is Barnouw (1966–70), from which I draw extensively here. More recent interpretive work includes Douglas (1987, 1999) and Smulyan (1994). Barnouw (1975) covers the history of television broadcasting.

politan Opera House, using the new microphone technology, was locally transmitted. Telephones, connected by wire, were in use since 1876; the ability to transmit sound without wires was revolutionary. After the government passed its first licensing law in 1912, the number of licensed amateur radio operators jumped from 322 in 1913 to over 10,000 in 1916. By 1916 American Telephone and Telegraph (AT&T) bought out De Forest's patents and began to move into radio.

The Radio Corporation of America (RCA) was formed in 1919, taking hold of American Marconi's assets and operations. The following year General Electric (GE) and RCA pooled their patents with AT&T and its subsidiary Western Electric. The November 1920 Westinghouse Corporation broadcast of returns of the presidential election from their newly licensed station KDKA at their Pittsburgh plant was a milestone. They soon made daily broadcasts and began selling home receivers to a curious public. Westinghouse joined GE, RCA, and AT&T in 1921, pooling about two thousand patents and controlling the radio industry in a monopoly. GE and Westinghouse would manufacture receivers and parts, RCA would market them under their trademark, and AT&T would sell the transmitters and control telephone service. Each of these corporations would soon begin operating their own radio stations.

Smulyan (1994: 1) opens her book on commercial radio broadcasting as follows: "When the first radio station began in 1920, no one knew how to make money from broadcasting." That would change in 1921, when the U.S. Department of Commerce began issuing licenses in a new class of station, called broadcasting, to twenty-eight stations that year. In the initial boom year of 1922, over five hundred new broadcasting stations were licensed. Sales of radio sets and parts went from $60 million in 1922 to $640 in 1928.

In 1922 ASCAP began a fight with broadcasters to be paid royalties, in the form of an annual licensing fee, for the public performance (radio broadcast) of music composed by its members. Fees were negotiated station by station, ranging from a few hundred dollars up to $5,000 within several years. The radio boom had a devastating impact on the sales of recordings, excepting race records—African Americans had not abandoned records to purchase radio sets for programming that was excluding black musical genres (Smulyan 1994: 25). The sales of Bessie Smith's blues records may have kept Columbia Records in business at this time (Barnouw 1966: 129).

Stations in the South and Midwest offered country music programs, including WSB in Atlanta in 1922, WLS in Chicago in 1924 (National Barn Dance), and WSM in Nashville in 1925 (which would become the Grand Ole Opry). National networks date to 1926, when AT&T left the broadcasting business and sold its New York station WEAF to RCA, which formed its subsidiary National Broadcasting Company (NBC) to operate the growing web of independent stations. At that point about five million homes in the United States had radios. By 1927 RCA had two networks: Red (WEAF) and Blue (WJZ, which became WABC).

Network radio and then television would provide a new model for the dispersion of U.S. culture. Music of a single artist or group could be instantly disseminated across the nation for the first time. President Franklin D. Roosevelt took advantage of the new medium with his first "fireside chats" in 1933, the intimacy of which helped push through his New Deal agenda.

The Radio Act of 1927 established the Federal Radio Commission, which would become the Federal Communications Commission (FCC) in 1934. All radio licenses were to be voided, impacting the 732 stations broadcasting at the time (including about 90 operated by educational institutions), and new applications would provide a fresh start. In 1927 six hundred sponsors had supported the programming of a quarter of the NBC network's hours, providing revenue to support noncommercial programming such as religious programs, talks, classical music concerts, and music-appreciation broadcasts.

United Independent Broadcasters was formed in 1927, which that year joined with Columbia Phonograph Record Company to form the Columbia Phonograph Broadcasting System, the birth of the second national network. CPRC soon pulled out, and their name was shortened to Columbia Broadcasting System (CBS) in 1928. In the late 1930s a major dispute between ASCAP, which was planning to significantly raise the rates of their blanket licenses to radio stations, and the National Association of Broadcasters (NAB) led to the NAB founding the second performing rights organization, Broadcast Music, Inc. BMI attracted younger composers and especially those in nonmainstream styles not served by ASCAP.

As a result of an FCC monopoly probe, NBC's red and blue networks split in 1943, and so NBC sold its blue network to American Broadcasting System, soon to be renamed American Broadcasting Company (ABC). Three major radio networks were now in place: CBS, NBC, and ABC. All three began commercial broadcasting on television in the 1940s, and to this day they remain the three major television networks (joined by Fox as the fourth in the 1990s).

In 1946 RCA put its black-and-white television sets on the market. By 1954, 354 television stations were broadcasting to more than half of U.S. households (twenty-six million). Contrary to fears of television putting them out of business, AM radio stations went from 948 in 1946 to 2,824 in 1954 (Douglas 1999: 219, 223). Popular music got a major boost in 1948, when CBS launched *Toast of the Town*, hosted by Ed Sullivan, soon renamed the *Ed Sullivan Show*, the most important single venue for launching national music acts from the mid-1950s through the 1960s (see figure 5). *American Bandstand*, hosted by Dick Clark in Philadelphia, became the first major show exclusively devoted to teen music. In 1957 it went on the air for ninety minutes every day. Within two years it was being broadcast to 101 affiliates to an audience of twenty million. Television began to be broadcast in color in 1965. A series of short-lived shows in the 1960s featured musical performances, and in the 1980s new cable networks, such as MTV and VH1, came on the air to broadcast music full-time, aimed at teens.[12]

As television initially expanded, taking advertisers with them, radio began to specialize in response. The immediate post–World War II era saw the rise of the disc jockey, who introduced and played records on the air. Radio stations playing R&B and jazz significantly expanded during this time, catering to an African American audience unable to afford the new TV sets and finding little interest in white middle-class television programming (Smulyan 1994: 159).

FM radio, with a better overall sound quality than AM, took off in 1965, when the FCC required that all AM/FM stations in markets of more than a hundred thousand people broadcast different material at least half of their airtime; this impacted more than half of the almost thousand FM stations. Some AM stations devoted FM to noncommercial programming. Tom Donahue (1967), a disc jockey and program director in San Francisco, was a pioneer in playing a wide variety of music on his eight-to-midnight FM show, including longer cuts with less chatter. It became known as free form, underground, or progressive radio, an alternative to AM. By 1972 about 400 of the 2,700 FM stations on the air were programming this format (Sanjek 1996: 543).

In the mid-1960s African Americans, long excluded from starring roles in television (with few exceptions such at Nat King Cole), began starring in a limited number of ongoing TV network prime-time series (see figure 6). In the early 1970s a flurry of Hollywood films with predominantly black casts and directors appeared, with several of them featuring strong musical soundtracks, including *Shaft* (music by Isaac Hayes) and *Super Fly* (music by Curtis Mayfield). This coincided with the rise of the style

---

12 For information on Dick Clark and *American Bandstand*, see Jackson (1997); for MTV, see Tannenbaum and Marks (2012).

called funk. A similarly remarkable flurry occurred in the late 1980s and early 1990s, coinciding with increasing public attention to rap, this time including rap artists such as Ice Cube and Tupac Shakur as stars (see figure 42).

See figure 4. Growth of radio in the United States

See figure 5. Music on television, 1940s–1980s

See figure 6. African Americans in starring roles in television

See figure 42. Blaxploitation films and the next generation

MAGAZINES, CHARTS, AND INDUSTRY AWARDS

Billboard magazine has long been the standard weekly publication for news about the music industry. In the latter half of the 1960s, magazines devoted to rock began to be published, with journalists treating the music as a serious cultural phenomenon for the first time. The monthly *Rolling Stone* magazine, established in 1967 with a countercultural aura about it, is the longest-lasting magazine of this type (see figure 7).

Commercial success in the music industry can be measured by sales figures and popularity charts, although this should not be confused with artistic merit, which is a matter of subjective critical debate. Record sales figures are registered with the Recording Industry Association of America (RIAA), which certifies gold (half a million) and platinum (one million) awards.[13]

Popularity charts are published weekly by *Billboard* magazine, which is the standard measure for the industry (see figure 8). When new markets opened in the 1920s, record companies advertised and distributed them to specific demographics, and so the categories of hillbilly and race records were born. In the early twentieth century the term *race* had some positive connotations: "She was what is termed a 'race woman,' and desired to work for her own people" (Lilian Wald 1915, qtd. in *OED* 2019c). "A 'Race Man' was somebody who always kept the glory and honor of his race before him. . . . It was a mark of shame if somebody accused: 'Why you are not a Race Man (or woman).' . . . They were champions of the race" (Zore Neale Hurston 1942, qtd. in *OED* 2019c).[14] The category was definitively relabeled in 1949 as rhythm and blues (or R&B). Hillbilly, a pejorative term, was relabeled as country.

---

13 RIAA (2019a) has a searchable database for gold and platinum records.

14 The references are to Wald's *House on Henry Street* and Hurston's *Dust Tracks on the Road.*

In the 1950s separate charts tracked record sales, radio airplay, and jukebox plays. Since the 1960s sales figures and radio airplay were combined into a single chart. *Billboard* published separate charts for the three primary markets: pop; rhythm and blues; and country (or country and western, C&W). In recent decades many new markets have been added, including dance, Latin, world, and Christian/gospel. Popularity charts matter for several reasons. They are the clearest measure of the exposure that a record is receiving. Reaching the Top 40 indicates a significant degree of national airplay and sales and consequently public attention. The Top 10 in any chart signifies a more elite status of getting massive national exposure.

Two significant industry awards are decided by vote of industry personnel. The National Academy of Recording Arts and Sciences (NARAS) has offered Grammy (originally Gramophone) Awards in a wide assortment of categories since 1959 (see figure 9). The Rock and Roll Hall of Fame Foundation has inducted honorees since 1986, and a dedicated physical space, the Rock and Roll Hall of Fame, opened in 1995 in Cleveland, Ohio (home of disc jockey Alan Freed's radio show in the early 1950s).[15]

A series of reference books compiled by Joel Whitburn (1990–2013b) provides quick and easy access to an artist's or group's various *Billboard* chart rankings, with one series reproducing the actual Hot 100 singles charts. AllMusic (2019) lists Grammy Awards for artists, and Wikipedia typically includes artist discographies that provide *Billboard* chart rankings.

See figure 7. Magazines

See figure 8. Industry popularity charts (*Billboard*)

See figure 9. Grammy categories

TECHNOLOGY

Technological innovations have been a driving force in the music industry (e.g., recording devices and audio-storage formats) and in musical performance. New solid body electric guitars and basses, guitar amplifiers, keyboard synthesizers, drum machines, and samplers would all contribute to significant, sometimes revolutionary, musical change (see figure 10).

---

15 See Recording Academy (2019) for listings of Grammy Award winners and Rock and Roll Hall of Fame (2019) for inductees.

CP
bearing
Vinyl)

Commercial recording onto magnetic tape dates to 1948, when Ampex released its first model (200A), with the new medium improving audio fidelity and adding the ability to edit, erase, and reuse tape. By 1950 magnetic tape recording became the professional standard. In 1956 guitarist Les Paul began experimenting with an eight-track tape recorder, and in 1958 Atlantic Records engineer Tom Dowd was using an Ampex eight-track recorder. Multitrack recording enabled individual instruments or voices to have their own unique track of tape to be mixed with the other tracks down to two-track stereo in a separate mixing session. It also allowed some tracks to be recorded in one session and additional tracks to be added at later sessions (called overdubbing). This kind of flexibility opened up the recording studio to new creative possibilities. The industry in general did not move to eight-track recording until 1968 (Horning 2013: 174–80, 203).[16]

For decades the primary audio-storage format was a disc made of thick fragile shellac, ten inches in diameter, spinning at 78 rpm (revolutions per minute), and holding about three minutes of music. In 1948 Columbia introduced a ten-inch (soon to be twelve-inch) 33⅓ rpm long play (LP) record made of lightweight unbreakable vinyl, which could hold twenty-plus minutes of music. RCA responded in 1949 with its seven-inch 45 rpm single vinyl record holding three minutes. By 1952 their patents were pooled, and jazz and classical music drifted toward LPs and 45s became the format for pop. Stereo record releases date from the mid-1950s, and by 1961 seven million of the thirty million phonographs in U.S. homes could play stereo discs (Sanjek 1996: 363). Vinyl discs remained the standard until the 1970s, when prerecorded cassette tapes (introduced in the early 1960s) started gaining popularity. In 1983 cassette sales ($237 million) passed those of vinyl ($209 million), and digitally recorded compact discs (CD) hit the U.S. market. By 1988 CDs outsold vinyl and by 1992 outsold cassettes. Emotional attachment to the format that birthed and nurtured rock and roll kept vinyl alive (barely), and it has been making a comeback since the early 2000s, hitting its highest point since 1991 again in 2017 at 8.5 percent of all album sales (physical and downloads).[17]

The first electric guitars hit the market in the early 1930s. Gibson Guitar Corporation's ES (Electric Spanish) series debuted in 1936 with the ES-150, a favorite of

---

16 Mayfair Recording, the second New York studio (after Atlantic) to go eight-track (in 1965), was used by the Velvet Underground and Frank Zappa in 1966–67. Motown went eight-track in 1964.

17 Plasketes (1992: 117–18); Christman (1999, 2007); Caulfield (2018); RIAA (2019b). See also Osborne (2012).

Fleetr baby

jazz guitarist <u>Charlie Christian</u>. The ES series were hollow (later semihollow) body guitars, essentially acoustic jazz guitars with one or more electromagnetic pickups to amplify the strings. T-Bone Walker played an ES-250; B. B. King played a variety of ES models, eventually settling on the ES-335 (issued in 1958), the first semihollow body or thinline model; and Chuck Berry played an ES-350T and later 335.[18]

In the early 1950s a new type of electric guitar, with a completely solid body, came on the market, eliminating the resonance of the hollow sound box and amplifying the strings with pickups that had electromagnetic coils embedded in them (one for each string). The solid body allowed the instrument to be played at a louder volume with more even response and longer sustain. The early guitars became classics and have maintained their reputation to this day.

Leo Fender's company issued its first solid-body guitar, with a single pickup in 1950 (the Esquire), adding a second pickup in 1951, which came to be called the Telecaster.[19] In 1954 Fender released the three-pickup Stratocaster, with a different body design. The Telecaster had its proponents in country (Buck Owens), rockabilly (James Burton), and blues (Muddy Waters, Albert Collins).[20] The Stratocaster was a favorite in blues and rock, played by Buddy Holly, Buddy Guy, Dick Dale, and, most famously, Jimi Hendrix. The Fender Precision bass, issued in 1951 became the standard model for most bass players. Gibson introduced its first solid-body model in 1952, the Les Paul, which became a favorite of <u>Jimmy Page</u> and Duane Allman. Eric Clapton played a Les Paul in the mid-1960s and switched to a Stratocaster by the early 1970s. As a result of the rise of rock and roll, surf music (Dick Dale, the Beach Boys), and the Beatles, guitar sales jumped in the first half of the 1960s to 1.5 million in 1965. *Guitar Player* magazine began publishing two years later.[21]

Love

Fender led the pack in guitar amplifiers with its Twin model, issued in 1952, with twenty-five watts of power and two twelve-inch speakers. By 1963 it had developed

---

18 Berry's ES-350T from 1959 is on display at the National Museum of African American History and Culture. This section on electric guitars and amplifiers draws from Hunter (2005) and Tolinski and di Perna (2016).

19 The Telecaster was briefly called the Broadcaster, but they had to change the name, as Gretsch had their own Broadkaster.

20 Jeff Beck played an Esquire in the Yardbirds, and later a Les Paul on his solo debut LP *Truth* (1968).

21 A 1993 New York Apollo Theater all-star blues concert (B. B. King and others 1993-v) showcases three guitar models: Gibson ES-335 (B. B. King); Fender Stratocaster (Buddy Guy, Eric Clapton, and Jeff Beck); and Fender Telecaster (Albert Collins).

into the eighty-watt Twin Reverb model, which Hendrix had used before he left for England in 1966. The main competition was British Marshall amps, which debuted in 1962, developing into the hundred-watt Marshall Super Lead model 1959 in 1965. Marshall was marked by a separate amplifier head and cabinet holding four twelve-inch speakers, which could be stacked on top of one another to provide a massive wall of sound. Both Marshall and Fender amps rely on vacuum-tube amplification, which, when overdriven at full volume, create an electronic distortion that is one of the most prized and sought-after sounds. By placing the guitar's pickups close to the speakers, a feedback loop occurs and guitarists in the 1960s discovered how to sustain tones as long as they wanted. This power to control an electrified sound that at any moment could leap above the threshold of pain has given the electric guitar, and those who play it, a special status.

The first major commercial analog synthesizer, named after its inventor Robert Moog (pronounced *mohg*), hit the public consciousness in 1968 with keyboardist Wendy Carlos's *Switched on Bach*, an album of works by J. S. Bach played exclusively on the Moog.[22] Released on Columbia, it reached #10 on the pop album chart, an unlikely development for a classical or electronic album. Rock groups picked up on it right away, in the studio and in concert with the portable Minimoog (launched in 1969). The Beatles used the Moog on *Abbey Road* (1969), at the ends of "Because" and "Maxwell's Silver Hammer," and it became a staple of progressive rock bands, such as Emerson, Lake, and Palmer ("Lucky Man," 1970) and Yes ("Excerpts from 'The Six Wives of Henry VIII,'" 1973). Stevie Wonder embraced the new technology from his first album once he renegotiated his contract when he turned twenty-one ("Superwoman," "Evil," 1972).[23]

Analog synthesizers utilize voltage-controlled oscillators, filters, and amplifiers to create and shape waveforms based on the overtone series. At first they were monophonic, with the Moog and Arp 2600 (1971) dominating the field. Duophonic (two tones at a time) synthesizers soon came (Arp Odyssey, 1972) followed by polyphonic, which could play up to five tones (Prophet 5, 1978) or eight tones (Yamaha CS-80,

---

22 The following paragraphs on synthesizers and samplers draw from Pinch and Trocco (2002), Jenkins (2007), Russ (2008), Milner (2009: 308–46), Fintoni (2016), Twells (2016), S. Wilson (2016), and Linn (2019).

23 The iconic bass line to Michael Jackson's "Thriller" was played on two Minimoogs (*Keyboard* 2009: 25).

1976) at once. The Casio VL-1, a children's toy (at $70), was one of the first digital synthesizers to hit the market, in 1979. The Casiotone MT-40, released in 1981 (at $150) had a similar low-tech sound, although in 1985 it was used for Jamaican Wayne Smith's "Under Me Sleng Teng," moving Jamaican music from reggae to a new electronic dancehall era; its instrumental track was used in many subsequent recordings (called *versions* in Jamaica). ↓ Drum machine

The Roland TR-808 drum machine, which hit the market in 1980 (at $1,000), used synthesized drums sounds, which could be programmed in a sequence and endlessly looped. This led to revolutionary changes in the way in which music was conceived and produced (A. Dunn 2015-v). Early examples include Yellow Magic Orchestra's "1,000 Knives" (1981), Marvin Gaye's "Sexual Healing (1982), Afrika Bambaataa's "Planet Rock" (1982), Run-D.M.C.'s "It's Like That" (1983), and Cybotron's "Clear" (1983). Boss, a division of Roland, had come out with the DR-55 in 1979 (at $200), making it an easily affordable unit. Depeche Mode used the DR-55 in live performance.[24]

Professional quality digital synthesizers used frequency modulation (FM), in which a sound carrier (generally a sine wave, a pure tone with no overtones) is operated on by a modulator (another sine wave), creating a complex waveform, enlivening the sonic spectrum, which can change over time. Adding more carriers and modulators to the mix can create an extraordinary variety of sounds. The first digital FM synthesizer was the Synclavier, which went public in 1978 (at $13,000). Soft Cell's "Tainted Love" (1981) helped put the Synclavier onto the 1980s soundscape. Michael Jackson's "Beat It" (1982) opens with sounds created on the Synclavier II (released 1980). Prices soon dropped dramatically, and the Yamaha DX7 digital FM synthesizer released in 1983 (at $2,000) was widely embraced; its sound was pervasive in the 1980s (e.g., the bass line to Kenny Loggins's 1985 hit "Danger Zone," which also uses a LinnDrum).[25]

Whereas synthesizers create new sounds (whether by analog or digital means), samplers record existing sounds digitally (e.g., a snare drum hit, a one-bar drum pattern, a vocal grunt, a bird chirp), play them (or prerecorded presets) back using a keyboard or programming interface, and can loop the recorded sounds. Samplers were initially marketed either as drum machines or keyboard instruments that could

---

24 For a detailed history of Roland and its products, see Reid (2004–5).

25 See Twells (2016). *Synth Britannia* (Whalley 2009-v) covers the synthesizer in the 1970s–80s in the United Kingdom.

play melodies (monophonic) and soon chords (polyphonic). In 1979 both types went on the market.[26]

The first drum machine to use digital samples hit the commercial market in 1979: the Linn LM-1 (at $5,000). It had a store of sampled drums sounds but could not record new ones. Prince used it extensively, including on The Time's "777–9311" (1982) and his own "1999" (1982) and "When Doves Cry" (1984). The next generation LinnDrum hit the market in 1982 (at $3,000) adding crash and ride cymbal sounds. E-Mu's Drumulator (also just playing prerecorded samples) debuted in 1983 (at $1,000). The E-Mu SP-12 (for twelve-bit sampling) debuted in 1985, as the first drum machine that could record its own samples (though at half the rate of CD quality), an extraordinary innovation. The first generation of sample-based hip hop producers used it, including Marley Marl (for MC Shan) and Rick Rubin (for the Beastie Boys). The SP-1200, which debuted in 1987, greatly expanded the capability to record samples, which was exactly what hip hop producers were searching for; it quickly became a staple of the genre. Although it was designed to sample (record) short drum sounds, Hank Shocklee of Public Enemy's Bomb Squad hacked it to record and loop longer segments of 1970s vinyl records on their second album (*It Takes a Nation of Millions*, 1988), which put the machine on the map. Its low-tech twelve-bit, 26 kilobyte sampling rate was a plus in this world, adding some noise in its reproduction, and it remained a vital tool into the 1990s, even after new technology (e.g., sixteen-bit sampling) surpassed it.[27]

The Fairlight CMI (computer musical instrument), released in 1979 (at $25,000), had a keyboard and monitor interface and could record and play back any sound. One prepackaged sample, an orchestral chord from Stravinsky's *The Firebird Suite*, has gained some unlikely dispersion: a Fairlight was in the studio where Arthur Baker and Afrika Bambaataa recorded the early hip hop classic "Planet Rock" (1982), and they used that sample in the opening and throughout the whole piece (Fink 2005b). The cost of commercial samplers would quickly drop. The E-Mu Emulator digital sampler debuted in 1981 (at $10,000), with Stevie Wonder as one of the first customers. It was on an Emulator in 1984 that Marley Marl made his history-making discovery that a drum sound could be isolated, sampled, and combined with other sampled sounds.

---

26 For an explanation of the science of digital sampling, see Audacity (2019). At the May 1980 Audio Engineering Society meeting the Synclavier II, Linn LM-1, and Fairlight CMI all had official debuts (Milner 2009: 317).

27 See Milner (2009: 330–34), J Dilla (2014-d), Fintoni (2016), and E-MU Systems (2019).

Polyphonic sampling (multiple keys triggering samples) arrived in 1984 with up to eight simultaneous voices in the Emulator II (at $8,000). The Ensoniq Mirage debuted in 1984 as the first keyboard sampler that sold for under $2,000.

Questlove points to Stevie Wonder sampling voices on the Cosby Show (aired February 20, 1986) with his Synclavier (a later model that sampled) as "the first time that 99 percent of us who went on to be hip-hop producers saw what a sampler was." Soon after (in his midteens) he got a Casio SK-1, a toy keyboard sampler, synthesizer, and sequencer released in 1985 (for under $100), on which he learned the fundamentals of isolating and combining sounds, setting him on his path that would bear fruit with the Roots, one of the most innovative groups of the 1990s (Questlove and Greenman 2013: 66–69).

The Akai series of samplers designed by Roger Linn would eventually displace the E-Mu SP-1200, starting with the MPC 60 in 1988, with sixteen-voice polyphony, an upgraded 40 kHz stereo sample rate, Linn's trademark quantize and swing rhythm correction, and the ability to play and record sequences in real time, combining a drum machine, sampler, and sequencer into one. The MPC 3000 (1994), which defined the sound of hip hop in the 1990s, featured CD quality sixteen-bit, 44.1 kHz sampling, and much more memory. Wu-Tang Clan cofounder and producer RZA has effectively summarized the role of technology in the development of hip hop with reference to the Akai MPC 3000: "If there's ever a hip hop hall of fame Roger Linn has to be inducted within the first year. . . . He's like the motherfucker who made the piano. He's a genius that should never stop getting props. It's like how Grandmaster Flash came with the [turntable] scratch—these guys are the true foundation of our culture. Even to this day 80 percent of hip hop is produced on that machine" (qtd. in Noakes 2014).[28]

The sound of 1980s rock and pop was deeply imbued with synthesized and sampled sounds. While British synthpop bands were overtly exploiting the potentials of the new technology, even guitar, bass, and drums-oriented bands were being enhanced. The massive snare drum, electronically enhanced by engineer and producer Bob Clearmountain, on dance-oriented music like David Bowie's "Let's Dance" (1983) and Hall and Oates's album *Big Bam Boom* (1984) was pervasive in the decade. In 1984 Clearmountain produced Bruce Springsteen's highest-ever charting single, "Dancing in the Dark" (pop #2), which, along with "Born in the USA" (pop #9), left

---

28 The original print version (Noakes 2006: 215) edits one of RZA's terms for a general audience.

Springsteen's trademark electric guitar by the wayside in favor of that 1980s ubiquitous snare drum sound (Milner 2009: 326–27).

Personal computers came on the market in the late 1970s, using a keyboard interface. In 1984 the Apple Macintosh debuted as the first to use a mouse that could manipulate a graphic cursor in the monitor, a major development that opened up the possibilities for new music-related software, such as Soundtools, which came out in 1989. Pro Tools software (still an industry standard), allowing four tracks of digital recording, came on the market in 1991 (at $4,000); by 1997 digital audio workstations (DAW) with forty-eight tracks came on the market. The instant easy editing capabilities of DAWs may have had some unintended consequences for musicianship: "The most common charge is that DAWs have dealt a fatal blow to the idea of musical spontaneity. Why get it right the first time when you can always fix it through plug-ins or judicious editing?" (Milner 2009: 299). That jury is still out, although it may be related to plummeting electric guitar sales in the past decade, from 1.5 million sold annually (the same amount sold in the mid-1960s) to just over 1 million in 2017 (Edgers 2017).

See figure 10. Innovations in sound and musical instrument technology, 1948–2001

Rock emerged out of the confluence of many streams that have nourished it, each with their own histories of assimilating streams that have in turn fed them. Tin Pan Alley, blues, early rhythm and blues, gospel, and country flourished in various regional and national forms before rock took over as the primary musical language. The major events that provide the backdrop for this era are the birth of the recording industry in the late nineteenth and early twentieth centuries, World War I, the boom in commercial radio broadcasting and growth of markets aimed at blacks and southern whites in the 1920s, the Great Depression, and World War II and the immediately ensuing postwar prosperity.

TIN PAN ALLEY

Tin Pan Alley (West Twenty-Eighth Street in the vicinity of Broadway, between Fifth and Sixth Avenue in Manhattan) was an important distribution center for sheet music in the early twentieth century and has come to stand in as a name of the predominant style of popular songwriting at the time. The string of shops located there would feature pianists (song pluggers) demonstrating the latest compositions for the general public to purchase and play on their own home pianos. The origins of the term *Tin Pan Alley* are wrapped up in myth, but it is generally believed to be a description reported by a journalist around 1900 of the piano sounds filtering out of the publishing houses along Twenty-Eighth Street (Mathieu 2017).

The exact location of the concentration of sheet-music publishers followed the movement of theaters north along Broadway, initially around Union Square (Fourteenth Street and Broadway) in the 1880s, then beginning in the mid-1890s to Twenty-Eighth Street, and finally north of Forty-Second Street in the 1920s.[1] Many of the songs came from the world of musical theater, generically known as Broadway because of the concentration of theaters initially around Broadway downtown, eventually moving north to Midtown (roughly between Forty-Second Street and Fifty-Second Street). Songs coming of out Broadway shows set the standard for popular music in the first half of the twentieth century.

The model for what would later be called *payola*, an illegal practice in which record

---

1   A plaque commemorating the location is embedded in the sidewalk on West Twenty-Eighth Street near the southeast corner with Broadway.

companies would pay disc jockeys to play recordings of their contracted artists, was set by Tin Pan Alley publishers, who would financially reward vaudeville vocalists to popularize their songs in their shows. (Vaudeville is a concert-show form in which a variety of music, comedy, dance, and other acts would perform.)

Composers and lyricists in the golden age of Broadway musicals in the 1920s–30s were overwhelmingly first-generation American-born Jews from New York City of parents emigrating from Russia, eastern Europe, and Germany. They included composers Irving Berlin (born in Russia), George Gershwin, Richard Rodgers, Harold Arlen (born in Buffalo), and Jerome Kern; and lyricists Ira Gershwin, Oscar Hammerstein II (Jewish father, raised Episcopalian), Yip Harburg, and Lorenz Hart, all four of whom were born within two years of one another (1895–96). Almost all had changed their last names to assimilate and avoid discrimination in the industry. The most notable exception in this crowd was composer and lyricist Cole Porter, born in Indiana in 1891, who experienced a wealthy white Anglo-Protestant upbringing in small town Indiana, earning a Yale college degree. The musical style had roots in European popular song, especially the musical theater (comic operas) of the British team of lyricist W. S. Gilbert and composer Arthur Sullivan, who were active in the 1870s–90s. In general, the lyric content and song style reflected a northern urban white middle-class lifestyle, filled with romance and occasional humor.

One of the most widespread musical forms in this genre can be diagrammed as AABA (as in the Gershwins' song "I Got Rhythm"), wherein each letter represents eight bars of musical material, for a total of thirty-two bars. In this form the A sections present the same melody and chords, but with different lyrics, and the B section (or bridge) presents a contrasting melody and accompanying chords. In terminology used in the jazz world, each time through the AABA form is called a *chorus*. A jazz performance might consist of playing the melody once (one AABA chorus), improvising over several choruses of the AABA form, and then playing the melody one more time to end the song. The thirty-two-bar AABA form (or other related thirty-two-bar forms) dominated popular music until twelve-bar blues forms became common currency in the 1950s, although it still retained relevance in the vocal group style called *doo wop*.[2]

---

2   For more on Tin Pan Alley and Broadway, see Hamm (1979), Gottlieb (2004), Gilbert (2015), Yagoda (2015), Furia and Patterson (2016), Mathieu (2017), Kantor (2004-v), and savetinpanalley .org.

BLUES

The most important musical stream that has fed rock and R&B in their early years is blues. An expression of southern African American lifestyle changes over the many decades following emancipation, blues existed as a form of musical expression at least a few decades before the first recordings of it were made in the 1920s. In his 1963 classic, *Blues People*, Amiri Baraka identifies a number of features of postslavery life in the later part of the nineteenth century that led to the development of the blues:

1. increased leisure time and opportunity for solitude;
2. a new personal freedom to travel;
3. work songs no longer responding to the new experiences of black life, which included new opportunities for choosing partners;
4. a lesser hold of the Christian church on black life leading to less communal and more individual social experiences;
5. a new search for employment and struggle for economic security;
6. and the use of new musical instruments. (1963: 61–69)

The new individual forms of musical expression, which grew out of postemancipation experiences and lifestyles, were informed by older communal forms but developed beyond them. Just as communally sung spirituals eventually gave way to composed gospel songs and then recordings featuring star vocal soloists, communal work songs (as well as field hollers) gave way to individual blues musicians singing their own stories. The guitar, which became available through inexpensive mail order by the end of the nineteenth century, replaced the slavery-era banjo and fiddle as the instrument of choice among southern rural blacks.

In the course of making a strong case for the historical conditions that gave rise to the blues, Baraka (1963: 82) also suggested that "musical training was not a part of African tradition—music like any art was the result of natural inclination." Nowadays, one might note two sides of a claim like this (besides the fact that African musicians can indeed go through rigorous apprenticeship and training). On the one hand, the statement could be taken to reflect racial pride in artistic abilities. On the other hand, suggesting that a people are born with certain inclinations (that they have an inner essence) can also serve to reinforce stereotypes, with the potential implication that they are not born with certain other capabilities.

Blues probably initially developed in the Mississippi Delta region, the two-hundred-mile stretch between Memphis in the north and Vicksburg in the south between the Mississippi and Yazoo Rivers (in the east and west) in the late nineteenth and early twentieth centuries. (The actual river delta is several hundred miles farther south.) It was an especially saturated region of cotton farming, with one of the highest concentrations in the country of black tenant and sharecropping farmers. The towns chronicled by Charley Patton (billed as both "Founder" and "King" of the Delta blues) in "High Water Everywhere, Part 1," about the devastating river flood of 1927, reads like a guide to the region: Sumner and the county it's in (Tallahatchie) in the north on the Yazoo side; Rosedale (to the west) and Greenville (farther south) on the Mississippi River and nearby Leland; Sharkey County in between the two rivers in the south; and Vicksburg, where the two rivers meet (see figure 11).

The earliest documentation of the blues appeared in writings in the early part of the first decade of the 1900s. Country blues, performed by men singing and accompanying themselves on the guitar, developed in three southern regions:

- Mississippi Delta (Charley Patton, his protégé Son House, and next generation Robert Johnson);
- East Texas (Blind Lemon Jefferson); and
- Piedmont or southeastern United States (Blind Willie McTell, Blind Boy Fuller).

The Delta branch is especially significant for rock. The impact of those who remained in the region has been deeply felt: the reissue of Robert Johnson's 1930s recordings by Columbia in the 1960s strongly influenced Bob Dylan and spawned covers by Cream ("Crossroads"), the Rolling Stones ("Love in Vain"), and Led Zeppelin ("Travelling Riverside Blues"). But those who left the region were among the early pioneers of rock: Muddy Waters moved to Chicago, as did harmonica player and vocalist James Cotton and Willie Dixon, one of the great songwriters for Chess Records; B. B. King moved to Memphis; and John Lee Hooker moved to Detroit. Alan Lomax, an important documenter of blues in the 1930s and 1940s (he made the first recordings of Lead Belly and Muddy Waters, for the Library of Congress) reports the lineage.

[Son House, interviewed in the early 1940s]: "Little Robert [Johnson] learnt from me, and I learnt from an old fellow they call Lemon down in Clarksdale, and he was called Lemon because he had learnt all Blind Lemon's pieces off the phonograph." Now *I* [Lomax] felt like shouting. Son House had laid out one of the main lines in the royal lineage of America's great guitar players—Blind Lemon of Dallas to his double in Clarksdale to Son House to Robert Johnson. "But isn't there anybody alive who plays this style?" I asked. "An old boy called Muddy Waters round Clarksdale, he learnt from me." (Lomax 1993: 16–17)

A.L. [in an early 1940s interview with Muddy Waters]: Did you know the tune before you heard it on record [Robert Johnson's "Walking Blues"]?
M.W.: Yessir, I learned it from Son House; that's a boy that picks a guitar. I been knowing Son since 'twenty-nine. He was the best. . . . I followed after him and stayed watching him.[3] (411)

Waters had a special reputation among British rock and rollers: "At the Beatles' first press conference in New York, a reporter asked them what they most wanted to see. They immediately replied, 'Muddy Waters and Bo Diddley.' . . . Mick Jagger named his Rolling Stones after a line from one of the blues Muddy recorded at Sherrod's [plantation] on that long-ago day [1941–42; rerecorded for Chess in 1950]" (406). Son House also reinforced stereotypes about bluesmen: "'Bob [Robert Johnson] was a terrible man with the women, like all us guitar players.' Son looked at his sweet-faced wife and they both laughed. 'And I reckon he got one too many down there in Lou'sana. So this last one, she gi'n him poison in his coffee. And he died'" (16).

The recording industry did not see any commercial value in recording blues artists until 1920, when it began recording women blues singers, who had developed another, more urbane style variously called city, vaudeville, or classic blues, typically accompanied by pianists or small jazz bands. A wave of women classic blues singers was recorded starting in 1923. The most renowned were Ma Rainey, known as "The Mother of the Blues," as she came from an early generation, and the next generation Bessie Smith ("The Empress of the Blues"). Recordings of men country blues singers followed in 1926. The 1920s became a golden era of early blues recordings (see figure 12). The following decade the music eventually fell out of fashion, to be replaced by big band jazz (also called swing) and, by the mid 1940s, small group rhythm and blues.

---

3 See also Waters interviewed in Murray (1977) and Lomax and Work's Library of Congress recordings of Muddy Waters (1993-d) and Son House (2013-d).

When the women blues singers were first recorded in the 1920s, the genre had gelled into a standard twelve-bar form: one line of lyrics was sung over four measures (of four beats each measure), the same line was repeated over another four measures, and a responding line was sung over the final four measures. This lyric pattern can be diagrammed as *aab*. Each of these four-measure sections had a distinguishing chord pattern, played on the piano or guitar (see figure 13). "Down Hearted Blues," recorded by Bessie Smith in New York for Columbia in early 1923, follows this pattern strictly, although it is preceded by a four-line verse (wherein each line is four measures, totaling sixteen measures), which sets up the story. This practice of an introductory verse is borrowed from the Tin Pan Alley songs of the day. The presence of a separate vocalist and accompanist (or ensemble) dictated that a standardized format be followed.

The earliest country blues singers, however, had no need to standardize the musical form. As solo singer-guitarists, they could expand or contract their guitar accompaniment at will, according to how they felt at the moment. When Charley Patton was finally recorded in 1929, he was still playing blues forms that were open ended. In "High Water Everywhere, Part 1," for example, he used the *aab* lyric scheme, with the usual chord pattern associated with each line, but he would expand or contract each line at will to more or fewer than four measures. In this piece he systematically turns the beat around (moving the accented strong beat from the downbeat to the offbeat) at the end of the first line and then turns it back around at the end of the response line as he moves into the next verse (see figure 11, which shows the number of beats in each measure for each verse).

Blues forms and vocal and guitar styles laid the foundation for rock through the 1960s. The three-line *aab* lyric structure can be called a *verse* or a *chorus* depending on its function within a song. In American popular song, the term *verse*, which refers to lyrics that typically move the story line ahead, is contrasted with *chorus* (sometimes called a hook or refrain), which alternates with verses and repeats the same lines throughout the piece. (The term *chorus* can refer to a full AABA form or, as here, a repeated line or section that contrasts with the verse—see the glossary for clarification.) Blues developed independently of this verse-chorus tradition and did not initially follow it, but in the 1940s it assimilated mainstream popular song forms to do just that. For example, Chuck Berry's "Maybelline" opens with a twelve-bar blues chorus ("Oh Maybelline") that alternates with a twelve-bar blues verse, which pushes the story along. Berry's "Roll over Beethoven" uses the first two lines of the *aab* form as a verse (with two separate lines rather than repeating the first line) and the response line ("Roll over Beethoven") as a chorus.

Blues lyrics are often marked by strong sexual references, almost always couched in metaphor using double entendre, wherein a phrase or line could be interpreted two ways. This led to consumption of certain forms of blues recordings by whites in the 1920s that would be similar to the pattern for certain forms of rap music in the 1990s. The first widely recognized professional blues composer W. C. Handy ("Memphis Blues," 1912; "St. Louis Blues," 1914) wrote in his autobiography, "A flock of low-down dirty blues appeared on records, not witty double entendre but just plain smut. These got a play in college fraternities, speakeasies and rowdy spots. Their appeal was largely to whites, though they were labeled 'race records'" (1941: 209).

Not only did blues styles, forms, and lyrics cast a long shadow over rock, but so also did the actual compositions, which were covered by young white British and American groups in the 1960s. This brought them into their most direct contact with the musical materials and also opened up the ears of their fans, stimulating some of them to seek out the original sources. Two of the more well-known examples from virtuoso electric guitarists (Duane Allman and Eric Clapton) are the Allman Brothers Band's 1971 cover of Blind Willie McTell's "Statesboro Blues" (1928) and Cream's 1968 cover of Robert Johnson's "Cross Road Blues" (1937).

Blues forms are malleable and can be open-ended. John Lee Hooker's "Boogie Chillen'" (1948), for example, does not strictly follow the chord pattern or form of blues but rather pares down the form to just two (rather than three) chords and is a vehicle for spoken storytelling. Here boogie can refer to dancing, partying, having a good time, or, perhaps more abstractly, following your passion in life ("cause it's in him and it got to come out").

In addition to referring to a musical form, blues refers to a more general aesthetic about music making, a feeling, and an attitude toward life. Baraka's book *Blues People* was one of the first to explore this aesthetic and attitude in depth. Angela Y. Davis's *Blues Legacies and Black Feminism* has further explored the significance and cathartic and empowering role of the blues in African American life. Referring to blues women in particular, Davis notes, "Naming issues that pose a threat to the physical or psychological well-being of the individual is a central function of the blues. . . . Through the blues, menacing problems are ferreted out from the isolated individual experience and restructured as problems shared by the community. As shared problems, threats can be met and addressed within a public and collective context" (1998: 33).[4]

See figure 11. "High Water Everywhere, Part 1," by Charley Patton

See figure 12. Early blues singers

See figure 13. Twelve-bar blues form

RHYTHM AND BLUES

The designation *rhythm and blues* (R&B) replaced Harlem Hit Parade (1942–45) and *race records* (1945–49) in the *Billboard* charts beginning June 25, 1949, continuing the tradition of categorizing music made by African Americans aimed at an African American audience.[5] But now it no longer covered gospel and other religious music and sermons. Independent record labels flourished in the decade after World War II to cater to local tastes, with many of them specializing in R&B (see figure 14). They had a close relationship with the new independent radio stations exploding in local markets. Several tributaries were covered under the umbrella category R&B.

As the large swing bands, which provided the dance music of the 1930s, became impractical to support in the 1940s because of war rationing, a new style of dance music developed called jump blues, played by a smaller jazz ensemble, with a piano (and sometimes guitar), bass, and drums rhythm section, and a few horns (trumpet and saxophone). The most successful artist in this genre was Louis Jordan and his Tympany Five, who crossed over to the pop charts frequently between 1944 and 1949, hitting #1 there with "G. I. Jive" in 1944.[6] Figure 15 shows how Jordan's 1946 recording of "Choo Choo Ch-Boogie" integrates a twelve-bar blues form into a verse-chorus structure. Vocalists in this style who were particularly forceful, often with more sexually oriented lyrics, were called shouters, exemplified by Big Joe Turner ("Roll 'em Pete," 1938; "Shake, Rattle and Roll," 1954) and Wynonie Harris ("Good Rockin' Tonight," 1948), both of whom were covered in the early rock and roll era by white artists Bill Haley and Elvis Presley.

---

4   For more on blues, see Titon (1977), Palmer (1981), Barlow (1989), Santelli (1993), the documentary by Dall (1989-v), and a rare film performance of Bessie Smith (Murphy 1929-v).

5   The term *rhythm and blues* appeared sporadically in *Billboard* in 1947 (Csida 1947: 22; Ackerman 1947) and was used as a style heading in an RCA Victor ad in early 1949.

6   Jordan's short film *Caldonia* (Crouch 1945-v) includes several performances.

Many songs in the jump blues style were based on a boogie woogie rhythm, typically played by the bass player or left hand of a pianist (at the bass end). Boogie woogie was first popularized by virtuoso solo pianists in the late 1920s and 1930s, including Meade Lux Lewis ("Honky Tonk Train Blues," 1927), Pinetop Smith ("Pinetop's Boogie Woogie," 1928), and Albert Ammons ("Boogie Woogie Stomp," 1936).[7]

A major blues scene developed in Chicago, where first-generation migrants from the South modernized their southern roots with the electric guitar, bass, and drum set. Chess Records, located in the black South Side of Chicago, was the primary label, featuring songwriter and bassist Willie Dixon and guitarist and vocalist Muddy Waters, who often teamed up (e.g., "Hoochie Coochie Man," 1954). Other major artists include B. B. King (based in Memphis), John Lee Hooker (based in Detroit), and Howlin' Wolf and Little Walter (both in Chicago). This strand of R&B, called Chicago blues or urban electric blues, thrived from the late 1940s through the mid-1950s (see figure 16). It was enormously influential on rock in the 1960s in both its vocal styles and electric guitar styles, which established the model for both singing and guitar soloing.

A smoother and more restrained R&B style was pioneered by pianist and vocalist Nat King Cole (1919–65), who was one of the earliest artists to cross over onto the pop charts; vocalist Charles Brown; and electric guitarist and vocalist Aaron "T-Bone" Walker (1910–75), who is credited with reintroducing the guitar into black dance music. Cole's "Straighten Up and Fly Right" topped *Billboard*'s Harlem Hit Parade chart (not yet called R&B) for ten weeks starting April 29, 1944; spent six weeks at the top of the Juke Box Folk chart (not yet called country); and reached the Top 10 of Best Selling Retail Records chart (July 1, 1944) and Top 20 of the Juke Box Pop chart, an extraordinary accomplishment. Walker's 1947 single "Call It Stormy Monday (But Tuesday Is Just as Bad)" had an immediate impact on R&B, helping along the postwar rise of the electric guitar.

African American male vocal groups began recording a style just after World War II, which a decade later would become known (retrospectively) as doo wop. They were preceded in the 1930s by the very popular Mills Brothers and Ink Spots, who both had a broad audience. The first commercially successful groups in the post–World War II

7   Seven-year-old child prodigy Frankie "Sugar Chile" Robinson performing Louis Jordan's "Caldonia" in the 1946 Hollywood film *No Leave, No Love* provides an extraordinary example of a boogie woogie bass in the left hand, given his age.

style were the Ravens (New York), with their Top 10 Harlem Hit Parade (R&B) hit "Ol' Man River" in 1947, followed by the Orioles (from Baltimore) with their #1 R&B hit "It's Too Soon to Know" in 1948. Clyde McPhatter, lead singer with the Dominoes ("Have Mercy Baby," 1952) before moving on to a solo career, is often credited with introducing gospel-style singing into R&B, preceding Ray Charles by a few years. The name *doo wop* comes from a phrase that was used by the background singers. Early examples, from the mid-1950s, include the Clovers ("Good Lovin'," 1953); the Drifters ("Let the Boogie Woogie Roll," 1953, not released until 1960); the Turbans ("When You Dance," 1955, R&B #3, pop #33); and a song called "Do Wop" by the De Villes (1958).

Women vocalists, including Dinah Washington (the most commercially successful), Ruth Brown, LaVern Baker, and Etta James, would have a major and defining presence in R&B in the 1950s (see figure 17). They would occasionally cross over to the pop charts (which expanded to a hundred slots beginning 1955), gaining a greater audience, but reaching the pop Top 40 was much more difficult. For example, Dinah Washington placed forty-seven songs in the R&B charts between 1944 and 1961, thirty-five of which rose to the R&B Top 10; after a single pop crossover in 1950, she finally began crossing over to the pop charts in 1959, placing twenty-one songs (in 1959–63), seven of which reached the pop Top 40. Ruth Brown placed twenty-four songs in the R&B charts between 1949 and 1960, twenty-one of which rose to the R&B Top 10; she too, did not cross over until the late 1950s, placing seven songs (1957–62), two of which reached the pop Top 40.

Ruth Brown's records sold so well that she is credited with keeping her record label, Atlantic, afloat in the early 1950s. But with twenty-one Top 10 R&B hits and only two hitting the pop Top 40, one can get some sense of the frustrations of R&B artists in the 1950s, especially in the face of bland cover versions by white singers reaching larger audiences. Eventually learning that she was not receiving her share of royalties, Brown enlisted an attorney and testified before Congress at a federal racketeering law hearing in 1986, putting some pressure on Atlantic; her activism had a major impact for her peers. Atlantic Records settled with Brown and many other artists from her era, and as a direct result of her actions the Rhythm and Blues Foundation (2019) was established in 1988 to provide financial assistance, educational outreach, and performance opportunities, seeded by a $1.5 million grant from Atlantic cofounder Ahmet Ertegun. Brown's (1996) autobiography provides a vivid firsthand account of the R&B generation of the 1950s.

R&B Music and Society

In his book on R&B in the 1950s and 1960s, Brian Ward (1998) suggests significant parallels between the concurrent historical developments of the civil rights movement and rhythm and blues. His starting point was 1954: the Supreme Court *Brown v. Board of Education of Topeka* decision (separate public school facilities for black and white children were inherently unequal) in May and the Chords' "Sh-Boom" crossing over to the pop charts a few months later in July. From about 1956 to 1963 there was a mood of optimism for integration reflected in crossover success and black admiration for some of the white pop of the era.

Ward lays out three premises of his book: (1) both production and consumption patterns are important in understanding R&B (the music industry does not just initiate and sustain trends that do not have relevance for its audience); (2) blacks are not just passive consumers—by actively purchasing recordings, going to concerts and clubs, and choosing to listen to various radio stations they can impact musical production; and (3) Americans are acculturated into attributing certain musical techniques and devices to blacks and to whites. These techniques are generally agreed-on codes, clearly recognized by some adult whites, for example, who initially objected to rock and roll, and by some blacks in the later 1960s who wished to assert less assimilated identities.

R&B of the 1950s–60s challenges notions of authenticity or purity of earlier styles, such as blues and gospel, which were also commercial enterprises, perhaps more removed from the pressures of mass media but still commodities packaged as recordings. Commercial success could indicate a special kind of relevancy to African Americans, similar to what less mediated blues and gospel might have offered in earlier decades. Furthermore, African American music has long been in a mutually engaging relationship with other musical influences around it. Reducing it to a "pure" style (or an inborn essence, sometimes critiqued as racial essentialism) can devalue the breadth of vision and syncretic nature of African American culture.

Until the late 1960s many blacks may have believed, as Ward notes, that white interest in R&B would lead to increased racial understanding. But admiration for black music did not necessarily challenge white stereotypes about blacks, and indeed it could also serve to reinforce them. Characterizations such as physical, passionate, ecstatic, emotional, and sexually liberated could serve both to praise and to stereotype black music. While white audiences with little real-world exposure to African

American culture might take these as defining characteristics of African American music and culture, blacks would be less susceptible to consider these as the sum total of a much more rich and diverse existence (e.g., jazz may contain all of this and more: restraint, understatement, technical sophistication, intellectual experiment, and exploration). In general, through the early 1960s black entrepreneurs and performers (with the exception of some in the jazz world) were reluctant to get publicly involved in civil rights causes or to address such issues in their music for fear of limiting their commercial acceptance and opportunities. That would soon change.[8]

See figure 14. Some key independent record labels, 1940s–1950s (date founded and artist's debut recording)

See figure 15. "Choo Choo Ch-Boogie," by Louis Jordan

See figure 16. Electric blues guitarists, 1950s–1960s (R&B Top 10 single hits and pop LP debuts)

See figure 17. Women R&B singers, 1940s–1950s (R&B Top 10 single hits and crossovers to pop Top 40)

GOSPEL

African American gospel music has provided a pervasive influence on R&B, and consequently on rock and roll, primarily in the form of vocal and bodily expression. This is in contrast to blues, which has additionally influenced musical forms, guitar-playing styles, and lyric content (as well as vocal styles). As part of a more racially segregated religious experience, and one that became increasingly vital in the 1930s–1950s, gospel had a strong and direct impact on African Americans growing up in those decades, right when country and classic blues were falling out of favor. Compared to the more publicly visible secular blues, gospel remained relatively hidden from the view of whites.

It is the rule rather than exception for black vocalists to credit the formative impact of early church and gospel music experience on their later careers. B. B. King sang with a gospel quartet about 1946, before moving on to become one of the great blues electric guitarists and vocalists. Soul pioneer Ray Charles sang spirituals since he was three,

---

8   For more on R&B, see A. Shaw (1978), George (1988), Gillett (1996), and Mahon (2011). See Kohn (1955-v) for performances by Dinah Washington, Ruth Brown, and Nat King Cole and Price (1956-v) for LaVern Baker.

sang with gospel quartets later in school, and eventually took gospel lines and turned them into secular songs: "Nothing was more familiar to me, nothing more natural [than spirituals and gospel]" (Charles and Ritz 1978: 149). Little Richard sang with the Penniman singers and toured churches; his grandfather and uncle were preachers, and he went to Baptist, AME, and Holiness churches. James Brown went to a lot of churches as a child, taking note of charismatic preachers: "I'm sure a lot of my stage show came out of the church" (1986: 18). Ruth Brown's formative vocal experiences were in the church, and Clyde McPhatter adapted the style of women gospel singers for the Dominoes and his later solo career. Sam Cooke was a gospel star with the Soul Stirrers before leaving them to help establish the genre that came to be called soul in the late 1950s. And perhaps most famously, Aretha Franklin's father, Rev. C. L. Franklin, was a nationally known Baptist minister, due in part to his sermons released on disc; gospel greats James Cleveland and Clara Ward were important influences on Aretha, and she toured early on with gospel choirs. She boldly went back to her roots in her acclaimed double-LP *Amazing Grace*, recorded in 1972 with Rev. James Cleveland and his gospel choir at the height of her initial reign as Queen of Soul. Perhaps one key to Elvis Presley's success in adapting African American musical styles was that he grew up going to a Pentecostal church.

Gospel music in black communities developed in urban areas in the late nineteenth and early twentieth centuries out of slave-era spirituals, which were communal religious songs. In the 1890s alternatives to Baptist and Methodist churches arose, with denominations such as Holiness, Pentecostal, Church of God in Christ, and Sanctified. Pentecostal churches arose in the first decade of the twentieth century from the interracial Azusa Street Revival in Los Angeles, led by an African American preacher. The following decade whites had formed their own Pentecostal denomination, the Assemblies of God (the church that Elvis belonged to). They all featured ecstatic singing and dancing, where congregants often became possessed by the Holy Spirit. They were the first black churches to encourage the use of musical instruments in church, following Psalm 150: "Praise him with the sound of the trumpet . . . psaltery and harp . . . timbrel [tambourine] and dance . . . stringed instruments and organs . . . loud cymbals."[9]

The gospel music world is marked by composers, vocal soloists (both men and women), and vocal groups. Methodist minister Charles Albert Tindley (1851–1933)

---

9   King James version.

was the first major black gospel composer, with classics such as "I'll Overcome Some Day" (1901) and "Stand by Me" (1905). Thomas A. Dorsey (1899–1993), son of a Baptist minister, initially played blues piano (as "Georgia Tom") with Ma Rainey in the 1910s and 1920s, and he was a prolific blues composer: "In the early 1920s I coined the words 'gospel songs' after listening to a group of five people one Sunday morning on the far south side of Chicago. This was the first I heard of a gospel choir. There were no gospel songs then, we called them evangelistic songs" (qtd. in Heilbut 2002: 27). From 1929 on he committed himself solely to gospel music, and his music began to flourish. In 1932 he and Sallie Martin (1895–1988), the first of the great women gospel singers, founded the Gospel Singers Convention. Throughout the 1930s she and Dorsey set up the first gospel choruses in many of the major black communities of the South and Midwest. In 1932 Dorsey was appointed choral director of Pilgrim Baptist Church (with three thousand seats) in Chicago, where he stayed for forty years. That same year he composed "Precious Lord," moved by the death of his wife and child. His music was also popular with white southerners, and by 1939 his music was published in anthologies by white publishers of gospel music. His adaptation of the spiritual "We Shall Walk through the Valley in Peace" later became a hit when Elvis Presley recorded it.

Sister Rosetta Tharpe (1915–73) was a pioneering guitarist and singer in the gospel field (G. Wald 2007; Csaky 2011-v). Born in Arkansas, she grew up in the sanctified Church of God in Christ with her mother, who was a singer and mandolin player. Her family moved to Chicago in the mid-1920s, where her career as a gospel performer and guitarist took off. She signed with Decca Records in 1938 and her recording "Rock Me" that year had a major impact on the rise of the gospel-record industry as well as on the first generation of rock and rollers. Little Richard, who performed with her once when he was a boy, has credited her with inspiring him, as have many others. She performed in the groundbreaking 1938 "Spirituals to Swing" concert in Carnegie Hall and became known for bringing gospel music to secular audiences. She reached the Harlem Hit Parade Top 10 chart with "Strange Things Happening Every Day" (#2) in 1945. Filmed performances from folk and blues festivals in the 1960s of her playing electric guitar and fronting choirs ("Down by the Riverside," "Didn't It Rain," "Up above my Head") give some sense of her power and excitement. A U.S. Postal Service stamp was issued in her honor in 1998.

Mahalia Jackson (1911–72), the most beloved of all gospel singers, was born and raised in New Orleans into a devout Baptist family. Her early influences were the

Mahalia The Goddess

classic hymns composed by Isaac Watts in eighteenth-century England, Bessie Smith, jazz, and the Sanctified Church (but she remained Baptist). She moved to Chicago in 1927, made her first records in 1937 with Decca, and joined Thomas Dorsey in the early 1940s. In 1946 she signed a contract with Apollo Records and her third record with them, "Move on Up a Little Higher" (1948), sold over a million copies. In 1954 she signed with Columbia Records, for whom she recorded another version of the song (her piano accompanist was Mildred Falls). The high profile of black gospel music can be seen in the career of Mahalia Jackson, who sang the national anthem at the 1961 Kennedy inaugural celebration and "Precious Lord" at the funeral of Rev. Dr. Martin Luther King Jr., who loved her music. Aretha Franklin sang "Precious Lord" at Jackson's funeral in Chicago in 1972.[10]

COUNTRY

The prehistory of country music, going back a few centuries to folk traditions of the rural southern United States, provides one of the most vivid examples of the symbiotic cultural relationship between Anglo-Americans (those coming from the British Isles) and African Americans. The banjo was an invention of enslaved Africans in the Caribbean, with early forms used on plantations in North America by the eighteenth century (Conway 1995). In the early nineteenth century, whites began to play it, adding technical innovations to its construction. In the 1830s it was used in small minstrel troupes in a genre in which whites blackened their faces with burned cork and caricatured blacks by singing in exaggerated dialect. African Americans eventually dropped the banjo in favor of the guitar in the latter half of the nineteenth century, although a few have maintained banjo traditions to this day.

The fiddle, the other characteristic instrument in country music, was brought over from Europe, with an especially strong tradition from Scots-Irish immigrants (Ritchie and Orr 2016). While whites had picked up the banjo from blacks, the complementary process occurred with the fiddle, with some African Americans achieving a degree of local fame for their ability on the instrument. The fiddle, banjo, and guitar form the nucleus of string-band traditions (called old-time music) that were central in the rise of country music in the 1920s.

The first commercial recordings featured virtuoso fiddle-contest champions. Eck

---

10 For more on gospel music, see Reagon (1992), Schwerin (1992), and Boyer (1995).

Robertson (1887–1975), born in Arkansas and raised in Texas, recorded four fiddle duets with Henry C. Gilliland (1845–1924), who was born in Missouri and grew up in Texas, for Victor in New York in June 1922.[11] Robertson recorded solo (and with piano) the following day. Victor released two records from those sessions: "Sally Gooden" (Robertson solo) and "Arkansas Traveler" (duet with Gilliland) in 1922, and "Ragtime Annie" (Robertson solo) and "Turkey in the Straw" (duet with Gilliland) in 1923. They were the first country music recordings.

"Sally Gooden" is replete with a short-long rhythmic pair called a Scotch snap (at the end of every two bars), historically associated with Scottish language and fiddle music, which has filtered into a variety of American musics. Fiddlin' John Carson (1868–1949), from Georgia, recorded "The Little Old Log Cabin in the Lane" and "The Old Hen Cackled and the Rooster's Going to Crow" on portable recording equipment in Atlanta brought by Ralph Peer of Okeh Records, who was scouting talent in 1923. Carson played solo fiddle and sang along. He had played the previous year on Atlanta's WSB radio, probably the first station to broadcast country music, but his success in this untapped market was extraordinary. The initial run of five hundred copies quickly sold out, and he would record over 120 sides for Okeh between 1923 and 1931 (and 24 more for Victor in 1934), opening up a new market that was initially called hillbilly in 1925. *Billboard* charts later used the term *folk* until it was replaced by *country and western* in 1949.

An important landmark in country music came when Ralph Peer visited Bristol, Tennessee, in 1927 to record local talent for Victor. The discovery there of singer-guitarist Jimmie Rodgers (1897–1933), born in Mississippi, and the Carter Family (husband, A. P.; wife, Sara, and A. P.'s sister-in-law, Maybelle), from Virginia, yielded the first two major stars of country music, representing opposite poles of the spectrum (the road-wise traveler and the domestic family). The Carters recorded over 300 sides for several record labels from 1927 to 1941, and Maybelle's daughter June would marry Johnny Cash, a major star who started out on Sun Records in 1955. Rodgers's career was meteoric, recording over a hundred songs for Victor and selling more than most of Victor's pop artists, but brief due to his early death just six years after his recording debut.

In the 1930s country expanded to include the westernmost southern states (Oklahoma, Louisiana, Texas) and California, which drew in part on cowboy imagery and songs. The most successful artist was Gene Autry (1907–98) from northern Texas, who went to Hollywood in 1934 and made over ninety movies. Autry popularized

---

11 This section on country music is based on Malone and Neal (2010).

the image of a cowboy who wielded both a gun and guitar. Honky-tonks, drinking establishments that featured music, dancing, and jukeboxes, became an important part of the landscape in the 1930s, especially in Texas, where oil attracted workers with cash to spend. Southwestern bands electrified in this environment and developed a style that after World War II became known as western swing.

In 1939 Nashville's radio show *Grand Ole Opry* on WSM was picked up for national broadcast by NBC, making it the most visible face of country music. When Decca began recording country musicians there starting in 1946, Nashville would soon become the center of the country music world. Just after the war a virtuosic uptempo instrumental ensemble style called bluegrass surfaced in the hands of Kentucky mandolinist Bill Monroe and his band, including future stars Earl Scruggs (1924–2014) from North Carolina on banjo and Lester Flatt 1914–79) from Tennessee on guitar, and a fiddle and bass player. Their recordings from 1946 to 1947 for Columbia defined the style. Monroe's "Blue Moon of Kentucky" was covered by Elvis Presley on his very first recording for Sun Records in 1954.

In the late 1940s Hank Williams (1923–53), from Alabama, emerged in a style known as honky tonk (named after the bars where the music was played). Williams's recording career was short (similar to Rodgers), due to his early death at age twenty-nine in January 1953, but he had an enormous impact on the generations after him. Williams began recording professionally (on the Sterling label) in December 1946, and after recording eight songs (including "Honky Tonkin'"), he moved to MGM in April 1947, when he recorded "Move It on Over," his first recording to register on a *Billboard* chart (country #4). The same session also yielded "I Saw the Light." He recorded another version of "Honky Tonkin'" for MGM in November 1947 and remained with the label for the rest of his life, placing a total of thirty-eight records on the country charts through the year he died, all recorded in Nashville. He had seven #1 country hits during his lifetime, including "Hey Good Lookin'" (1951) and "Jambalaya" (1952), and another four the year he died, including "Your Cheatin' Heart" (1953). He crossed over into the pop charts only twice in his lifetime ("Lovesick Blues" and "Jambalaya"). After joining the Shreveport radio show *Louisiana Hayride* in 1948 and Nashville's *Grand Ole Opry* in 1949, Williams had become, by virtue of his singing and songwriting abilities, the most famous and most emulated country singer, even though he rarely broke into the pop charts. He averaged earnings of $200,000 per year from recordings and appearances the last few years of his life.

Williams's clever songwriting was similar in some ways to that of Chuck Berry, the master craftsman of early rock and roll a decade later. "Move It on Over" (1947) and Berry's "Roll over Beethoven" (1955) both insert a verse-chorus structure into a single twelve-bar blues form: "Move it" has a four-bar verse and eight-bar chorus, and "Roll Over" has an eight-bar verse and four-bar chorus. Each time Williams sings the chorus, he slightly alters it: move, get, scoot, ease, drag, pack, tote, scratch, shake, slide, sneak, shove, and sweep, keeping listeners on their toes. The all-string ensemble, including a fiddle, and solos on the electric guitar and steel guitar exude a signature Nashville sound.

Kitty Wells (1919–2012), from Nashville, was country music's first woman star, initially registering on the charts with the answer song "It Wasn't God Who Made Honky Tonk Angels" (country #1) in 1952. Between 1952 and 1965 she placed fifty-nine singles on the country charts, thirty-four of which hit the Top 10. After that she was still placing on the country charts, but only occasionally breaking into the country Top 40. Wells crossed over into the pop charts even less then Hank Williams, just once, in 1958 ("Jealousy"). Wells was succeeded by Patsy Cline and Loretta Lynn. Beginning with "Walkin' After Midnight," which hit country #2 in 1957, Cline (1932–63), from Virginia, had eight Top 10 country hits between 1957 and 1963, two of which reached #1. Sixteen of her songs crossed over into the pop charts in this same period, with four breaching the Top 20. Loretta Lynn (1932–), from Kentucky, debuted in 1960 with her single "I'm a Honky Tonk Girl" hitting #14 on the country chart. Lynn had an extraordinary run of more than sixty-five Top 40 country hits through the 1960s, 1970s, and 1980s, with sixteen at #1. She rarely crossed over into the pop charts (just five times), never breaching the Top 40.

Elvis Presley's recording career started out on the country charts. His first five releases, on Sun Records in Memphis, moved up the regional country charts, with his fifth record ("I Forgot to Remember to Forget" and "Mystery Train") hitting #1 and #10 on the national country chart in early 1956. At that point, after he had moved to RCA Victor, he immediately hit the top of the pop (and country) charts. Elvis placed sixty-seven songs on the country charts in his lifetime, ten of which hit #1 (almost all between 1955 and 1957).[12]

---

12 For more on country music, see Crichton (1938), Green (1965), Peterson (1997), Russell (2010), Pecknold (2013), Hubbs (2014), Stimeling (2014), and H. Gleason (2017).

Rock and roll (often stylized as rock 'n' roll) as a distinct named genre emerged in the mid-1950s, with 1955 being a key year for its commercial breakthrough. The term was used in blues and R&B recordings since the 1920s, typically as a double entendre referring to both dancing and sexual activity. The earliest title may be "My Man Rocks Me (with One Steady Roll)," written by J. Berni Barbour and recorded by Trixie Smith in 1922 for the African American–owned Black Swan label (musically, the song is closer to New Orleans style jazz than blues). In the post–World War II era, such references became more common: Manhattan Paul Bascomb's "Rock and Roll" (1947); Wild Bill Moore's "We're Gonna Rock, We're Gonna Roll" (1947) and "We're Gonna Rock and Roll" (1949); Roy Brown's "Good Rockin' Tonight" (1947), covered by Wynonie Harris (1947) and Elvis Presley (1954); and Wynonie Harris's "All She Wants to Do Is Rock" (1949). Country singer Buddy Jones recorded "Rock and Rollin' Mama" in 1939.

Let's be clear at the outset about the origins of rock and roll: no one person invented it and no single record was the first rock and roll recording. A cohort of individuals converged on a sound (and an audience for it), and there are too many candidates for the first rock record. Any designation of "king" devalues the communal effort and should be viewed with skepticism. Three artists stand out, however, and there was enough shared brilliance among them. Chuck Berry's songwriting, guitar playing, and singing provided a model of elegance in its simplicity; Little Richard channeled outrageous youthful energy with his songwriting, piano playing, and singing and an irresistible signature beat; and Elvis Presley pulled disparate streams together with a youthful, magnetic charisma and versatile singing capabilities, achieving unprecedented mass impact (see figure 18). They all have cited earlier artists from whom they drew in their own development.

One arrival point, in terms of the music industry, came in the summer of 1955, several months after the release of *Blackboard Jungle*, a film about juvenile delinquency set in an urban high school. The film's theme song, "Rock around the Clock," performed by Bill Haley and His Comets, shot to #1 on all three of *Billboard*'s pop charts in July: Best Seller in Stores, Most Played by Jockeys, and Most Played in Juke Boxes. For all of August 1955 it was at the top of the three charts. It was a ripe moment, allowing veteran R&B artist Fats Domino ("Ain't It a Shame") and newcomer Chuck Berry ("Maybelline," his debut recording) into the pop charts that summer for the first time. Little Richard debuted on the R&B chart in November ("Tutti Frutti") and then crossed over to the pop chart two months later. Elvis Presley, who debuted on the national country chart in July with his fourth single on the independent Sun Records label, would hit #1 on that chart with his fifth and last single, entering in September and taking many months to reach the top, in February 1956. He would not debut on the pop chart until March 1956 ("Heartbreak Hotel"), after he moved to the major RCA Victor label.

The year 1956 would see the domination of the pop charts by twenty-one-year-old Elvis Presley and the significant presence of the first generation of solo black artists to be called rock and roll: Fats Domino, Chuck Berry, Little Richard, and Bo Diddley (see figures 19 and 20). Film musicals began capitalizing on the sudden rise of rock and roll, featuring Chuck Berry, Little Richard, Bill Haley and His Comets, Frankie Lymon, LaVern Baker, Clyde McPhatter, and disc jockey Alan Freed, and Elvis's Hollywood film career began this year.[1]

Not only were black artists more frequently appearing on the pop charts, but some southern white rockabilly artists began appearing on the R&B charts. Carl Perkins ("Blue Suede Shoes") was the first to do so, hitting #2 on both the pop and R&B charts and #1 on the country and western chart in early 1956; Presley ("Don't Be Cruel") hit #1 on all three charts later that year; and in 1957 Jerry Lee Lewis ("Whole Lotta Shakin' Going On") hit all three charts: pop #3, R&B #1, C&W #1. About the same time, Buddy Holly ("That'll Be the Day") hit #1 on the pop chart and #2 on the R&B chart.[2]

The initial energy of this era would dissipate by the end of the decade, in part because of a series of unrelated events that took the major players off the scene with no generation behind them to pick up the slack. Or, rather, the music industry caught on and promoted photogenic clean-cut white teen idols in their wake. Elvis was drafted and then inducted into the army in March 1958, several months after Little Richard had given up rock and roll for the ministry and then gospel music. Also in 1958 Jerry Lee Lewis was blacklisted for marrying his young teen cousin. In February 1959 Buddy Holly, Ritchie Valens ("La Bamba"), and J. P. "The Big Bopper" Richardson Jr. ("Chantilly Lace"), who were all touring together, died in a small plane crash in Iowa. (Don McLean memorialized the event in 1971 with "American Pie," calling it the day the music died.) Later that year Alan Freed was fired due to the payola scandal,

---

1   See Sears (1956-v, 1957-v), Price (1956-v), and Dubin (1957-v).

2   Simon (1956) noted that, before Carl Perkins, no country artist ever appeared on the R&B charts. Despite being from Texas, Holly never registered on the country charts.

and Chuck Berry was arrested and ultimately convicted in 1961, after a mistrial, of transporting a minor across state lines for prostitution.[3]

A number of factors converged in the decade following the end of World War II that enabled rock and roll to develop: (1) rapid changes and growth in the music and related media industries, including recording, radio, and television; (2) the rise of teenagers as a new consumer demographic; and (3) a new cohort of creative individuals who captured the imaginations of teens.

THE MEDIA

Changes in the media in the 1940s and 1950s included the growth of independent radio stations, disc jockeys, and Top 40 formats; the addition of another performing rights organization (BMI); the entrance of two new distribution formats for audio recordings (vinyl albums and singles); the growth of television; and the growth of independent record labels (Peterson 1990). They all contributed to opening up the access of rhythm and blues and country recordings to broader audiences.

In the 1930s the Federal Communications Commission tightly restricted the number of radio stations licensed to broadcast, which typically resulted in five or fewer stations broadcasting in each local market: the major networks—NBC (Red and Blue), CBS, and Mutual—plus one independent station.[4] In effect, there was a single national market with four networks competing for that audience. In 1940, when the FCC temporarily stopped licensing new stations, there were 813 licensed AM stations. In 1947 the FCC began approving a backlog of applications, and by 1949 the number of AM stations jumped to 2,127, with small independent stations making the biggest gain. In February 1953 *Variety* (1953) magazine featured a front-page story—"Negro Jocks Come into Own: Play Key Role in Music Biz"—noting that five hundred black R&B disc jockeys were working across the country, with twelve in New York City alone. Their standing in the community pointed to a new role for disc jockeys, beyond just playing records. By 1956 the total number of AM stations grew to almost 3,000, and by the end of the decade about one hundred autonomous local markets had materialized,, with each having 8 to 12 or more stations competing for local audiences.

---

3   The first two classes of inductees into the Rock and Roll Hall of Fame (1986, 1987) is populated by many of the people covered in this chapter (Rock and Roll Hall of Fame 2019).

4   This paragraph draws from Peterson (1990: 101, 105) and Ennis (1992: 136–37).

White teens could hear R&B in the early 1950s through local disc jockeys like Alan Freed, whose Cleveland radio program the *Moondog House*, beginning in 1951, drew many listeners. When Freed moved to WINS in New York City in the fall of 1954, soon calling his show *Rock 'n' Roll Party*, he became one of the most influential deejays in the music business. Other disc jockeys in the early 1950s, such as Dick "Huggy Boy" Hugg in Los Angeles and Rufus Thomas and Dewey Phillips in Memphis (who played Elvis Presley's first recordings in 1954), fueled the growing interest. A Top 40 radio format, wherein radio stations would play a limited list of the forty most popular songs in the nation each week, dates to the mid-1950s. The format is credited to station director Todd Storz, in Omaha, who noted people repeatedly putting coins in jukeboxes to hear the same songs over and over (Fong-Torres 1998; Rasmussen 2008).

A 1939 dispute over increased licensing fees that radio stations should pay to ASCAP (representing composers and publishers) led to radio station owners forming their own competing Broadcast Music, Inc., performing rights organization. BMI attracted songwriters working in genres that were underrepresented or excluded from ASCAP, such as rhythm and blues and country. Throughout much of 1941 network radio stations played BMI-licensed music exclusively, giving a strong boost to previously ignored musical styles.

The debut of ten-inch (soon to be twelve-inch) 33⅓ rpm long-play records from Columbia in 1948 and seven-inch 45 rpm single records from RCA in 1949 (both made from vinyl) immediately displaced the heavier and fragile ten-inch 78 rpm shellac records and had a major impact on the industry. The LP became the primary medium for jazz and classical recordings and the 45 was the one for pop music and jukeboxes. The smaller, lighter, and virtually indestructible 45s enabled independent record labels to affordably and reliably ship their product nationwide.

The growth of television had both direct and indirect effects on rock and roll. Television had made significant inroads into U.S. homes by 1949, and 65 percent of U.S. households had a TV by 1955. Thinking that television would displace radio, the major broadcast networks loosened their objections to licensing additional radio stations, and local radio exploded by the mid-1950s. While the major radio networks were using live bands for their music broadcasts, independent stations were playing recordings. Cheap lightweight compact Japanese transistor radios flooded the market about this time, further contributing to the growth of radio.

In 1948 the four major record labels—RCA, Columbia (CBS), Capitol, and American Decca (MCA)—released 81 percent of all records that reached the weekly Top 10. Independent record labels grew exponentially beginning in the late 1940s (see figure 14), and by 1959 the major labels' share of the Top 10 pot had dropped to 34 percent. Record sales grew steadily during the first part of the 1950s and then almost tripled between 1954 and 1959, when it reached $604 million. Rock and roll releases, including those on independent labels, fueled much of the growth (Gillett 1996: 39).

YOUTH CULTURE

Post–World War II economic prosperity in the United States led to teenagers having the time and means to participate in and influence American consumer culture by the 1950s. *The Wild One* (1953), starring thirty-year-old Marlon Brando; *Rebel without a Cause* (1955), starring twenty-four-year-old James Dean; and *Blackboard Jungle* (1955), with twenty-eight-year-old Sidney Poitier in his breakout role, reflected a growing concern about post–World War II youth culture. Toward the end of the decade, however, a series of films featuring rock and roll began to show a lighter side to teen life, and rock and roll had become the soundtrack for this generation.

Desegregation of the U.S. armed forces ordered by President Harry S. Truman in 1948 also contributed indirectly to the birth of rock and roll. Of the 5.7 million U.S. military personnel involved in the Korean War (1950–53), six hundred thousand were African American, a significant number in a country with a population of 150 million in 1950. Whites were exposed to the listening tastes of their black counterparts during the war, and when they returned home some of them passed those new listening experiences to their younger siblings.

NAMING A STYLE

The definitive arrival of the term *rock and roll* to name a multifaceted musical phenomenon can be tracked to late 1954, just after Alan Freed moved to WINS in New York and was forced to drop the label *Moondog* for his show (a local artist with that name had sued him). Freed began calling his program the *Rock and Roll Show* by December (*Billboard* 1954), and by January 1955 the term had caught on, as can be seen in two *Billboard* notices.

Disc Jockey Alan Freed's first 'Rock 'n' roll' Ball in this city was a complete sell-out for both nights at the St. Nicholas Arena [capacity six thousand]. (*Billboard* 1955a: 13)

[Advertisement for Alan Freed's WINS radio program:] America's #1 'Rock 'n' roll' disc Jockey (*Billboard* 1955b)

The profile of the new style by the mainstream *Life* magazine in April 1955 provided a brief explanation as to how the style arose: "During the past years as the big record companies concentrated on mambos and ballads, the country's teen-agers found themselves without snappy dance tunes to their taste. A few disk jockeys filled the void with songs like *Ko Ko Mo, Tweedlee Dee, Hearts of Stone, Earth Angel, Flip, Flop, and Fly, Shake, Rattle and Roll*, and the name rock 'n roll took over. On a list of 10 top jukebox best-selling records last week, six were r 'n r" (*Life* 1955: 168). All the songs named were R&B hits in 1954, except "Flip, Flop, and Fly," which was released in early 1955. By early 1956 rock and roll was no longer a novelty; in a trend that would forever mark rock, it had gained respectability and was being co-opted, as *Billboard* had noted: "The shouting and tumult has died, but rhythm and blues or, as the teen-agers call it, rock and roll, has not departed. Rather, it may be stated that it has received respectability. The true measure of this development is the extent to which the idiom is being used in more or less pedestrian areas of the entertainment and advertising world" (Ackerman 1956: 1).

CROSSOVERS

Crossing over from the R&B or country charts to the pop charts was a major concern of many artists and their record labels. It meant exposure to a much broader audience and greater economic returns. The Mills Brothers, Louis Jordan, and Nat King Cole were some of the very few black artists to cross over from the race charts (called Harlem, then R&B) to the pop charts in the 1940s. A new crossover trend accelerated by the mid-1950s with black male vocal groups: the Dominoes' "Sixty-Minute Man" (1951) hit #17; the Orioles' "Crying in the Chapel" (1953) hit #11; the Crows' "Gee" (1954) hit #14; and the Chords' "Sh-Boom" (1954) broke into the pop Top 10 at #5. These were the first new R&B groups or artists of the 1950s to cross over into the upper reaches of the pop charts. The Tin Pan Alley–based pop styles and forms they used most likely facilitated their entry. The two high-profile crossovers of "Gee" and "Sh-Boom" in such close succession, in May and June 1954, were a harbinger.

Solo artists who were more blues and R&B-based would soon follow. The axis between New Orleans (Fats Domino, Little Richard), Mississippi Delta and Memphis (Ike Turner), Saint Louis (Chuck Berry), and Chicago (Bo Diddley) was crucial in providing the first generation of black R&B artists to cross over. (Turner did much work behind the scenes in the 1950s as a musician, scout, and producer, but did not hit the pop charts until 1960, with his wife, Tina.) Black artists crossing over became common from 1956 onward: "Whereas during the forties and early fifties there were rarely as many as three black singers simultaneously in the popular music hit parades, after 1956 at least one fourth of the best-selling records were by black singers" (Gillett 1996: xix).

COVERS

Bill Haley and His Comets' 1954 cover of R&B singer Big Joe Turner's "Shake, Rattle and Roll," three months after the original entered the R&B charts, could be taken as another sign that a new era was emerging. Turner hit #1 on the R&B jukebox chart in June 1954, but he did not cross over to the pop charts at the time (he would later cross over three times between 1956 and 1960). In August Haley's cover broke into the pop Top 10 in all three charts (Best Seller, Juke Box, and Jockey). The previous year (1953), Haley debuted on the pop chart with his "Crazy Man, Crazy" at #12, and so he had already laid some groundwork with his sound—different from Turner's, for sure—a sound that would become one of the most emblematic of the early rock and roll era (see figure 21).

A notorious case, because the cover came in such close succession and sounded so similar to the original, was "Tweedlee Dee." First recorded by R&B artist LaVern Baker (on the independent Atlantic label), the original entered both the pop and R&B charts on January 15, 1955. Just two weeks later, on January 29, white singer Georgia Gibbs's cover version (on the major Mercury label) entered the pop charts. And just as Baker's original hit #4 on the R&B charts and was rising up the pop charts, Gibbs's cover surpassed it, rising to pop best seller #3; Baker's original stalled at #22. Baker wrote her Congress representative, protesting that her arrangement (and, presumably, style) should be protected by copyright, but to no avail (*Billboard* 1955c). The African American songwriters Jesse Stone ("Shake, Rattle and Roll") and Winfield Scott

("Tweedlee Dee") received their share of composer royalties from any cover versions; the vocalists, however, received royalties only on sales of their own recordings.

In 1950 a test case had opened the door for this common practice of pop cover versions of R&B hits, ruling that musical arrangements were not considered as copyrightable property. The independent label Supreme tried, unsuccessfully, to sue the major Decca for $400,000. Supreme claimed that Decca had stolen their arrangement of "A Little Bird Told Me," sung by Paula Watson, when Decca had issued an almost indistinguishable cover by Evelyn Knight (*Billboard* 1950).

Gibbs's cover of Baker's "Tweedlee Dee" may have prompted Langston Hughes's (1955) article later that year in the African American newspaper *Chicago Defender*: "Highway Robbery across the Color Line in Rhythm and Blues." Imitation can be a form of flattery, Hughes noted, but blacks did not have the same access to venues, radio, and film, and so the practice was inherently unfair. The week after Hughes's article was published, Pat Boone, who was perhaps the most notorious practitioner of producing bland pop covers of R&B hits, entered the pop charts covering Fats Domino's "Ain't It a Shame," with Domino following close behind. Domino's original had been at #1 on the R&B charts for eleven weeks in the early summer. While he crossed over to pop best seller #16, Boone's cover hit #2 and remained there for many weeks as the original fell off the charts (see figure 21). Boone's cover may have inadvertently pulled Domino into the otherwise impermeable pop charts. Domino had placed twelve songs in the Top 10 of R&B charts since 1950, with none crossing over. He had performed earlier in 1955 at Alan Freed's first Rock 'n' Roll Ball in New York City, so perhaps the time was right for him to reach a new audience, under the banner of rock and roll. According to Boone, years later Domino called him up to the stage to thank him. "This man bought me this ring with this song," Domino said pointing to one of his diamond rings, and they sang "Ain't That a Shame" together (J. Miller 1999: 101). Composer royalties earned from Boone's cover may have taken some of the sting out.

Ray Charles, whose style was much less threatened by pop cover versions, had a generous attitude in his assessment of the practice: "White singers were picking up on black songs on a much more widespread basis. They had always done it, but now it was happening much more frequently. Georgia Gibbs and Pat Boone and Carl Perkins and Elvis were doing tunes which originally had been rhythm-and-blues hits. It didn't bother me. It was just one of those American things. I've said before that I believe in mixed musical marriages, and there's no way to copyright a feeling or a rhythm or a style of singing. Besides, it meant that White America was getting hipper" (Charles and Ritz 1978: 176).

The case of Boone and Little Richard may illustrate Ray Charles's point about getting hipper. Boone's early 1956 cover of Little Richard's "Tutti Frutti" reached pop best seller #6, surpassing the original, which had stalled at #17 and dropped off the chart. But, very soon after, Little Richard's "Long Tall Sally" spent a few months on that same best-seller pop chart, reaching #6, while Boone's cover barely registered there, appearing for just two weeks and only reaching #23.[5] Little Richard later spoke of this moment back in 1956: "When Pat Boone come out, I was mad . . . because, to me he was stopping my progress. I wanted to be famous. And here this man done came and took my song. . . . Now, in later years I thought about that, and said, that was good. But back then I said, oooh I can't stand him. . . . I wanted the whole world to know that that's not the way it went."[6] Bo Diddley continued that thought in conversation with Little Richard: "I felt about the same way you did, until I learnt that, hey, I *am* important, very important, because if these cats think enough of me to imitate me, that's pretty good. Because I know guys out here can't even get arrested" (Hackford 1987-v, disc 3).

Cover versions coming out many months, or even years, later can have positive effects, as when in 1963 the Beatles, for example, covered Chuck Berry's 1956 "Roll over Beethoven," not only bringing Berry composer royalties, but also stimulating interest in his music for a younger generation. Many other British Invasion bands covered Berry early in their career, including the Rolling Stones ("Come On," "Carol"), Animals ("Memphis, Tennessee," "Around and Around"), and Yardbirds ("Too Much Monkey Business"). Berry noted that his fee jumped from $1,200 to $2,000 a night when he returned to performing after a prison term (1962–63) and the Beatles had arrived in the United States.[7]

A key question concerns the creativity of the cover version—does it offer anything new? Ruth Brown voiced a pragmatic approach: "My gripe would never be

---

5 Boone's cover had a similar fate on the Disc Jockey chart, but fared better on the Juke Box chart (#8), surpassing Little Richard (#14). One can only speculate whether white teens would have been okay with purchasing and requesting airplay of Little Richard's recording but less comfortable listening to it in public spaces on jukeboxes.

6 Little Richard had a similar take on another cover: "Elvis took my 'Tutti Frutti' and I was very disgusted. But by him singing it, he really made it bigger, and made *me* bigger" (Wharton 2002-v).

7 See Hackford (1987-v, disc 4, Robertson interview).

with legitimate covers, or subsequent versions like [British singer] Cliff Richard's, but with bare-faced duplicates, with no artistic merit whatsoever. Everybody in the business accepted covers as fair game. . . . I covered several songs myself . . . but they were never by any stretch of the imagination mere duplicates. We *contributed* to the songs" (1996: 110).

FIVE PRIMARY STYLES

It can be convenient to get a handle on the first wave of early rock and roll (1954–56) by categorizing its diverse streams into five primary styles, as suggested by Gillett (1996: 23–35). Each of these styles has strong regional associations (see figure 22).

Northern Band Rock and Roll

Bill Haley (1925–81) and His Comets exemplify this stream with their hits "Crazy Man, Crazy" (1953), "Shake, Rattle and Roll" (1954), and "Rock around the Clock" (1955). Comparing Haley's "Shake, Rattle and Roll" with Joe Turner's original, one can hear one way in which R&B was reshaped for a young white mainstream audience, taking off some of the blues-drenched edge from both the musical beat and the lyrics. The saxophone, a staple of R&B, is still present, although paired with a country-style electric guitar and given less room for improvisation on recordings. Sam "The Man" Taylor's saxophone solos on R&B recorded in New York City in the mid-1950s set a standard difficult to retain in the new world of rock and roll (e.g., his baritone sax solo on Turner's original and his tenor sax solo on the Chords' "Sh-Boom" recorded the following month). Haley, born in 1925 in Michigan, was pushing thirty years old during his initial years of popularity (1953–56), no match for Elvis, who was a decade younger. Haley moved to the major label Decca in 1954 after his first hit.

New Orleans Dance Blues

The two major artists in this stream are pianists Fats Domino (1928–2017) from New Orleans and Little Richard (1932–) from Macon, Georgia, who made his first commercially successful recordings in New Orleans with some of Fats Domino's musicians. They recorded at the famed studios run by Cosimo Matassa: J&M Studio, open from 1945 to 1956, and then Cosimo's Studio at a new location.

Fats Domino's debut record, "The Fat Man," the B side of a ten-inch 78 rpm single on the New Orleans Imperial label, hit #2 on the R&B Juke Box chart in 1950. Featuring Earl Palmer, a future Rock and Roll Hall of Famer and one of the most recorded drummers who contributed much to the development of rock and roll (Scherman 1999), the song established Domino and his signature laid-back New Orleans–based boogie woogie sound as a major force. Domino was the most experienced and commercially successful (excepting Elvis), and one of the oldest (behind Bill Haley and Chuck Berry) of the first generation of rock and rollers, with thirteen songs in the R&B Top 15 before he crossed over to the pop charts with "Ain't It a Shame" in 1955. That initiated an extraordinary run of thirty-six Top 40 songs in the pop charts between 1955 and 1962. Domino recorded exclusively on the Imperial label from his debut through the peak of his recording career (1950–63); his *Complete Imperial Singles* collection contains over 130 songs.

Little Richard Penniman was born and raised in Macon, Georgia, singing in various churches (African Methodist Episcopal, Baptist, Pentecostal) and playing saxophone in his high school marching band. Richard has attributed his unique piano style to capturing the sound of the train rolling by his home as a child. After touring with various bands (occasionally appearing in drag attire), he recorded with RCA Victor in 1951 (no chart success) and Houston-based Peacock in 1953 (not released at the time) and then regrouped with a new band, the Upsetters. He signed with the Los Angeles–based Specialty label, which sent him to New Orleans to record at J&M Studio in October 1955 with Specialty producer Bumps Blackwell and Fats Domino musicians Lee Allen (saxophone) and Earl Palmer (drums). That session yielded "Tutti Frutti," a lewd song with lyrics cleaned up on the spot by songwriter Dorothy LaBostrie, which hit #2 on the R&B charts and crossed over to #18 on the pop Best Seller chart. His next session (February 1956) yielded "Long Tall Sally," his greatest crossover success (R&B #1, pop #6) (see figure 20). He made appearances in three films in 1956–57 (*Don't Knock the Rock*, *The Girl Can't Help It*, and *Mister Rock and Roll*) and enjoyed some financial success as a result of his touring and record sales. Little Richard left rock and roll in late 1957 to study for the ministry at a Seventh Day Adventist university, returning in 1962. His peak recording years, just 1955–57 on Specialty, yielded close to forty songs.[8]

---

8 Little Richard established the terms of a public queer persona in rock, no mean feat given his religious background (C. Malone 2017). For more on Little Richard, see C. White (1984).

Memphis Rockabilly

In the mid-1950s southern white artists, primarily on independent Memphis-based Sun Records, merged country (formerly called "hillbilly") with R&B, typically featuring string instruments: acoustic and electric guitars and bass. Jerry Lee Lewis playing piano would be the exception. Saxophones were absent. The style came to be known as *rockabilly*, a term that *Billboard* magazine began using about June 1956, two years after Elvis Presley's first recordings. By early 1957 *Billboard* noted the dominance of both rock and roll and rockabilly on the pop charts (see figure 23).[9]

The genre was kicked off on Sun with Elvis Presley's (1935–77) first single, "That's All Right Mama" (backed with "Blue Moon of Kentucky"), recorded and released in July 1954.[10] Elvis would release a total of five seven-inch 45 rpm singles for Sun over the next year, each with an R&B cover on one side and a bluegrass or country cover on the other side. Five additional songs recorded at Sun would be released on his first album (*Elvis Presley*), on RCA Victor in early 1956. His group initially consisted of a trio, with Elvis on acoustic guitar and vocals, Scotty Moore on electric guitar, and Bill Black on acoustic bass; various drummers joined the trio for his fourth ("I'm Left, You're Right") and fifth ("Mystery Train") releases, until D. J. Fontana settled in by the time Elvis moved to RCA Victor. The sequence of Elvis's Sun singles and his entry into the country charts is as follows:

"That's All Right"/"Blue Moon of Kentucky" (rec. July 5, 1954;
  rel. July 19, 1954)
"Good Rockin' Tonight"/"I Don't Care If the Sun Don't Shine"
  (rec. September 10, 1954; rel. September 25, 1954)
"Milkcow Blues Boogie"/"You're a Heartbreaker" (rec. December 8, 1954;
  rel. December 28, 1954)

---

9 Early uses of the term *rockabilly* in *Billboard* include the following. "The wave of 'rock-a-billy' imitators (which accompanied Presley's rise) has sharply receded during the last couple of weeks" (Bundy 1956: 17). "The phenomenon of the charts, of course, is the presence of three rockabilly platters on the R&B list [by Presley and Perkins]" (Simon 1956). "The current domination of rock and roll and rockabilly tunes in the pop music field" (*Billboard* 1957).

10 Sixteen-year-old Oklahoman Wanda Jackson's debut, "You Can't Have My Love," was released two months earlier, in May on Decca, reaching #8 on the C&W Juke Box chart. More in the realm of country, she would not cross over to the pop charts until 1960, with "Let's Have a Party."

"Baby Let's Play House" (#5 country)/"I'm Left, You're Right,
    She's Gone" (rec. February 1 and March 5, 1954; rel. April 10, 1955)
"I Forgot to Remember to Forget" (#1 country)/"Mystery Train" (#10 country)
    (rec. July 11, 1955; rel. August 6, 1955)

In late 1955, after a year of Elvis breaking out of *Billboard*'s regional country charts
to the top of its national country chart, the major label RCA Victor bought his contract from Sun recording studio and record-label owner Sam Phillips for $35,000
plus $5,000 in owed royalties. Phillips's quote—"If I could find a white man who
had the Negro sound and the Negro feel, I could make a billion dollars"—is one of
the most famous in rock and roll history.[11] Elvis's massive success beginning from his
very first single on RCA Victor in early 1956 marked the arrival of rock and roll as a
high-profile commercial recorded product. That single ("Heartbreak Hotel") entered
the pop charts in early March, reached #1, and stayed there for eight weeks. His first
album, *Elvis Presley*, was released in March and hit #1, staying there for ten weeks;
it was the first rock and roll album to hit #1. This was an era of independent record
labels scouting talent and bringing them to national audiences before the major
labels caught on. The majors had the influence and finances to market Presley, and
he appeared on national television shows almost every month in 1956, culminating
with three appearances on the *Ed Sullivan Show* toward the end of the year.

Presley's standing in the history of rock and roll can be appreciated by looking
at his recording track record: he had nineteen Top 10 hits between 1956 and 1959,
twelve of which went to #1. "Don't Be Cruel" (backed with "Hound Dog") stayed at
#1 for eleven weeks in the summer of 1956 and hit #1 on the pop, R&B and C&W
charts, indicating that a broad cross section of American youth was listening to him.
His Sun recordings (1954–55), made when he was nineteen to twenty years old, are
among the most seismic in the history of rock. Drawing deep from country, gospel,
R&B, and the blues, Elvis created a unique mix that reflected the mood and optimism
of young America in the second decade after the Great War.

Growing up in Tupelo, Mississippi, about a hundred miles east of the Mississippi
Delta region, exposed Elvis early on to deeply rooted southern culture, including
African American culture, which he drew on. After he moved with his family to
Memphis at the age of thirteen, he would occasionally attend the church services

---

11 Phillips is quoted from his studio partner Marion Keisker in Guralnick (1971: 172).

and evening radio broadcasts of the great black gospel composer and preacher Rev. W. Herbert Brewster, who was popular among blacks and whites.[12] Elvis's African American audience can be gauged by his R&B chart standings: between March 1956 and early 1961, he had twenty-two Top 10 hits in the R&B charts, six of which went to #1.

In April 1957 white-owned *Sepia* magazine, which catered to a black readership, published "How Negroes Feel about Elvis," registering opinions that ran the gamut from condemnation to admiration. The article contained a racist comment rumored to have been said by Elvis. That summer, black-owned *Jet* magazine, also catering to a black audience, sent editor Louie Robinson (1957) to interview Elvis and others who knew him, including African Americans in his hometown Tupelo and in Memphis. Robinson found no credible basis for the rumor and offered up a sympathetic picture of his standing among African Americans. The article estimated that Fats Domino, his closest peer, would earn $700,000 in 1957 and that Elvis stood to earn twice that amount. (For comparison, earlier in the decade the biggest star in country music, Hank Williams, was earning $200,000 a year until his death in 1953 at age twenty-nine.) The *Sepia* magazine quote may be the original basis for rumors about Elvis that still persist.

Robinson also interviewed Brooklyn-based songwriter Otis Blackwell: "The lion's share, or an estimated $900,000, of the Presley income is from records, two of the best of which were penned by a New York Negro, Otis Blackwell: *Don't Be Cruel*, which has brought Presley a not-at-all cruel $202,500, and *All Shook Up*, which shook $135,000 into Elvis' jeans. Blackwell refuses to disclose his earnings on the songs, but he says: 'I got a good deal. I made money, I'm happy'" (1957: 61). Blackwell himself, according to his obituary in the *New York Times*, "from an early age crossed a cultural color line. At home, his family gathered around the piano to sing gospel songs, but while working at a nearby movie theater he became obsessed with the singing cowboy movies of Tex Ritter. 'Like the blues, it told a story,' he once said of country music. 'But it didn't have the same restrictive construction. A cowboy song could do anything.' … Many of the songs he wrote for Presley gave both men songwriting credit, because

12 Louie Robinson (1957: 61); Guralnick (1994: 75); see also Reagon (1992: 201) and Heilbut (2002: 101).

of an arrangement with Presley's management. 'I was told that I would have to make a deal,' Mr. Blackwell later said" (*New York Times* 2002).[13]

Some of the animosity toward Elvis among African Americans may be due to a perception that he did not publicly acknowledge his sources. The songwriters he covered, though, received copyright credit on his records (and presumably royalties from his sales and performance rights), and early interviews should dispel any doubts.

> The colored folks been singing it and playing it just like I'm doin' now, man, for more years than I know. They played it like that in the shanties and in their juke joints and nobody paid it no mind 'til I goose it up. I got it from them. Down in Tupelo, Mississippi, I used to hear old Arthur Crudup bang his box the way I do now and I said if I ever got to the place I could feel all old Arthur felt I'd be a music man like nobody ever saw" (Presley, qtd. in Gary 1956).

Presley was frank about his own contribution: "A lot of people seem to think I started this business,' he muses, 'but rock 'n' roll was here a long time before I came along. Nobody can sing that kind of music like colored people. Let's face it: I can't sing it like Fats Domino can. I know that. But I always liked that kind of music. I used to go to the colored churches when I was a kid—like Rev. Brewster's [Baptist] church [in Memphis]" (Presley, qtd. in Louie Robinson 1957: 61).

Presley recognized here another source of animosity: getting credit for inventing a musical style. Referring to Elvis as the king of rock and roll, suggesting that he either invented the style or did it better than anyone else, does a disservice to his African American contemporaries and predecessors. This was Chuck D's point when he later reflected back on his incendiary lines in Public Enemy's 1989 "Fight the Power," lines that reinforced negative perceptions of Elvis for later generations: "Elvis [Presley] was an icon to America but he ain't invent Rock & Roll. There were other Black heroes

---

13 Presley's publisher required songwriters to give up a third of their credit if they wanted their songs recorded, something that embarrassed Presley: "I've never written a song in my life. . . . It makes me look smarter than I am" (qtd. in Guralnick 1994: 386–87). Blackwell states, "There had to be a deal, share this and that. I said no at first, but they said Elvis is gonna turn the business around, so I said okay. . . . It turned out we sounded alike, had the same groove. . . . The cat was hot, that's why his name is on the songs. Why not? That's the way the business is anyway" (qtd. in Giddens 1976: 48).

[that did]. . . . And that aspect was racist I thought, that people just obscured the Black foundation of what Elvis evolved from. . . . He started off being quite humble . . . hearing from people speaking that knew him and knew his beginnings: from Bobby 'Blue' Bland, I had conversations with Little Richard, Ike Turner. He started out being this cat that loved Black music, the Black environment, the Black way of dress and all that" (qtd. in P. Arnold 2012).

From a commercial point of view, Presley was in a class by himself. His artistic contribution, a unique mix of styles drawing not only from R&B but also from country and white and black gospel can be readily heard by comparing his cover version of "Mystery Train" (1955) with Herman "Little Junior" Parker's original from 1953. One would be hard pressed to doubt his talent and charisma as an entertainer. His age, eight years younger than Chuck Berry and two years younger than Little Richard, was also a major factor among a teen market that was asserting itself for the first time.

Presley's appeal across generations, after an initial shock, was in part due to his lack of pretense: "One big element, it is clear, is his lack of all pretensions. A recurrent theme among the adult minority interviewed at Tuesday night's show was expressed by Mrs. G. E. Anderson of Charlotte. 'I didn't like Sinatra in his day but I like Elvis. He's country and I am too,' she said. Nearly all the adults who expressed delight with Presley had 10 years before scorned the smooth Frankie boy" (Oberdorfer 1956: 1B).

Some quotations posted on the website of Graceland (2019), Elvis's home since 1957 and now a major tourist site, provide a sense of his standing among his African American peers. Most are unsourced, but some can be tracked down, which can lead to many more. James Brown and Muhammad Ali, in particular, both icons of black identity and achievement, world famous, and born into poverty, have expressed close kinship with, and love and respect for, Presley. Muhammad Ali remembered, "All my life, I admired Elvis Presley. When I was in Las Vegas, I heard him sing, and it was a thrill to meet him" (qtd. in Hauser 1991: 481). "When I was 15 years old [about 1957] and saw Elvis on TV, I wanted to be Elvis. Other kids in the neighborhood were listening to Ray Charles and James Brown, but I listened to Elvis. I admired him so much and I decided that if I was going to be famous I'd do it just like him" (qtd. in Shanahan 2016: 138–39).

The year after Presley died, James Brown paid tribute to him, covering one of his early hits, "Love Me Tender," saying in the introduction, "I want to talk about a good friend I had for a long time and a man I still love, brother Elvis Presley" ("Love Me Tender," 1978). Brown wrote in his autobiography, "[in 1966] we threw everybody out of the room, and Elvis and I sang gospel together. . . . That's how we communicated. . . . I could tell Elvis had a strong spiritual feeling by the way he sang that music. . . . His death hit me very hard. We were a lot alike in many ways—both poor boys from the country raised on gospel and R&B. . . . I went to Graceland that night" (1986: 165, 166, 247). B. B. King, who knew Elvis in his early days in Memphis, had this to say: "Respect, respect, respect. And he sorta earned it, earned that respect from me at that time. Finally I had a chance to meet him and I found out that he really was something else" (PBS 2001). Memphis all-black-formatted WDIA radio deejay Rufus Thomas stated, "I was the first black jock to play Elvis records. . . . We were doing a WDIA show at Ellis Auditorium, and Elvis was backstage. I took him by the hand and led him onstage, he made that twisting of the leg, and the people, these were all black people now, they stormed that stage trying to get to Elvis. After that, the show was really over. Elvis was doing good music, blues and rhythm and blues, because that was his beginning." And R&B bandleader Roy Brown recalled, "Elvis followed us, from Tupelo to Vicksburg to Hattiesburg, and he just watched us. Later on, when I first saw him on 'The Ed Sullivan Show,' all that wiggling and stuff, man, the blacks had been doing that for years. But there was something about Elvis that was different from the Fabians and them other guys. Elvis could *sing*. And he had a heart. . . . He had style, and he had soul" (qtd. in Palmer 1995: 27–28).

Elvis's recording success immediately led to his film career, with over thirty films made from 1956 (*Love Me Tender*, released in November) through 1969, including *Jailhouse Rock* (1957), *King Creole* (1958), *Kid Galahad* (1962), and *Viva Las Vegas* (1964). After devoting much of the 1960s to acting, Presley made a comeback with an NBC television special in December 1968, hitting the Top 10 twice in 1969 (rare since 1963) with "In the Ghetto" (#3) and "Suspicious Minds" (#1). This led to his Las Vegas career and eventual declining health due to prescription drug abuse (Guralnick 1999).[14]

Immediately following the initial success of Elvis, several other Sun Records artists moved onto the national scene, notably guitarist Carl Perkins ("Blue Suede Shoes," pop #2, 1956) and pianist Jerry Lee Lewis ("Whole Lot of Shakin' Going On," pop #3, 1957). Johnny Cash ("I Walk the Line," country #1, 1956) would top the country

---

14 Raymond and Raymond (1987-v) focuses on 1956, when Elvis first burst into national celebrity; Wharton (2002-v) contains many tributes on the twenty-fifth anniversary of his death; and Zimmy (2018-v) takes a deep dive into his life and career.

charts, and Roy Orbison, having only minimal success debuting at Sun (1956–58), would eventually break through when he left for Monument Records ("Only the Lonely," pop #2, 1960). A photo of a chance meeting of Presley, Lewis, Perkins, and Cash at Sun Studios in December 1956 was captioned "Million Dollar Quartet" (R. Johnson 1956); recordings of the impromptu session were not released until 1981.

Chicago Rhythm and Blues

While a potent urban electric blues scene catering to the black community developed in the 1950s in Chicago, with many of the musicians coming from the South (e.g., Muddy Waters, Willie Dixon, and Howlin' Wolf), other musicians were able to create a more youthful music, crossing over into the pop market. The most successful was Chuck Berry (1926–2017), born and raised in Saint Louis, perhaps the most musically influential of all the early rock and roll artists. Berry was unique in his mastery of three realms: songwriting, singing, and guitar playing. He has cited Carl Hogan, guitarist with Louis Jordan, as an important influence, which can be heard on the introduction to Jordan's "Ain't That Just Like a Woman" (1946).

Berry's father was a contractor and church deacon, and his mother was a public school principal, and so he grew up in a middle-class neighborhood. He married in 1948 and worked various jobs to support his family (his daughter was born in 1950). By 1953 Berry was playing in Johnnie Johnson's trio regularly at the Cosmo Club in Saint Louis. On a recommendation from Muddy Waters he brought a demo tape to Chess Records and made his first record there in May 1955 ("Maybelline," an adaptation of the country tune "Ida Red"), with Johnson on piano and Willie Dixon on bass. To push "Maybelline" in the New York City market, Chess gave Alan Freed cosongwriting credit (without Berry's knowledge), and it worked: his debut record became a #1 R&B hit, crossing over to #5 on the pop chart. Berry (1987: 90–91) had a clear understanding of his audiences (he catered to both blacks and whites at the Cosmo Club), drawing his diction from both Nat King Cole and Muddy Waters. He had nine pop Top 40 hits through 1959 (out of a lifetime total of fourteen), five of which were in the Top 10 (see figure 20). Berry is widely recognized as the great songwriter of the early rock and roll era. His only #1 pop hit, though, came in 1972 with the novelty song "My Ding-a-Ling."

"I don't think there's any group in the world, white or black. . . . You name any top group, and they've all been influenced by him. His lyrics that were very intelligent lyrics in the fifties, when people were just singing virtually about nothing, he was writing social comment songs. He was writing all kinds of songs, with incredible meter to the lyrics, which influenced Dylan and me and many other people. The meter of his lyrics is tremendous. He's the greatest rock and roll poet, and I really admire him" (John Lennon in the 1970s, in Hackford 1987-v).

Bo Diddley (1928–2008), born Ellas Bates in McComb, Mississippi (changing his name to McDaniel when he was adopted by relatives), moved to the South Side of Chicago at the age of seven. Like his label-mate Chuck Berry, McDaniel was the other transplant to Chicago who was a major part of this early rock and roll era. He learned and played violin at the famed three-thousand-member Ebenezer Baptist Church and later picked up the guitar. His first record, "Bo Diddley," recorded and released on Chess subsidiary Checker, hit #1 on the R&B chart in 1955. In November 1955 he appeared on the *Ed Sullivan Show* as part of New York deejay Dr. Jive's *Rhythm and Blues Revue* from the Apollo Theater. Bo Diddley had several trademarks: a signature rhythm, sometimes called hambone (same as the Cuban clave); a percussive style of playing rhythm guitar even during his solos ("Bo Diddley," "Pretty Thing"); and a band that included a maracas player (Jerome Green) and a woman guitarist (Peggy "Lady Bo" Jones, succeeded by Norma-Jean "The Duchess" Wofford). He had the least commercial success of the early rock pioneers, in part because he put out fewer recordings, but his original, quirky sound, guitar style, personality, and look (he wore glasses and played a rectangular-shaped guitar) has given him an enduring visibility. He was inducted into the second class of the Rock and Roll Hall of Fame (2019) in 1987.

Although not based in Chicago, Ike Turner, from Clarksdale, Mississippi, brought his band to Sun Studio in Memphis to record "Rocket 88," which was issued on Chicago's Chess Records in 1951 under vocalist Jackie Brenston's name. It hit #1 on the R&B chart and is often pointed to as a key recording in rock history, due in part to the prominence of the distorted electric guitar in its boogie woogie rhythm. Turner subsequently worked for several years with Sun owner Sam Phillips, who formed Sun Records the following year.

Vocal Groups (Doo Wop)

Primarily a genre associated with northern urban African American communities (especially in New York City), doo wop developed in the mid-1950s from male vocal groups. The Dominoes and Crows were from Harlem, and the Chords were from the South Bronx. Doo wop typically drew not on blues forms but rather on Tin Pan Alley styles of songwriting. This involved a thirty-two-bar verse-verse-bridge-verse structure (diagrammed as AABA), wherein each letter refers to eight bars, and the bridge features a contrasting melody and chords.

Doo wop was an optimistic music that looked to the future, especially with romantic lyrics that pointed to life together as a couple. Whereas R&B and blues were
rooted in the past, doo wop represented a more modern urban and cosmopolitan
outlook: "The group singers dealt with a completely different situation. For them
and their audience, the past was, if not rejected and despised, then often ignored.
The present was of greatest importance, and the future was looked at with wonder:
Does she love me?—it's too soon to know. The songs were invariably about unfulfilled
relationships—the period after acquaintance has been established, before romance
has been confirmed. A smaller number of songs concerned the aftermath of a broken
relationship" (Gillett 1996: 162–63).

A series of crossovers from R&B to the pop world in the mid-1950s firmly established the genre and led to a glut on the market, reflecting its popularity in urban
neighborhoods. Two of the more well-known groups in the later 1950s, both affiliated with Atlantic Records and the songwriting team of Leiber and Stoller were the
Drifters (1953–), featuring Clyde McPhatter (who had left the Dominoes) and then
Ben E. King ("This Magic Moment" and "Save the Last Dance for Me," 1960); and
the Coasters (1955–), with hits including "Young Blood" and "Searchin'" (1957),
"Yakety Yak" (1958), and "Charlie Brown" (1959).

_____

*Buddy Holly (1936–59), from Lubbock, Texas, and the Crickets are missing in
Gillette's (1996: 23–35) first-wave five primary styles (1954–56), because they came
on the scene in 1957, in a second wave of early rock and roll. Neither do they fit into
any of the previously mentioned categories, as a white electric guitar–based quartet
with drums coming from Texas, hitting the R&B charts and never making the country
charts. After two misses in 1956, they hit #1 ("That'll Be the Day") and #3 ("Peggy
Sue") on the pop chart in 1957. They set the model for 1960s rock: they were a distinct unit (a band) that wrote their own songs, and they had a two-guitar (lead and
rhythm), bass, and drums quartet format.*

PAYOLA

In 1959, on the heels of television quiz-show inquiries, a House of Representatives
subcommittee began investigating the practice of payola, the payment of cash by record
promoters to radio disc jockeys to play their records. The highest-profile targets were
Alan Freed and Dick Clark. Freed was arrested along with seven other radio figures in
May 1960 for receiving over $100,000 in bribes from twenty-three record companies

over the past two years—it was front-page news for the *New York Times* (Roth 1960). He had already been fired from his radio and television jobs in 1959 and eventually pled guilty to two of the ninety-nine counts, paying a small fine in 1963. Freed was indicted in 1964 for income-tax evasion and died the following year of cirrhosis of the liver. Clark, who was the subject of an intense hearing in April 1960 and *Life* magazine profile, managed to escape unscathed by divesting his questionable industry holdings: "Dick Clark . . . did not rely on conventional cash payola but worked out a far more complex and profitable system. It hinged on his numerous corporate holdings which included financial interests in three record companies, six music publishing houses, a record pressing plant, a record distributing firm and a company which manages singers. The music, the records and the singers involved with these companies gained a special place in Clark's programs, which the [congressional] committee [investigating payola] said gave them a systematic preference" (Bunzel 1960: 120).

Freed and Clark had differing reputations in the African American press at the time (1959–60):

> If there's one shining star in the constellation of Alan Freed's career, it has been his determined, quiet, but effective war on racial bigotry in the music business. Largely as a result of his efforts, several Negro singing groups are top successes today because of his encouragement and fairness. . . . His "Big Party" has always had Negro kids right in there putting down a tough "slop" with the best of them. Have you ever seen Negro kids on Dick Clark's program? . . . Someone should raise the question as to whether there was ever any payola to keep Negro kids off of Dick Clark's American Bandstand TV program?[15] (*New York Age* 1959)

SOCIAL IMPACT

Gathered around a piano in the mid-1980s with Chuck Berry and Bo Diddley, discussing life on the road in the 1950s in a one-hour filmed conversation, Little Richard suggested that rock and roll had a stronger social impact than many people might be aware of.

> Little Richard: In some of the shows that I did in the early days, when I was drawing more blacks, they would have white spectators ([to Bo Diddley:]

---

15 Delmont (2012) has more on payola and Clark (143–47) and African American newspapers noting segregation on *American Bandstand* (184–87); see also Jackson (1997).

I know you used to play like that too, I'm sure that we all did), and the
white people would jump over the balcony and come down, and rock and
roll really brought integration about.

Chuck Berry: It helped.

Little Richard: It was a big force and a big help in integration coming about.
Today a lot of people don't know that.

Bo Diddley: That's right.

(Hackford 1987-v, disc 3)

In addition to the more private kinds of listening activities, such as in the home or in
a car, large-scale public rock and roll concerts—even those in segregated venues in the
South—may indeed have had a positive impact in the path toward racial integration.
Although, as we will see in a story related by Eric Burdon of the Animals, those teens
crashing the color line in the next decade did not necessarily represent all their peers
who loved rock and roll.

———

*Just looking through the prism of the number of pop Top 40 hits from 1954 to 1959, the
contributions of the first-generation architects of early rock and roll have registered very
unevenly. In chronological order of breaking through, they include Bill Haley (fifteen),
Fats Domino (twenty-one), Chuck Berry (nine), Little Richard (nine), Elvis Presley
(thirty-two), and Bo Diddley (one). Popularity chart recognition is just one, albeit
essential, part of a multifaceted story. Some parts of the story resist measurement, such
as originality, innovation, and feel (groove). And still other parts, such as the virulent
opposition on the part of some adults, may be hard to fathom. The contribution of this
generation of rock and roll pioneers to a new vision of U.S. culture and society is well
documented and generally recognized, yet still incalculable.*

———

See figure 14. Some key independent record labels, 1940s–1950s (date founded
and artist's debut recording)

See figure 18. Birth years of early rock and roll, soul, and funk leaders

See figure 19. Elvis Presley Top 10 hits

See figure 20. Top 40 crossover pop hits by black rock and roll artists

See figure 21. Five cover comparisons, 1954–1956

See figure 22. Five styles of early rock and roll, 1954–1956

See figure 23. Rockabilly artists and their debut recordings

Too much happened in the 1960s to cover in a single chapter. The first half of the decade saw the rise of a small independent Detroit record label (Motown) that would have an enormous impact way beyond its humble beginnings. By the time the Beatles arrived in the United States in February 1964, quickly taking over the pop charts and leading a British Invasion that saw a new British group enter the Top 40 almost every month for two years, Motown had launched two of its four most successful artists, Stevie Wonder and Marvin Gaye. The other two were the Supremes, who would begin an extraordinary run of #1 pop hits that year, and the Jackson Five (featuring eleven-year-old Michael Jackson), who would do the same at the end of the decade. The decade opened with an urban folk revival that provided the backdrop for the sudden celebrity of Joan Baez, followed by Bob Dylan, whose sophisticated songwriting cast a long shadow in all directions. James Brown's star would rise in the first half of the 1960s, matched by Aretha Franklin in the second half. Independent producers, girl groups, surf rock, and southern soul round out the picture.

All this took place in conversation with the increasingly urgent civil rights movement, fear of a nuclear war with the Soviet Union (weapons testing resumed in Nevada in September 1961 after the USSR broke a three-year worldwide moratorium), and gradual awareness that the United States was surreptitiously entering into what would be one of the most controversial wars in its history, in Vietnam. The assassination of President Kennedy in November 1963 added further distress to unsettling, yet economically abundant, times. A youth counterculture would gel by mid-decade, setting the terms of youth engagement with authority for many decades, deeply entwined in the new styles of rock and soul.

INDEPENDENT PRODUCERS, THE BRILL BUILDING, AND TEEN IDOLS

One of the major developments that took shape in the years between Elvis and the Beatles (late 1950s–early 1960s) was the surge of pop songs associated with independent songwriters and producers working in Midtown Manhattan.[1] The Brill Building, located at 1619 Broadway (at Forty-Ninth Street), was part of a small network of buildings on Broadway between Forty-Ninth and Fifty-Third Streets, including 1650 Broadway (at Fifty-First Street, home to Aldon Music), which housed offices

---

1 See Emerson (2012) for the full story.

for songwriters, publishers, arrangers, producers, talent agencies, and record labels. The Brill Building gave its name to a genre, which kept the focus on the single pop song that could be shopped around to different labels and artists. It was the major music-production center in New York City in the late 1950s and 1960s wherein songwriters would work during the day and pitch their product to a publisher, record label, and talent agent (who would supply the artists) and even record a demo (using in-house arrangers) all in one place. Production values were generally high.

The Brill Building gave rise to the independent producer, not attached to any single record label. The most well known of the early independent record producers were Jerry Leiber (1933–2011, from Baltimore) and Mike Stoller (1933–, from Long Island, New York), who met as teens in Los Angeles in 1950 and began writing songs together. Their first hit was in 1953, "Hound Dog," sung by Big Mama Thornton (and later covered by Elvis). Atlantic Records hired them, and they wrote and produced many hits for the Drifters and the Coasters. They moved to New York City about 1957 and about 1961 set up an office in the Brill Building. The role of the producer can be heard to good effect in Leiber and Stoller's arrangement of Ben E. King's 1960 "Stand by Me": the sparse opening gives way to a subtle and steady buildup of instrumental forces that dramatically highlight King's voice (see figure 24).

About 1960 Phil Spector (1939–, from Bronx, New York) apprenticed with Leiber and Stoller before moving out on his own to become one of the most important producers of the early and mid-1960s. Spector set up his own record label (Philles) and primarily recorded in Gold Star Studios in Los Angeles, where he created his trademark "wall of sound," fully saturating his productions. The group of LA studio musicians that Spector (and many others, including the Beach Boys and the Byrds) employed were known as the Wrecking Crew, including conductor-arranger Jack Nitzsche, drummers Hal Blaine and Earl Palmer, bassist Carol Kaye, guitarists Glen Campbell and Tommy Tedesco, and pianist Leon Russell. The Wrecking Crew was the house band for the T.A.M.I. Show held in Santa Monica, California, in October 1964, one of the first live rock concert films (Binder 1964-v).

Brill Building songwriters typically worked in teams (composer and lyricist), writing in small offices.[2] Some of the more successful writers included Burt Bacharach and Hal David ("What the World Needs Now Is Love," "I Say a Little Prayer"), whose writing was largely a vehicle for singer Dionne Warwick (niece of Cissy Houston,

---

2 Many songwriters worked at 1650 Broadway for publisher Aldon Music.

Whitney's mother); Doc Pomus and Mort Shuman ("This Magic Moment," "Save the Last Dance for Me"); Carole King and Gerry Goffin ("Will You Love Me Tomorrow," "Up on the Roof"); Barry Mann and Cynthia Weil ("You've Lost That Lovin' Feeling," "On Broadway"); and Ellie Greenwich and Jeff Barry ("Be My Baby," "Da Doo Ron Ron"). These were some of the most memorable hits of the early and mid-1960s (see figure 25).[3]

The legacy of the Brill Building style was far-reaching (Inglis 2003). It provided an unprecedented voice for young woman songwriters: Carole King, Cynthia Weil, and Ellie Greenwich (part of three songwriting pairs) placed over two hundred songs on *Billboard*'s Hot 100 singles chart. It provided important vehicles for African American singers, and particularly women, to reach the top of the pop charts: the Shirelles were the first African American women group to reach #1 on *Billboard*'s pop chart, with Goffin and King's "Will You Love Me Tomorrow"; and Dionne Warwick, fueled by the songwriting of Bacharach and David, had the most Top 40 hits of any woman in that era (until Aretha Franklin surpassed her in the 1970s). It provided the songwriting and production model for Motown. And it provided an important context for the rise of the Beatles: they had about a dozen Brill Building songs in their repertory in the early 1960s; they covered three Brill Building songs on their first album; and Lennon and McCartney have expressed great admiration for the songwriting team of Carole King and Gerry Goffin.

In the void left by the dissipation of the early waves of rock and roll by the late 1950s, a cohort of predominantly white male singers in their mid and late teens, projecting a cleaned-up wholesome version of rockabilly Elvis, helped define a brief post–rock and roll era (see figure 26). Many were Italian Americans from South Philadelphia (Frankie Avalon, Bobby Rydell, and Fabian), New Jersey (Connie Francis, Frankie Valli), and New York City (Dion, Bobby Darin). Eight vocalists produced 174 Top 40 hits between 1957 and 1965. Those from Philadelphia (and the surrounding region) enjoyed exposure on Dick Clark's *American Bandstand* television show, which was based there. Frankie Avalon, Ricky Nelson, Fabian, and Bobby Darin also had major careers starring in Hollywood teen films and TV shows. A related trend at the time was white male vocal groups, including Danny and the Juniors ("At the Hop," 1957);

---

3 Like many of their Tin Pan Alley predecessors, most Brill Building composers, lyricists, and producer were Jewish, including all those listed in this paragraph (and in figure 25) as well as Leiber, Stoller, and Spector (Stratton 2009).

Dion and the Belmonts ("A Teenager in Love," 1959); and one of the most successful vocal groups of all time, the Four Seasons, led by Frankie Valli ("Sherry" and "Big Girls Don't Cry," 1962).[4]

See figure 24. "Stand by Me" form and arrangement

See figure 25. Brill Building songwriting teams and select pop hits

See figure 26. Teen idols: Late 1950s–1960s Top 40 hits

GIRL GROUPS

In the late 1950s all-women vocal groups combining elements of R&B and rock and roll began to appear on the pop charts. Most were young, often starting their singing careers in high school. Primarily a northern urban African American phenomenon, early signs of this genre were the Bobbettes (from Harlem) in 1957 with "Mr. Lee" (pop #6) and the Chantels (from the Bronx) in 1958 with "Maybe" (pop #15). In 1960 the Shirelles (from Passaic, New Jersey) were the first group in this cohort to hit pop #1 ("Will You Love Me Tomorrow"). The Shirelles inaugurated a new era and had nine more Top 40 hits over the next three years. Their initial pop success was immediately followed by three all-women groups on the new Motown label: the Marvelettes ("Please Mr. Postman," pop #1, 1961); Martha and the Vandellas ("Heat Wave," pop #4, 1963); and the Supremes ("Where Did Our Love Go," pop #1, 1964). The Supremes were the most commercially successful of the groups in this genre (and of any Motown artist) with twenty Top 10 hits through 1970 (see figure 27). Supremes lead vocalist Diana Ross went on to a major solo career beginning in 1970.

Motown's girl groups were rivaled by two New York groups produced by Phil Spector, who recorded them at Gold Star Studios in Los Angeles, yielding eleven Top 40 hits between 1962 and 1964: the Crystals and the Ronettes (with lead-singer Ronnie Bennett). "Da Do Ron Ron" (pop #3, Crystals, featuring LaLa Brooks) and "Be My Baby" (pop #2, Ronettes), both released in the second half of 1963, were emblematic of Spector's wall of sound. The Ronettes had a brief but meteoric celebrity, illustrating differences between how record labels invested in their artists. After "Be My Baby," they had four Top 40 hits in 1964 (all Spector productions), none of which

---

4   For more on this era, see Aronowitz (1963), Fox (1986), Rohlfing (1996), M. Brown (2008), Leiber and Stoller (2009), Hartman (2012), and Tedesco's (2008-v) documentary.

breached the Top 20, and that was it for them. They were hot in 1964, touring with both the Beatles and the Rolling Stones. The Shirelles had a slightly longer trajectory (all on the Scepter label): their Top 40 success lasted from 1960 to 1963, with twelve hits, five of which were in 1962. By contrast, the most successful of these groups, the Supremes, heavily supported by Motown, had twenty-nine Top 40 hits from 1963 to 1970 (twelve of which hit #1), with an average of four hits per year.

Some girl groups were associated with Brill Building writers, such as the Chiffons (from the Bronx), whose "One Fine Day" (written by Carole King and Gerry Goffin) hit #5 in 1963. The Shangri-Las (from Queens, New York) were one of the few white (and Jewish) groups in the genre, with "Leader of the Pack" (Jeff Barry, Ellie Green-wich) hitting #1 in 1964. Darlene Love, who sang with Bob B. Soxx and the Blue Jeans, the Blossoms, and surreptitiously with the Crystals ("He's a Rebel"), had three solo songs in the pop charts in 1963, all Ellie Greenwich–Phil Spector productions. By the mid-1960s girl groups were a major presence on the musical landscape, with African American groups predominating.

O'Brien (2002: 68) has noted that three Brill Building husband-and-wife song-writing teams were the "nucleus of the girl-group industry" until Motown moved in: Carole King and Gerry Goffin, Barry Mann and Cynthia Weil, and Ellie Greenwich and Jeff Barry (see figure 25). She has succinctly summarized part of the significance of this moment in the early 1960s: "Women love telling stories—they read them to children at night, they relate them to girlfriends in the ladies' room—the girl-group era is a gigantic narrative full of morality tales locked up like charms in a crystallized sound" (2002: 67).[5]

See figure 25. Brill Building songwriting teams and select pop hits
See figure 27. Motown pop Top 10 singles, 1960–1970

MOTOWN

In 1959 Detroit native Berry Gordy Jr. (1929–) founded the Tamla and then Motown record labels in his hometown. Several additional subsidiaries were folded into Mo-town, including Anna, Gordy, and Soul. Tamla had its first hits the following year

5 For more on this style, see Betrock (1982), Spector (1990), Warwick (2007), Love (2013), and MacLeod (2015).

with Barrett Strong's "Money (That's What I Want)" (pop #23) and the Miracles' (featuring Smokey Robinson) "Shop Around" (pop #2). Gordy had initially entered the music business cowriting the hits "Reet Petite" (1957) and "Lonely Teardrops" (1958) for Jackie Wilson. In 1961 Motown had its first pop #1 hit with the Marvelettes' "Please Mr. Postman."

Berry Gordy and Motown, a predominantly black corporation, were known for their investment in their artists and full in-house production, including a recording studio (Hitsville U.S.A.); songwriters, producers, sales and promotion personnel; a choreographer (Cholly Atkins); charm and poise instructor (Maxine Powell); publishing company (Jobete); and a house band. That band was known as the Funk Brothers and featured Benny Benjamin (drums), James Jamerson (bass), Earl Van Dyke (piano), and Robert White (guitar), among many others, most of whom had a significant jazz background. Jamerson in particular is highly regarded as one of the most sensitive and creative bass players of his era. Motown began recording on eight tracks in 1964 (with the Supremes' "Baby Love"), increasing the clarity and giving a more prominent role to Jamerson, whose bass had its own track.[6]

Gordy's whole Motown operation consciously resembled the Detroit auto-plant assembly lines on which he worked. As Gordy has noted, "Every day I watched how a bare metal frame, rolling down the line would come off the other end, a spanking brand new car. What a great idea! Maybe, I could do the same thing with my music. Create a place where a kid off the street could walk in one door, an unknown, go through a process, and come out another door, a star" (Motown Museum 2019).

Motown songwriters included the teams of Brian Holland, Lamont Dozier, and Eddie Holland ("Heat Wave," "Baby I Need Your Loving," "How Sweet It Is," "You Can't Hurry Love") and Nickolas Ashford and Valerie Simpson ("Ain't No Mountain High Enough," "Reach Out and Touch"); and individuals, including Smokey Robinson ("The Way You Do the Things You Do," "My Guy," "My Girl," "Get Ready") and Norman Whitfield ("Ain't Too Proud to Beg," "I Heard It through the Grapevine," "Papa Was a Rollin' Stone").

The Funk Brothers and their producers were largely responsible for the recognizable Motown sound. Animated by Jamerson's prominent dynamic bass lines (e.g., "Ain't No Mountain High Enough"), tambourines or handclaps, and relatively sophisti-

---

6   See Justman (2002-v) for a documentary on the Funk Brothers, and see Dr. Licks for more on Jamerson as well as information about Motown's recording studio at the time (1989: 81–83).

cated musical forms (that rarely drew on the blues), the Motown sound reflected an upwardly mobile, rather than down home southern, aesthetic. Although Motown singers could draw on deep gospel inflections (e.g., "Heat Wave"), their delivery was typically smoother (often complemented with orchestral strings by mid-decade) than that of singers coming out of the southern soul Stax and Fame studios.

Between 1960 and 1970 Motown had ten artists or groups with three or more pop Top 10 hits (see figure 27). A roster of about two dozen artists produced about a hundred pop Top 10 hits during this decade, making the label one of the most vital musical forces of its time. The most commercially successful artists and groups were the Supremes, Temptations, Marvin Gaye, Stevie Wonder, and the Jackson Five, who had their first hit in 1969.

Motown moved to Los Angeles in 1972 and in 1983 celebrated its twenty-fifth-year anniversary with a television special that reunited many artists and groups who had left the label, including Michael Jackson and the Jackson Five. Michael Jackson's performance of "Billie Jean" was particularly iconic as he performed the moonwalk to a large national audience for the first time. While Gordy is widely respected as one of the most successful and visionary entrepreneurs in the music business with a label that has won exceptional and enduring critical acclaim, he has also been the target of lawsuits regarding improprieties with royalties by some Motown artists, including Barrett Strong, Mary Wells, Mary Wilson, and the songwriting team of Holland, Dozier, and Holland, who left the label in 1968.[7]

See figure 27. Motown pop Top 10 singles, 1960–1970

URBAN FOLK REVIVAL

In the late 1950s and early 1960s a second wave of an urban folk revival hit. The initial high point took place at the July 1963 Newport Folk Festival, with rousing renditions of "Blowin' in the Wind" and "We Shall Overcome" at the end of Bob Dylan's set, where he was joined by Joan Baez; the acoustic guitar and vocal trio Peter, Paul, and Mary; the SNCC (Student Nonviolent Coordinating Committee) Freedom Singers; and Pete Seeger. The following month Dylan, Baez, and Peter, Paul, and Mary sang

7   For more on Motown, see Gordy (1994), Fitzgerald (1995, 2007), S. Smith (1999), Abbott (2001), and Early (2004).

at the March on Washington before several hundred thousand people. When Dylan played an electric guitar set at the 1965 Newport Folk Festival, many saw this as the end of an era.

The first wave took place in the 1930s and 1940s with the arrival in Greenwich Village of Louisiana singer-guitarist Lead Belly in 1935, New England–bred Harvard dropout Pete Seeger in the late 1930s, and Oklahoma singer-songwriter-guitarist Woody Guthrie in 1940. Seeger apprenticed with Guthrie and formed the Almanac Singers, recording together in 1941. Guthrie, who wrote "This Land Is Your Land" within weeks of arriving in New York City in early 1940, would suffer from a debilitating disease that would put him out of commission by the early 1950s and in hospital care for much of the rest of his life (he died in 1967). Seeger formed the Weavers in 1949, and the following year they became the first folk group to have major commercial success, hitting #1 on the pop charts in the summer with "Goodnight Irene" (the flip-side "Tzena Tzena" hit #2 at the time).

That same summer of 1950, however, a right-wing organization issued the publication *Red Channels*, which named 151 people in the media (including Seeger and other musicians and actors) and listed their alleged communist sympathies (including membership in peace and other democratic organizations). This contributed to a wave of anticommunist paranoia that was earlier exacerbated in 1947 with the House Un-American Activities Committee investigating alleged communist infiltration in Hollywood, questioning the loyalty of actors, directors, and screenwriters. The blacklists that ensued denied employment in the entertainment industry, typically on the basis of being associated with progressive organizations that were fully legal.

Just as quickly as the Weavers had risen to stardom, so nightclubs and organizations were afraid to hire them for fear of a backlash. Folk music, which had strong pro-union and socialist leanings, was driven underground during this era, the high (or low) point of which were hearings led by Senator Joseph McCarthy in 1953–54. Pete Seeger was called before the House Un-American Activities Committee in 1955 and lectured his inquisitors about questioning his loyalty. He was indicted for contempt of Congress in 1957, convicted in 1961, and sentenced to ten one-year terms in prison (one for each question he did not answer) to be served concurrently, but in 1962 the conviction was overturned. In December 1954 the Senate had voted to censure Senator McCarthy.

The release of the six-LP set *Anthology of American Folk Music* (edited by Harry Smith) on the Folkways label in 1952 was a major event in the reemergence of folk music later in the decade. Consisting of reissues of recordings of a diverse range of American music from 1927 to 1932 (blues, white and black gospel, jug bands, old-time fiddle), the *Anthology* provided a blueprint for the generation growing up in the 1950s.

The second wave of the urban folk revival was spurred on in part by the Kingston Trio, a clean-cut collegiate group who enjoyed a six-month run at the Purple Onion in San Francisco in the second half of 1957. "Tom Dooley," a single from their first album, hit #1 on the pop charts in the summer of 1958, leading the album into the #1 slot. Their next four albums hit #1.

The key moment, however, was eighteen-year-old Joan Baez (1941–) guest singing with Bob Gibson at the first Newport Folk Festival in 1959. She represented a new generation of singers who drew on a diversity of folk material and sang in their own intimate interpretive voices. Baez quickly gained a recording contract with the independent downtown New York–based Vanguard label (turning down an offer from Columbia), hitting the Top 40 with ten of the twelve albums she released in the 1960s (four were in the Top 10). A *Time* magazine cover story on Baez in fall 1962 announced that the folk revival had swept the nation. She was the first folksinger star of this generation and introduced Bob Dylan (1941–) to her large audiences following the 1963 Newport Folk Festival. Dylan emerged as a star at that festival. Peter, Paul, and Mary had just given Dylan his first pop Top 10 chart appearance with their recording of "Blowin' in the Wind," which had become something of an anthem for the times. Within a few months they would do it again with Dylan's "Don't Think Twice" (see figures 28 and 29).

Dylan's "A Hard Rain's A-Gonna Fall," from his second album (*The Freewheelin' Bob Dylan*, 1963), can illustrate his songwriting brilliance, in both form and content. The model for the song, the British ballad "Lord Randal," is built on four-line stanzas, each consisting of (1) a question; (2) repeated with a term of endearment; (3) a response; and (4) a refrain (a line that reappears at the end of each stanza). Dylan's rewrite retained the form of the first two lines (asking questions) and then entered into a stream-of-consciousness–like flow of responses ranging from five to seven lines per stanza, followed by a refrain, which functioned as the chorus for the song ("And it's a hard . . . rain's a-gonna fall"). In a world where songwriting strictly observed formal symmetry, this was a revolutionary move. In the final stanza, he further broke open the mold, by entering into a six-line stream-of-consciousness expansion on one of his responses and then picking up where he left off, but now adopting the activist stance that captured the New Left politics of his youth cohort. The content of Dylan's responses consist of chains of vivid imagery, with little narrative thread. They are each meant to evoke, or perhaps provoke, rather than tell a story. No matter the cliché, songwriting would be forever be changed by songs like "A Hard Rain's," "Masters of War," "The Times They Are a-Changin'," and "Mr. Tambourine Man" from those early albums of Dylan. Swift and effusive peer admiration was one sign. A Nobel Prize in Literature in 2016 was another.[8]

See figure 28. Birth years of singer-songwriters
See figure 29. Bob Dylan Top 40 pop singles and LPs in the 1960s

THE BEACH BOYS AND SURF ROCK

In the early 1960s a number of bands and artists from Southern California converged in a style that came to be called surf rock. Many of the songs' lyrics were devoted to a Southern California beach lifestyle, and surfing was a prime topic. Guitarist Dick Dale (1937–2019), with his group the Del-Tones, was a pioneer of the genre with his first two albums, *Surfer's Choice* (1962) and *King of the Surf Guitar* (1963). His guitar style was notable for trying to emulate the sound of big waves, using extensive reverb and a tremolo-picking technique (very fast up and down strokes). Dale helped bring the genre to national attention with performances in the films *Beach Party* (1963) and *Muscle Beach Party* (1964). His recording of "Miserlou" (1963), which did not register on national charts at the time, gained wide recognition when it was used as a theme song in the film *Pulp Fiction* (1994).

Before Dale and surf rock, guitarist Link Wray (and his Wraymen) hit pop #16 with "Rumble" (1958), an unusual guitar instrumental that shares a similar overdriven guitar aesthetic with Dale. (Wray both strums his guitar with tremolo technique and electronically simulates it with a setting on his guitar amplifier.) "Rumble" featured a heavy metal-like sound way before its time and has been cited by many (in Bainbridge and Maiorana's [2017-v] film *Rumble*) for opening them up to a new direction, including vocalist and bandleader Iggy Pop and guitarists Jimmy Page, Pete Townshend, and Robbie Robertson.

---

8   For more on this era, see Baez (1968), Scaduto (1971), Shelton (1986), R. Cohen (2002), and Dylan (2004).

The Beach Boys were the most well-known group in this style, and the cover artwork on their first three albums featured surfing or them carrying surfboards: *Surfin' Safari* (1962), *Surfin' USA* (1963), and *Surfer Girl* (1963). From Hawthorne, just southwest of Los Angeles and next to Manhattan Beach, the Beach Boys were a family affair, led by songwriter, bassist, and producer Brian Wilson. The band included Wilson's two younger brothers, Dennis (drums) and Carl (guitar); cousin Mike Love (vocals); and friend Al Jardine (guitar). In 1962, the year of their first album, the Wilson brothers turned sixteen (Carl), eighteen (Dennis), and twenty years old (Brian). Their main song themes were cars, surfing, and girls.

The Beach Boys, whose first hit ("Surfin' Safari," #14) came out in fall 1962, were probably the most popular rock group by the time of the arrival of the Beatles in the United States in early 1964. Their rivalry with the Beatles extended through the decade, ending with a tally of twenty-seven Top 40 hits for the Beach Boys compared to forty-six for the Beatles (see figure 30). In early 1965 Brian Wilson withdrew from live performing (due in part to mental health issues) and began concentrating on songwriting, eventually showing a maturity (leaving behind surfing themes) that in turn stimulated the Beatles. His album *Pet Sounds*, released in May 1966 and featuring "Sloop John B" and "Wouldn't It Be Nice," revealed a new personal intimacy and experimental recording studio work. Wilson was stimulated in part by the Beatles' *Rubber Soul* (released in December 1965). The Beatles in turn took notice of Wilson's work. Wilson's masterpiece "Good Vibrations," featuring extensive experimentation in the recording studio, took months to record and was released in October 1966, quickly rising to #1 and becoming the Beach Boys' first million-selling single.

The other main surf rock group, which had just fleeting, although massive, success, was Jan and Dean, with early albums *Jan and Dean Take Linda Surfing* (1963) and *Ride the Wild Surf* (1964). A series of Hollywood films, beginning with *Beach Party* (1963), starring Frankie Avalon and Annette Funicello, accompanied the fad, which ended about three years later.[9]

See figure 30. Beach Boys, Beatles, and Rolling Stones pop Top 40 comparisons, 1962–1971

---

9   For more on surf rock, see Crowley (2011), Blair (2015), and McKeen (2017); for Brian Wilson, see Cromelin (1976) and B. Wilson (2016).

THE BEATLES AND THE BRITISH INVASION

It would be difficult to overstate the importance of the Beatles, not only in twentieth-century music history but also in shaping youth culture in the 1960s. Formed in the late 1950s when they were still teenagers, the Beatles gigged in clubs extensively for several years (in their native Liverpool and in Hamburg, Germany) before releasing their first commercial single in late 1962 ("Love Me Do" with "P.S. I Love You"). Over the course of the next eight years, until their breakup in 1970, the Beatles dominated the pop music industry, both in terms of commercial success and critical reception. The combination of their string of consecutive #1 singles and albums (and consequently their mass audience) along with their creative artistic experimentation, growth, and influence has secured their place in rock history and has yet to be matched (see figures 30 and 31).

One key to understanding the aura of the Beatles is that they are a classic example of the sum being greater than the parts. The unique mix of John Lennon (1940–80, guitar), Ringo Starr (1940–, drums), Paul McCartney (1942–, bass), and George Harrison (1943–2001, lead guitar), all from Liverpool, shepherded by their extraordinary producer, George Martin, and manager, Brian Epstein, along with being in the right place at the right time, can be a starting point to understand what they did and how they did it. Key ingredients to their success include the especially strong songwriting team of Lennon and McCartney; their hard-earned early experience in clubs performing as a band; their combined vocal abilities (they all sang); the shaping of their songs and sound in the recording studio by Martin; their look and presentation, overseen by Epstein; their constant artistic openness and growth as they moved through the decade of their twenties in the decade of the 1960s; and their understanding of how to reconcile their own individual personalities with that of a group. Their arrival in the United States several months after the November 1963 assassination of President John F. Kennedy may also help to explain part of the great enthusiasm and welcome of masses of young people coming out of a period of national mourning (Kennedy was the second-youngest U.S. president, elected at age forty-three in 1960).

The Beatles finished recording their first album (*Please Please Me*) in February 1963, which yielded their first UK Top 10 single ("Please Please Me"). The song was released in the United States at the time but did not chart until it was rereleased in January 1964, at which point it went to #1. The Beatles' arrival in the United States, at JFK airport on February 7, 1964, was a major news event, and they made their U.S. debut on the *Ed Sullivan Show* two days later, on February 9 (they appeared on the show two more times that February). Two months later (April 4) they owned the top five slots in the *Billboard* Hot 100 singles pop chart. Their first film, *A Hard Day's Night*, released that summer, is a classic and was a major catalyst for stimulating the growth of rock bands.

The commercial success of the Beatles was unprecedented and remains rare. Thirteen of their total of fifteen albums released in the United States between 1964 (*Introducing*) and 1970 (*Let It Be*), went to #1 on the *Billboard* pop chart; the exceptions were their debut and *Yellow Submarine* (1969), both of which hit #2. Ten of these albums stayed at #1 for two or more months. The tally of their U.S. Top 40 singles between 1962 and 1970 shows them clearly in a separate class: forty-six compared to their closest rock band peers, the Beach Boys (twenty-seven) and the Rolling Stones (twenty).

Three consecutive Beatles albums, released in December 1965 (*Rubber Soul*), August 1966 (*Revolver*), and June 1967 (*Sgt. Pepper's Lonely Hearts Club Band*), mark a major shift in the maturity of their music and in rock music in general.[10] The album-cover artwork shows increasingly psychedelic and countercultural images. Leaving behind lyrics about boy-girl romantic relationships, they moved into more abstract and psychedelic topics, and they began using the recording studio as a unique forum for composition, not just as a place to capture what they performed live. On *Rubber Soul* "The Word" deals with love as an abstract idea not attached to a one-on-one personal relationship ("All You Need Is Love," released July 1967, codified the concept) and "Norwegian Wood" features a sitar. On *Revolver* "Tomorrow Never Knows" marks a major exploration of experimental compositional techniques, including the use of drones, recording tape loops faded in and out, and distorted vocals (fed through a rotating Leslie organ speaker).

Sgt. Pepper's is widely considered to be their masterpiece, along with the *White Album* released the following year (so-called because of its all-white cover with just "The Beatles" in small print on it), and one of the most important albums in all of rock. Conceived as a single unified album based on a fictional band, the songs lead

---

10 *Yesterday ... and Today* was released between *Rubber Soul* and *Revolver*, but it is a compilation album.

directly into one another and draw on a variety of styles utilizing the recording studio in new ways. They had just given up live concerts after their third U.S. concert tour in August 1966 and had no need to reproduce their recordings in performance. One of their most experimental musical forays was in "A Day in the Life," in which a section consisted of having a full orchestra play a passage beginning at the lowest note of their instrument and gradually rise to the highest note (of an E major chord) following the cue of a conductor. This building crescendo and ensuing chaotic sound gets abruptly cut off and the song moves in a starkly different direction. The final chord of the piece, played on several keyboards, is one of the longest fade-outs in the history of recorded music, made possible by gradually increasing the sensitivity of the microphones as the acoustic sound decayed.

The sequence of *Sgt. Pepper's* (1967), *The Beatles* (also called the *White Album*, 1968), and *Abbey Road* (1969) marks another major shift in the Beatles' output and, again, for rock more generally. Moving beyond a psychedelic peak of 1967, the Beatles found a new kind of maturity in their explorations of the artistic possibilities of the medium of a rock album. These three albums and the preceding *Rubber Soul* (1965) and *Revolver* (1966) are placed within the first fourteen slots of *Rolling Stone* (2012) magazine's 500 Greatest Albums list (Dylan has three in the first sixteen slots).

Until October 1963 all the Beatles recordings (their first two albums) were done on a two-track tape recorder. "I Want to Hold Your Hand" was their first on a four-track. They did significant amounts of overdubbing, which usually meant mixing the four tracks down to two, then adding more to tracks 3 and 4, and then repeating the whole process if necessary. An eight-track recorder was used for the first time on a few pieces on the *White Album* (1968) and all of *Abbey Road* (1969) (Everett 2001: 122–25).

The appearance of the Beatles on the U.S. pop charts in January 1964 stimulated a British Invasion, in which over twenty British bands or solo artists appeared in the U.S. Top 40 through January 1966, a rate of almost one new band or artist per month for two years (see figure 32). While many of the bands and artists were short-lived, some have proven to have longevity (e.g., vocalists Dusty Springfield and Tom Jones) and even a major impact on the shape of rock. Examples of the latter include the Animals, Rolling Stones, Kinks, and Yardbirds (a training ground for guitarists, including Eric Clapton, Jeff Beck, and Jimmy Page). The Who were latecomers, not breaking into the U.S. Top 40 until April 1967 ("Happy Jack"). Their "I Can't Explain" (May

1965, #93) and "My Generation" (January 1966, #74) had earlier shown up on the hundred-slot pop chart (they both reached the UK Top 10). "Anyway, Anyhow, and Anywhere" (released May 1965, no U.S. charting) and "My Generation" trafficked in a gritty, noisy, and electronically distorted sound that would later be exploited in heavy metal and punk.

The Rolling Stones, the second-most popular British rock band at the time (and probably the longest-running rock and roll band ever, with three original members still touring as of 2019), were seen and heard as a foil to the Beatles. They projected a tougher image and more blues-infused sound, with lyrics that were less romantic, more erotic and sexually suggestive, and more aggressive. Lead singer Mick Jagger, the quintessential front man and sixties rock star, was unencumbered by a musical instrument and therefore became the focal point of the band as he moved around the stage. The quintet, which released their first single in 1963, consisted of Mick Jagger (lead vocals), Keith Richards (lead guitar), Brian Jones (guitar), Bill Wyman (bass), and Charlie Watts (drums). Mick Taylor (guitar) replaced Jones very shortly before his untimely death in 1969, and Ronnie Wood (guitar) replaced Taylor in 1975. Nine of their ten albums released in the 1960s were in the U.S. Top 5 (their self-titled 1964 debut album hit #11), and all six of their albums released in the 1970s hit #1. Their primary songwriting was done by the team of Jagger and Richards. After *Their Satanic Majesty's Request* (1967), released six months after *Sgt. Pepper's* and showing its influence, they returned to a more blues-based rock and roll sound (bucking trends that would soon yield progressive rock and heavy metal) and released a series of their most highly acclaimed albums: *Beggars Banquet* (1968, #5), *Let It Bleed* (1969, #3), *Sticky Fingers* (1971, #1), and the double album *Exile on Main Street* (1972, #1), which some consider their best.

With London as a fashion capital in the 1960s, including designer Mary Quant introducing the miniskirt in 1964 and model Twiggy gaining international stardom in 1966, the look of British bands at the time contrasted with those in the United States (just view Beach Boys videos from the time for a stark comparison). One of the forces behind this contrast has recently been recognized as a profusion of gay managers who helped shape the look of their bands (Farber 2017), including Brian Epstein (the Beatles), Simon Napier-Bell (the Yardbirds), Kit Lambert (the Who), and Robert Stigwood (Cream, Bee Gees). For a general framework and point of comparison, figure 33 shows the years of birth of the three top rock groups (Beach

Boys, Beatles, Rolling Stones) and top vocal group (Supremes) of this era and the year of their first Top 40 hit.[11]

See figure 30. Beach Boys, Beatles, and Rolling Stones pop Top 40 comparisons, 1962–1971

See figure 31. Beatles U.S. albums: Pop album chart positions

See figure 32. British Invasion groups/artists and debuts in U.S. pop singles Top 40

See figure 33. Birth years of early 1960s groups

SOUL

In the mid and late 1950s the term *soul* began to be used to describe a trend in the jazz world in which musicians drew deeply from down-home gospel and blues traditions. Ray Charles was a major figure in this regard, secularizing gospel musical and vocal styles. Song titles and then album titles began appearing with the word soul in them, such as Charles's "A Bit of Soul" (1955) and two albums recorded in 1958 with vibraphonist Milt Jackson: *Soul Brothers* and *Soul Meeting*. Sam Cooke represented a smoother and more restrained line than Charles, and his 1963 album, *Mr. Soul*, gave a broader presence to the designation. Subsequent albums by James Brown (*Grits and Soul*, 1964), Otis Redding (*Sings Soul*, 1965), and Aretha Franklin (*Soul Sister* and *Queen of Soul*, 1966) announced a new genre and style firmly rooted in African American aesthetics (see figure 34).

In his autobiography Ray Charles defines soul as follows: "Some people told me that I'd invented the sounds that they called soul—but I can't take any credit. Soul is just the way black folk sing when they leave themselves alone" (Charles and Ritz 1978: 268–69). About 1953–55 Charles began a process, "when I became myself.... I started taking gospel lines and turning them into regular songs" (148). He was not alone: Clyde McPhatter's gospel-drenched singing on the Dominoes' "Have Mercy Baby" (1952) was an important step. (McPhatter joined Atlantic Records in 1953, just after Charles.) Charles has identified a few of the sources for his songs at that time,

---

11 For more on the Beatles, see Adler (1964), Beatles (2000), Everett (1999, 2001), the documentaries by Lindsay-Hogg (1970-v), Smeaton and Wonfor (1996-v), and Hanly (2017-v), the films *A Hard Day's Night* and *Help!* (Lester 1964-v, 1965-v), and the complete scores for their music (Beatles 1993); for the Rolling Stones, see Margotin and Guesdon (2016); for the British Invasion, see Miles (2009) and Perone (2009).

but he points to "I Got a Woman," his first record to hit #1 on the R&B charts (in early 1955): "That's where it all started from, because a lot of people said, 'Ohh, that's a religious, and you just changed the words around, and so you're being sacrilegious'" (Espar and Thomson 1995-v, episode 4).[12]

"I Got a Woman" is an instructive song to single out, as it is based on a sixteen-bar chord progression that is common in gospel. Charles's immediate source may have been the melody and chords from the Southern Tones' "It Must Be Jesus" (1954), which is similar to that of the Spirit of Memphis Quartet's "He Never Left Me Alone" (1949) and the Pilgrim Travelers' "Good News" (1947).[13] Here Charles is going beyond bringing gospel-style vocalizing to secular music to actually bring in musical forms and melodies associated with the genre.

Two southern recording studios in particular helped to define the sound of soul in the 1960s: Stax (also the name of its record label) in Memphis and Fame in Muscle Shoals, Alabama. New York City–based Atlantic Records sent its artists to both studios to record, most notably providing Wilson Pickett with his first hit, "In the Midnight Hour" (R&B #1, pop #21), recorded at Stax in 1965; and Aretha Franklin's breakthrough debut Atlantic album, *I Never Loved a Man The Way I Love You* (pop #2, R&B #1), which included her first Top 10 hits, "I Never Loved a Man (the Way I Love You)" (pop #9, R&B #1), recorded in early 1967 at Fame, and "Respect" (pop #1, R&B #1), recorded in New York City with musicians flown in from Fame. Otis Redding's breakthrough album, *Otis Blue/Otis Redding Sings Soul* (R&B #1, pop #75), featuring his first Top 40 hits "Respect" (pop #35, R&B #4), "Satisfaction" (pop #31, R&B #4), and "I've Been Loving You Too Long" (pop #21, R&B #2), was recorded at Stax in 1965.

The studio band at Stax, Booker T. and the MGs, had their first hit with "Green Onions" in 1962. They were one of the few racially integrated bands at the time (keyboardist Booker T. Jones and drummer Al Jackson Jr. were black; guitarist Steve Cropper and bassist Lewie Steinberg—replaced by Donald "Duck" Dunn in 1964—

---

12 Examples of secular rewrites of gospel songs include "Leave My Woman Alone" (1956) from "Let That Liar Alone," and "Lonely Avenue" (1956), composed by Doc Pomus, from the Pilgrim Travelers' "How Jesus Died" (1956) (Charles and Ritz 1978: 149; Heilbut 2002: 83–84). The Golden Gate Quartet (1938) and Sister Rosetta Tharpe (1947) recorded earlier versions of "Let That Liar Alone."

13 Stumpel (2014). Speculation about the source of the lyrics includes "I've Got a Savior (Way over Jordan)," recorded by the Bailey Gospel Singers in 1950, with Charles changing "savior" to "woman."

were white). The studio musicians at Fame were all white. The phenomenon of an all-white (Fame) and an integrated (Stax) studio band helping to produce some of the most important statements of 1960s soul music, while Motown, using an almost all-black roster of musicians (excepting guest classical musicians), produced some of the most important crossover pop statements of its time, suggests some fluidity of roles and aspirations in 1960s U.S. musical culture.

Aretha Franklin's (1942–2018) career is especially illustrative of the importance of a sympathetic record label and producer. Born in Memphis in 1942, she moved to Detroit in 1946 when her father, the renowned preacher Rev. C. L. Franklin, became pastor of the 4,500-member New Bethel Baptist Church. She grew up in Detroit singing in church, befriended Mahalia Jackson and Sam Cooke, and went on tour in 1958 with Martin Luther King Jr., who became a fan of hers. She would sing "Precious Lord" at his memorial service ten years later. Franklin signed with Columbia and released nine albums between 1961 and 1967, singing lighter pop and jazz material, registering in the Top 10 of the R&B charts but barely making a dent into the pop charts. As soon as she moved to Atlantic in 1966, producer Jerry Wexler sent her to Fame for her first recording, and she immediately gained her greatest commercial success up to that point. Between 1967 and 1974 she had thirty-two pop Top 40 hits (all on Atlantic), fourteen of which were in the Top 10. Franklin was in a class by herself among solo vocalists of her era, having a more commercially successful track record than pop vocalist Dionne Warwick, who had twenty-two Top 40 hits between 1963 and 1970. Only Marvin Gaye, who had thirty-five Top 40 hits, but within the longer time span of 1963–73, and James Brown (who led his own band), with forty-three Top 40 hits in the even longer span of 1960–74 surpassed this record at the time. By the late 1960s Brown had gained the unofficial titles of Soul Brother #1 (subtitle of his 1966 album *It's a Man's Man's Man's World*) and the Godfather of Soul (the subtitle of his 1986 autobiography).

Franklin was featured on the cover of *Time* magazine the week of June 28, 1968, two and a half months after the assassination of Martin Luther King Jr., with the heading "The Sound of Soul." She was the fourth African American woman ever featured on the cover up to that time. Previous covers of *Time* featuring African Americans are instructive: boxers Joe Louis (1941), Sugar Ray Robinson (1951), and Muhammad Ali (1963); baseball and tennis pioneers Jackie Robinson (1947) and Althea Gibson (1957); classical concert singers Marian Anderson (1946) and Leontyne Price (1961); jazz musicians Louis Armstrong (1949), Duke Ellington (1956), and

Thelonious Monk (1964); writer James Baldwin (1963); *Brown v. Board of Education* lawyer and future Supreme Court justice Thurgood Marshall (1955); U.S. secretary of Housing and Urban Development Robert C. Weaver (1966); and Martin Luther King Jr. (1957, 1964).

By the early 1970s gospel singers crossing over to the secular world or soul singers secularizing gospel music was no longer news. In this context Aretha Franklin reversing sail, and recording a live gospel double album, *Amazing Grace* (1972), was a landmark event. It won a Grammy Award for Best Soul Gospel Performance and was, and still is, her best-selling album, going gold within months, platinum in the CD era (1992), and now certified at two-times platinum.

Soul music production was not just limited to the Detroit (Motown), New York (Atlantic), and Memphis (Stax) axis. Chicago boasted the Impressions, formed in 1958 with Curtis Mayfield and initially led by Jerry Butler, who recorded on the local Vee-Jay label, one of the few black-owned labels at the time. After Butler left, Mayfield became the lead vocalist and composer, and the group signed with ABC-Paramount in 1961; in 1963 they teamed up with African American producer Johnny Pate, who had a strong jazz background. Their biggest hits were "It's All Right" (pop #4, 1963), "Keep on Pushing" (pop #10, 1964), and "People Get Ready" (pop #14, 1965). Mayfield went solo in 1970, and his soundtrack album for the 1972 film *Super Fly* reached #1 on the pop album chart. Mayfield is especially appreciated for his unique compositional and vocal sensibility, socially sensitive lyrics, and highly distinctive tasteful guitar style.

In addition to Ray Charles, who was firmly rooted in the 1950s, Sam Cooke (1931–64) stands out as one of the great pioneers of the genre. Born in Clarksdale, Mississippi, and raised in Chicago, Cooke grew up in a religious home (his father was a Holiness Church minister), and he joined the gospel group Soul Stirrers as lead singer in 1950. After some hesitation for fear of alienating his audience, Cooke left the gospel field and hit #1 on both the R&B and pop charts with "You Send Me" in 1957, initiating a string of twenty-nine Top 40 hits between 1957 and 1965. Cooke's "A Change Is Gonna Come" (1965), spurred by his recent encounter with racism in the South and inspired by Dylan's "Blowin' in the Wind," is one of the most profound statements of its kind in the era. At funeral services in Chicago and then Los Angeles in December 1964, an estimated one hundred thousand mourners paid their respects to Cooke.

From November 30, 1963, until January 30, 1965, *Billboard* did not publish R&B charts. The magazine never explained why, but some have theorized that faulty methodology led to unlikely white artists flooding the R&B charts. When the R&B chart reappeared, black artists predominated, perhaps better reflecting black listening audience tastes (Molanphy 2014).[14] In October 1965 *Billboard* reported on a new trend of R&B stations playing white artists, using the term "blue-eyed soul," pointing to the Righteous Brothers as possibly initiating the trend. Their first three albums registered slightly higher on the R&B charts than the pop charts, and their biggest hit, "You've Lost That Lovin' Feelin'" (1964), by Brill Building writers Barry Mann, Cynthia Weil, and Phil Spector and recorded and produced by Spector in his Gold Star Studios, hit #1 (pop) and #2 (R&B). A Washington, DC, radio music director was quoted as saying, "The Negro audience is no longer a specialized 'in' group. Musically, they have grown out of the strictly heavy-accented R&B field limited only to Negro artists" (C. Hall 1965: 49). Although groups like the Rolling Stones (who received positive notices in the black press at the time) and Sonny and Cher were named, the term more typically referred in the 1960s to artists like the Righteous Brothers, Tom Jones, Dusty Springfield, and the Spencer Davis Group ("I'm a Man," "Gimme Some Lovin") with vocalist Steve Winwood.[15]

See figure 34. Soul: Naming a genre in song and album titles

---

14 See also Brackett (1994).

15 For more on soul, see Garland (1969), Guralnick (1986), Pruter (1991), Bowman (1997), Werner (2004), R. Gordon (2013), and C. Hughes (2015). See also the biographies of Ray Charles (Evans 2005), Sam Cooke (Guralnick 2005), Aretha Franklin (Ritz 2014), and Otis Redding (Gould 2017); Camalier's (2013-v) documentary on Fame Studios in Muscle Shoals; and the performances of Otis Redding (Pennebaker, Hegedus, and Dawkins 1986-v) and Aretha Franklin (Pollock 2018-v).

Tensions escalated in the latter half of one of the most turbulent decades in U.S. history. Key areas of conflict included inner-city riots; escalation of the war in Vietnam and massive antiwar protests; a dramatic increase in recreational drug use; the widening of a generation gap; free speech on college campuses and the rise of underground newspapers; a sexual revolution related to the introduction of the birth control pill; and, toward the end of the decade, gay and women's liberation movements.

Civil rights events during this decade began with peaceful civil disobedience: a sit-in at the all-white Woolworth's lunch counter by black students from North Carolina Agricultural and Technical College in Greensboro, North Carolina, in February 1960. In the second half of the decade, events included the signing of civil rights legislation in 1964–65; the coining of the term *Black Power* and the founding of the Black Panthers (both in 1966), who carried out armed citizen's patrols and offered community social services; the assassination of Martin Luther King Jr. in April 1968; and dogged counterintelligence infiltration by the FBI. Riots, sparked by high unemployment and oppressive policing tactics, broke out in many major cities in mid-decade and again across the country in the aftermath of King's murder. James Brown's "Say It Loud—I'm Black and I'm Proud," recorded and released in August 1968, rose to #1 for six weeks on the R&B chart and #10 on the pop chart, highlighting a shift in consciousness that had already been underway for several years.

The war in Vietnam revealed a major split in the country. U.S. helicopter units first arrived in 1960. Agent Orange, an herbicide that defoliated the country and turned out to be contaminated with deadly dioxin, began to be sprayed by U.S. troops in 1962, and in 1965 the U.S. was officially at war, with 60,000 troops in Vietnam. By the end of 1966 there were 385,000 troops in Vietnam and 60,000 sailors offshore. In 1967 the largest antiwar protest yet took place in New York City with 400,000 people. In November 1969, 500,000 protesters gathered in Washington, DC. The following month the draft lottery (based on birthdate) was introduced. The United States would finally get out of the war in 1973.

Music and the counterculture went through rapid changes. One set of milestones can be heard (and seen) on Beatles albums: *Rubber Soul* (1965), *Revolver* (1966), *Sgt. Peppers Lonely Hearts Club Band* (1967), the *White Album* (1968), *Abbey Road* (1969), and *Let It Be* (1970), their final album. Not only did the Beatles' sound get increasingly experimental and eclectic, but one also can track the increasing length of hairstyles and presence of facial hair, as well as psychedelic lettering and design on their album covers. Their *White Album* cover provided a stark contrast.

The summer of 1965 saw the takeover of folk rock, with Dylan songs permeating the airwaves and the release of his *Highway 61 Revisited*. Three debut albums recorded in 1966 point to new radical tendencies: Frank Zappa and the Mothers of Invention's *Freak Out!* (recorded March 1966, released June 1966); *The Velvet Underground and Nico* (recorded throughout 1966, released March 1967); and *The Doors* (recorded August 1966, released January 1967). The year 1967 was marked by Aretha Franklin's swift ascendance as Queen of Soul, with her debut album on Atlantic and her first #1 pop single "Respect," which *Ebony* magazine suggested was "the new Negro national anthem" (Garland 1967: 47), as well as the "Summer of Love," with the Monterey Pop Festival (featuring Jimi Hendrix's and Otis Redding's stunning performance) and release of the Beatles' *Sgt. Pepper's*. The next year, 1968, was marked by James Brown's "Say It Loud—I'm Black and I'm Proud," reflecting and driving a new black pride. Finally, 1969 was the year of the Woodstock and Altamont music festivals, marking countercultural highs and lows.

CROSS-FERTILIZATION

Langston Hughes's July 1955 *Chicago Defender* article voiced what was a widespread concern for African Americans—that is, whites imitating and profiting off of African American cultural production, exacerbated by unfair access to mainstream media (radio, television, record distribution, performance venues). Ten years later the same newspaper presented a youth perspective on rock and R&B, with a series of a dozen articles published from April to October 1965 in a section headlined *Defender's Younger Set*, written by, it seems, five young black women, named Terry, Penny, Pip, Brandy, and Tee. Called "The Low Down," their first column began, "Today our music (R&B) is by far the most sought after, imitated and enjoyed. In my opinion, our guys, the 'Howlin' Wolf,' 'Bo Diddley,' 'Muddy Waters,' and others have promoted this sound well, but have not all claimed the high rewards they should be receiving." Then came an unexpected twist. Terry Joe wrote, "Since there is also a trend towards English groups and since these groups often use R & B material, I feel the goal of this column should be to study the effects of our famous singers on the different English groups. I hope, too, that those who have mental blocks concerning these groups will become a little more open minded towards all types of musical expressions." Penny then chimed in: "[These] British groups . . . haven't been given a chance, 'They are moving in and taking over!' . . . is what I hear too much. I'm a D.O.B.G! I'm proud of it too. By the way it means 'Defender of British Groups'" (Terry et al. 1965a).

In one entry they interviewed the Kinks, who were playing at the convention center (Terry et al. 1965c). In May the Rolling Stones, on their third American tour, performed in Chicago and recorded at Chess. "We went to the show (man can they get down with R & B!) After the show we went to the hotel and got up to see them. . . . They treated us with such courtesy and respect. . . . They love and feel this music. . . . The Stones are R & B men in the truest sense" (1965b). Several months later they talked to "the King himself, Muddy Waters." Being under twenty-one, they could not get into the venue, and so Waters came out to see them. "Muddy sends this message. . . . We've got some great kids, wonderful kids, I'm only sorry more of them are not interested in music." By music, he must have meant blues. "Muddy thinks those long hairs are okay. . . . 'The Rolling Stones, sure I dig them, they're a part of me, you know they're named after one of my records. Those boys jam'" (1965d).

How can one understand young black women and an aging blues legend who no longer registered on the charts praising a young generation of British whites playing music rooted in the black culture of Chicago, a city that put both early rock and roll and electrified blues on the map? They each had their own type of authority that could offer legitimacy and authenticity: Waters was the pioneer who lived the life and provided the model; and the young women were loyal R&B fans from its targeted community, as well as members of the Beatlemania generation, which it seems spared few (Ehrenreich, Hess, and Jacobs 1986). "When we got up there Pip and Keith [Richards] were sitting down with shoes off. YES I SAID WITH SHOES OFF! Mick, Keith, Bryan, Bill and Charlie are all-right. Mellow, girls, mellow" (Terry et al. 1965b).

In the 1970s, Muddy Waters had not changed his opinion, crediting the Rolling Stones with creating

a whole wide open space for the music. They said who did it first and how they came by knowin' it. They told the truth about it, and that really put a shot in my arm with the whites. I tip my hat to 'em. They took a lot of what I was doin', but who care? . . . The Beatles did a lot of Chuck Berry, The Rolling Stones did some of my stuff. That's what it took to wake up the people in my own country, in my own state where I was born, that a black man's music is not a crime to bring in the house. . . . Those kids didn't give a damn what your colour is; they just want to hear the records. Then the college kids started comin' to see me in places where I was afraid for 'em even to be there. . . . They had more nerve than I woulda had, man. (qtd. in Murray 1977: 30)[1]

Muddy Waters's best charting pop LP, *Fathers and Sons* (Chess, 1969, #70), was a collaboration with young white Chicago blues musicians Paul Butterfield (harmonica) and Mike Bloomfield (guitar), and Donald "Duck" Dunn (bass player with Booker T. and the MGs).[2] Blues guitarist B. B. King, who had major R&B success in the 1950s, credits the Rolling Stones and other English groups for "re-importin' the blues." At the end of the 1960s, he provided a very sober and thoughtful analysis of the situation:

> They had a little bit of a different sound, simply by them being white and English, but they were playing them [blues] with *soul* in the way they could feel it, and enough so that *I* could feel it, though maybe not as deeply as some of the people I know, because most of them are kids. . . . And so a lot of the white kids—American kids—started to doing research on the blues. . . . They started listenin' and tryin' to understand what kind of message *we* were trying to get over. To me, some of these people are beginnin' to feel a *part* of it. Naturally, they can't feel it as we do, because we've *lived* it. . . . You can step on a person's foot. You know it hurt, but you don't know how deeply or how *pain*ful it is. But you *do* know it hurt, because you've had people maybe to step on *your* feet. (qtd. in Garland 1969: 108–9)

King credited this younger generation for "openin' the door for people that *really* know the blues" and appreciated a certain kind of respect that he had not seen before. "I never had a standin' ovation in my life until last year. It first happened at the Café Au Go Go in New York and . . . in San Francisco at a place called the Fillmore. . . . I was at a disc jockey convention last year and that was the *first* time I'd seen *my* people give me a standing ovation. And I *cried*!" (109–10).[3]

---

1   Hamilton (2016) discusses the Stones and race in depth.
2   Other collaborations of this type at the time include *Hooker 'n Heat* (Liberty, 1971, pop #73) featuring John Lee Hooker with LA rock band Canned Heat; *The London Howlin' Wolf Sessions* (Chess, 1971, pop #79) with Eric Clapton and members of the Rolling Stones; and *The London Muddy Waters Sessions* (Chess, 1972) with Steve Winwood and Irish guitarist Rory Gallagher (the album did not chart, but won a Grammy Award for Best Ethnic or Traditional Folk Recording).
3   See PBS (2001) for other similar comments from B. B. King.

Guitarist Carlos Santana was similarly impressed when he had seen British guitarist Peter Green with the original lineup of Fleetwood Mac at the Fillmore in San Francisco in January 1969. The group had just come from Chicago, where they recorded with Chess label artists Willie Dixon (bass), Otis Spann (piano), and Buddy Guy (guitar) (*Blues Jam at Chess/Fleetwood Mac in Chicago*, 1969). Santana would record Green's composition "Black Magic Woman" on his second album *Abraxas* (1970). Green had earlier passed through John Mayall and the Bluesbreakers, one of the most important British electric blues revival bands, playing on their third album (*A Hard Road*, 1967), replacing Eric Clapton, who played on their second album (*Blues Breakers with Eric Clapton*, 1966). "The white British dudes . . . zeroed in on two things—B. B. King and Elmore James—and they played the shit out of that music. . . . They lived the blues. They weren't wearing it like a suit. That's all they wanted to do; that's all they did, and they did it so well. I couldn't believe they were white" (Santana 2014: 111).

In the latter part of the 1960s some currents in rock moved further away from its blues roots, while others moved more deeply into them. The greater commercial success of young whites drawing on a tradition pioneered by blacks a generation or two older than them has provoked a variety of responses, which can vary according to when they were offered and the position of the writer. Muddy Waters continued to see the benefits in the 1970s. Margo Jefferson (1973), however, a peer of the *Chicago Defender* crew—she was roughly their age and grew up in the same city—had a very different take at that point.

A significant number of black musicians had both generous and pragmatic responses to musical cross-fertilization. When asked in 1967 why he thought white blues performers were so much more successful than the originals, Otis Redding replied, "Because the white population is much larger than the colored. I like what these rock and roll kids are doing. Sometimes they take things from us, but I take things from them, too. The things that are beautiful, and they do a lot of beautiful things" (qtd. in Delehant 1967: 57). Redding—1960s soul personified—here elegantly summons common sense: sales demographics favor the majority; everyone takes from everyone; and black soul musicians can appreciate the cultural expression of white rock musicians (who drew deeply from the well of black music).

Redding was in England with a Stax Records tour at the time of the March 1967 interview. He had by then placed sixteen songs on the R&B charts over the past four years, fourteen of which crossed over to the pop charts (with five hitting the

Top 40). His musical curiosity was probably typical for black musicians from the South.

> JD: Do you like country and western music?
> Otis: Oh, yeah. Before I started singing, maybe ten years ago, I loved anything that Hank Williams sang. Eddy Arnold does some groovy things, too. Everybody's got their own bag and if they're doing something good, I can hear it (qtd. in Delehant 1967).[4]

Black artists in the later 1960s were occasionally covering white artists such as Bob Dylan (Sam Cooke, Stevie Wonder, "Blowin' in the Wind"); the Rolling Stones (Otis Redding, "Satisfaction"); the Beatles (Wilson Pickett, "Hey Jude," Ike and Tina Turner, "Come Together"); Simon and Garfunkel (Aretha Franklin, "Bridge over Troubled Water"); and the Band (Aretha Franklin, "The Weight"). The all-white studio band at Fame in Alabama backed up some of these efforts and had a remarkable ability to move between the worlds of soul and country (C. Hughes 2015).

In a radio documentary broadcast in 1969, Little Richard was asked about whites and soul: "The average person when he see a black man they will say, 'Man he got soul cause he's colored!' But I disagree with that. . . . [God] lets his blessings fall on all races. I think that there are different types of souls like there are different types of cars. But they all are cars. When a white guy sing, if he have soul, that don't mean that he have to copy no Negro to *get* it. If he feels, when one sings from the heart and it reaches another heart, that's *soul*" (qtd. in Gilliland 1969b).[5]

One promise of the early rock and roll generation was breaking down racial and ethnic barriers. Much progress was made, although Eric Burdon, lead singer of the British group the Animals, reported a disturbing encounter in 1966 from the still-segregated South. Burdon related a conversation, in an extraordinary profile he wrote for *Ebony* magazine, he had with a "young white girl" in Mobile, Alabama. When he mentioned that Otis Redding had played there the previous night, she said, "Yeh, man, he's too much, isn't he? I think his recording of *My Girl* is fantastic." Burdon asked if she went to see him. "Did I see him? You got to be joking, man, the place was

---

4   Chuck Berry and Ray Charles listened to country music growing up. Charles's biggest LP, the only one to hit #1 on the pop chart, was *Modern Sounds in Country and Western Music* (1962); volume 2, released the same year, hit #2. C. Hughes (2015) documents a number of black artists who had strong country roots in the early 1970s.

5   In the same radio program gospel great Clara Ward expressed a similar sentiment.

full of n-ggers" (1966: 168). How can this be reconciled with Muddy Waters's report about white college kids seeking him out in black clubs? There are no easy answers.

A national mood of optimism, brought on by the Beatles and dozens of British Invasion bands (many of whom were informed by American R&B), in the wake of the assassination of President Kennedy, may have lent a degree of cultural open-mindedness in mid-decade. There may have been some immediate resentment too, in the midst of the 1964–65 British onslaught: "There was a bit of jealousy, because we were cut off at a time we was just getting ready to become stronger than strong ourselves. . . . And then all of a sudden these kids came along and stopped all that. It was a strong pill to swallow" (Ben E. King, qtd. in Espar and Thomson 1995-v, episode 2). But Motown thrived in this era, as did southern soul created by racially integrated units. With the assassination of Martin Luther King Jr. in 1968, riots across the country, a national day of mourning declared by President Johnson, and a nationally televised funeral, that openness became more difficult.

FOLK ROCK

The cover version of the folk classic "House of the Rising Sun" (recorded earlier by Lead Belly, Woody Guthrie and Pete Seeger, Joan Baez, and Bob Dylan) by the British group the Animals opened the doors to a new genre when it hit #1 on the pop charts the first week of September 1964. The genre flowered the following summer, largely fueled by Bob Dylan's songwriting, and acquired the label *folk rock*. Between May and October 1965 six Dylan songs made seven appearances in the Top 40—two by Dylan himself, the others by the Byrds, Turtles, and Cher (see figure 29). In all, Dylan songs generated fourteen Top 40 hits in the 1960s, half of which were cover versions by others. The Byrds were the primary group that defined the jangly (twelve-string) electric guitar sound of the style with #1 hits in 1965, in the summer (Dylan's "Mr. Tambourine Man") and fall (Pete Seeger's "Turn, Turn, Turn").

Although Dylan first used a drummer (with acoustic guitars and upright bass) in an October 1962 session for "Corrina Corrina" on his second album (*The Freewheelin' Bob Dylan*), he did not use one again until his electric January 1965 sessions for his fifth album (*Bringing It All Back Home*), on songs including "Subterranean Homesick Blues" (his debut as a performer on the Top 40) and "Maggie's Farm." His June 1965 sessions for his sixth album (*Highway 61 Revisited*) had a full-blown rock band, yielding "Like a Rolling Stone," which hit #2 in early September (blocked from #1 by the Beatles' "Help!"), the highest he would rise as a performer on the singles chart in the 1960s ("Rainy Day Women #12 and #35" also hit #2 a year later).

Billboard (1964b) first noted a trend in July 1964, referencing Hoyt Axton's "Heartbreak Hotel," which his label (Vee-Jay) called *folk rock*. Another article in the same issue used the term "folk rock," putting it in quotation marks as if it were something unfamiliar, and referred to "the gimmick of fusing folk material with a rock beat" (1964a: 36). This was just a few months before the Animals hit #1 with "House of the Rising Sun." By the following June folk rock was a national phenomenon: "With Bob Dylan as the stimulus and the Byrds as disciples, a wave of folk-rock is developing in contemporary pop music.... The race is on to get on the folk-rock band wagon.... If the folk-rock movement takes hold, a song's lyrical content could become as respected as the dominating beat" (Tiegel 1965a: 1, 10). *Billboard*'s reporting continued in August 1965: "Rock + Folk + Protest = an Erupting New Sound" (Sternfield 1965). Two weeks later *Billboard* recognized the significance of Dylan and his role in the new shift in rock:

> West Coast recording companies are rushing to cut Bob Dylan songs, with his message-protest material all but killing surfing, hot rod and other teen topics this summer.... 48 different Dylan records have been cut within the past month.... There are seven Dylan tunes on the charts, and the movement toward a folk-rock sound (*Billboard*, June 12) using Dylan as the chief prognosticator began with the Byrds' single of "Tambourine Man." Then the avalanche began.... All the Beach Boys-type groups have been washed out to sea by the Dylan-influenced groups who have also begun imitating Dylan's droning, monotonous vocal style.... The newest teen topic is protesting about a person's abnormally long hair. (Tiegel 1965b: 12, 47)

Dylan's April–May 1965 solo acoustic concert tour of England was the basis for a documentary by filmmaker D. A. Pennebaker (*Dont Look Back*, 1967-v), a new genre of film that by the 1970s would yield a related genre of staged concert films, such as *The Last Waltz* (Scorsese 1978-v), the farewell concert of his former backup group, the Band (Dylan made a guest appearance singing "Forever Young" and several of his other compositions). The innovative influential opening scene in *Dont Look Back* shows Dylan in an alley (with Allen Ginsberg off to the side) flipping through cue cards to the soundtrack of his recently released "Subterranean Homesick Blues." Dylan's Royal Albert Hall performance of "It's Alright, Ma (I'm Only Bleeding)," which closes the film, provides a vivid illustration of the sheer sonic brilliance of his lyrics, including the assonance (similar vowel sounds) and alliteration (similar consonant sounds) that is a hallmark of his style.

At the end of July 1965, Dylan played an electric guitar set (with members of the Paul Butterfield Blues Band) at the Newport Folk Festival, including his recently released "Like a Rolling Stone." The audience reaction to hearing a rock band, with Dylan no less, at the premier folk festival was mixed, with journalists reporting that he was booed. Captured on film and not released until decades later (Lerner 2007-v), this was one of the defining moments in rock history. Two years later rock critic Ellen Willis wrote an extended assessment of Dylan's career: "As composer, interpreter, most of all as lyricist, Dylan has made a revolution. He expanded folk idiom into a rich, figurative language, grafted literary and philosophical subtleties onto the protest song, revitalized folk vision by rejecting proletarian and ethnic sentimentality, then all but destroyed pure folk as a contemporary form by merging it with pop" (1968: 37).[6]

See figure 29. Bob Dylan Top 40 pop singles and LPs in the 1960s

PSYCHEDELIC ROCK

Psychedelic rock refers to a trend beginning in mid-decade toward more expansive instrumental solos (especially featuring electric guitar distortion) and recording studio effects (such as reverb, echo, tape loops, altered-tape playback speed) that somehow mimicked the experience of the distortion of time and perception as induced by psychedelic drugs, both chemically synthesized (LSD) and naturally occurring (psilocybin mushrooms, peyote cactus), and marijuana. Song lyrics too began to address such drug use.

Examples of studio experimentation include the Beatles ("Tomorrow Never

---

6   Dylan's LP output in the 1960s can be broken down into his debut in 1962 (mostly covers), three acoustic classics of social commentary (1963–64), three electric classics reaching the Top 10 (1965–66), a Greatest Hits compilation (1967) issued while recuperating from a motorcycle accident, and then a move toward country rock with two albums (1968–69). For Dylan at Newport 1965, see Wald (2015); for his 1966 UK tour, see Dylan (1972-v) and Scorsese (2005-v); for his 1975 Rolling Thunder Revue tour, see Dylan (1978-v). For more on folk rock, see Unterberger (2002).

Knows," 1966); the Beach Boys ("Good Vibrations" 1966); and Jimi Hendrix ("Third Stone from the Sun," 1967). Examples of lyric content include the Byrds ("Eight Miles High," 1966); Jefferson Airplane ("White Rabbit," 1967); and Jimi Hendrix ("Purple Haze," 1967). Iron Butterfly's 1968 one side of an album's length "In-A-Gadda-Da-Vida" would come to exemplify the genre. San Francisco, and its Haight Ashbury neighborhood, was an important center with many groups emerging there in the second half of the sixties associated with the rapidly growing psychedelic drug culture (see figure 35). By the end of the decade subgenres began to splinter off, including acid rock, hard rock, heavy metal, and art rock. The initial boundaries among these styles were quite fluid until the 1970s, when listeners began to more heavily invest in subgenres of rock.[7]

See figure 35. Mid to late 1960s U.S. rock (psychedelic and hard)

EXPERIMENTAL, UNDERGROUND, AND PROTOPUNK

In the spring of 1966 the Velvet Underground (New York City) and Frank Zappa and the Mothers of Invention (Los Angeles) recorded their debut albums, *Velvet Underground and Nico* and *Freak Out!*, both released on Verve and produced by Tom Wilson, one of the few African Americans working in that role at the time. Wilson had earlier produced albums by Simon and Garfunkel and Dylan. Both Velvet Underground and Zappa represented new, innovative, and different directions pushing the boundaries of rock and roll, appreciated by critics, but with little commercial visibility or viability (see figure 44).

Formed by vocalist, guitarist, and songwriter Lou Reed and Welsh viola player and composer John Cale, the Velvet Underground represented a gritty side of downtown urban New York City life in their lyrics and music. Cale brought in his experimental music background, introducing drones and sonic distortion. Reacting to Dylan and drawing on the dirtier, noisy sound of the Kinks, the Velvet Underground laid the foundation for what would be known as punk rock in the mid-1970s. With songs from their debut album, such as "Heroin" and "I'm Waiting for the Man," they were establishing a rock and roll aesthetic that was not aimed toward mainstream com-

7   For more on the music and scene, see Henke and Puterbaugh (1997), Hicks (1999), Unterberger (2003), Zimmerman (2008), and S. Hill (2016).

mercial success. Cale's noise-drenched viola solo toward the end of "Heroin" was unprecedented in rock and is still a sonic rarity. Cale left after their second album (*White Light/White Heat*, 1968), producing the debut albums of the Stooges (led by Iggy Pop) in 1969 and Patti Smith in 1975; in 1972 he produced many of the songs that would wind up on the 1976 debut album of the Modern Lovers (led by Jonathan Richman) (see figure 48). After two VU studio albums post-Cale, Lou Reed moved on to a solo career in the early 1970s. His second solo album (*Transformer*, 1972) was produced by David Bowie, five years Reed's junior (they both were on the RCA record label and admired each other's work), yielding the extraordinary "Walk on the Wild Side," Reed's only Top 40 hit.

Frank Zappa introduced virtuosic ensemble writing, requiring a high level of musicianship, into rock, including unusual time signatures (5/4 and 7/4 in "Flower Punk," 1968) and extended ensemble breaks. His satirical lyrics targeting the commercialization of rock (e.g., his fourth album, *We're Only in It for the Money*, 1968) and the shallowness of the new youth counterculture contributed to his reputation as working along the critical margins of rock. Zappa's musical sensibilities were especially informed by the work of experimental music composer Edgard Varèse. Zappa was an outspoken proponent of free speech in the music industry, testifying before Congress at the PMRC hearings in 1985, and a staunch critic of the conservative forces inherent in the music industry. Reflecting on the generational shifts in which 1960s know-nothing record executives were replaced by hipper younger ones, he noted, "The young guys are more conservative and dangerous to the art form than the old guys with the cigars ever were" (Zappa 1987-v). A prolific and boundary-smashing composer, creative guitarist, and witty lyricist, Zappa released over sixty albums in his lifetime with almost fifty more released posthumously. Nine of his albums reached the Top 40, with *We're Only in It for the Money* (1968) the highest at #30; he breached the Top 40 singles chart once, in 1982 with "Valley Girl," featuring his daughter Moon Unit.

Two Michigan bands, both with noisy in-your-face debut albums in 1969 on the Elektra label, were outrageously protopunk in their own unique ways. "If the Velvets can be considered to have fathered art-rock, then Detroit's two chief rock exponents, the MC5 and the Stooges, represented a more primitive tradition—rock & roll as the people's music, requiring nothing more than commitment from its participants" (Heylin 2005: 32). MC5 may be best known for being the only group that showed up to play outdoors at the August 1968 Democratic National Convention protests, which ended in a police riot, and for the opening line of the title track of their debut album, which their record label censored.[8] That debut album, recorded live in Detroit's Grande Ballroom in 1968, *Kick Out the Jams* (1969, #30), and its title track "Kick Out the Jams" (1969, #82) achieved some chart success, but the band was dropped by their label and recorded just two more albums before breaking up. The Stooges (initially based in Ann Arbor) did not last much longer (just three albums as a group), but leader Iggy Pop (James Osterberg, 1947–) had much greater career longevity, known for giving his all in performance, bordering on jumping off a cliff. Their debut album, *The Stooges* (1969, #106), reflected a disaffected suburban white teen ethos well before punk kicked in five years later. Iggy Pop's highest-charting album (until *Post Pop Depression* in 2016 at #17) was his debut solo album *The Idiot* (1977, #72), produced by and co-composed with David Bowie, on RCA.[9]

See figure 44. Progressive, art, experimental, and glam rock

See figure 48. Punk and new wave groups and their debut LPs

WOMEN AND 1960S ROCK

The visibility of women in rock and roll increased in the 1960s in several arenas. Girl groups thrived throughout the decade, especially on Motown. British vocalists Petula Clark and Dusty Springfield and American Dionne Warwick were major presences on the pop charts, as were soul singers Aretha Franklin and Gladys Knight. In the world of folk rock, Sonny and Cher and the Mamas and the Papas (a quartet with Cass Elliot and Michelle Phillips) both debuted in 1965, putting forward the novel presence of duos and groups with men and women equally balanced. Women folksingers (Joan Baez) and then singer-songwriters backed up with bands (Joni Mitchell, Judy Collins) had a presence in the 1960s, laying the groundwork for an explosion in the early 1970s.

A very different kind of presence occurred in the second half of the decade, with women leading rock bands. The two pioneers both date to about 1966 in San Francisco: Grace Slick fronting Jefferson Airplane and Janis Joplin fronting Big Brother and the Holding Company. They were moving into an all-male environment defined at the time by the Rolling Stones and the Animals with front men Mick Jagger and

---

8   The opening line is "Kick out the jams, motherfucker."

9   For more on the Velvet Underground, see Cale and Bockris (2000), DeCurtis (2017), and Unterberger (2009); for Frank Zappa, see Zappa (1989); for the MC5, see Callwood (2010); for Iggy Pop, see Trynka (2007) and D. Thompson (2009).

Eric Burdon providing the model. Closer to home Jim Morrison fronting the LA-based Doors was their closest peer.

The sequence of the appearances of Slick, Joplin, and Morrison (for comparison) on the pop charts can highlight their convergence on the scene. Jefferson Airplane's second album (their first with Grace Slick), *Surrealistic Pillow* (March 1967, #3) yielded their first (and biggest) singles: "Somebody to Love" (April 1967, #5) and "White Rabbit" (June 1967, #8). At that same moment the Doors' debut album *The Doors* (March 1967, #2) was released, with "Light My Fire (June 1967) reaching #1. Big Brother and the Holding Company's self-titled debut album on a small independent label arrived that fall (September 1967, #60); their performance at Monterey Pop earlier that summer gained them a Columbia Records contract, and their follow-up *Cheap Thrills* (August 1968) hit #1, containing "Piece of My Heart" (August 1968, #12). Joplin left the band in 1968, breaking into the Top 40 one more time, with "Me and Bobby McGee" (January 1971), which hit #1. Both the Doors and Jefferson Airplane released a string of high-charting albums through the early 1970s. Joplin died in 1970, and Morrison died in 1971. Grace Slick went on to an extended career with Jefferson Starship through the 1980s.

Joplin's status as a culture hero was captured at the time by *New Yorker* critic Ellen Willis (1969): "At the Fillmore East last August [1968], Janis Joplin put on the most exalting, exhausting concert I have ever been privileged to see, hear, and feel. . . . She sang four encores, and the audience, standing on the seats, wouldn't go home. Finally, she came back onstage. 'I love you, honey,' she said, gasping, 'but I just got nothing left.' . . . I felt a little like a vampire. From now on, I decided, after two encores I stop clapping." In a *Rolling Stone* profile six years after Joplin's death, Willis analyzed Joplin's legacy:

[She was] the only Sixties culture hero to make visible and public women's experience of the quest for individual liberation, which was very different from men's. . . .

Joplin's metamorphosis . . . [meant] that a woman who was not conventionally pretty, who had acne and an intermittent weight problem and hair that stuck out, could not only invent her own beauty . . . out of sheer energy, soul, sweetness, arrogance, and a sense of humor, but have that beauty appreciated. Not that Janis merely took advantage of changes in our notions of attractiveness; she herself changed them. It was seeing Janis Joplin that made me resolve, once and for all, not to get my hair straightened. And there was a direct line from that sort of response to those apocryphal burned bras and all that followed. (Willis 1976: 258)

Joplin was one of the few white artists singled out for praise by Jefferson, writing in 1973: "She was a misfit from Port Arthur, Texas . . . and she discovered early that identifying with archetypal misfits makes life a little easier. . . . Janis's life has echoes of Bessie Smith's, both being small-town Southern girls who took the cities with their singing, drinking, and swearing; both being dubbed Queen of the Blues. . . . Janis was a white woman using a black woman's blues to get to her own. . . . [At her best] the mimicry stopped and her own pain came out in her own way. . . . [She] purchased a tombstone for Bessie Smith some thirty years after the fact" (1973: 44).[10]

FUNK

The genre known as funk was pioneered by James Brown, who set the standard over the course of the mid and later 1960s. The term *funk* has a long history in jazz, and by 1967 the word was being consistently used for this newer style coming out of soul (see figure 36).[11] By the early 1970s the genre had gelled, with new bands emerging rapidly from all across the United States with no single geographic center (see figure 43). Being a dance-oriented style firmly rooted in African American aesthetics, it placed a strong emphasis on rhythm, with sharp percussive playing, offbeat syncopation, and dance-oriented lyrics.

Funk, as defined by James Brown's music, is marked by the following:

- a prominent bass line (sometimes doubled by the guitar or matched with a contrasting rhythm guitar line);
- sharp attacks on all the instruments;
- one or two rhythm guitars, one of which could play chords, quickly choking off the strings to emphasize a percussive effect, and the other could either double the bass line or play a contrasting line;

---

10 For more on Joplin, see Echols (1999) and Berg (2016-v).

11 See *OED* (2019a) for the English-language history of "funk" and "funky" (dating back to the seventeenth century) meaning a pungent odor, which conforms with its musical usage here, as in bad or nasty can refer to a particularly sharp (good) groove.

- an obligatory horn section (some combination of trumpet, trombone, and saxophone); and
- a dialogue, conversation, or call and response, often on several levels (most prominently between the vocalist and horns but also between any of the other instruments), which is reminiscent of the conversations among the instruments in virtually any kind of African drum ensemble.[12]

These features were laid out in a series of Brown's mid-1960s singles that crossed over into the upper reaches of the pop charts, including "Out of Sight" (#24) in 1964, "Papa's Got a Brand New Bag, Part 1" (#8), and "I Got You (I Feel Good)" (#3) in 1965, all three of which were in a twelve-bar blues form; and "Cold Sweat" (#7) in 1967. By the late 1960s Brown had let go of blues forms, paring down his structures to just a short melodic line played over and over on the guitar or bass or a short pattern alternating between two chords on the rhythm guitar. Examples include "Give It Up or Turnit Loose" (#15) and "Mother Popcorn" (#11) in 1969; "Get Up (I Feel Like Being a) Sex Machine" (#15) in 1970; "Hot Pants" (#15) and "Make It Funky" (#22) in 1971; and "Get on the Good Foot" (#18) in 1972. Brown is probably the most sampled artist in hip hop, in large part due to his two drummers: Clyde Stubblefield (1965–71), "Cold Sweat," "Say It Loud," "Mother Popcorn," and "Funky Drummer" (famous break at 5:21); and John "Jabo" Starks (1965–75), "Super Bad," "The Payback," and "Sex Machine."

By the late 1960s Sly and the Family Stone had developed their own brand of funk in San Francisco, giving even more presence to the bass player (Larry Graham); expanding the diversity of song forms, due to the keyboard skills of Sly Stone (born Sylvester Stewart) and group vocals (several band members sang); and combining elements of gospel music and San Francisco–based rock. They were one of the few bands at the time that were integrated in terms of both race and gender.

See figure 36. Funk: Naming a genre in song and album titles
See figure 43. Funk bands: Their debut LP year and their first pop Top 10 single

---

12 James Brown's music director, Bobby Byrd, recalls, "It was the syncopation of the instruments. . . . We winded up with a seven-piece band, but everybody had a different part to play. That's where the funk part of it became. Everybody playing a different part and it's all fitting together like a glove" (qtd. in Sublette 2007: 91). For an in-depth theoretical look at Brown's musical practice, see Brackett (1995).

The second half of the 1960s saw the elevation of the lead guitarist to a status that has defined rock up to the present time. Virtuoso guitarists of this era, all of them blues-based, set the standard in taste, timing, and craft. Seven guitarists stand out, four British and three American. On the British side Eric Clapton (Cream, Blind Faith, Derek and the Dominos), Jeff Beck (Jeff Beck Group, Beck, Bogert, and Appice), and Jimmy Page (Led Zeppelin) all played in the Yardbirds before moving on:

Clapton (October 1963–February 1965), "For Your Love" (*For Your Love*, 1965)

Beck (March 1965–November 1966), "I'm a Man" (*Having a Rave Up*, 1965)

Page (June 1966–July 1968), "White Summer" (*Little Games*, 1967)

Guitarist Pete Townshend spent most of his career with the Who. Townshend used feedback and other distortion techniques early on ("My Generation," "Anyway, Anyhow, Anywhere," 1965) and began literally destroying his guitar about 1964, at first by accident, then by design (something that Hendrix brought to new heights at Monterey Pop in 1967): "The guitar was . . . a metaphor for a machine gun. And the only thing you could do with a machine gun in the sixties was break it across your legs. . . . [Because] the guitar was a weapon, most of the techniques I used were very violent, virulent, and aggressively expressive. . . . I was at an art school where the course was dedicated to breaking the rules, and I just drafted that into my work as a guitar player" (Townshend, qtd. in Tolinski and di Perna 2016: 209–10).

The power trio Cream (Clapton, bassist Jack Bruce, and drummer Ginger Baker) released their debut album (*Fresh Cream*, U.S. pop #39) in December 1966, surely inspiring Jimi Hendrix, living in London at the time and whose debut album with his trio (*Are You Experienced?*) was released six months later, reaching #5 on the U.S. pop album chart. Power trios, the minimal rock group size (guitar, bass, drums), dating from this era, demand extraordinary constant effort from all three group members. The rapid-fire succession of releases by these two guitar-driven trios gives some sense of the peak year of their commercial success: Cream (*Disraeli Gears*, December 1967, #4); Hendrix (*Axis: Bold as Love*, February 1968, #3); Cream (*Wheels of Fire*, July 1968, #1); and Hendrix (*Electric Ladyland*, October 1968, #1).[13] The week of November 23,

---

13 The dates here indicate their entry into the U.S. album charts.

1968, they were saturating the upper reaches of the *Billboard* album chart, with four albums in the Top 25: *Electric Ladyland* (#1), *Are You Experienced?* (#6), *Wheels of Fire* (#9), and *Disraeli Gears* (#25). This was album-oriented rock. Hendrix had only one pop Top 40 single: "All Along the Watchtower" (*Electric Ladyland*); Cream hit the Top 40 three times: "Sunshine of Your Love" (*Disraeli Gears*) and "White Room" and "Crossroads" (*Wheels of Fire*).

On the U.S. side Jimi Hendrix, Duane Allman, and Carlos Santana all led their own bands, emerging just after the British guitarists. Before forming the Allman Brothers Band with brother Greg in 1969, Duane Allman (1946–71) played sessions at Fame Studios in Muscle Shoals, Alabama, most notably soloing on Wilson Pickett's "Hey Jude" (rec. November 1968) and Aretha Franklin's "The Weight" (rec. 1969). A chance meeting in 1970 brought in Allman to guest on Clapton's *Layla and Other Assorted Love Songs* (the debut album of Clapton's group called Derek and the Dominos), a rare cross-Atlantic recording collaboration at the time of two of the greatest guitarists of their generation. Allman died in a motorcycle accident in October 1971. Carlos Santana (1947–) was born in Mexico and moved to San Francisco with his family in his teens. Santana's debut album (*Santana*) was released the same month they played Woodstock in 1969, one of the highlight performances of the festival.[14]

Jimi Hendrix (1942–70), the lone African American in the bunch, probably has the greatest stature among rock guitarists, releasing four albums during his lifetime, with dozens more released in the many decades after his death in September 1970 (choking on his vomit in his sleep brought on by an overdose of sleeping pills). Born and raised in Seattle with distant Cherokee ancestors on both sides of his family (Hendrix 2008), Hendrix joined the airborne division of the army and then apprenticed for several years with R&B bands, including the Isley Brothers and Little Richard. After moving to Harlem, he played in Greenwich Village clubs, where he met ex-Animals bass player Chas Chandler, who brought him to London in the fall of 1966, the center of the rock world at the time due to the influence of the Beatles, Rolling Stones, and the aforementioned British guitarists. Hendrix formed his own trio and recorded his first album there. Hendrix returned to the United States with his trio in June 1967 to play at the Monterey Pop Festival. He built his own state-of-

---

14 Santana is discussed further in chapter 8.

the-art recording studio in Greenwich Village, Electric Lady Studios, completed in summer 1970, shortly before he died.[15]

ROCK FESTIVALS, 1967–1969

Outdoor rock festivals helped to define late 1960s counterculture. The first major one took place about 110 miles south of San Francisco: the Monterey International Pop Music Festival, held the weekend of June 16–18, 1967. Crowd estimates range from fifty thousand to one hundred thousand people on the festival grounds, with an actual arena seating capacity of just seven thousand. Highlights included Jimi Hendrix's U.S. debut (after spending nine months in London), in which he burned his guitar with lighter fluid, and Ravi Shankar performing Indian classical music on the sitar. The roster included bands from England (the Who, the Animals); San Francisco (Grateful Dead, Jefferson Airplane, Big Brother and the Holding Company, Quicksilver Messenger Service); Los Angeles (Buffalo Springfield, Mamas and the Papas, Canned Heat); New York City (Simon and Garfunkel, Laura Nyro); Georgia (Otis Redding); and South Africa (Hugh Masekela).[16]

The Woodstock Music and Art Fair, held the weekend of August 15–17, 1969, was the biggest of its kind, attracting approximately four hundred thousand people (estimates ranged from three hundred thousand to five hundred thousand), an un-anticipated number, resulting in food shortages and major transportation difficulties, including shutting down local exits on the New York State Thruway. Musical high-lights included Sly and the Family Stone ("I Wanna Take You Higher"); Santana ("Soul Sacrifice"); and Jimi Hendrix's solo guitar rendition of the "Star Spangled Banner." A novel documentary film (Wadleigh 1970-v), with the screen often split into three different camera shots, and a three-LP soundtrack album (the first triple album), which hit #1 on the pop charts, were both released in 1970, capturing these and many more classic performances that have come to stand in as symbols of the 1960s (e.g., performances by Crosby, Stills, Nash, and Young; Richie Havens; Joe Cocker; and the Who).

The euphoria of Woodstock was literally beaten down several months later with

---

15 For more on Hendrix, see Henderson (1981) and the documentary *Jimi Hendrix* (Boyd, Head, and Weis 1973-v).

16 Pennebaker, Hegedus, and Dawkins (2002-v).

the Altamont Speedway Free Festival held December 6, 1969, at a motor speedway track about sixty miles east of San Francisco. Originally conceived as a free concert given by the Rolling Stones at Golden Gate Park in San Francisco, the venue had to be changed, finally landing just a few days before the event at the inhospitable Altamont site. A very low, too-easy-to-access stage and the decision to employ members of the Hells Angels motorcycle club as stage security in exchange for $500 worth of beer, led to excessive violence and a murder, captured in the documentary film of the tail end of the Rolling Stones' 1969 U.S. tour, *Gimme Shelter* (Maysles, Maysles, and Zwerin 1970-v). Compounded by little thought given to the needs of the approximately three hundred thousand attendees, it turned out to be a disaster. Local bands Santana and Jefferson Airplane performed, but the Grateful Dead, who were an integral part of organizing the event, declined to go on at the last minute. It was everything that Woodstock was not and symbolically marked the shutting down not only of the decade but also of the aspirations of the 1960s youth counterculture.[17]

ROCK JOURNALISM

In the second decade of its existence, rock began to be treated as a mature form of artistic expression by a new generation of writers, who established an enduring legacy. Most had earned college degrees (unusual in the world of the musicians), and many were affiliated with *Rolling Stone*, which was cofounded as an underground counter-cultural magazine by Jann Wenner and Ralph J. Gleason in 1967 in San Francisco.[18]

Al Aronowitz (1928–2005) established the mold, writing about the Beatles for the mass-circulation general-interest *Saturday Evening Post* in 1964. Ellen Willis (1941–2006) was the first pop music critic at the *New Yorker* beginning in 1968 and one of the few women rock journalists at the time. Another was Ellen Sander (1944–), who wrote regularly on rock for the *Saturday Review* from 1968 to 1972.[19] Lilian Roxon (1932–73) published a *Rock Encyclopedia*, the first of its kind, in 1969 and then

---

17 For more on Woodstock, see Collier (1969) and Lang (2009); for Altamont, see R. Gleason (1970), *Rolling Stone* (1970), and Selvin (2016).

18 Dates in this section indicate either an individual's life span or career stages. The References section provides some of the early publications of each person discussed. See Gendron (2002: 190–224) for a study of early rock criticism.

19 For Sander's *Saturday Review* articles, see Sander (2019). Rhodes (2005) has an extended analysis of the work of Willis and Roxon.

published in various venues until her death in 1973. Robert Christgau (1942–) began writing for *Esquire* in 1967 and then the *Village Voice* in 1969, and Richard Goldstein (1944–) began writing for the *Village Voice* in 1966. Peter Guralnick (1943–) wrote for *Crawdaddy!* (1967) and *Rolling Stone* (1969), but he is primarily known for his well-researched biographies, including those of Elvis Presley, Sam Phillips, and Sam Cooke. Greil Marcus (1945–) was *Rolling Stone*'s first record reviews editor and has written one of the most widely acclaimed early histories of rock (*Mystery Train*, 1979). Richard Meltzer (1945–) started out at *Crawdaddy!* before moving to *Rolling Stone* and the *Village Voice*, Ben Fong-Torres (1945–) and Jim Miller (1947–) began writing for *Rolling Stone* in 1968, and Lester Bangs (1948–1982) began writing for *Rolling Stone* in 1969. As a seventeen-year-old college student in 1966, Paul Williams (1948–2013) founded and edited *Crawdaddy!*, the very first of the crop of magazines to take rock criticism seriously. Dave Marsh (1950–) was a founding editor of *CREEM* magazine (1969) before joining *Rolling Stone* (1975) and then founding *Rock and Roll Confidential* (1983). Cameron Crowe (1957–) first published in *Rolling Stone* at age sixteen (a cover story) in 1973 and eventually wrote and directed a semiauto-biographical film about his experiences (*Almost Famous*, 2000).

African American writers are noticeably absent in the rock press in this era, although several were occupied with the jazz world, including Amiri Baraka (1934–2014) and A. B. Spellman (1935–). Phyl Garland (1935–2006) wrote about soul for the general-interest *Ebony* magazine after she joined them in 1965. She would become the first woman and first African American to gain tenure at Columbia University's School of Journalism. This absence would only gradually be addressed, as with the dearth of women writers, over the next several decades.

END-OF-DECADE TRENDS

Several trends can be noted at the end of the decade, some subtle, some not so subtle. The organ became more prevalent, with a marked shift from a mid-decade use of the Farfisa (Sam the Sham and the Pharaohs, early Pink Floyd, Sly and the Family Stone) and Vox Continental (Animals, the Doors, the Zombies) brands to a late decade use of the richer-sounding Hammond B3 brand (Booker T. and the MGs, Allman Brothers, Santana) (see figure 37). Integrated groups gradually appeared, and Latin percussion became almost standard fare after Santana (see figures 38 and 39).

A series of deaths of high-profile artists before they reached the age of thirty—some by accident (plane or motorcycle), most related to drug abuse—clustered within just a few years, a phenomenon rarely seen again (see figure 40). Five died at the age of twenty-seven within a space of two years: Rolling Stones guitarist Brian Jones in 1969; Canned Heat cofounder Alan Wilson, Jimi Hendrix, and Janis Joplin in 1970; and Jim Morrison in 1971. With the gruesome murders committed by the Charles Manson family (July–August 1969) and the ugly outcome of the Altamont music festival (December 1969), a decade marked by optimism, prosperity, widespread social engagement and protest, and excess gave way to one that would be marked by retreat. Jefferson Airplane's *Volunteers*, released in November 1969, captured the moment, with both protest ("Volunteers," "We Can Be Together") and retreat ("The Farm").

During the 1960s a significant number of artists and groups began to rack up large numbers of Top 40 hits (see figure 41). This is one measure of popularity, different than Top 10 hits, which is a much more exclusive achievement, or hit albums, which might not generate hit singles. Elvis Presley is the leader in this field, with almost twice as many Top 40 hits (113) as the next in line, Elton John, with fifty-nine. This list is helpful in evaluating the relative presence of men, women, blacks, whites, soloists, and groups.

———

See figure 37. Groups with organ, 1960s

See figure 38. Integrated groups, 1960s to early 1970s

See figure 39. Groups with Latin percussion

See figure 40. Birth and death years of 1960s musicians

See figure 41. All-time Top 40 hits: Soloists and groups (through 1999)

The promise of the 1960s youth counterculture was deferred as the realities of the 1970s set in, including the continuing Vietnam War, persistent inner-city poverty and lack of opportunity, oil shortages, and a recession. A fragmentation process accelerated in the late 1960s and early 1970s as rock developed into more specialized subgenres: hard rock, progressive rock, glam rock, country rock, heavy metal, and punk. Both punk and disco emerged about the same time in the mid-1970s, offering stark points of comparison. Funk, a dance music, continued through the whole of the 1970s, with sometimes blurred and contested boundaries between it and the dance music that marked the second half of the decade: disco.

Key social and political events include the following. In 1970 the first annual Earth Day was held in April, and the first annual Gay Pride march in June marked the one-year anniversary of the riot at Greenwich Village's Stonewall Inn. In April National Guard troops fired on protesting students at Kent State University, killing four; Crosby, Stills, Nash, and Young's "Ohio," released two months later, reached #14 on the pop chart. In March 1973 U.S. involvement with the war was officially over. More than three million Americans had served: almost 58,000 were killed; 150,000 were seriously injured; and 1,000 were missing in action. About one and a half million Vietnamese were killed in the war. Also in 1973 a six-month oil embargo was imposed by Arab nations as part of the Arab-Israeli (Yom Kippur) war in October, leading to an energy crisis in the United States and an economic recession with high unemployment and high inflation (late 1973–early 1975). Alex Haley's 1976 *Roots*, a novel (that he termed *faction*), tracing his family origins from eighteenth-century West Africa, and its six-episode television miniseries, which aired the following year, both enjoyed massive popularity, with the miniseries remaining one of the most watched in television history.

Two other major events marked the decade: President Nixon resigned in August 1974, before the conclusion of the House of Representatives impeachment hearings on the Watergate scandal; and students supporting the Iranian revolution took over the U.S. embassy in Tehran (November 1979–January 1981), holding over fifty Americans hostage, contributing to incumbent Jimmy Carter's loss of the presidential election to Ronald Reagan (November 1980).

The early 1970s witnessed a surge of Hollywood films that featured African American directors and casts targeted at predominantly African American audiences. Dozens were released in the first half of the decade, with two of the most prominent films featuring major soundtrack albums: *Shaft*, with music by Isaac Hayes; and *Super*

Fly with music by Curtis Mayfield (see figure 42). A local NAACP leader coined the term *Blaxploitation* for these films in 1972, initially objecting to their depictions of criminal life (Repino and Allen 2013). The term has since taken on a more positive (or at least neutral) spin. A second wave (but without the term *Blaxploitation*) began in the late 1980s, prominently featuring hip hop, including *Do the Right Thing* ("Fight the Power," 1989) and *Boyz n the Hood*, featuring Ice Cube (1991).

See figure 42. Blaxploitation films and the next generation

FUNK IN THE 1970s

Funk in the 1970s blew up, becoming the major African American style by mid-decade and a powerful and lasting symbol of black music around the globe. The accompanying flurry of African American–oriented films early in the decade provided a mutually reinforcing cultural current. From 1967 to 1977 funk bands flourished, with about a dozen of them hitting the pop Top 10 (figure 43 shows the more well-known ones). Funk from this era provided much of the soundtrack of sample-based hip hop beginning in the second half of the 1980s. In the early part of the 1970s, very tightly rehearsed horn sections (typically trumpet, trombone, and saxophone) out front in the mode of James Brown's band were the norm (e.g., Tower of Power's "What Is Hip?," 1973). Toward the later 1970s and into the 1980s, the driving role of horns gave way to synthesizers (or a string section) and a more prominent role for rhythm guitar, blurring the border at times with disco (e.g., Chic's "Le Freak," 1978, and "Good Times," 1979).

After Sly and the Family Stone, the most innovative and unusual funk band was Parliament Funkadelic (P-Funk), led by vocalist and composer George Clinton (1941–) with his co-conspirators Bootsy Collins (bass, 1951–) and Bernie Worrell (keyboards, 1944–2016). Recording under two different names (Parliament and Funkadelic), Clinton's vivid imagination, driven by Collins and Worrell, provided legendary stage shows with dozens of costumed performers taking on fictional character roles, proselytizing for the transformative power of funk: "Maybe funk itself was a form of evolution. Maybe if you refused to participate in it, you were holding yourself back. We had already created and deployed Star Child, an agent of interplanetary funk. Did he have the secret for improving the species, funkateer by funkateer? . . . Ever since *Chocolate City* [1975], I had been moving toward a complete, comprehensive funk opera. . . . Why couldn't soul or funk music be just as sophisticated, just as wide-ranging, just as artistically successful?" (Clinton 2014: 179, 181).

Funkentelechy vs. the Placebo Syndrome (1977) was "a collection of funk anthems about the anthemic power of funk" (Clinton 2014: 181). Clinton's classic anthem came the following year, "One Nation under a Groove," which hit the pop Top 40. Between 1975 (*Mothership Connection*) and 1979 (*Gloryhallastoopid*) Parliament Funkadelic had a string of eight Top 10 R&B albums, seven of which crossed over to the Top 40 pop chart. The large outer space mothership prop from their 1976–77 P-Funk Earth Tour, following the release of *Mothership Connection*, currently resides at the National Museum of African American History and Culture.

The importance of the electric bass guitar in 1970s funk can be appreciated in the episode devoted to it in the ten-part WGBH/BBC *Rock and Roll* documentary (Espar and Thomson 1995-v, episode 8). It is the only episode that prominently features bass players, with two standing out: Larry Graham, a driving force in Sly and the Family Stone; and Bootsy Collins, who apprenticed with James Brown in 1970 before teaming up with George Clinton. Stevie Wonder made a key move by playing the bass line on a keyboard synthesizer in "Maybe Your Baby" (1972) and "Boogie on Reggae Woman" (1974). Embracing technology in a live funk band context, Clinton and Bernie Worrell took it a step further with "Flashlight," lowering the range of the bass and bringing it front and center: "We had always heard groups like Emerson, Lake, and Palmer and them play [synthesizers], but not use it as a bass that would play those real low sounds on it. And I would hear Bernie hittin' it, so I told [him] could you actually do the bass line, and he started doing [Sly Stone bassist] Larry Graham for me. Bernie was a real Larry Graham freak" (Clinton, qtd. in Espar and Thomson 1995-v, episode 8).

Clinton has become an elder statesman of funk, given a boost by Dr. Dre's debut solo album *The Chronic* (1992, pop #3, R&B #1), which drew heavily from Parliament's *Mothership Connection* LP.[1] Permeating the sound of the album that launched Dr. Dre's solo career as well as that of guest Snoop Dogg (his debut album in 1993

---

1 Dr. Dre's "The Roach (The Chronic Outro)," with the line "Make my bud the Chronic," parodies Parliament's "P Funk," with the line "Make my funk the P-funk," including the style of delivery, lyric content, form, and instrumental backing; and the chorus on Dr. Dre's "Let Me Ride" comes from a line in "Mothership Connection (Star Child)." Many samples are credited in the album liner notes. For further details see Who Sampled (2019). Clinton's memoir (2014: 292–95) discusses East and West Coast sampling of his music.

would hit #1 on the pop chart), Parliament Funkadelic gained new generations of listeners.

———

See figure 43. Funk bands: Their debut LP year and their first pop Top 10 single

PROGRESSIVE ROCK

The studio experiments of the Beatles beginning with *Revolver* (1966) had a major impact on other British bands, especially those moving further away from the blues. In his autobiography, drummer Bill Bruford (Yes, King Crimson, Genesis) notes a merging of psychedelic and pastoral folk styles by bohemian middle-class youth in southeast England, many of whom had early musical experiences in the Anglican Church. The kinds of contrasts these bands were exploring begged for longer forms: technical and pastoral; present and past; male and female (equated with nature, romantic, and pastoral). Groups began to outdo each other with more ambition and more sound equipment, in what Bruford (2013: 116) called an "arms race."

Primarily a British phenomenon, in the space of four years nine major groups (other than the Beatles) released albums that came to define progressive rock: Moody Blues (*Days of Future Passed*) and Pink Floyd (*The Piper at the Gates of Dawn*) in 1967; Soft Machine (*The Soft Machine*) in 1968; King Crimson (*In the Court of the Crimson King*), the Who (*Tommy*), Yes (*Yes*), and Jethro Tull (*Stand Up*) in 1969; and Emerson, Lake, and Palmer (*Emerson, Lake, and Palmer*) and Genesis (*Trespass*) in 1970 (see figure 44). Roxy Music (*Roxy Music*) came out in 1972, and their keyboardist Brian Eno soon began collaborating with King Crimson guitarist Robert Fripp and going solo; Eno became one of the most important collaborators and producers later in the decade with his work on David Bowie's Berlin Trilogy albums (1977–79) and Talking Heads' second through fourth albums (1978–80).

Bruford notes that from about 1966 to 1971 the socioeconomic background of both the musicians and their American following were similar, "singing from the same high-cultural song sheet." By about 1972 the genre was popular enough to accommodate stadium tours in the United States and left its subcultural status behind for the mainstream. Bruford suggests that its popularity in the United States was primarily "in the Northeast and Midwest, both regions with a strong WASP [White Anglo-Saxon Protestant] population. The young white audience found a resonance in the nationalism of the music and a kind of surrogate ethnic identity at a time when the question of what it meant to be a white person in America was coming under scrutiny. . . . The neo-Marxist critics—Bangs, Marsh, Christgau, and the rest—were deeply suspicious in three main areas: the lack of a political stance within the music; its overreliance on high culture; and its commercial success. In the critical court of law, the progressive rockers were guilty on all three counts" (Bruford 2013: 118, 119).

Progressive rock was largely album oriented, featuring ambitious song forms whose lengths were less conducive to a Top 40 radio commercial format. Consequently, bands generally had higher chart rankings for their albums than their singles. The most commercially successful bands in this regard include the following (with the number of albums in the Top 10 during the period indicated): the Who (nine, 1969–82); Jethro Tull (seven, including two at #1, 1971–77); Yes (six, 1972–78); Moody Blues (five, including two at #1, 1968–81); Pink Floyd (five, including three at #1, 1973–83); and Emerson, Lake, and Palmer (four, 1971–74). For comparison, the top glam bands at the time were Alice Cooper (five, including one at #1, 1972–75); Queen (five, including one at #1, 1975–80); and Kiss (four, 1975–79).

Germany spawned its own scene in the 1970s, an outgrowth of the 1968 International Essen Song Days, the first major rock festival in Europe (responding to the previous year's Monterey Pop Festival). Along with the Fugs and Frank Zappa, fledgling German rock groups, including Tangerine Dream, performed. Can was formed the same year. *Krautrock* (named by British deejay John Peel in the early 1970s) would have a profound impact on later generations, particularly those involved in electronic dance music (EDM), ambient music, and the early days of hip hop beat making. Harmonia's electronic-based drones with a beat (*Musik von Harmonia*, 1974) had a strong impact on Brian Eno, who recorded with them briefly in 1976. The electronic synthesizer and drum machine quartet Kraftwerk laid a sonic foundation for hip hop pioneer Afrika Bambaataa and his producer Arthur Baker in the early 1980s. The drum beat in Bambaataa's biggest hit, "Planet Rock" (1982), was based on Kraftwerk's "Numbers" (1981), which had entered the R&B charts six months earlier, rising to #22.

By comparison, the North American progressive rock legacy was much attenuated. Both Kansas (from Topeka) and the trio Rush (from Toronto) debuted albums in 1974 and would enjoy sustained chart success as the decade wore on.[2]

See figure 44. Progressive, art, experimental, and glam rock

---

2   For more on progressive rock, see Covach (1997), Macan (1997), Holm-Hudson (2002), and Weigel (2017); for the German scene, see Stubbs (2015) and Adelt (2016).

GLAM ROCK

Glam (for glamour) rock arose in the early 1970s, marked by men wearing makeup, flirting with cross-dressing and flamboyant fashion, and challenging images of masculinity posed by their predecessors in rock. It was characterized less by its sound than by its theatricality, that is, performers taking on various personas on stage that pointed out the artificiality of our identities. Auslander (2006: 10) calls it "the first post-counterculture rock style to solidify as a genre," arising out of the political and social disappointments and gloom of the turn into the new decade. A late 1960s rock aesthetic associated with the youth counterculture prized authenticity in the form of free expression and spontaneity (extended improvised guitar solos); participatory democracy (gatherings, such as be-ins and love-ins, and festivals); and a singular persona on stage representing one's inner self. Performers appeared as themselves, in everyday life, identifying with their audiences down to their stage attire. Glam was the antithesis (Auslander 2006: 10–18).

The March 1971 appearance of Marc Bolan with his group T. Rex (formerly Tyrannosaurus Rex) on the British *Top of the Pops* television show to lip synch "Hot Love" is often cited as the moment of origin (see figure 44). The wife of T. Rex manager Tony Secunda, Chelita, daubed glitter beneath Bolan's eyes (Hoskyns 1998: 18). Later that year David Bowie (born David Jones, 1947–2016) recorded his fifth album, *The Rise and Fall of Ziggy Stardust and the Spiders from Mars*, inventing an alien rock star character, injecting the new genre with a story and moving it beyond just the spectacle.[3] Bowie was especially appreciated in that his diverse personas in the 1970s pointed up the artifice or artificiality of who we project ourselves to be, that we wear masks and our identities are in a state of flux: "'It's no surprise Ziggy Stardust was a success,' David later explained, 'I packaged a totally credible plastic rock'n'roll singer—much better than the Monkees could ever fabricate. I mean, my plastic rock'n'roller was much more plastic than anybody's. And that was what was needed at the time'" (Bowie, qtd. in Pegg 2016: 352). Madonna would gain similar attention for this a decade later.

From his very first album (*David Bowie*, 1967), Bowie drew on a British music-hall popular song tradition of playing characters or parts in a song: "Bowie changes his delivery and vocal tone according to the character he is describing. . . . He neither presents a consistent persona on the album nor sings in a single voice. . . . Some of

---

3   See the concert documentary by Pennebaker (1973-v).

his lyrics are in the first person, some in the third. His voice and accent change according to the character he portrays. . . . One can hear this album as anticipating in miniature Bowie's basic performance strategy" (Auslander 2006: 110–11). He had a strong fascination for both Lou Reed ("He gave us the environment in which to put our more theatrical vision. . . . He supplied us with the street and the landscape, and we peopled it") and Iggy Pop (he "unleash[ed] the animalistic parts of rock" and represented "the wild side of existentialist America") (Bowie, qtd. in Pegg 2016: 353). His biographer has contrasted Bowie's style with more mainstream American rock: "Bowie's music has seldom gone mainstream in America, where honesty and denim and Bruce Springsteen are what rock music is all about: 'I'm not a guy that gets on stage and tells you how my day's just gone. . . . I feel like an actor when I'm on stage, rather than a rock artist. . . . Sometimes I don't feel like a person at all,' he said in 1972, 'I'm just a collection of other people's ideas'" (Pegg 2016: 5). Bowie has addressed this in other ways: "I think there's a real continuity with what I do, and it's just about expressing myself in a contemporaneous fashion. . . . The chameleon is always trying to blend into his surroundings, and I don't think that's exactly what I'm known for" (6). Regarding his eclectic tastes, Bowie has explained, "There's no point in just ripping something off, but if you hear something and think, 'I like what this guy is doing; I know what I can do with that,' it's like having a new colour to paint with, and I think it depends very much on what you do with that colour once you've found it" (4).

Bowie's mainstream presence is curious; his highest-charting albums came at the end of his long career. Out of almost twenty albums released from his debut in 1967 through 1980, only four songs entered the Top 40 (including the single "Fame," which hit #1 in 1975). After an initial creative burst in the early 1970s, which yielded the albums *Hunky Dory* (1972, #93), his most famous *Ziggy Stardust* (1972, #75), and *Alladin Sane* (1973, #17), he reached his commercial recording peak between 1974 and 1976, marked by a string of five consecutive Top 10 albums. In 2013, after a recording hiatus of ten years, his album *The Next Day* reached his highest chart position at #2. His final album, *Blackstar*, released January 8, 2016, two days before he would die of liver cancer (on January 10) would become his first #1 charting album.

Bowie's significance was due in part to his transience: "No other artist of his stature straddled and thereby defied the conflict between the opposing camps of 'rock' and 'pop.' . . . Bowie challenged the tribalism of such allegiances. . . . Leading by example, his career actively encouraged his followers to reject uniforms and movements, to shed

their skins, to revel in the transience of musical and sartorial fashion. In so doing . . .
it enabled his music to defy categorization" (Pegg 2016: 6).[4]

Bowie's 1972 collaboration as producer on Lou Reed's second solo LP (*Transformer*,
#29) resulted in one of the most compelling statements in rock: "Walk on the Wild
Side" (1973, #16), an extraordinary combination of a stark and elegant arrangement
with risk-taking lyrics. The acoustic bass overdubbed with an electric bass moving in
opposite tonal directions is one of the most recognizable sonic fingerprints in rock.
Each verse is devoted to a member of Andy Warhol's orbit (his superstars), deni-
zens of New York City's underground: transgender actors Holly Woodlawn, Candy
Darling, and Jackie Curtis and gay icons Joe Dallesandro and "Sugar Plum Fairy"
Joe Campbell. It was a ripe moment, coming three years after the Stonewall Inn riot
that led to increasingly public calls for acceptance of lifestyles outside of mainstream
heterosexual norms.

> Reed: "I don't know of any other song where you have a character per verse."[5]
> David Byrne: "I'd hear it on radio all the time, you'd hear it in restaurants,
>   in bars, in bus stations, wherever, and I wondered, 'Do any of these people
>   realize what this song is talking about? Who is being talked about and what's
>   going on?'"
> Patti Smith: "They were the ragtag queens of Max's Kansas City [New York
>   City club where Warhol held court] and they got very little in return for all of
>   the groundbreaking things that they did, and to be heralded by someone like
>   Lou was lovingly compassionate without being syrupy." (Greenfield-Sanders
>   1998-v)

Other artists and groups that exemplify glam rock include the New York Dolls,
Alice Cooper (the stage name of singer Vincent Furnier, born in Detroit), and Kiss
(New York City) on the U.S. side and the British groups Roxy Music (led by Brian
Ferry) and Queen, led by vocalist Freddie Mercury (1946–91). Born Farrokh Bulsara
in Zanzibar and educated in India, Mercury moved to England when he was seventeen.
In contrast to most of his peers in the genre, he was gay. "His queerness, like the name
of his band, was so in-your-face that no one even noticed it," notes Hoskyns (1998:
99). This is remarkably similar to Little Richard. Mercury was the first major rock

---

4   For more on Bowie see Broackes and Marsh (2013).
5   Joni Mitchell's "Ladies of the Canyon" (1970) features this technique.

star to die of AIDS, publicly acknowledging the cause of his illness the day before he died in November 1991. Queen's legacy includes "Bohemian Rhapsody" (1975, #9); "We Are the Champions" (#4) and "We Will Rock You" (two sides of a single, 1977); "Crazy Little Thing Called Love" (1979, #1); "Another One Bites the Dust" (1980, #1); and "Under Pressure" (with Bowie) (1981, #29; #1 in the United Kingdom).

———

See figure 44. Progressive, art, experimental, and glam rock

HARD ROCK

Hard rock, as it took shape in the 1970s, is generally considered loud, aggressive, oriented toward the spectacle of stadiums, and simpler in construction and in rhythmic conception than either progressive rock or heavy metal. It is more apt than other genres to be marked with memorable sing-along choruses. The lyrics alone can often distinguish it from other genres: it is party music, typically celebrating heterosexual masculinity. Exhibit A: the chorus to Grand Funk Railroad's 1973 #1 single:

> We're an American band [two times]
> We're comin' to your town
> We'll help you party it down
> We're an American band.

Robbins's (2000) harsh critique of Grand Funk Railroad ("The Band That Killed Rock 'n' Roll"), whose eight of their first eleven albums reached the Top 10, represents a classic rock critic's response to the dashed utopian dreams of the Woodstock generation:

> Arriving on the scene too late to grasp rock's pivotal role in shaping the '60s, they observed a landscape of no-account hippies, foreign [British] influence and dissipating idealism and didn't like what they saw. . . . Grand Funk inadvertently knocked down the wall that had divided rock self-expression from market-driven factory pop. . . . Their sales as much as their sensibilities cleared a path to football stadiums, where rock, sports and other testosterone-fueled mass gatherings could finally meld into one universal crud culture. What Grand Funk did was establish banality as a mass-market ideal. . . . For a brief, exciting time, rock could not bear to stand still, and its greats

were those who constantly sought new challenges. Between 1966 and 1969, it was swept by waves of psychedelia, sitar, folk, blues, country and more. The arrival of Grand Funk stopped progress dead in its tracks.[6]

Letters-to-the-editor responses to Robbins weighed in pro and con, with one widening the blame: "if Robbins had looked a little harder at the fingerprints on the many knives in the back of rock 'n' roll, the more likely offenders would turn out to be the legions of deeply pretentious art rockers that plodded right alongside GFR" (Grogan, qtd. in Salon Staff 2000). On the other hand, writing right when Grand Funk Railroad was entering into its height of mass popularity, Willis noted a "frontlash" (at least at the Detroit-based *Creem* magazine) in which the critical disdain for GFR was likened to the disdain that parents in the 1950s expressed toward early rock and roll, and GFR was positioned as the voice of teens in the 1970s, perhaps the band to consolidate a fragmenting audience. Willis saw them as an "antidote to James Taylor and the other upper-class brats; their adrenalin is bound to do us all good," but still she did not enjoy their records, conceding that it may be because she is "fifteen years older than the average Grand Funk enthusiast" (1972: 80).[7]

As rock bands played to larger and larger crowds from the early 1970s on, sports arenas (both indoor and outdoor) came to be the venues of choice, giving rise to the pejorative designation *arena rock* (see figure 45). Bands in this category were commercially oriented and radio-friendly and frequently went on expensive massive tours. Grand Funk was one of the first to draw such large crowds, along with Led Zeppelin. Later bands included Journey, REO Speedwagon, Boston, Foreigner, Styx, Aerosmith, and Queen.

See figure 45. Early to mid 1970s rock: Top 40 singles and albums

SINGER-SONGWRITERS

Artists who sang their own introspective compositions, accompanying themselves on acoustic guitar or piano, made a concerted appearance in the early 1970s, establishing the genre simply known as *singer-songwriter* (see figure 28). Joan Baez provided

---

6   See Archer (1996-v) for television cartoon character Homer Simpson defending his love for Grand Funk Railroad with backhanded compliments, epitomizing the points made here.

7   See also Waksman's (2009: 19–69) discussion of Grand Funk.

the early model in terms of sound and image in the early 1960s, but she was not a songwriter; rather, she had an original interpretive style (she began recording her compositions on her 1970 album *One Day at a Time*). Dylan laid the groundwork, increasingly evident from his fourth album *Another Side of Bob Dylan* (1964), cited at the time as marking a shift in personal style, moving away from protest or "finger pointin'" songs. In an "Open Letter to Bob Dylan" in the urban folk revival magazine *Sing Out!*, editor Irwin Silber complained, "You seem to be in a different kind of bag now, Bob. . . . Your new songs seem to be all inner-directed now, inner-probing, self-conscious—maybe even a little maudlin or a little cruel on occasion" (1964: 22). Bromell tied this shift into a broader cultural current in the mid-1960s of moving from liberal politics, calling out injustices, to a "radical politics conceived in terms of one's own loneliness . . . a politicalization of the private sphere—making the personal political as feminists would teach people to say—and it meant that a turn *inward* was a turn toward, not away from, politics" (2000: 130).

Joni Mitchell set the standard for the next generation with her first three albums: *Song to a Seagull* (1968, #189, "The Cactus Tree"); *Clouds* (1969, #31, "Chelsea Morning," "Both Sides, Now"); and *Ladies of the Canyon* (1970, #27, "Big Yellow Taxi," "Woodstock," "Circle Game").[8] The year 1971 marked the time of the woman singer-songwriter: Carole King's monumental second solo album *Tapestry* (which would win four Grammys) entered the charts in early April, hitting #1 and generating two #1 singles ("It's Too Late," "I Feel the Earth Move"); Carly Simon's debut album (*Carly Simon*, #30) entered the charts a few weeks later (she would receive a Grammy for Best New Artist the following year); Joni Mitchell's fourth LP *Blue* (#15) entered the charts in July; and Carly Simon's second album (*Anticipation*, #30) entered in November. Simon's next album *No Secrets*, released in late 1972, would hit #1, as would the single "You're So Vain."[9]

Joni Mitchell's *Blue* is the highest-ranking album by a woman on *Rolling Stone* magazine's "500 Greatest Albums of All Time" list (#30) and the #1 ranked album on National Public Radio's "150 Greatest Albums Made by Women" list.[10] David Crosby (of the Byrds and Crosby, Stills, Nash, and Young), who was close with Mitchell in the

---

8 "Big Yellow Taxi" (#67) was Mitchell's only song to make the singles chart from these three albums.

9 For a comparative study of Carole King, Joni Mitchell, and Carly Simon, see Weller (2008). See also the documentaries on Mitchell (Lacy 2003-v) and King (Neville 2011-v; Scott 2016-v).

10 See *Rolling Stone* (2012) and NPR (2017).

late 1960s, has expressed the kind of widespread peer admiration that Mitchell had gained: "When I was with Joni, I'd write a song like 'Guinnevere'—probably the best song I ever wrote—I'd play it for her, and she'd say, 'That's wonderful, David, here, listen to these ones.' Then she'd sing me four that were that good. It was a humbling experience for a writer" (Crosby, qtd, in Lisa Robinson 2015: 270).

On the men's side, Crosby, Stills, and Nash gave a lightning jolt to the genre in 1969 with their self-titled debut album, which entered the charts a month and a half before Woodstock, rising to #6 and yielding two Top 40 singles ("Marrakesh Express" and "Suite: Judy Blue Eyes"). Their Woodstock performance, adding Neil Young, moved an acoustic guitar-based supergroup of singer-songwriters into rock royalty. David Crosby (with the Byrds), Stephen Stills and Neil Young (with Buffalo Springfield), and Graham Nash (with the Hollies) had all hit the upper reaches of the pop charts a few years earlier. Their second album (their first with Young), *Déjà Vu* (1970), hit #1, as did a follow-up concert tour album (*4 Way Street*, 1971) and a compilation after they had broken up (*So Far*, 1974). Capitalizing on the success of *Déjà Vu*, they each released solo albums in 1970–71, all debuts except for Young, who had released his debut the previous year. All four albums moved into the Top 20. Young's fourth album, *Harvest*, hit #1 in 1972, as did its single "Heart of Gold."

Crosby, Stills, Nash, and Young had an unusual mix of intricate solo and group acoustic guitar work; exquisite three-part vocal harmony (reminiscent of an earlier Southern California group, the Beach Boys); a deep well of four accomplished song-writers to draw from; a combination of youth and experience (they ranged from twenty-five to twenty-nine years old in 1970); and soulful electric guitar and organ playing by Stills. As a group, they were short-lived and unique to their times. But they were not alone as male singer-songwriters in the rock world.

Shumway (2016: 15–17) notes that a key aspect of the rise of singer-songwriters in the late 1960s is a confessional mode (autobiographical, direct conversational style of address, stark in its despair), exemplified by James Taylor's 1970 "Fire and Rain," from his second album *Sweet Baby James* (1970), both of which hit #3. Joni Mitchell's *Blue* "cemented the confessional stance of the singer-songwriter" (16). Taylor's next album, *Mud Slide Slim* (1971), hit #2, and its single, "You've Got a Friend" written by Carole King, hit #1. British-born Cat Stevens's fourth album, *Tea for the Tillerman*, hit #8 in 1971, leading to a string of Top 10 albums (he became Yusuf Islam in the late 1970s). In 1972 Jackson Browne hit the Top 10 with "Doctor My Eyes" (#8) from his self-titled debut album, the same year his "Take It Easy" (cowritten with Glenn Frey) was released on the Eagles' debut album. The song also appeared on their record-setting 1976 *Greatest Hits* album.

The peak decade for these singer-songwriters was the 1970s, with the following tally of Top 10 albums in this decade: Cat Stevens (seven; one at #1); Carole King (six; two at #1); James Taylor (six); Carly Simon (four; one at #1); Neil Young (four; one at #1); Joni Mitchell (three); and Jackson Browne (two; another album would hit #1 in 1980). The most successful group in this category was Crosby, Stills, Nash, and Young, with their first six albums (1969–82) all hitting the Top 10, reaching #1 three times. Dylan placed eight albums in the Top 10 in the 1970s, with *Planet Waves* (1974), *Blood on the Tracks* (1975), and *Desire* (1976) all hitting #1.

The genre came to be incorporated into the larger heading *soft rock*, contrasting with hard rock, pointing out how musical styles can be strongly marked by gender stereotypes. Laurel Canyon, a neighborhood in the Hollywood Hills region in northwest Los Angeles, attracted a significant body of singer-songwriters living and working alongside one another in the late 1960s and 1970s, including Joni Mitchell, Neil Young, David Crosby, Stephen Stills, Graham Nash, Chris Hillman, Roger McGuinn, the Mamas and the Papas, Carole King, and the Eagles (Walker 2006; Lisa Robinson 2015).

In 1972 Bruce Springsteen auditioned for John Hammond at Columbia Records (the same person who signed Dylan ten years earlier) on acoustic guitar, right in the tradition of singer-songwriters. After weak sales figures for his first two albums (twenty-three thousand for his debut album *Greetings from Asbury Park*), he moved into the rock mainstream with his third album *Born to Run* (1975, pop #3). Regarding his first album, he says, "I never wrote completely in that style again. Once the record was released, I heard all the Dylan comparisons, so I steered away from it. But the lyrics and spirit of *Greetings* came from an unself-conscious place. Your early songs emerge from a moment when you're writing with no sure prospect of ever being heard. Up until then, it's been just you and your music. That only happens once" (2016: 178).[11] *Born to Run* pushed Springsteen into rock star status. He would become one of a handful of superstars beginning in the 1980s. His self-awareness about this change is instructive:

> [The single] "Born to Run" was more condensed; it maintained the excitement of "Rosalita" [from his second album] while delivering its message in

---

11 An almost identical passage is in his earlier book (Springsteen 1998: 7).

less time and with a shorter burst of energy. This was a turning point, and it allowed me to open up my music to a far larger audience. . . . The characters on *Born to Run* were less eccentric and less local than on *Greetings* and *The Wild, the Innocent* [second LP]. They could have been anybody and everybody. When the screen door slams on "Thunder Road," [from *Born to Run*] you're not necessarily on the Jersey Shore anymore. You could be anywhere in America. These were the beginnings of the characters whose lives I would trace in my work for the next two decades" (Springsteen 1998: 44, 47).

The style of songwriting discussed in this section is not the stuff of consistent Top 40 singles success, although Paul Simon and Art Garfunkel were able to bridge that gap beginning in the 1960s. Pianists Elton John and Billy Joel, who led their own rock bands and had massive success as pop stars, could be considered as part of this singer-songwriter tradition (see figure 41 for the Top 40 success of these artists). John's U.S. debut in 1970 at the Troubadour in Los Angeles, one of the most important centers for singer-songwriters at the time (Springsteen also performed there in 1973), firmly places his early career in this environment.

See figure 28. Birth years of singer-songwriters
See figure 41. All-time Top 40 hits: Soloists and groups (through 1999)

COUNTRY ROCK

Southern California, a center of folk rock (Byrds, Buffalo Springfield), maintained its status into the 1970s, with Laurel Canyon (in the mountains surrounding Los Angeles) and the Troubadour (a nightclub in West Hollywood several miles away) as key locations.[12] As harder rock styles developed in the later 1960s, one response was to draw on an authenticity represented by country music and its sources, idealizing rural southern and especially southwestern U.S. lifestyles (Mather 2013). One clear sonic marker was the steel guitar, a hallmark of country and western music since at least Hank Williams in the late 1940s. Occasionally a fiddle or mandolin would be added to the mix. The banjo was less common. The sentiments expressed

---

12 See Walker (2006), Hoskyns (2009), Lisa Robinson (2015), and Troubadour (2019).

tended toward the simplicity and directness of country music and social and political retreat.[13]

The crowning commercial success was the formation of the Eagles (a Southern California group), whose 1976 *Greatest Hits* LP went neck and neck with Michael Jackson's 1983 *Thriller* as the best-selling album in the United States. The recording industry (RIAA) gave the top selling U.S. album of the twentieth century award to the Eagles at twenty-six million copies (*Thriller* had twenty-five million); a recent recalculation has *Greatest Hits* at 38 million and *Thriller* at thirty-three million (CNN 1999; RIAA 2019a). Members of the Eagles had played in bands alongside former members of the Byrds and Buffalo Springfield, establishing a genealogical connection to the source.

The formative wave of country rock, between 1966 and 1969, was driven by members of the Byrds and Buffalo Springfield along with two young outsiders, virtuoso bluegrass guitarist Clarence White (1944–73) and budding singer-songwriter Gram Parsons (1946–73). A network of about two dozen musicians, recording and performing with one another in varied combinations, initially defined the field (see figure 46). Bob Dylan (who recorded in Nashville) and the Band worked outside this California orbit. Byrds bass player (and bluegrass mandolinist) Chris Hillman (1944–) can be credited with some key moves: his composition "Time Between" with guest guitarist Clarence White, released in early 1967 on the Byrds' fourth album, *Younger Than Yesterday* (#24), is often cited as the first major example of melding country and rock. Later that year Buffalo Springfield made a similar move with "A Child's Claim to Fame" (*Buffalo Springfield Again*, #44), composed and sung by band member Richie Furay, with guest James Burton on dobro (a relative of the steel guitar). Burton was a legend, helping to define rockabilly electric guitar playing with his solos on Dale Hawkins's "Susie Q" (1957) and as a long-term member of Ricky Nelson's band ("My Bucket's Got a Hole in It" and "Believe What You Say," 1958).

The Byrds' sixth LP, *Sweetheart of the Rodeo* (August 1968, #77), now with Gram Parsons as a member, and White guesting again, augmented with pedal steel guitar and fiddle, was the first major album-length statement, in instrumentation, vocal and instrumental style, and compositions (featuring country songwriters). The album was

---

13 Examples of retreat include early hits of the Eagles, "Take It Easy" and "That Peaceful, Easy Feeling" (1972), and a lyric from the Flying Burrito Brothers' "My Uncle" (1969): "So I'm headed to the nearest foreign border."

recorded in Nashville. Hillman and Parsons left the Byrds that year and formed the Flying Burrito Brothers, whose first album, *Gilded Palace of Sin* (May 1969, #164) thoroughly integrated band member "Sneaky" Pete Kleinow's pedal steel guitar and was the first major statement primarily featuring a country rock band's own songwriting.[14] A few months later a similar move capping this first wave came from the debut album of Poco (*Pickin' Up the Pieces*, June 1969, #64) comprising Buffalo Springfield veterans Richie Furay and Jim Messina, pedal steel guitarist Rusty Young, and future Eagles bass player Randy Meisner.[15]

Some under the radar developments with Parsons and White before they recorded *Sweetheart* with the Byrds fill in the story. Gram Parsons, born and raised in Florida and dropping out of Harvard after a semester, formed the International Submarine Band in Boston and recorded their only album (*Safe at Home*) in 1967 after relocating to Los Angeles. As the debut recording of an unknown twenty-one-year-old on a small independent label, it provides a window into the early process before Parsons teamed with more experienced peers. Guitarist Clarence White began releasing albums in 1963 with his bluegrass group the Kentucky Colonels and guesting on other projects. By the age of twenty (1964) his style of playing fiddle tunes on the guitar was rivaled only by his predecessor Doc Watson.[16] White soon went electric and formed Nashville West, a group named after a club where they were the house band. A recording of one of their gigs in 1967 (released as *Nashville West* in 1978) provides another window into how in-demand studio musicians were working out the process in public. White and drummer Gene Parsons (no relation to Gram) would join the Byrds in 1968 after Hillman and Gram Parsons left to form the Flying Burrito Brothers.[17]

Also coming from bluegrass, the Dillards, with brothers Douglas (banjo) and Rodney (guitar) from Missouri, began releasing albums in 1963, the year they began appearing on the Andy Griffith television show (as the Darlings). They moved into

---

14 Sneaky Pete occasionally used an electronic fuzzbox, simulating electric guitar distortion.

15 Meisner left Poco in a dispute before the album release, and most of his contributions were erased from the recording.

16 Examples of White's virtuoso bluegrass playing include "Sally Goodin'" and "Soldier's Joy" recorded in the studio and live in the mid-1960s, and "Black Mountain Rag/Soldier's Joy" from *The Byrds Live at Royal Albert Hall* (1971). See Aubrunner (2019) for a comprehensive biodiscography of White.

17 White was killed by a drunk driver in July 1973, and Parsons died of a drug overdose in September 1973.

country rock with *Wheatstraw Suite* (1968), recorded just after Rodney left and formed Dillard and Clark with recent ex-Byrds singer and songwriter Gene Clark; *The Fantastic Expedition of Dillard and Clark* (1968) was yet one more entry into the field. Joining D&C on guitar and banjo was Bernie Leadon, who would move on to the Flying Burrito Brothers for their second and third albums, then to Linda Ronstadt, and finally the Eagles.

On the East Coast the personnel involved were much more circumscribed: Dylan and his 1965–66 touring group, the Hawks (soon to be renamed the Band). Dylan recorded his third electric album *Blonde on Blonde* (July 1966, #9) in Nashville, which became his base of operations for his next two albums: *John Wesley Harding* (January 1968, #2) and *Nashville Skyline* (May 1969, #3). Unlike the West Coast bands, every album Dylan produced in this era hit the Top 10. His contributions to country rock with *Blonde* and *John Wesley* were more subtle, drawing on Nashville session musicians to brilliantly bring his own music to life and changing attitudes about the town and country music by his celebrity presence.[18] Nashville multi-instrumentalist legend Charlie McCoy, leader of the *Blonde on Blonde* sessions, noted, "The fact that Dylan came here, it sent a message around the folk-rock world that, 'Hey, it's OK to go [to Nashville]. These guys can do this.' And it was after he came, that all the others came. . . . They descended on us" (McCoy, qtd. in Sanders 2011). It was not until *Nashville Skyline* that Dylan drew on the already-established sonic signifiers of country rock, adding a prominent pedal steel guitar and dobro.[19]

Dylan's former band, now called the Band, relocated to a pink house outside Woodstock, New York, near Dylan, where they worked on their landmark debut album *Music from Big Pink* (August 1968, #30), which yielded their single "The Weight" (#63).[20] Aretha Franklin recorded a cover of "The Weight" (February 1969, pop #19, R&B #3) at Fame Studios in Muscle Shoals, Alabama, with Duane Allman on guitar, highlighting deeper connections between country rock and southern soul. Recordings that the Band made with Dylan in 1967 were eventually released in 1975 as *The Basement Tapes*.

---

18 *Rolling Stone* (2012) ranked *Blonde on Blonde* at #9 in their "500 Greatest Albums of All Time" list.

19 *John Wesley Harding* featured just a pared-down trio, excepting "I'll Be Your Baby Tonight," which has a pedal steel guitar in the background.

20 See Aronowitz (1968) for an informative review of the album, and Hoskyns (2016) for the scene in Woodstock at the time.

While Nashville was an important recording destination on the East Coast, a sound associated with Bakersfield, California, had a major impact on first-generation West Coast country rock musicians. As a destination for depression-era dust bowl refugees, Bakersfield, in the oil- and agriculture-rich San Juaquin Valley, provided a fertile ground for country and western music by the time Texas-born Buck Owens (1929–2006) settled there in the early 1950s. Owens's electric guitar playing on Tommy Collins's "You Better Not Do That" (1954, country #2) helped established his reputation, and by the end of the decade he was recording on his own with Capitol Records. Owens's singing, songwriting, tasteful (Fender Telecaster) guitar playing, and pared-down group arrangements defined a Bakersfield sound of country music in the 1960s, an alternative to a slicker and more highly produced Nashville sound. Between 1959 and 1975 he had sixty-nine Top 40 country hits, nineteen of which hit #1 between 1963 and 1969. That sound, featuring members of his band (the Buckaroos) Don Rich (fiddle and lead guitar) and Tom Brumley (pedal steel guitar), made a deep impression locally. They attracted a pot-smoking crowd at the Carousel Ballroom in early 1968, just before it was rechristened the Fillmore West by impresario Bill Graham, and the Byrds played Owens's #1 country instrumental hit "Buckaroo" (1965) in concert there in 1969 (with Clarence White on guitar).[21]

The country rock–defining pedal steel guitar has origins in late nineteenth-century Hawaii, where a guitar would be placed on the lap and played with an object (comb or steel bar) sliding across the strings. Hawaiian Joseph Kekuku is widely credited with developing and disseminating this style in the early twentieth century (Troutman 2016). By the 1920s country groups were recording with this Hawaiian-style guitar (Jimmie Rodgers's "Treasures Untold," 1928). In the 1930s electric tabletop models were manufactured, and in the late 1940s Hank Williams featured steel guitar player Dale "Smokey" Lohman in his group taking solos ("Move It on Over," 1947). As steel guitarists were limited by the open tuning of a single chord, instruments with several necks (tuned to different chords) were built; in the late 1940s pedals that could change the tuning of individual strings to allow greater flexibility of chord choice were added. Players used the pedals to bend individual strings, resulting in the

---

21 Rich began playing lead with "Act Naturally" (1963). Brumley's playing on "Together Again" (1964) is considered a classic. For more on Owens and the Buckaroos, see Kienzle (2007). The Bakersfield connection is discussed in Einarson (2001: 21–26); Stimeling (2014: 179–204); and Malone and Neal (2010: 290–98). Owens was honored with a Fender Telecaster model named after him in 1998, as was James Burton in 1991.

classic sound that characterizes country music.[22] The list of pedal steel guitar players in country rock is deep and rich: Tom Brumley (Buck Owens, Ricky Nelson); Jay Dee Maness (International Submarine Band, the Byrds); Lloyd Green (the Byrds); Sneaky Pete Kleinow (Flying Burrito Brothers, Linda Ronstadt); Rusty Young (Poco); Buddy Emmons (the Dillards, Linda Ronstadt); and Pete Drake (Dylan). A dobro is an acoustic guitar, fitted with a large metal resonator ring, played on the lap like a steel guitar, dating from the late 1920s.[23] Clarence White adapted his Fender Telecaster so that the B string could be loosened or tightened (lowering or raising the pitch) with a finger-button push, emulating a pedal steel guitar (Schu 2017). Perhaps the only country rock group that did not have a steel guitar–like instrument was the Band, who made up for it with a fiddle and mandolin.

The shift from folk rock to country rock can be heard between Crosby, Stills, and Nash's self-titled debut album (1969), laden with acoustic guitars and complemented with rock guitar, drums, and organ and their second album, adding Neil Young (*Déjà Vu*, 1970), on which a pedal steel guitar appears on "Teach Your Children," played by Jerry Garcia.

A plethora of bands emerged in the 1970s (some very short-lived) that explored various paths merging country and rock. Most remained on the margins of the rock world. The Eagles came out of this nexus. The combination of first-wave veterans (Leadon and Meisner), newcomers Don Henley (drums) and Glenn Frey (guitar), radio-friendly group songwriting with memorable hooks (with contributions from Jackson Browne and J. D. Souther), clean and clear three- and four-part ("Take it Easy," "Witchy Woman") vocal harmonies, Southwest cowboy and Native American imagery, groundwork laid by first-wave groups in terms of artistic direction and market testing, and a young and ambitious David Geffen behind them with his new Asylum Records label led to unprecedented commercial success in country rock. Their self-titled debut album (1972, #22) generated three Top 40 singles, something that eluded their predecessors. After two more albums they produced a string of four straight #1 albums between 1975 and 1979. As of 2019 two of them—*Greatest Hits* (1976, thirty-eight million copies) and *Hotel California* (1976, twenty-six million copies)—have more combined U.S. sales (sixty-four million copies) than anyone else's top two albums, including Led Zeppelin (thirty-nine million), Pink Floyd

---

22 Budd Isaacs's playing on Webb Pierce's "Slowly" (1954) is an early example of pedal steel.
23 The name *dobro* is a contraction of the brothers who invented it: DOpyera BROthers.

(thirty-eight million), Garth Brooks (thirty-eight million), the Beatles (thirty-six million), and Whitney Houston (thirty-one million).[24]

Linda Ronstadt (1946–), who had inadvertently put together the Eagles in 1971, defied categories, drawing from folk, country, rock, and pop.[25] Born and raised in Tucson, she moved into the Southern California scene and began releasing solo albums on Capitol Records in 1969, covering songwriters such as Bob Dylan, Carole King and Gerry Goffin, Johnny Cash, Jackson Browne, Neil Young, and J. D. Souther. She began including pedal steel guitarists (Sneaky Pete Kleinow and Buddy Emmons) on her albums beginning in 1972 (*Linda Ronstadt*). Her first four albums had little to moderate pop chart appearances, but she struck gold with her fifth album, *Heart Like a Wheel* (1975, pop #1, country #1), which yielded four Grammy nominations (winning Best Country Vocal Performance, Female) and three hits: "You're No Good" (pop #1), "When Will I Be Loved" (pop #2, country #1), and Hank Williams's "I Can't Help It (If I'm Still in Love with You)" (country #2), an unusual mix of pop and country success. She was a fixture on the rock-touring circuit, becoming the most well-known and commercially successful woman singer of the 1970s, appearing on the cover of *Time* magazine in February 1977.[26]

Emmylou Harris (1947–), born in Alabama and raised there and in North Carolina and Virginia, also straddled categories, starting out as a singer-songwriter in Greenwich Village before joining Gram Parsons on his solo debut album (*GP*, 1973). Her major label debut album, *Pieces of the Sky* (1975, pop #45, country #7), with "If Only I Could Win Your Love" (country #4, pop #58), picked up where Parsons left off, using some of the same musicians, including Bernie Leadon, Byron Berline, and Elvis Presley's current band member James Burton. Her next two albums hit #1 on the country charts and broke into the pop Top 30. By 1980 she had thirteen Top 10 country singles, four of which hit #1. Harris's albums typically crossed over from country to the pop charts, but not often breaching the Top 40. In 1978 she began recording a trio album with Dolly Parton and Linda Ronstadt, but the project

---

24 See RIAA (2019a). None of the country rock bands mentioned so far appeared on the country charts, with the exception of the Eagles' *Hotel California* (#10), their only album to do so. For more on the Eagles, see Ellwood (2013-v).

25 The album *Linda Ronstadt*, recorded in 1971, included Frey and Henley from her touring band, as well as contributions from Leadon and Meisner; see also her memoir (Ronstadt 2013: 69–70).

26 Ronstadt's recording of "Farther Along" with Dolly Parton and Emmylou Harris (*Trio*, 1986) is discussed in chapter 9.

stalled until almost a decade later: *Trio* (1987, country #1, pop #6) gave both Harris and Parton their greatest pop success. "Three years into her Warners [record label] deal [1975–78], she'd reached deeper into the country audience than any rock-based performer since Jerry Lee Lewis, without sacrificing an ounce of her country-rock credibility" (Doggett 2000: 397).

The Grateful Dead came up with a hybrid style all their own, still rooted in country rock. Their extended instrumental sections, featuring guitar solos by Jerry Garcia, helped establish the category *jam band*, first exemplified on "Dark Star," a twenty-three-minute-long performance recorded live at the Fillmore West in San Francisco in February 1969 and issued on their fourth album, *Live/Dead*. A 1970 *Rolling Stone* magazine review of *Live/Dead* may be responsible for the label: "A jamming band (and the Dead are that, if nothing else) has to rely on its sense of Flow, on its talent in taking that small series of steps which will ultimately bring it to some entirely different place from where it started" (Kaye 1970). Fellow San Francisco band Santana, with their 6:30 minute "Soul Sacrifice" from their debut album (*Santana*, 1969) and almost twelve-minute live Woodstock version, and the southern boogie Allman Brothers Band, with the 5:15 minute "Whipping Post" from their self-titled debut album (1969) and twenty-three-minute live version *At Fillmore East* (1971), also emerged right at this moment with a similar jam aesthetic. In these three cases jam bands rely on the brilliance and inventiveness of their lead guitarists (Jerry Garcia, Carlos Santana, and Duane Allman). Jimi Hendrix's fifteen-minute-long "Voodoo Chile" (*Electric Ladyland*, 1968) is right in line with this kind of expansive thinking.

The Grateful Dead formed in 1965 from former members of a folk jug band (popular in the southern United States in the early twentieth century): Jerry Garcia (lead guitar), Bob Weir (guitar), and Ron "Pigpen" McKernan (keyboards, harmonica), plus Phil Lesh (bass) and Bill Kreutzmann (drums). Their early gigs included author Ken Kesey's acid tests (parties where LSD was taken) in December 1965 and the three-day January 1966 Trips Festival in San Francisco (along with Jefferson Airplane and Big Brother and the Holding Company), where the beginnings of a hippie counterculture developed. (Possession of LSD became illegal in California in 1966 and nationally in 1968.) Second drummer Mickey Hart joined in 1967. Their fifth and sixth albums—*Workingman's Dead* and *American Beauty*—both recorded in 1970 right after the Altamont festival disaster, are considered classics and represent a new turn away from blues-based psychedelic rock, now accentuated with acoustic guitars, mandolin, and pedal steel guitar. In May 1977 they gave a series of concerts at Cornell

University, one of which has gained mythical status, recorded for posterity by their sound engineer Betty Cantor and the subject of a recent book (Conners 2017). The Grateful Dead established an alternate model in the music industry, encouraging audience members to make high-quality recordings of their live concerts, even setting aside physical space at their concerts for doing so. As a result, they are one of the most documented bands in rock.[27]

The boundary between country rock and southern boogie bands like the Allman Brothers appears to be demarcated by their relationship to blues. Speaking about auditions for Poco, founding member Rusty Young recalled, "Gregg [Allman] was going to play piano and sing in our band. He had a great voice. But we were more into country, and he was into a blues-based music" (qtd. in Einarson 2001: 106). In Einarson's history they are distinct styles: "Even some of the southern blues-based rock bands, like the Allman Brothers and the Marshall Tucker Band, dabbled in country rock" (250).

An alternate kind of crowning success took place the same year as the Eagles debut album when the more acoustically oriented Nitty Gritty Dirt Band invited an unusual cohort of legends of country and bluegrass for a collaboration, resulting in a three-album set recorded in Nashville, *Will the Circle Be Unbroken* (1972, country #4). The unlikely mix was both cultural (conservative traditional South meets West Coast counterculture) and generational. Maybelle Carter (of the original Carter Family) rose to fame in the 1920s; Grand Ole Opry star Roy Acuff in the late 1930s; guitarist, composer, and vocalist Merle Travis, bluegrass banjo pioneer Earl Scruggs, and vocalist guitarist Jimmy Martin in the 1940s; and hillbilly jazz fiddler Vassar Clements and guitar virtuoso Doc Watson in the 1950s. The critically acclaimed album stayed on the pop charts for over half a year, during which time it rose to #68 and was certified gold, unusual for an all-acoustic album digging deep into Americana.

Other country crossovers have a Texas connection. Texas-born singer-songwriter Willie Nelson (1933–) regularly appeared on the country charts from the mid-1960s, before moving to Austin in the early 1970s. When he changed record labels to Columbia in 1975, he began moving into the pop charts. About this time he produced and starred in the PBS television show *Austin City Limits*, which is still on the air.

---

27 Grateful Dead Internet Archive Project (2019) contains over thirteen thousand audience and band soundboard recordings. See Meeske (2001-v) and Bar-Lev (2017-v) for documentaries on the Grateful Dead.

In 1976 the compilation album *Wanted! The Outlaws*, which included Nelson and fellow-Texan Waylon Jennings, hit #1 on the country chart and #10 on the pop chart. Texas-born singer-songwriter Kris Kristofferson ended up in Nashville, releasing a series of Top 10 country albums in the early 1970s that crossed over to the pop Top 40, including a duo with his wife Rita Coolidge, *Full Moon* (1973, country #1, pop #26). Coolidge's solo album *Anytime . . . Anywhere* (1977) crossed over from pop (#6) to country (#23).

Developing out of an intense wave of artistic exploration in the late 1960s, country rock struck a balance between generational and cultural differences, eventually asserting itself into the mainstream of rock by the mid-1970s. Artists from this era have provided the model for alternative takes on country music ever since.

———

See figure 46. Folk rock and country rock groups

STEVIE WONDER

Stevie Wonder (1950–), born in Saginaw, Michigan, is one of the few artists who transcends genre and category. Whereas some artists exemplify a genre, such as James Brown and funk or Ray Charles and Aretha Franklin and soul, Wonder's breadth, which draws from funk, soul, rock, pop, and jazz, puts him in a rarified class. Motown, as a record label, enjoys a similar reputation as defining a genre of music rather than being defined by a genre. Wonder has been a Motown recording artist for his whole life, but calling his sound Motown does not really capture his range. He is a singer-songwriter who is also a multi-instrumentalist, playing all the instruments on many of his recordings from the 1970s, including the new electronic synthesizers, a trademark of his sound. That alone puts him in a rarefied category, with few peers.

Wonder was a child prodigy, with a #1 pop hit at the age of thirteen in 1963 ("Fingertips Part 2") on Motown (he grew up in Detroit). His cover of Dylan's "Blowin' in the Wind" hit #9 on the pop chart in 1966. Before turning twenty-one, when his career would take a dramatic turn, Wonder had recorded hits with his own compositions (cowritten with other Motown songwriters, including his mother Lula Hardaway), such as "Uptight (Everything Is Alright)" (1965, pop #3, R&B #1); "I Was Made to Love Her" (1967, pop #2, R&B #1); "My Cherie Amour" (1969, pop #4, R&B #4); and "Signed, Sealed, Delivered I'm Yours" (1970, pop #3, R&B #1).

When Wonder turned twenty-one in 1971, he was able to tap into his trust fund and renegotiate his Motown contract. This immediately led to a series of classic solo albums that showed him in his full maturity, as one of America's great composers and performers, speaking to contemporary issues: *Music of My Mind* (1972, pop #21, R&B #6); *Talking Book* (1972, pop #3, R&B #1); *Innervisions* (1973, pop #4, R&B #1); *Fulfillingness' First Finale* (1974, pop #1, R&B #1); and *Songs in the Key of Life* (1976, pop #1, R&B #1), which stayed at #1 on the pop charts for fourteen weeks. These five albums all resulted from close collaboration with associate producers and engineers Bob Margouleff and Malcom Cecil, an electronic music duo whose 1971 Tonto's Expanding Head Band debut album led Wonder to seek them out. Wonder embraced the new electronic synthesizer technology, and they in turn helped shape his sound (C. Williams 2013).

Wonder's innovative embrace of technology, consummate musicianship, unique harmonic and melody sensibility, ability to seamlessly integrate diverse styles, and endless fount of compositional creativity puts him in a class all his own. Between 1973 and 2006 Wonder won twenty-five Grammy Awards, including four each in 1973, 1974, and 1976, winning Album of the Year in each of these three years (*Innervisions*, *Fulfillingness'*, and *Songs*). As of 2019 his Grammy tally is surpassed only by Quincy Jones (twenty-eight), Alison Krauss (twenty-seven), and two classical music artists; he is tied with pianist Vladimir Horowitz. Next in line are composer John Willliams (twenty-four), Beyoncé (twenty-three), and Jay-Z, Chick Corea, and U2 at twenty-two Grammys each (Recording Academy 2019).[28]

DISCO

Disco as a musical genre has immediate origins in early 1970s releases on the Philadelphia International Records label, cofounded in 1971 by songwriters-producers Kenneth Gamble and Leon Huff, featuring work by arranger and producer Thom Bell and the songwriting team of Gene McFadden and John Whitehead ("Back Stabbers," "Ain't No Stoppin' Us Now"). Philly International was marked by lush jazz-inflected orchestral arrangements (with strings and horns), including the O'Jays ("Backstabbers," "Love Train," 1972); Harold Melvin and the Blue Notes, with lead vocalist Teddy Pendergrass ("If You Don't Know Me by Now," 1972, "The Love I Lost," 1973, "Wake Up Everybody," 1975); and their house band MFSB ("TSOP," "Love

---

28 For more on Stevie Wonder, see Ribowsky (2010) and Love and Brown (2002).

Is the Message," 1973). Although as a named musical style disco reigned for about five years (1974–79), its repercussions were far-reaching, setting the terms of dance (and electronic dance) music from then on and opening up a public social space that challenged heterosexual norms.[29]

Disco deejays working in dance venues became the nexus for a dance-floor culture, which by some accounts approached a religious experience in its communal ethos. The three-minute song format for radio proved inadequate, and so deejays and producers (sometimes the same person) created extended mixes, at first in live performance with two turntables and then by recording vinyl onto tape and editing the tape. Once record labels caught on, they employed deejays and producers to work their original multitrack studio recordings into extended dance remixes.

The breakdown section of former Temptation Eddie Kendricks's Motown release "Girl You Need a Change of Mind" (February 1973, R&B #13) laid out a blueprint for the extended deejay dance edits and remixes that would mark the disco era. Beginning at 3:45, the band drops out, leaving just the guitar and tambourine; the bass soon enters, followed by a four-on-the-floor bass drum (the ultimate disco hallmark), then piano, and finally horns and organ. A second breakdown comes at 6:00, leaving just a conga and Kendricks, with another buildup of instruments entering. "People always ask me about the breakdown," the song's producer Frank Wilson explained. "Well, my background is the church. It's not unusual in a church song to have a breakdown like that. Here, the idea was spontaneous. I stood in the studio with the musicians, giving instructions as we were cutting for them to break it down to nothing, then gradually come in one by one and rebuild the fervour of the song" (qtd. in Brewster and Broughton 2006: 182).

Deejays took this concept and created new extended versions more conducive to long bouts on the dance floor. Deejay Walter Gibbons (1954–94), working at New York City's Galaxy 21 (on West Twenty-Third Street) in the mid-1970s, was a pioneer. "Prefiguring the amazing cut and paste skills later developed by the hip hop DJs, Gibbons would take two copies of a track . . . and mix and splice the drum breaks so adroitly it was impossible to tell that the music you were hearing hadn't been originally recorded that way" (Brewster and Broughton 2006: 168). Jellybean Benitez (who would produce for Madonna ["Holiday," 1983] and Whitney Houston) grew up in

---

29 In this section I draw extensively from Lawrence (2003) and Brewster and Boughton (2006). Lawrence's (2019) many articles are available online.

the South Bronx experiencing the early development of hip hop deejays: "I thought I was the best DJ in the world until I heard Walter Gibbons play . . . He was phasing records—playing two records at the same time to give a flange effect—and doubling up records so that there would be a little repeat. He would do tremendous quick cuts on records, sort of like b-boys do. He would slam it in so quick that you couldn't hear the turntable slowing down or catching up" (qtd. in Brewster and Broughton 2006: 168). "His style appealed to my Bronx sensibilities. He just blew me away" (qtd. in Lawrence 2003: 217).

Gibbons's 1976 remix of Double Exposure's "Ten Percent" extending the original four minutes to almost ten minutes, issued on the disco-oriented Salsoul Records label, was the first commercially available twelve-inch single, a format that would rule the disco era (Lawrence 2008: 293). Tom Moulton had laid the groundwork with his studio remix of B. T. Express's "Do It ('Til You're Satisfied)" (entered charts August 1974: pop #2, R&B #1, disco #8), extending it from three minutes to almost six minutes. A few months later Moulton famously mixed a suite of three songs together on one side of Gloria Gaynor's (1949–) debut album *Never Can Say Goodbye* (entered album charts February 1975: pop #25, R&B #21). Moulton extended the individual song lengths (initially totaling about ten minutes) to a total time of eighteen and a half minutes and blended them so that there was no break between songs. By the time the album was released, two of the songs were already disco hits: "Honey Bee" (entered charts April 1974: R&B #55, pop #103, disco #2) and "Never Can Say Goodbye" (entered charts October 1974: disco #1, pop #9, R&B #34); the extended three-song remix hit the disco charts in January 1975 (#2) and the third song, "Reach Out, I'll Be There," entered the singles charts that March (pop #60, R&B #56).

Brewster and Broughton (2006: 184) refer to Gaynor's single "Never Can Say Goodbye" (originally recorded by the Jackson 5 in 1971) as the first *identifiably* disco record to chart or, as Kopkind (1979: 11) put it, "the first big disco hit—*as disco*." It hit the charts in late October (disco), early November (pop), and late December (R&B) of 1974. *Identifiably* probably refers to the combination of sonic signifiers, starting with the bass drum on all four beats and the hi-hat cymbal closing on the offbeats (joined by the rhythm guitar), perhaps disco's most recognizable trademark and the one that would eventually sound its death knell in its clichéd predictability; pervasive and occasionally soaring strings; punctuating horns; gospel-tinged improvisatory musical comments; and, at 127 beats per minute, in the disco sweet spot between 120–130 bpm. As a music industry–recognized genre, disco can be traced to that same moment in the fall of 1974 when *Billboard* magazine inaugurated its weekly "Disco Action" charts and column, both by producer Tom Moulton (1974). "Never Can Say Goodbye" debuted at #1 in those very first *Billboard* disco charts (Hot at the Discos and Best Sellers at two record stores, all in New York City).

As a club culture, disco has its origins in New York City dance spaces catering to gay, black, and Latino patrons in the early 1970s. An important early venue was deejay David Mancuso's living space, the Loft (beginning in 1970 at Broadway and Bleecker), home to underground dance parties called "Love Saves the Day," which catered to a primarily gay crowd. The Gallery opened in 1973 (on West Twenty-Second Street), featuring seventeen-year-old deejay Nicky Siano. It was an "invitation-only mainly gay dance club . . . the world's first modern disco . . . a commercial club where admission was nevertheless on a members/friends-only basis, a crucible where room environment, social vibe, narrative-style song sequencing, sound effects, elaborate lighting, awesome sonics with extreme bass frequencies, and drugs combines to take people to places they'd never been before" (Hermes 2011: 29). In 1974 the Gallery moved downtown to Mercer and Houston Streets. Siano later deejayed at the famed Studio 54 in Midtown when it opened in 1977.

New York club deejays were initially predominantly Italian American. Two black teens, Larry Levan and Frankie Knuckles, were helping out in the Gallery before it moved downtown, watching Siano ply his craft, and later did the same at the Continental Baths, where they soon worked their way into the deejay booth. As Knuckles noted, "There weren't that many black DJs playing in New York City, let along black gay ones, and you could pretty well count us on one hand. . . . I guess we were like the second generation. We were the next wave" (qtd. in Lawrence 2003: 132). When the Paradise Garage (on King Street near Hudson in Soho), a former parking garage, officially opened in January 1978 with one of the best sound systems in the city, Larry Levan (1954–92) got the gig and would establish his reputation there as one of the most important deejays of the disco era, primarily for the way in which he moved his crowd. Frankie Knuckles went to Chicago to deejay at the Warehouse in 1977, eventually pioneering the music that came to be called *house*.[30]

The disco era promoted the producer and deejay to the role of star, deemphasizing live bands and shifting the energies from the stage to the dance floor. African American

---

30 Documentaries by Ramos (2003-v) and Sumner (2017-v) cover this era. For more on Levan and the Paradise Garage, see P. Shapiro (2014).

women vocalists (and their producers, such as Giorgio Moroder) reigned supreme: Gloria Gaynor ("Never Can Say Goodbye," 1974; "I Will Survive," 1978); disco queen Donna Summer ("Love to Love You Baby," 1975; "Last Dance," 1978; "Hot Stuff" and "Bad Girls," 1979); Vicki Sue Robinson ("Turn the Beat Around," 1976), who was biracial; and Evelyn "Champagne" King ("Shame," 1978) (see figure 47). Summer's 1977 "I Feel Love," with its electronic synthesizer–based instrumental track, established the foundation of what later became known as electronic dance music.

These singers attracted a large gay audience. Quoted in the *Village Voice* in 1979, New York deejay Danae elaborated on the preferences of this audience: "There's gay disco and straight disco, although there's overlap between the two. . . . Straight disco is heavy-duty funk, the driving sound, that has all the power without much of the emotion. Gays like to hear black women singers; they identify with the pain, the irony, the self-consciousness. We pick up on the emotional content, not just the physical power. The MFSB sound was gay, Barry White was a gay sound, so is Donna Summer, Gloria Gaynor" (qtd. in Kopkind 1979: 14).[31] In the same article Kopkind (11) contrasted 1970s disco with 1960s rock: "Disco places surface over substance, mood over meaning, action over thought. The '60s were a mind trip (marijuana, acid): Disco is a body trip (Quaaludes, cocaine)." The sales medium went from radio for rock to clubs for disco. New York's first major disco station was WBLS, featuring broadcasting aimed at African Americans.

The display of sexuality on the disco dance floor was one of its key attractions. Kopkind (1979: 13) notes that a disco club mix "is a sexual metaphor; the deejay plays with the audience's emotions, pleasing and teasing in a crescendo of feeling." The rise of disco, as *Village Voice* writer Braunstein noted in 1998,

> brought with it the mainstreaming of *gay*, possibly the opening salvo in the queering of America. Yet it wasn't homosexuality per se that disco ushered in but a sustained exploration of the sexual self, including the femme side of the male persona. With its fluid structure of crests and flows, disco music allowed men to imagine the wavelike and recurrent quality of the female orgasm. . . . The demise of glam made the polarization of rock and disco an inevitability, and for a while it looked as if disco would erode the willingness

---

31 The question of a gay sound in music has its analog in speech patterns, the subject of Thorpe's (2014-v) documentary *Do I Sound Gay?*

of young Americans to stand in stationary phalanxes at arena concerts, saluting bloated, burned-out superstars with lit matches. The kinetic ambiguity of disco demolished the boundary between performer and audience, and made the dancers the stars.

But the real animosity between rock and disco lay in the position of the straight white male. In the rock world, he was the undisputed top, while in disco, he was subject to a radical decentering. Disco was an extended conversation between black female divas and gay men. Straight men were welcome to join the party, but only if they learned the lingo. (1998: 55, 58)[32]

Disco's eroticism (invoking physical desire) was matched by a romanticism that was set in an era where homosexual contact was illegal in many states and legally recognized long-term same-sex partnerships were not on the horizon. Vocalist Diana Ross, in particular, expressed the intensity of fleeting emotional contacts. "No wonder Ross is (was?) so important in gay male scene culture, for she both reflects what that culture takes to be an inevitable reality (that relationships don't last) and at the same time celebrates it, validates it" (Dyer 1979: 23).

Block (1982: 45, 46), in "Confessions of a Gay Rocker," explained both the mainstream appeal and the eventual stultifying formulaic tendency of disco as follows: "Disco seemed like some secret gas—turn the stuff on and suddenly you were in a queer bar. . . . The trick seemed to be that America loved the gay spirit of outrageousness for its entertainment value, as long as the sex part didn't intrude. . . . The ugly thing about disco was that it seemed to announce and enforce an overwhelming conformity. . . . It hadn't occurred to me that homos might create a society as intolerant as the one they had escaped from." Regarding intolerance, "systems of exclusion were part of the disco scene from the very beginning. In the form of members-only policies, these were initially justified as self-protective and legally necessary—particularly for unlicensed venues—but later this turned into a form of elitist social curatorship, selecting and excluding people based on beauty, celebrity, glamour, and social connections" (Garcia 2014: 12).

No sooner had disco as a commercial genre arrived on the scene about 1975 and crossed over to the mainstream in a big way in 1977 with the blockbuster film *Saturday Night Fever* (Badham 1977-v), based on what turned out to be a fictionalized *New*

32 See Lawrence (2011) for an analysis of queerness and disco.

York Magazine account of a working-class Bay Ridge, Brooklyn, club scene (Cohn 1976; LeDuff 1996), than the style had died out by the beginning of the new decade. The mainstreaming of an underground cultural style eventually led to its collapse. The *Saturday Night Fever* soundtrack album, featuring the British band Bee Gees, entered the pop charts at the end of November 1977, hitting #1 and staying there for almost half a year, winning the Album of the Year Grammy Award in 1978. The Bee Gees had eight #1 pop hits between 1975 and 1979.

The Village People, a group fabricated by two New York producers featuring costumed gay fantasy stereotypes, cemented the move of disco into the mainstream. The Village People first appeared on the disco and then pop charts in July and October 1977, not reaching the R&B charts until a year later (and only twice). The specific dates of chart entry of their two biggest hits and their chart positions can illustrate the path reversal (from pop to R&B and disco) that can occur when an underground culture enters the mainstream in this way, as well as waning interest in the source communities (i.e., lower disco and R&B positions).

"Y.M.C.A." (October 21, 1978, disco #2, pop #2; November 4, 1978, R&B #32)
"In the Navy" (March 17, 1979, pop #3; March 24, 1979 R&B #30; April 7, 1979, disco #14)

The Village People presented a classic vision of camp: "Disco had become artificial, stylized, disengaged and apolitical, emphasizing texture, sensuous surface, and style at the expense of content, all of which made the music entirely consistent with the definition of the term [*camp*] outlined by Susan Sontag" (Lawrence 2003: 333–34). Sontag saw camp as an aesthetic sensibility marked by extravagance (1964: 522), distilling the essence of camp down to "its love of the unnatural: of artifice and exaggeration" (515). "To perceive Camp in objects and persons is to understand Being as Playing a Role. It is the farthest extension, in sensibility, of the metaphor of life as theater" (519). "There are two levels on which The Village People's campiness works," Kopkind suggested soon after they first hit the pop charts. "The first is with the 'knowing' gay audience, the listeners who are in on the joke, the images, the allusions. . . . The other is with the 'naive' straight audience, the listeners who either don't know (or mind) what's going on in the lyrics, or think it is all theatrical drag. In much the same way, disco music as a whole appeals to a 'knowing' audience that sees what [Casablanca Records label promoter] Friedman calls the 'cultural gayness' in it, and a naive audience that simply likes the fashion and the beat" (1979: 14, 16). Before the Village People's record label, Casablanca, was about to release a disco movie, *Thank God It's Friday*, Friedman screened parts of it across the country to gauge reaction to a scene of two men dancing together and sniffing amyl nitrate. He noted, "The straights don't see the gay culture, they've only seen what they've made—the styles. . . . I interviewed hundreds of people, showed it to thousands, and as far as I know not one straight person ever saw the men dancing, even after I showed the segment to them two or three times. . . . And yet the gay viewers saw it immediately" (qtd. in Kopkind 1979: 16).

The July 1979 disco demolition night at Chicago's Comiskey Park that caused a riot after the first game of a White Sox baseball doubleheader was one sign that the tide was turning. Just after the music industry caught on, with *Billboard* inaugurating its disco Top 80 chart in April 1979 and the first Disco Recording Grammy awarded in February 1980, disco was commercially dead by the following year and the Grammy category was discontinued. Gloria Gaynor ("I Will Survive") won in that single year of 1980, facing nominees Earth, Wind and Fire ("Boogie Wonderland"), Michael Jackson ("Don't Stop 'Til You Get Enough"), Rod Stewart ("Do You Think I'm Sexy"), and Donna Summer ("Bad Girls").

Disco had become formulaic, dulling initiatives for musical creativity, especially when major record labels moved in at the end of the decade. *Billboard's* expanded Disco Top 100 (September 1979) dropped back to 80 (fluctuating with 60) in August 1981 and was renamed Dance/Disco Top 80 in March 1982. The label *Disco* hung on as an appendage to *Dance* and was finally dropped in favor of Hot Dance Music–Club Play in October 1987. Donna Summer (1948–2012) got her due with "Carry On" when the Grammy category was revived in 1998, but now called Dance Recording. Winners since then shed light on the legacy of disco: Madonna, Cher, Janet Jackson, Britney Spears, Justin Timberlake, Lady Gaga, Rihanna, and the collaboration of Skrillex, Diplo, and Justin Bieber. We will pick up this thread in the next chapter (electronic dance music). The rise and fall of disco roughly parallels that of punk, a style that could hardly be more diametrically opposite (see figure 49).

See figure 47. Disco singers and groups and their debut disco LPs
See figure 49. Disco and punk comparisons

PUNK

Punk as a named genre is intimately associated with CBGB (Country BlueGrass Blues), a rundown bar-club on Bowery Avenue in the Lower East Side of New York City that Hilly Kristal opened in December 1973. Within several months the first punk rock band began playing there regularly: Television, formed in late 1973 with guitarist-vocalist Tom Verlaine, bassist Richard Hell, and guitarist Richard Lloyd.[33]

Verlaine (born Meyers from Wilmington, Delaware) and Hell (born Miller from Lexington, Kentucky) met in boarding school. Hell is widely credited with pioneering the 1970s punk look of ripped clothing and spiked short hair. Verlaine would soon collaborate with Patti Smith, playing guitar on her first single, "Hey Joe" (backed with "Piss Factory"), recorded in 1974 at Hendrix's Electric Lady Studios, and co-publishing a short book of poetry (*The Night*, 1976). Television's 1977 debut album, *Marquee Moon* (recorded after Hell left), and Hell with the Voidoids' 1977 debut *Blank Generation* are classics of this era. In the spring of 1975 Television and Patti Smith's group shared a residency at CBGB, and soon Smith got signed to the new Arista Records (founded by former Columbia Records president Clive Davis, who had signed Janis Joplin to Columbia in 1967 and would sign Whitney Houston to Arista in 1983). She was the first of her cohort to release an album: her debut, *Horses* (December 1975, #47), received great critical acclaim.

That summer of 1975 a critical mass of forty bands was presented in a festival at CBGB, none of whom had a recording contract.[34] The CBGB Rock Festival: Top 40 New York Unrecorded Talent was held from July 16 to August 3, featuring the Ramones, Talking Heads, and Blondie on the opening and closing three days. Television played the final weekend. The Ramones and Talking Heads signed with Sire Records. The Ramones' self-titled debut album was released on Sire in April 1976. Three months later, on July 4, the Ramones played at the Roundhouse in London, having an impact on the growing punk scene there.

That November (1976) the British Sex Pistols (lead singer Johnny "Rotten" Lydon), managed by Malcolm McLaren, released their debut single, "Anarchy in the UK." The following May (1977) the Sex Pistols released their single "God Save the Queen," coinciding with the silver (twenty-fifth-year) jubilee celebration of Queen

---

33 Lloyd's (2018: 179) informative autobiography dates the debut to March 29, 1974.
34 The schedule was published in ads in the *Village Voice* (CBGB 1975).

Elizabeth II's accession to the throne. The lyrics were seen by some as blasphemous ("the fascist regime . . . She ain't no human being / There is no future / In England's dreaming"); it was banned by the BBC even as it rose to #2 on the official BBC UK singles chart. They toured the United States (primarily in the South) in December 1977–January 1978, notoriously breaking up after their gig in San Francisco, having released just one album, *Never Mind the Bollocks, Here's the Sex Pistols* (December 1977, #106). Lydon formed Public Image Ltd later that year; bassist Sid Vicious died of a heroin overdose in 1979, while awaiting trial for the murder of his girlfriend Nancy Spungen, who died in the Chelsea Hotel in New York City. Although not originators of the genre, the short-lived Sex Pistols personified the punk aesthetic of their time, remaining one of the most prominent and enduring symbols of the style.

The term *punk* has a long history of pejorative usage, going back to Shakespearean times (meaning a prostitute) and since then referring variously to poor quality, a gay young man, a delinquent, hoodlum, or coward, and, in the 1960s, extending to some young rock music fans and musicians.[35] Frank Zappa's "Flower Punk" (on *We're Only in It for the Money*, 1968) satirized the San Francisco scene at the time using the term. By 1970 it increasingly took on a positive spin as applied to rock musicians with a garage band, do-it-yourself feel to their music, particularly Michigan bands MC5 and the Stooges (especially front man Iggy Pop), who both released their debut albums in 1969, and mid-sixties bands exemplified by ? [Question Mark] and the Mysterians, also from Michigan. *Creem* critic Lester Bangs (1970, 1971) embraced and self-identified with the term *punk*, perhaps encouraging others to do the same. Gendron (2002: 233–36) notes three themes of a punk aesthetic emerging in Bang's writing then: (1) aggressiveness, loudness, and shock; (2) minimalism, as in stripping rock down to its bare essentials; and (3) rank amateurism. Several other rock critics were using the term at the time, including *Creem* writer Dave Marsh (1971: 42, 43), who referred to a recent appearance of ? [Question Mark] and the Mysterians as a "landmark exposition of punk-rock."[36]

The following year guitarist Lenny Kaye (1972) used the term *punk rock* in the

---

35 In this section I draw on Gendron (2002: 230–73), Kugelberg and Savage (2012a), and J. P. Robinson (2018), who do deep dives into the etymology and 1970s usages of the term *punk*; see also *OED* (2019b).

36 See Gendron (2002: 230–33), Kugelberg and Savage (2012a), and J. P. Robinson (2018) for references to usages by Ed Sanders, Greg Shaw, John Mendelsohn, Metal Mike Saunders, and Ellen Willis through 1972.

liner notes to his now-classic double-LP compilation (called *Nuggets*) of relatively lesser known midsixties bands. A *Rolling Stone* review of *Nuggets* gave some weight to the designation, although the reference was to sixties garage bands (as in, they practiced in their parents' garages, maintaining a do-it-yourself aesthetic): "Punk Rock: The Arrogant Underbelly of Sixties Pop" (G. Shaw 1973). The first issue of *Punk* magazine was published in January 1976, canonizing the name, the aesthetic, and the protagonists of the genre. With a cartoon of Lou Reed on the cover, the issue contained an editorial headed "Death to Disco Shit! Long Live the Rock!" It read, "Kill yourself. Jump off a fuckin' cliff. Drive nails into your head. Become a robot and join the staff at Disneyland. OD. Anything. Just don't listen to discoshit.... The epitome of all that's wrong with western civilization is disco. Eddjicate yourself. Get into it. Read Punk" (Holmstrom 1976). The covers of the following issues featured cartoons of Patti Smith (twice), the Ramones, Iggy Pop, Richard Hell, the Sex Pistols, and Blondie (in the summer of 1977).[37]

Punk was a singles genre, and bands released albums once they had released enough singles to fill them out. Sire Records, formed by Seymour Stein and songwriter Richard Gottehrer in 1966 and initially issuing recordings by British bands, was an important independent label in the early New York punk and new wave scenes, releasing the debut recordings of the Ramones in 1976; Richard Hell and the Voidoids, Talking Heads, the Dead Boys, and Patti Smith (a seven-inch single), all in 1977; Tuff Darts! in 1978; Tom Tom Club in 1981; and Madonna in 1982.

Punk, and subsequently new wave, was a developing conversation across the Anglophone Atlantic (see figure 48). John Cale (from Wales) brought British Kinks records to the United States in the summer of 1965 to share with Lou Reed as they shaped the sound of the Velvet Underground. Cale produced the debut albums by the American group the Stooges (featuring Iggy Pop) in 1969 and Patti Smith in 1975. British manager and producer Malcolm McLaren worked with the New York Dolls in 1975 before returning to England and forming the Sex Pistols, who saw the Ramones perform in London in July 1976, months before their first single was released. David Bowie produced Lou Reed's *Transformer* (1972), and Roxy Music's Brian Eno would produce three albums by Talking Heads.

Defining punk as a musical aesthetic is not as easy as it might seem on the surface; the visual aspect is more clearly defined, especially regarding clothing and hairstyles

---

37 See Holmstrom and Hurd (2012) and Holmstrom (2019).

(see figure 49). The two quintessential American punk bands, the Ramones and the Patti Smith Group, both of whom emerged at the same time in the same club (CBGB), could not be more different in some aspects. The Ramones dealt in short forms: on their first album half of the songs were under two minutes, and no song even approached three minutes, extraordinary for its time. On Patti Smith's first album, over half of the songs were four minutes or longer (one clocked in at nine-and-a-half minutes), and only one song was under three minutes.

Patti Smith was a poet who formed a rock band; she was already performing her poetry publicly for several years and published several books of poetry before her first album. Few would lay that label on the Ramones, who largely dealt with teen angst. One of their songs (1:43 long) repeats, "I don't wanna walk around with you" over and over (with one variation) and an occasional response ("So why you wanna walk around with me?"). This nihilistic response to the excesses of 1970s rock could be taken as an iconoclastic and elegant poetic rejoinder. But it is a very different kind of response than Patti Smith's epic (nine-plus-minutes long) medley "Land," channeling writer William Burroughs, with references to violence, sexuality, heroin, cocaine, switchblade knives, and French poet Rimbaud. The Patti Smith Group prominently featured a keyboard, an instrument largely absent in the punk world, and explored a variety of dynamic levels and tempos. The Ramones's music was effectively summarized by the two-word title of their 2002 album compiled by Johnny Ramone: *Loud, Fast*. What unites these two groups, and the others who either claimed or were labeled with punk status, is attitude, an intangible yet perceptible characteristic. "Punk wasn't a musical style, or at least it shouldn't have been. To many people it turned into a particular musical style. It was more a kind of do-it-yourself anyone can do it, kind of attitude. If you only played two notes on the guitar, you can figure out a way to make a song out of that. And that's what it was about" (David Byrne, qtd. in Espar and Thomson 1995-v, episode 9).[38]

See figure 48. Punk and new wave groups and their debut LPs
See figure 49. Disco and punk comparisons

---

38 For more on this era, see Robins (1976), McNeil and McCain (1996), Heylin (2005), P. Smith (2010), and Worley (2017); documentaries by Kral and Poe (1976-v), Lommel (1979-v), Temple (1980-v, 2000-v), Fields and Gramaglia (2003-v), Stein (2009-v), and J. J. Miller (2019-v); and *Rock 'n' Roll High School* with the Ramones (Arkush 1979-v).

NEW WAVE

New wave, as a rock marketing category, refers to late 1970s–early 1980s bands informed by punk sensibilities but moving beyond, bringing back dance-oriented grooves and more ambitious songwriting. By this standard Television (*Marquee Moon*, 1977), intimately involved with the early CBGB punk scene, straddles punk and new wave or rather transcends their boundaries. Although Blondie, with lead vocalist Debbie Harry (1945–), and Talking Heads, with lead vocalist David Byrne (1952–), both gigged at CBGB in 1975 along with punk icons Patti Smith and the Ramones, they both exhibit postpunk sensibilities. Blondie (*Blondie*, 1976), Talking Heads (*77*, 1977), the Cars (*The Cars*, 1978), Devo (*Q: Are We Not Men?*, 1978), and the B-52s (*The B-52s*, 1979) initially defined new wave in the United States, and Elvis Costello (*My Aim Is True*, 1977) did the same in the United Kingdom (see figure 48).

The title *new wave*, canonized in a January 1978 *Billboard* magazine twenty-page feature (the same month the Sex Pistols broke up), covers a variety of artists and styles. Cateforis (2011: 12–13) suggests that the phrase "modern pop music" can be an effective lens, marked by a nervousness (reinforcing a white middle-class identity), "irreverent irony," and "nostalgic appreciation," and notes two phases: 1978–81 in a U.S. context; and 1981 through a decline in the mid-1980s, with a primary base in the United Kingdom. The term *new wave*, used by rock journalists in the early 1970s, was pushed by Sire Records head Seymour Stein in 1977 to distinguish his roster, most notably Talking Heads, from what had become known as punk rock (Cateforis 2011: 25).

The Boston-based Cars, breaking into the Top 40 with two songs ("Just What I Needed" and "My Best Friend's Girl") from their self-titled debut album (which broke into the Top 20) in the second half of 1978 marked the commercial rise of the genre. They were the first of any group marketed as punk or new wave to reach this far up the pop charts. Comparing the Cars with peer mainstream album-oriented rock groups like Foreigner, Journey, or Boston, who distilled early 1970s hard rock and progressive rock into a late 1970s FM radio-friendly format, Cateforis notes that the Cars (and other new wave bands) chose different lineages with different attitudes: "By depicting romance through an air of detachment rather than insatiable physical attraction, 'Just What I Needed' borders on the cynical, highlighting the conflict that many new wave musicians felt in dealing with rock's well-worn tropes of sex and love" (2011: 31). The Cars were also distinguished in their fashion: no denim, bell-bottom pants, or sports jerseys but rather button-down, tucked-in shirts, assorted skinny ties and jackets, and semicoordinated red, white, and black colors.

Cateforis (2000: iv, 11–12; 2011: 12–14) notes four themes that inform new wave: an avant-garde sensibility of irony (Talking Heads); drawing on past styles, including rockabilly (Elvis Costello); looking to the future, embracing synthesizer technology (Devo); and cross-cultural borrowing, with predominantly white bands drawing on African-based grooves and funk (Talking Heads' *Remain in Light*, 1980). Vocalist David Byrne, born in Scotland and raised in Ontario and then Maryland, bears an uncanny resemblance in his vocal delivery to David Bowie, evoking a similar kind of ironic detachment.

The rise of the personal computer in the late 1970s and early 1980s, coinciding exactly with new wave, was widely recognized when *Time* magazine renamed its "Man of the Year" award for 1982 to "Machine of the Year" and gave it to the personal computer.[39] This was accompanied by fears that the new technology would become an "alienating force and source of social anxiety" (Cateforis 2011: 77). Such technology was a flashpoint for a broader nervousness and anxiety that can be seen as a marker of "intellectual sensitivity and whiteness," channeled in the form of Talking Heads' front man, David Byrne, and his peculiar brand of spasmodic dance moves and physicality. "As a marker of whiteness, nervousness allowed new wave's white performers a space within which they could both celebrate and critique their cultural backgrounds, and also present a version of whiteness quite different from what had come to typify the societal norms of the 1970s" (80). Byrne characterized this phenomenon as "the groove was always there, as a kind of physical body-oriented antidote to this nervous angsty flailing, but the groove never took over. It served as a sonic psychological safety net, a link to the body. It said that no matter how alienated the subject or the singer might appear, the groove and its connection to the body would provide solace and grounding. But the edgy, uncomfortable stuff was still the foreground" (Byrne 2012: 51).[40]

The B-52s and the Go-Gos were unusual in the new wave pantheon. Consisting of three men and two women, the B-52s presented a different image, especially as they drew on early 1960s beach party nostalgia. The Go-Gos were an all-woman band—

---

39 See *Time* (1983) and Friedrich et al. (1983).

40 See Demme's (1984-v) Talking Heads concert film, *Stop Making Sense*; and Talking Heads (2011-v).

one of the few to gain significant commercial success. Their debut album, *Beauty and the Beat* (1981), hit #1, with two Top 40 singles, including "We Got the Beat" (#2).[41]

See figure 48. Punk and new wave groups and their debut LPs

WOMEN AND 1970S ROCK

The second half of the 1970s saw the increasing appearance of women leading rock bands, not just as vocalists but with some also playing electric guitar. Their predecessors were Grace Slick and Janis Joplin in the 1960s and rockabilly vocalist-guitarist Wanda Jackson in the 1950s (see figures 50 and 51). Suzi Quatro was the pioneer in the decade, playing electric bass and leading her own band. Born and raised in Detroit, she and her sisters formed and gigged in an all-women band before she moved in the early 1970s to England, which became her home base. Quatro had limited chart success (breaking into the Top 40 just once) and played the part of rock singer Leather Tuscadero on the sitcom *Happy Days* in 1977–78.

Patti Smith became an icon of punk rock with her critically acclaimed debut album, *Horses* (1975). Sisters Ann (vocals) and Nancy (guitar) Wilson were born and raised on the West Coast and released their debut album, *Dreamboat Annie*, in 1975, while their band, Heart, was based in Vancouver. Blondie, with lead vocalist Deborah Harry, released their debut album *Blondie* the following year, achieving mainstream success with several singles beginning in 1979 ("Heart of Glass").

In the space of three years (1979–81), Pat Benatar, Chrissie Hynde and the Pretenders, and Joan Jett released their debut albums, setting the standard for the era. Hynde played electric guitar, as did Jett, who had earlier cofounded the Runaways, an all-women band that included guitarist Lita Ford and vocalist Cherie Currie.[42] Siouxsie and the Banshees was a British punk band (led by vocalist Susan "Siouxsie Sioux" Ballion) that began releasing singles and albums in 1978 but did not break into U.S. charts until 1984. The Slits were a British all-women band that toured with the Clash in 1976, releasing their debut album in 1979 (*The Cut*), which charted in the

---

41 For more on new wave, see Majewski and Bernstein (2014); for the immediate postpunk era in the United States and United Kingdom, see Reynolds (2006).

42 Both Ford (2016) and Currie (2010) have published memoirs.

United Kingdom (#30), but not in the United States. Figure 51 shows some of the women who were breaking down the gender associations of the musical instruments used in rock.[43]

See figure 50. Women rock singers fronting bands, 1970s
See figure 51. Gendered instruments

JAZZ ROCK

Jazz was the popular dance music of the 1930s, when it was called swing. It was displaced from that role after World War II by R&B and then rock and roll. From 1955 to 1965 there were still about a dozen jazz artists who could place albums in the Top 40 (see figure 52). In the late 1960s trumpeter Miles Davis (1926–91), who had been active in the jazz world since the mid-1940s, moved in the direction of rock, adding electric keyboards, guitars, and bass to his ensemble. The rock-infused *Bitches Brew* (1970) became his best-selling album in his lifetime, gaining gold status (half a million copies sold) in 1976. It was eventually surpassed by his *Kind of Blue* (1959), one of the most popular albums in the jazz world, featuring tenor saxophonist John Coltrane and pianist Bill Evans, which hit four-times platinum in 2008.

Also in the late 1960s, two bands with jazz-trained instrumentalists drew on their experience and helped shape a style that has come to be known as jazz rock. Blood, Sweat, and Tears enjoyed some chart success, and Chicago released a string of albums in the early 1970s that either hit or came close to #1. Through the rest of the decade a significant number of jazz musicians crossed over into the pop charts.

See figure 52. Jazz and jazz rock albums in the pop Top 40

END-OF-DECADE MOMENT

The pervasive presence of the funk band Chic's "Good Times" in the summer and fall of 1979 was a catalyst for a new musical movement at end of the decade. The seductive and addicting bass (Bernard Edwards) and rhythm guitar (Nile Rodgers) combination

---

43 For more on women and rock, see Whiteley (2000), Gaar (2002), O'Brien (2002), and Carson, Lewis, and Shaw (2004).

provided a continuous loop soundtrack for a new style of making music, rapping lyrics rather than singing them (Budman and Bortolotti 2008-v). The Sugar Hill Gang's "Rapper's Delight," released in the fall, established the commercial viability of rapping over an instrumental soundtrack (in this case, Chic's "Good Times"). Blondie's "Rapture," released the following year, with an instrumental track indebted to Chic and rapping by lead singer Deborah Harry, gave some indication of a new meeting ground between musics coded black (funk, rap) and white (new wave). Parliament Funkadelic keyboardist, Bernie Worrell, joining Talking Heads on tour in 1980 was further evidence.

The 1980s were marked in the music industry by significant investment in individual highly profitable superstars: Bruce Springsteen, Michael Jackson, Prince, Madonna, and Whitney Houston. New digital synthesizer and sampling technologies had a major impact on the sound of the eighties, including a wave of British bands that leaned heavily on synthesizers, pervasive electronically enhanced snare drums sounds, and sample-based hip hop by the end of the decade. The parallel growth of rap and heavy metal, resulting in major commercial breakthroughs by the early 1990s for both, illustrated two alternate views of the new technologies. Hip hop deejays and producers embraced electronic drum machines and samplers as soon as they were affordable enough and pushed the limits of the technology. Heavy metal groups, on the other hand, were uninterested in these new developments and instead were pushing the limits of their musical instruments and voices, evincing their own strand of authenticity. Independent alternatives to the corporate rock world led to a commercial breakthrough for bands in the Pacific Northwest by the early 1990s.

Key social and political events in the 1980s include the following. Ronald Reagan served two terms as president (1981–89), cutting, among other things, federal funding to city governments, further contributing to urban decay. John Lennon was shot and killed outside his apartment building in New York City (December 1980). MTV went on the air, spurring the rise of music videos (August 1981). The first reports of crack cocaine use (1981) culminated in the height of the crack epidemic (1985–89). The #2 NBA college-draft pick Len Bias died of cocaine-induced heart failure (June 1986), leading to the Anti–Drug Abuse Act (October 1986), with mandatory five-year-minimum sentences for a first-time offense of trafficking powder (five hundred grams) versus crack (five grams) cocaine, a hundred-to-one disparity. An amendment to the act (September 1988) covered simple possession. The first use of the acronym AIDS was in response to reports to the CDC of over 450 cases in the United States (the summer of 1982); the number rose to 47,000 cases in the United States by the end of 1987. Actor Rock Hudson died of AIDS, bringing increased public attention (October 1985).

HIP HOP

In the 1970s in New York City, especially the borough of the Bronx, the four elements that make up hip hop culture were each developing on their own: deejaying, emceeing, break dancing, and graffiti tagging. Three deejays (from *disc jockey*) in particular, who were playing records at outdoor parties, community centers, and nightclubs, were especially significant for their pioneering contributions: Kool Herc, Afrika Bambaataa, and Grandmaster Flash.

When Clive "Kool Herc" Campbell (1955–) moved from Jamaica to the Bronx in 1967, he brought with him the practice of large sound systems being used for parties and dancing rather than live bands. In August 1973 Kool Herc first started publicly spinning records, for his sister's back to school party, in the recreation room of their apartment building (1520 Sedgwick Avenue, near 174th Street). Soon he moved outdoors to Cedar Park, about five blocks north along Sedgwick. Both the apartment building and park have been designated hip hop landmarks by the City of New York, naming the stretch at 1520 Sedgwick as Hip Hop Boulevard. Kool Herc would cue up records on dual turntables, moving back and forth between them to play short breaks (called *b-beats*) to keep the crowd dancing. His younger peer credited him early on as "the first DJ to take the Jamaican dub style and adapt it to a soul funk thing. He was the first DJ to spin b-beat records exclusively and was known at first just for that. Then together with the boys in the [Bronx street gang] Black Spades he applied rap . . . to the music. . . . He knows how to throw down b-beats and that's how he got the reputation of being the godfather of hip hop rock" (Afrika Bambaataa, qtd. in Holman 1982: 29). Herc's partner, Coke La Rock, is usually credited with being the first to take over the role from the deejay of exhorting the crowd, thereby laying the foundation for the independent art of the emcee (master of ceremonies).

Kevin "Afrika Bambaataa" Donovan (1957–), born to Jamaican and Barbadian parents, began deejaying for block parties where he lived at the Bronx River Houses (about three miles east of Herc) about 1977, playing an unusually eclectic mix of music. According to his producer, Arthur Baker,

> I'd be out in the park [in the Bronx] and Bambaataa and the guys would always play "Trans-Europe Express." . . . It would be so eerie to be sitting in the middle of these housing projects and there's this German sort of classical electronic music vibrating through the big buildings. . . . He would play any music as long as it had a beat. . . . At the time I was very aware of the whole downtown scene, which Talking Heads were a part of. There was a real cross-cultural thing of black kids in the downtown, all this interaction. Which is why the music was so interesting. Bands like Liquid Liquid (seminal alternative rock/dance fusion), and things like Grandmaster Flash opening for the Clash—stuff like that. (Qtd. in Kershaw 1996)

A former gang member, Bambaataa formed the Universal Zulu Nation, a cultural organization dedicated to breaking the cycle of gang violence. He is credited with publicly naming the genre *hip hop*, which appeared in print for the first time in 1982 (Holman 1982; Hager 1982).

Joseph "Grandmaster Flash" Saddler (1958–) moved from Barbados to the Bronx when he was a child and performed at Disco Fever (a club in the South Bronx) with his group by about 1977. He brought the art of scratching, a technique discovered by "Grand Wizard" Theodore Livingston (1963–) about 1975, as well as other techniques isolating beats and repeating them using two turntables, to a new level, pioneering a new performance genre that came to be called *turntablism* (see Katz 2012).

While deejays would initially verbally coax the crowd to participate, that function would be taken over by a second person, known as an emcee (or MC). Most of the first generation of emcees, active in the late 1970s and early 1980s, such as Curtis "Grandmaster Caz" Fisher (1961–) of the Cold Crush Brothers, featured in *Wild Style* (and who lived within blocks of Herc), were not able to cross over into the commercial recording sphere.[1] Kurtis "Blow" Walker (1959–), from Harlem, was the exception, although his success was short-lived. He was managed by Russell Simmons (1957–), whom he met when they were both students at City College.

The first commercially successful rap recording was "Rapper's Delight" by the Sugar Hill Gang (a trio of novices put together by label owner Sylvia Robinson), which hit #4 on the R&B singles chart in late 1979 and crossed over to #36 on the pop singles chart in early 1980. They rapped over the Sugarhill Records label's house band covering Chic's "Good Times," which was a #1 hit the summer of 1979. Kurtis Blow was the first bona fide rapper to hit the pop charts, with "The Breaks (Part 1)" (#87), which rose to #4 on the R&B chart in 1980 (see figures 53 and 54).

Two landmark recordings from 1982 moved the genre to a new level. "Planet Rock" (1982, R&B #4, pop #48) by Afrika Bambaataa and the Soul Sonic Force, with producer Arthur Baker, helped establish the sonic signature of hip hop tracks in the 1980s with the Roland TR-808, a programmable drum machine that used analog synthesis (rather than digital samples). Bambaataa called his style electro funk. "The Message" (1982, R&B #4, pop #62) by Grandmaster Flash and the Furious Five (featuring Melle

---

1   *Wild Style* (Ahearn 1982-v) is the earliest film about the scene; Splunteren (1986-v) documents the scene four years later. Hager (1982) provides one of the earliest detailed explorations of the birth of hip hop.

Mel), features lyrics that addressed some of the social situations experienced at the time ("Don't push me cause I'm close to the edge / I'm trying not to lose my head / It's like a jungle sometimes / It makes me wonder how I keep from goin' under").

Run-D.M.C. (from Queens, New York) was rap's first major group that broke through: the progression of their first three albums (culminating with their third album, *Raising Hell*) was #53, #52, and #3 on the pop album charts and #14, #12, and #1 on the R&B album charts. *Raising Hell* was certified platinum within two months of its May 1986 release (rap's first gold or platinum album) and hit three-times platinum the following year (RIAA 2019a). Their tougher aggressive sound, including harder drum machine beats and rock guitar (through their producer Rick Rubin) contrasted with the sing-song style that preceded them. So did their look, including black leather jackets and thick gold chains. Shortly after, the Beastie Boys' debut album, *Licensed to Ill*, hit #1 and went four-times platinum within a year of its October 1986 release.

Russell Simmons (older brother of Joseph "Run" Simmons) and Rick Rubin became the first major entrepreneurs of rap when they formed Def Jam Records in 1983, releasing records by LL Cool J (1984), the Beastie Boys (1985), and Public Enemy (1987). Rubin left later in the decade, forming his own record label, going on to cohead Columbia Records in 2007, winning Grammy Awards for his production work. Simmons formed Rush Communications in 1991, one of the largest African American–owned media companies, producing *Def Jam Comedy* on HBO (1992) and Def Poetry Jam (2002).

The instrumental backgrounds in early rap went through two stages before the era of digital sampling: live bands in the studio (Sugar Hill Gang, Kurtis Blow) and drum machines and keyboard synthesizers (Afrika Bambaataa, Run-D.M.C.). Queens-based producer Marlon "Marley Marl" Williams (1962–) is credited with realizing the potential of digitally recording (sampling) a previous recording and combining the individual sampled elements (e.g., a bass drum kick, snare drum hit, short instrumental sequence, snippet of a word) into loops to provide the background instrumental track. Marl has credited an unlikely source: "You know who my hero was before I even got into hip-hop? I just gotta lay it on the line: [Italian disco producer] Giorgio Moroder. I was into Giorgio like you would not believe. See, I was into electronic music. I was into triggering bass lines and making it sequence—I was a sequence head. That's how I beat people in hip-hop early because I was already sequencing. I already knew what a trigger was. I knew how to trigger anything off of anything" (qtd. in Muhammad and Kelley 2013). His work on MC Shan's "The Bridge" (1986) and Eric B. and Rakim's debut album, *Paid in Full* (1986, R&B #8, pop #58), opened up what has come to be known as the golden age of sampling, when producers were not yet hindered by copyright infringement lawsuits.[2] Rakim (1968–) is widely recognized as setting a new standard for rapping, in his innovative flow, word play, and storytelling style, which became the model for the 1990s generation.

Two other important emcees in the mid-1980s bear mention. Richard "Slick Rick" Walters (1965–), who was born in London and moved to the Bronx in his teens, established himself as one of the early storytellers with "La Di Da Di" (1985), with beatboxer Doug E. Fresh, and "Children's Story" (1988, R&B #5). Bronx-native Lawrence "KRS-One" Parker (1965–), whose "South Bronx" (1986) on his debut LP, *Criminal Minded* (1987), with his group Boogie Down Productions, asserted the primacy of his neighborhood in hip hop, has become an elder statesman and spokesperson for the positive power of hip hop. His Stop the Violence Movement yielded the all-star recording "Self-Destruction" (1988), an early effort at explicit and positive self-critique.

Three albums released in 1989–90 are considered to be masterpieces of sample-based hip hop: *3 Feet High and Rising* (De La Soul, entered charts March 1989: R&B #1, pop #24); *Paul's Boutique* (Beastie Boys, August 1989: pop #14, R&B #24); and *Fear of a Black Planet* (Public Enemy, April 1990: R&B #3, pop #10).[3] Public Enemy's classic 1989 "Fight the Power" (R&B #20), with perhaps a dozen or more unauthorized (and unacknowledged) samples, stands as a testament to the creative heights that producers can achieve with unhindered sampling (see figure 55). Their production team (called the Bomb Squad), according to Hank Shocklee, "would work like a conveyor belt. Eric [Sadler] and Keith [Shocklee] would make beats. Terminator [X] would come in with the scratch parts. . . . I [Hank] would organize and shape everything and mix everything" (qtd. in Chairman Mao 1998: 113). They were a different kind of group for its time, as Shocklee notes. "Public Enemy was . . . a street group. It was basically a thrash group, a group that was very much rock 'n' roll oriented. We very seldom used bass lines because the parallel that we wanted to draw was Public Enemy and Led Zeppelin. Public Enemy and the Grateful Dead.

---

2   See Carluccio (2012-v) for Marl recreating his work on "Eric B. Is President," and Dubspot (2014) for three other Marl recreations.

3   For more on sample-based hip hop, see Schloss (2014), Sewell (2014), and the documentary *Copyright Criminals* (Franzen 2009-v). Who Sampled (2019) is the standard reference for sample sources.

We were not polished and clean like any of the R&B groups or even any of our rap counterparts that were doing a lotta love rap. That just wasn't our zone" (113–14). In the documentary *Copyright Criminals* (Franzen 2009-v) Hank Shocklee addressed his practice of trying to hide the sources of his samples; the documentary also features the perspective of James Brown's drummer, Clyde Stubblefield, probably the most sampled drummer in hip hop, noting that he rarely received any royalties.

The infamous 1991 legal case of Gilbert O'Sullivan ("Alone Again, Naturally") objecting to Biz Markie's unauthorized sample (in "Alone Again"), which resulted in Markie's album *I Need a Haircut* being pulled from distribution (including taken out of record stores), put a chill on the practice. A similarly chilling case happened the same year when the Turtles ("You Showed Me") sued De La Soul ("Transmitting Live from Mars") for an unauthorized twelve-second sample, reaching an out-of-court settlement for a reported $1.7 million. Henceforth, all samples would need to be authorized (cleared) by the artists and their record labels.[4]

The first women rappers include fourteen-year-old Roxanne Shanté (1970–), whose 1985 single, "Roxanne's Revenge," hit #22 on the R&B chart, and the duo Salt-N-Pepa, whose 1986 debut LP, *Hot, Cool and Vicious*, hit #26 on the pop chart with its single "Push It" reaching #19. Dana "Queen Latifah" Owens (1970–) was the most successful of the early solo women emcees. Although her debut album, *All Hail the Queen* (1989, pop #124, R&B #6), with its single "Ladies First," had modest pop chart success, her third album, *Black Reign* (1993, pop #60, R&B #15), was the first gold album by a woman rapper. She later went on to a major career in television, starring in *Living Single* (1993–98) and her own talk show (1999–2001, 2013–15), as well as feature films (*Chicago*, *Hairspray*, *Ice Age*).

The art of the emcee can be appreciated on many levels. Bradley's (2007) chapter headings in his *Poetics of Hip Hop* provide a concise guide: "Rhythm" (or flow), "Rhyme," "Wordplay" (simile, metaphor, pun), "Storytelling," and "Signifying" (the art of the battle). This last item (verbal battling) has since at least the 1960s been the subject of much research among black inner-city youth (Labov 1972; Smitherman 1995) and is responsible in part for the public debates about the sometimes vulgar nature of the language and sentiments expressed. Within the in-group private context

---

4   For the Biz Markie case, see *Grand Upright v. Warner* (Music Copyright Infringement Resource 2019). Marshall (2006) covers the long-term ramifications of the sudden costs of sample clearance.

of street-corner verbal battles (also known as snapping, the dozens, signifying, and sounding) there are agreed-on codes: the words are not meant to be taken literally, and so hyperbole is required, the language is embellished and exaggerated, it provides an outlet for the emotions, and it is a contest between two individuals (Terkourafi 2010: 9–10).

By the late 1980s a new style emerged in Los Angeles, called *gangsta rap* for its hard-edged lyrics that portrayed street culture in some of the rawest language ever issued on commercial recordings. N.W.A.'s second album, *Straight Outta Compton* (1988, pop #37, R&B #9), with its title song and "Fuck tha Police," exemplified the genre in its violent imagery, foregrounding police brutality and their targeting of black youth, as well as routine misogyny. While the former is seen as a progressive political stance in calling attention to long-standing injustices in policing black communities, the latter has brought criticism from diverse corners, including African American clergy, parents, and academics. O'Shea "Ice Cube" Jackson (1969–), who left N.W.A. after *Straight Outta* for a solo career, was a lightning rod for praise and critiques, exacerbated by lyrics on his first three solo albums, which gained unlikely mainstream success: *AmeriKKKa's Most Wanted* (1990, pop #19, R&B #6); *Death Certificate* (1991, pop #2, R&B #1); and *The Predator* (1992, pop #1, R&B #1). The debut of *Yo! MTV Raps* as a daily two-hour show in August 1988, originally hosted by multidisciplinary artist, Brooklyn-based "Fab 5" Freddy Brathwaite (1959–), marks an initial maturity for hip hop, reaching a regular national audience.[5]

See figure 53. Rap groups and LPs moving into the mainstream, 1984–1990

See figure 54. Some key rap record labels

See figure 55. "Fight the Power" sample and lyric sources

Misogynist Lyrics in Hip Hop

How to interpret lyrics from Ice Cube and others in the 1990s has posed intractable questions to those who see rap as reflecting realities of inner-city African American life and therefore as a force for positive social critique and change. Contradictions abound, not only among young rappers but also among their audiences, who may ap-

---

5 Expansive documentaries on the history of hip hop include Perry (2004-v) and Wheeler, Dunn, and McFadyen (2016–18-v). Rose (1994) is an early classic study, and Chang (2005) covers the social and cultural history through the early 2000s.

preciate some, but not all, of their artistic expression. Six snapshots of debates within African American communities will help to articulate some of varied perspectives.

In an interview with Angela Y. Davis, one of the most outspoken political activists of the late 1960s and early 1970s, just before *Death Certificate* was released, Ice Cube was grilled on his views about women as espoused in his lyrics:

> IC: My first approach was holding up a mirror, you see yourself for who you are, and you see the things going on in the black community. Hopefully, it scares them so much that they are going to provoke some thought in that direction.
>
> AYD: Am I correct in thinking that when you tell them, through your music, what is happening in the community, you play various roles, you become different characters? The reason I ask this question is because many people assume that when you are rapping, your words reflect your own beliefs and values. For example, when you talk about bitches and "hoes," the assumption is that you believe women are bitches and hoes. Are you saying that this is accepted language in some circles in the community? That this is the vocabulary that young people use and you want them to observe themselves in such a way that may also cause them to think about changing their attitudes.
>
> IC: Of course. (Ice Cube and Davis 1992: 178–79)

On the other hand, in a magazine interview (published the same year) that referenced negative lyrics about Jews, Koreans, and gays from *Death Certificate*, Ice Cube responded, "So why are you taking rap music literally? . . . It's stupid to take anything that literally, other than the news. This is a form of *entertainment*. People keep forgetting that. I'm not a schoolteacher or a professor at any university. I'm a rapper. I entertain" (qtd. in Considine 1992: 38).

Not long after, an NBC TV (1993-v) special report noted some of the backlash, showing a now-infamous clip of Rev. Calvin Butts preaching to his Harlem Abyssinian Baptist Church congregation, revealing a generational divide: "We're not against rap. We're not against rappers. But we are against those thugs who disgrace our community."[6] In an interview Rev. Jesse Jackson expressed his perspective:

6　See also McDaniels (1993-v) for a televised debate with Butts, Ice-T, Cynthia Horner, and Coral Aubert.

We always had the oppressor wanting to call our women bitches. But we always fought against it, we didn't spread it. Or to call us niggas. We always fought against it. We didn't perpetuate it. Now we're getting paid to say that which we've always fought against. . . . We must take the profit out of pain. . . . Indeed, the rap artists have a responsibility. Those who pay them have a responsibility. Those who set the context have an even greater responsibility. If there were not such easy access to guns and drugs and so much unemployment and so much abandonment the rapper would be abstract. . . . Rap is an extension of the culture. Let's break up the violence in the culture. (Jackson, qtd. in NBC TV 1993-v)

A 1990 court case in which the group 2 Live Crew was accused of breaking a Florida obscenity law with sexually explicit lyrics in their album *As Nasty as They Wanna Be* (1989) was an initial flashpoint for debates among African American academics. Harvard (at the time, Duke) professor Henry Louis Gates Jr. was an expert witness for the defense and published an article in the *New York Times* explaining his viewpoint:

2 Live Crew is engaged in heavy-handed parody, turning the stereotypes of black and white American culture on their heads. These young artists are acting out, to lively dance music, a parodic exaggeration of the age-old stereotypes of the oversexed black female and male. Their exuberant use of hyperbole (phantasmagoric sexual organs, for example) undermines—for anyone fluent in black cultural codes—a too literal-minded hearing of the lyrics. This is the street tradition called signifying or playing the dozens, which has generally been risqué. . . . In the face of racist stereotypes about black sexuality, you can do one of two things: you can disavow them or explode them with exaggeration. . . . And we must not allow ourselves to sentimentalize street culture: the appreciation of verbal virtuosity does not lessen one's obligation to critique bigotry in all of its pernicious forms. (Gates 1990)

Harvard-trained UCLA professor of law Kimberlé Crenshaw responded, "Black women can hardly regard the right to be represented as bitches and whores as essential to their interests. Instead the defense of 2 Live Crew primarily functions to protect the cultural and political prerogative of male rappers to be as misogynistic and offensive as they want to be" (1991: 33).

The 2015 release of the Hollywood film *Straight Outta Compton*, an account of the rise of N.W.A., led to questions about what was left out of the film. Dee Barnes, an African American hip hop television show host who was assaulted in a nightclub by N.W.A. member Dr. Dre in 1991, had an especially sensitive perspective. Dr. Dre was convicted of a misdemeanor, and Barnes won an out-of-court civil-suit settlement at the time.

> Accurately articulating the frustrations of young black men being constantly harassed by the cops is at Straight Outta Compton's activistic core. There is a direct connection between the oppression of black men and the violence perpetrated by black men against black women. It is a cycle of victimization and reenactment of violence that is rooted in racism and perpetuated by patriarchy. . . . Straight Outta Compton transforms N.W.A. from the world's most dangerous rap group to the world's most diluted rap group. In rap, authenticity matters, and gangsta rap has always pushed boundaries beyond what's comfortable with hardcore rhymes that are supposed to present accounts of the street's harsh realities (though N.W.A. shared plenty of fantasies, as well). The biggest problem with Straight Outta Compton is that it ignores several of N.W.A.'s own harsh realities. (Barnes 2015)

Joan Morgan, trying to reconcile in the 1990s her identification as a hip hop feminist, notes that rap music is essential to the struggle against sexism,

> because it takes us straight to the battlefield. . . . The seemingly impenetrable wall of sexism in rap music is really the complex mask African-Americans often wear both to hide and express the pain. At the close of this millennium, hip-hop is still one of the few forums in which young black men, even surreptitiously, are allowed to express their pain. . . . [Hip hop's] illuminating, informative narration and its incredible ability to articulate our collective pain is an invaluable tool when examining gender relations. The information we amass can help create a redemptive, healing space for brothers and sistas. We're all winners when a space exists for brothers to honestly state and explore the roots of their pain and subsequently their misogyny, sans [without] judgment. (Morgan 1999: 72, 74, 80)

Gil Scott-Heron's 1994 "Message to the Messengers" (on *Spirits*) is one of the more moving statements in this regard, urging young rappers to know their history, respect their elders and women, speak out against gun violence, and curb profanity. Scott-Heron speaks with some authority. His spoken-word poetry, beginning with "The Revolution Will Not Be Televised" (on both *A New Black Poet*, 1970, and *Pieces of a Man*, 1971), set the standard, and he is widely admired as the model and inspiration for the socially conscious rap of the generations that followed.[7]

Epidemic, Economics, and Incarceration

The crack cocaine epidemic took a huge toll on African American communities in the 1980s.[8] It also set the context for some of the most powerful rap in the following decade. Powdered cocaine reemerged in the United States as a recreational drug in the 1970s, costing between $100 and $200 per gram (the 2001 Hollywood film *Blow* dramatizes the characters and events responsible for its widespread distribution in the United States). Crack is a crystalized form of cocaine that is smoked; a pebble-sized piece of crack, one-tenth of a gram of cocaine, sold for $5.00 to $10.00, delivering a highly addictive, intense but brief high. Because it was often sold in outdoor markets, street gangs took over the distribution. Gang violence grew to protect markets, and enormous profitability offered alternate models for success. A significant number of users were women, contributing to prostitution, the spread of AIDS, and low-birth-weight babies ("crack babies"). In the decade from 1984 to 1994 homicide rates (per 100,000) for black males more than doubled in both the fourteen-to-seventeen age group (from 5 to 12) and eighteen-to-twenty-four age group (from 13 to 28). The rate would decline dramatically for all groups in the next five years. Other quality of life spikes, which could be related to the impact of crack, included weapons arrests, low-birth weights, miscarriages, and placement of children in foster care. The percentage of arrests related to cocaine went from 2 percent to 6 percent between 1984 and 1989 and then went into a very slow decline. In the same five-year period, cocaine-related emergency room visits (per 100,000) jumped from 25 to 145. Cocaine-related deaths (per 100,000) made a similar jump but kept climbing, from 0.5 in 1984 to 4.5 in 1999.

The explosive growth of both rap and crack cocaine use in the late 1980s and early 1990s was an independent, although occasionally intertwined, phenomenon. The epidemic provided the backdrop for the early life of many rap artists, informing

---

7   See Hurt's (2006-v) documentary *Hip-Hop: Beyond Beats and Rhymes* for a compelling analysis of misogyny in hip hop.

8   Data for this paragraph comes from Fryer et al. (2013: 1651–56).

their personas. Some trafficked in cocaine, including Notorious B.I.G., Jay-Z, 50 Cent, RZA, Eazy-E, and Snoop Dogg, leaving it behind for careers in music. Some of the alarm raised by gangsta rap was related to a perception of a connection between street crime and rap, with no clear signals of repudiating such activity and possible interpretations of glorification with few consequences.

The 1983 Hollywood film *Scarface*, a remake of a 1932 film, is widely cited by rappers growing up in the 1980s as an important influence. It tells the story of Tony Montana (Al Pacino), who, as a Cuban refugee with nothing in Miami, ruthlessly rises up the chain to head a multimillion-dollar cocaine-trafficking operation, ultimately dying a violent death. Released just as crack trafficking was entering U.S. cities, it laid out a narrative in which some found resonance. The VH1 documentary *Planet Rock: The Story of Hip Hop and the Crack Generation* (Lowe and Torgoff 2011-v), narrated by Ice-T, the original gangsta rapper, clearly lays out the connection with persuasive interviews (also see Bogazianos 2012).

Reagan-era economic policies cutting back social programs (for example, school-lunch discounts, job-training programs, legal services for the poor, and funding for public transit), deregulating industries, and raising military spending contributed to the devastation of inner-city communities that provided the backdrop for the growth of hip hop culture. Many cities with limited property-tax bases depended on federal aid for basic services. Between the beginning and end of Reagan's two terms as president (1981–89) federal aid dropped from 22 percent to just 6 percent of big-city budgets. Schools and their after-school programs, libraries, hospitals, and sanitation, police, and fire departments all suffered. Reagan inherited a 7.4 percent unemployment rate (February 1981), which rose to 10.8 percent (November 1982) and then dropped to 7.5 percent (August 1984). By the end of his second term, it was 5.25 percent (Dreier 2011).

The United States has the highest incarceration rate in the world, both in absolute numbers and per capita.[9] Since Reagan announced the war on drugs in the early 1980s, the prison population exploded from around three hundred thousand to more than two million, with drug convictions accounting for the majority of the increase. Initially exacerbated by the Reagan-era Anti–Drug Abuse Act with mandatory-minimum sentencing targeting crack cocaine (with a hundred-to-one disparity) the Violent

9 This paragraph is based on Alexander (2012: 6, 51, 216). For 2019 statistics, see Sawyer and Wagner (2019).

Crime Control and Law Enforcement Act (1994) and other initiatives of the Clinton administration led to the largest increases in the federal and state prison populations of any president.[10] This in turn fueled the highest unemployment rates ever among noncollege black men in their twenties. This environment of a crack cocaine epidemic, Reagan-era economics, and mass incarceration is the backdrop out of which hip hop developed in the 1980s and 1990s.

HEAVY METAL

Heavy metal has its origins in late 1960s British bands, especially Deep Purple, Led Zeppelin, and Black Sabbath (lead vocalist Ozzy Osbourne), which enjoyed significant chart success in the United States. The term *heavy metal* was initially used sporadically by critics in the early 1970s.[11] The group Steppenwolf used the lyric "heavy metal thunder" in "Born to Be Wild" (1968), which figured prominently in the film *Easy Rider* (1969), which may have attached both the term and the sound of heavy metal to motorcycles. By the time of Jim Miller's 1974 *Rolling Stone* record-review survey, the term was firmly in place: "Since the late Sixties, two opposing commercial strains have dominated pop: the singer/songwriters and 'heavy metal' . . . (Led Zeppelin, Deep Purple, Grand Funk Railroad, Black Sabbath). . . . Rock writer Lester Bangs named the genre. . . . The musical hallmarks of heavy metal are extraordinary volume, distortion, riffing . . . and a blatant disregard for swing. . . . Singing and lyrics are generally subordinated to instrumental sound. . . . The genre emphasizes chaos over coherence. . . . Metal employs a piledriver approach more expressive of an assembly line gone berserk" (1974: 72).

Miller's (1974: 73) Heavy Metal Hall of Fame included the Yardbirds (*Greatest Hits*, 1967); Cream (*Fresh Cream*, 1966); Jimi Hendrix (*Are You Experienced?*, 1967; *Electric Ladyland*, 1968); Led Zeppelin (*II*, 1969); Deep Purple (*In Rock*, 1970; *Machine Head*, 1972); Black Sabbath (*Paranoid*, 1970); and Blue Öyster Cult (*Blue Öyster Cult*, 1972), all British, with the exception of Hendrix and Blue Öyster Cult. He also named others, which would soon be associated with punk: Velvet Underground, MC5, the Stooges, and New York Dolls (all American).

---

10 The Obama-era Fair Sentencing Act (2010) repealed and revised the Anti–Drug Abuse Act.

11 Weinstein (2014) traces the term *heavy metal* to album reviews by Lester Bangs and Mike Saunders in *Rolling Stone* in 1970. A. Brown (2015) offers further analysis.

In the mid-1970s the next-generation British bands Judas Priest and Motörhead cemented the connection with a biker ethos. Motörhead initiated a metal-punk crossover trend that by the end of the decade would be called the new wave of British heavy metal (or NWOBM), exemplified by Def Leppard and Iron Maiden (Elliott 2007; Waksman 2009: 146–209). The 1970s bands had very limited chart success in the United States, and so the genre was still on the margins of the rock industry. That would soon change, when Def Leppard hit #2 with their third album, *Pyromania*, and Iron Maiden reached #14 with their fourth album, *Piece of Mind*, both in 1983.

In the 1980s four U.S. bands (three from California) defined to define what came to be called thrash or speed metal: Metallica (Los Angeles/San Francisco), Slayer (Huntington Beach, California), Anthrax (New York), and Megadeth (Los Angeles). These were the bands that moved U.S. heavy metal into the mainstream, with Metallica being the most successful: their first album (*Kill 'Em All*, 1983) did not chart, and their next three albums steadily rose until their fifth album (*Metallica*, 1991) hit #1 (see figure 56).

After the first wave of guitarists in the first-generation bands noted earlier by Miller—Jeff Beck (Yardbirds), Eric Clapton (Cream), Jimi Hendrix, Jimmy Page (Led Zeppelin), Ritchie Blackmore (Deep Purple), and Tony Iommi (Black Sabbath)—Eddie Van Halen expanded the possibilities of the electric guitar right from the 1978 debut album (*Van Halen*) of the group he cofounded (Van Halen) with his brother drummer Alex. "Eruption" from that album is a one-minute, forty-two-second virtuosic display of guitar technique that draws from the European classical tradition of Bach and Paganini (who wrote violin etudes), further moving the genre away from its blues roots. Initially with lead singer David Lee Roth (from 1978 to 1985), Van Halen defined a more radio-friendly style, achieving mainstream pop status, consistently hitting the Top 10 from their second album on, thereby attracting the somewhat pejorative term lite or pop metal, along with their British contemporaries Def Leppard (Weinstein 2000: 45–48).[12]

Weinstein (2000: 22–43) has described features of heavy metal in three separate dimensions: sonic, visual, and verbal. In the sonic dimension, loud volume saturates the recording or performance space, and bands feature virtuosic solo guitar playing, an elaborate drum set, and bass; keyboards are rare. Screaming vocals and the guitar are in rivalry with each other. Visually, bands feature logos that are angular and thick.

---

12 For more on Van Halen, see Renoff (2015).

The thunderbolt is important and the dominant color in artwork is black, then red. The imagery conjures up horror movies, gothic horror tales, heroic fantasies, and technological science fiction. Bands favor studded, black leather biker wear. Fans identify with jeans and black T-shirts. The biker look (metal-studded leather fashion) was a symbol of rebellion, masculinity, and outsider status. Verbally, band names, album and song titles, and lyrics contain ominous images, themes of mayhem and cosmic evil.

Weinstein (2000: 33) lists band names, noting that they show "some uniformities of signification and sensibility," and Walser (1993: 2) has identified categories, such as electrical and mechanical power; dangerous or unpleasant animals, people, or objects; powerful auras of blasphemy or mysticism; and the terror of death itself. Their combined lists are instructive: AC/DC, Annihilator, Anthrax, Black Sabbath, Blue Öyster Cult, Dark Angel, Death, Death Angel, Grim Reaper, Iron Maiden, Judas Priest, Malice, Manowar, Mayhem, Megadeth, Mötley Crüe, Motörhead, Nuclear Assault, Poison, Quiet Riot, Ratt, Scorpions, Slayer, Trouble, Twisted Sister, Vengeance, Venom, and W.A.S.P. Weinstein (2000: 35–43) suggests two major themes in the lyrics: Dionysian (Greek god of wine) and chaos. The Dionysian experience celebrates the vital forces of life through various forms of ecstasy (sex, drugs, and rock and roll). Romantic love is out. Chaos challenges the order and hegemony of everyday life: monsters, the underworld and hell, the grotesque and horrifying, disasters, mayhem, carnage, injustice, death, and rebellion (see figure 57).

A description from the late 1980s of what would become the most commercially successful heavy metal band captures some of the flavor of the genre:

> Ulrich and Hetfield formed Metallica in Los Angeles in 1981 as a hard-edged response to late-Seventies mainstream rock. Inspired in equal parts by the so-called "new wave of British heavy metal" and by the Southern California hardcore scene, Metallica stripped away the gothic excesses of the former and expanded the short-form song structures of the latter to produce five- to eight-minute mini-epics of ear-shattering volume and mind-boggling speed. They compounded multiple riffs within single tunes, linking them with subject matter that rejected "gonna-rock-ya-all-night-long" HM cliches (not to be confused with "gonna-love-ya-all-nite-long" HM cliches) in favor of darker meditations on power, violence, aggression and death. (Gehr 1988: 44)

Headbanger's Ball, a two-hour show that aired weekly at night on MTV beginning April 1987, expanding to three hours in 1990, marked an arrival for heavy metal in the United States. It replaced and expanded on *Heavy Metal Mania*, which began airing monthly in June 1985.[13]

_____

See figure 56. Early metal groups, new wave of British heavy metal,
   and American metal
See figure 57. Hard rock, metal, and punk comparisons

SECOND BRITISH INVASION

In July 1983 eighteen of the U.S. Top 40 (and six of the Top 10) singles were from the United Kingdom. Two years later (May 1985) eight UK singles were in the U.S. Top 10, something that had not happened for twenty years (May 1, 1965), when the first British Invasion occurred. The era of 1982–85 is marked by this second British Invasion. British presence on U.S. pop charts comes and goes: in April 2001 there was not one UK single in the whole U.S. Top 100 singles chart, the first time since October 1963.

Elvis Costello and the Police opened the doors in the late 1970s. MTV spurred the wave when it went on the air in August 1981. British groups realized the importance of promotional videos sooner than their American counterparts and immediately reaped the benefit. Beginning in the spring of 1982 new British groups and artists began breaking into the U.S. pop Top 10 at the average rate of more than one every two months—twenty in all (see figure 58). At the end of 1982, *Billboard* noted a "new British Invasion," referring to them as techno-pop groups, because of their electronic synthesizer orientations (Kozak 1982). A little over a year later (January 23, 1984), *Newsweek* magazine featured Boy George and Annie Lennox on their cover, with the headline, "Britain Rocks America—Again."

Most of the groups drew heavily on electronic keyboard and drum synthesizers (e.g., the duo of vocalist Annie Lennox and synth player Dave Stewart, who made up Eurythmics), hence the term *synthpop*. Synth player Gary Numan opened up that door on his 1979 debut solo album, *Pleasure Principle* (#16), with its Top 10 single "Cars" (no guitars were used on the album, other than bass). The synth-driven group

_____

13 For an oral history of metal with hundreds of interviews, see Wiederhorn and Turman (2013); for documentaries, see Warren (2006-v), Johnstone (2008-v), and Heyn's (1986-v) quirky look at fans outside a Judas Priest concert.

Orchestral Manoeuvres in the Dark had a significant impact in the United Kingdom from their self-titled 1980 debut album (#27 in the UK) onward. Their next four LPs were in the UK Top 10, but they did not breach a U.S. pop chart until their third album (*Architecture and Morality*, #144, February 1982). They eventually had a Top 10 U.S. hit in 1986 ("If You Leave," #4), entering the chart weeks after its appearance in the film *Pretty in Pink*. Depeche Mode had a similar profile: their 1981 debut album (*Speak and Spell*, #192) barely broke into the U.S. Top 200, and it was not until their seventh studio album (*Violator*, 1990, #7) that they broke into the Top 10; all of their studio albums (through 2017) hit the UK Top 10. They had two U.S. Top 40 hits in the 1980s and their first Top 10 single came in 1990 ("Enjoy the Silence," #8).

Like the first British Invasion, not all the groups and artists had the staying power to last. While it would be difficult to characterize such a large collection of groups and artists, a few features stand out: as it was the early years of MTV, there was little narrative content in their videos; they were for the most part young and similarly telegenic; electronic synthesizers were common; and their singing approached an emotionally cool and detached style. Dave Hill (1986: 31) refers to this era as an eighties rebirth of glam ("icy cool and raging hot"), epitomized by Annie Lennox, whose "Sweet Dreams (Are Made of This)" is a "mesh of coolly opposed contradictions . . somehow both austere and desirous."

The guitar-bass-drums trio the Police (with Sting as lead vocalist and bassist) predated this era by a few years, releasing five albums between 1978 and 1983, which steadily brought them to the #1 slot as the invasion was in full swing: *Outlandos d'Amour* (1978, #25); *Regatta de Blanc* (1979, #23); *Zenyatta Mondatta* (1980, #5); *Ghost in the Machine* (1981, #2); and *Synchronicity* (1983, #1).

At the tail end of this infusion, Brits Peter Gabriel ("Sledgehammer"), formerly of Genesis, and Robert Palmer ("Addicted to Love") both hit #1 in 1986 with unusually innovative music videos that went well beyond the standard fare of their earlier compatriots.

See figure 58. Second British Invasion groups: Artists and first pop Top 10 singles

SUPERSTARS: MICHAEL JACKSON, PRINCE, AND MADONNA

About one dozen solo vocalists in the fields of rock, R&B, and pop had major commercial success in the 1980s (not including groups such as Journey, with vocalist Steve Perry). Five of them were in a class of their own, in terms of visibility: Michael Jackson, Prince, Madonna, Whitney Houston, and Bruce Springsteen (see figure 59).

Michael Jackson (August 29, 1958–June 25, 2009); Prince (June 7, 1958–April 21, 2016); and Madonna (August 16, 1958–) were born within several months of one another in 1958, all in the Midwest: Gary, Indiana; Minneapolis; and Bay City, Michigan, respectively. By the mid-1980s, when they were in their mid to late twenties, they were dominating the pop charts. Jackson is by far the most commercially successful artist since Elvis Presley, and the two of them are in a category of their own.

Jackson was a child star, with sixteen Top 40 pop hits on Motown as lead singer with the Jackson Five from 1969 to 1974. The group made history with their first four singles hitting #1 ("I Want You Back," "ABC," "The Love You Save," and "I'll Be There"). They were not able to maintain that level of chart success and moved to Epic in 1976. Jackson released four solo albums on Motown from 1972 to 1975 with mixed chart success. His solo albums on Epic all hit pop #1 (with the exception of his first): *Off the Wall* (1979, pop #3); *Thriller* (1982); *Bad* (1987); *Dangerous* (1991); *HIStory* (1995); and *Invincible* (2001). Quincy Jones, who had an earlier career as jazz trumpeter, composer, arranger, and record-label executive, produced Jackson's first three Epic albums. Jackson was unusual in the long amount of time between album releases.

Thriller is the second best-selling album of all time in the United States, with thirty-three million copies certified sold as of 2019. It won eight Grammys in 1983: album, record ("Beat It"), male pop vocal ("Thriller"), male rock vocal ("Beat It"), male R&B vocal ("Billie Jean"), R&B song ("Billie Jean"), producer (MJ and Quincy Jones), and engineering. He lost best song (for songwriting) to Sting ("Every Breath You Take"), possibly because his two nominations ("Beat It" and "Billie Jean") split his vote.

Jackson's style in the 1980s was the ultimate mix that appealed to a broad cross-section of listeners. *Thriller* in particular enjoyed widespread critical acclaim for its musical sensibilities, drawing from funk, rock, and postdisco dance music. A duet with Paul McCartney ("The Girl Is Mine") and guitar solo by Eddie Van Halen ("Beat It") on the album helped broaden his appeal. Jackson's unique talent for singing and dancing, honed since childhood and in the public eye for much of his early life, made him one of the greatest entertainers ever, probably the one with the highest global presence in the second half of the twentieth century.

Jackson from the 1980s on was surrounded by controversy on two fronts: plastic surgery on his face (and possible purposeful skin lightening) and allegations of child sexual abuse, resulting in a civil-suit out-of-court settlement (1993) and an acquittal after a grand jury indictment (2005). He was briefly married to Elvis Presley's daughter Lisa Marie in the mid-1990s. Jackson died in 2009 from an overdose of the anesthetic propofol, which was prescribed by his physician to help him sleep. The physician was convicted of involuntary manslaughter in 2011.

Prince Rogers Nelson was a guitarist (and multi-instrumentalist), vocalist, songwriter, dancer, and producer, similar in some ways to Stevie Wonder in terms of his breadth of talents and influences, but updated for the 1980s. Combining the 1960s funk and showmanship of James Brown with the rock virtuosity of Jimi Hendrix, the 1970s theater and sexual exploration of David Bowie with the dance music of Sly Stone, Prince debuted in 1978 on Warner Bros., a major label with which he would have a public legal battle in the mid-1990s to be released from his contract. His early albums progressed up the R&B and then pop charts until his fifth album *1999* (pop #9, R&B #4) broke into the pop Top 10 in 1983, with its singles "1999" (pop #12) and "Little Red Corvette" (pop #6). His next album, the soundtrack to his semiautobiographical film *Purple Rain*, hit pop #1, spawning four Top 10 singles: "When Doves Cry" (pop #1), "Let's Go Crazy" (pop #1), "Purple Rain" (pop #2), and "I Would Die 4 U" (pop #8).

Prince opened up his own Paisley Park recording, performance, and rehearsal studio complex in Minneapolis in 1988, where he recorded prolifically on his own. His sexually oriented lyrics on "Darling Nikki" (on *Purple Rain*) were in part responsible for Tipper Gore founding the Parents Music Resource Center. A virtuoso guitarist, he was able to play all the instruments and produce his own recordings. He died in 2016 of an accidental overdose related to opioid painkiller addiction. In the weeks after his death, five of his albums moved into the pop Top 10 (nineteen albums in total appeared in the two-hundred-position chart). Only Michael Jackson surpassed this, with six albums in the Top 10 immediately following his death in 2009. The Beatles had five albums in the Top 10, also in 2009, when their studio albums were remastered and reissued on CD.

Madonna Louise Ciccone's star power was second only to Michael Jackson in the mid and late 1980s. Between 1984 and 1987 she had fourteen Top 10 pop singles (beginning with "Borderline"), six of which hit #1 (beginning with "Like a Virgin"). Her streak resumed with eleven Top 10 hits between 1989 and 1992 (beginning with "Like a Prayer"). Moving to New York City in 1977, Madonna danced professionally and formed a band, eventually signing to Sire Records in 1982. A magnetic presence on video, Madonna mastered the medium, increasingly pushing the envelope of acceptability.

Defending Madonna's sexually explicit "Justify My Love" (1990) video, Camille Paglia (1990) published an op-ed in the *New York Times*:

> Madonna is the true feminist. She exposes the puritanism and suffocating ideology of American feminism, which is stuck in an adolescent whining mode. Madonna has taught young women to be fully female and sexual while still exercising total control over their lives. She shows girls how to be attractive, sensual, energetic, ambitious, aggressive and funny—all at the same time. . . . Madonna has a far profounder vision of sex than do the feminists. She sees both the animality and the artifice. Changing her costume style and hair color virtually every month, Madonna embodies the eternal values of beauty and pleasure. Feminism says, "No more masks." Madonna says we are nothing but masks. Through her enormous impact on young women around the world, Madonna is the future of feminism.

On the other hand, reacting to the video for "Like a Prayer" (1989), bell hooks saw less progressive politics in Madonna's drawing on black culture: "Given the importance of religious experience and liberation theology in black life, Madonna's use of this imagery seemed particularly offensive. For she made black characters act in complicity with her as she aggressively flaunted her critique of Catholic manners, her attack on organized religion. . . . Black people in the video are caricatures reflecting stereotypes. They appear grotesque. The only role black females have in this video is to catch (i.e., rescue) the 'angelic' Madonna when she is 'falling.' . . . In her own way Madonna is a modern day Shirley Temple" (1992b: 162).

Madonna's albums initially did well on the R&B charts but then dropped until *The Immaculate Collection* (1991, R&B #81), after which she no longer appeared on them. One of the highlights of Madonna's career in this era was "Vogue" (1990), a widely appreciated song and video, which brought mainstream attention to a Harlem underground drag fashion ball and dance culture.[14] Madonna's "Dress You Up" (1984) was on the Parents Music Resource Center's filthy fifteen list for sexually explicit lyrics. As of 2019 Madonna has sold the second-most number of units (album equivalents) in the United States of all women singers at 64.5 million, behind Barbara Streisand (68.5 million), and ahead of Mariah Carey (64 million), and Whitney Houston (58.5 million).

Whitney Houston (1963–2012), from Newark, New Jersey, daughter of gospel and soul singer Cissy Houston, grew up singing in church. In her teens she sang with her mother in nightclubs and modeled (appearing on the cover of *Seventeen* in 1981). Her debut self-titled album hit #1 on the R&B and pop charts, and she would become the top-selling woman R&B artist of the twentieth century and the fourth top-selling woman pop artist (measured by albums). In the 1990s she starred in the films *The Bodyguard*, *Waiting to Exhale*, and *The Preacher's Wife*. Her 1992 cover of Dolly Parton's "I Will Always Love You"—in particular her virtuosic use of gospel-tinged melismas—is often pointed to as the source for the generations of women vocalists who followed in her footsteps. Houston battled addictions later in life and died in 2012 from an accidental drowning in a bathtub.

The other major vocalists include the following. Tina Turner, Janet Jackson, Luther Vandross, and Lionel Ritchie (formerly of the Commodores) had R&B roots. British Nigerian vocalist Sade drew from R&B and jazz. John Mellencamp was rooted in rock, as was British vocalist and drummer Phil Collins (formerly of Genesis). George Michael (formerly of Wham!) was rooted in dance (postdisco) and pop.[15]

See figure 59. Superstars of the 1980s

BAND AID, "WE ARE THE WORLD," AND LIVE AID

In 1983–85 a devastating drought and famine in Ethiopia resulted in one million dead. British rock musician Bob Geldoff (Boomtown Rats), along with the help of Midge Ure (Ultravox), was moved to form Band Aid, a supergroup of several dozen

---

14 See Livingston's (1990-v) documentary *Paris Is Burning*.

15 For more on Michael Jackson, see Vogel (2011) and *Motown 25* (Mischer 1983-v); for Prince, see Hawkins and Niblock (2011) and *Purple Rain* (Magnoli 1984-v); and for Madonna, see Benson and Metz (1999) and *Madonna: Truth or Dare* (Keshishian 1991-v).

high-profile primarily British musicians to record the single "Do They Know It's Christmas" (released November 1984) to raise funds for famine relief. American artists responded by forming United Support of Artists (USA) for Africa and recording "We Are the World," composed by Michael Jackson and Lionel Ritchie and conducted by Quincy Jones. The main recording session took place in Hollywood the night of the American Music Awards in January 1985, ensuring that an A-list of participants would be available, including Stevie Wonder, Bruce Springsteen, Bob Dylan, Billy Joel, Dionne Warwick, Ray Charles, Michael Jackson, and many others.

That summer a major television event called *Live Aid* was broadcast live via satellite with simultaneous concerts on July 13, 1985, in Philadelphia (John F. Kennedy Stadium) and London (Wembley Stadium). The roster of dozens of headliners would ensure a huge audience, including Black Sabbath, Crosby, Stills, and Nash, Judas Priest, the Beach Boys, Santana, Madonna, Kenny Loggins, the Cars, Led Zeppelin, and Duran Duran in Philadelphia; and Elvis Costello, Sade, Sting and Phil Collins, U2, David Bowie, the Who, Elton John, Paul McCartney, and Queen (recognized as one of the great performances in rock and roll) in London. Over 1.5 billion viewers in 150 countries are believed to have tuned in (the largest ever TV audience at the time). Run-D.M.C. performed in Philadelphia before the broadcast began and was not televised. USA for Africa raised over $80 million the first year. Between 1985 and the release of the DVD in 2004, the Band Aid Trust and Live Aid Foundation spent over $144 million on famine relief in Africa.

The song "We Are the World" and the trust and foundation have come in for criticism, despite their good intentions. Music critic Greil Marcus (1985) pointed out that the repeated line in the song "There's a choice we're making" conflates with Pepsi's slogan "The choice of a new generation," suggesting that Pepsi was getting collateral publicity from the composers (Michael Jackson and Lionel Ritchie), who were paid endorsers for Pepsi at the time. Furthermore, Marcus stated, "I think the subliminal message of 'We Are the World' is destructive. The message is, ye have the poor always with you; that there is a 'We,' you and I, who should help a 'Them,' who are not like us; that as we help them we gain points for admission to heaven ('We're saving our own lives'); that hunger, whether in the USA or in Africa, is a natural disaster, in God's hands." In 1986 *Spin* magazine published a series of articles that questioned the efficacy of the actual aid relief in Ethiopia, which was undergoing a civil war with the government diverting international aid efforts (Keating 1986a, 1986b; Guccione 1986).

The year 1985 was a banner year, with two other similar events, although on a smaller scale. Willie Nelson, John Mellencamp, and Neil Young organized Farm Aid, to help U.S. farmers, putting on a marathon concert at the University of Illinois in September. The annual event is still going on (Farm Aid 2019). Guitarist Steven Van Zandt and producer Arthur Baker cofounded United Artists Against Apartheid and recorded the song "Sun City" and album *Sun City* with an all-star cast in October in support of the cultural boycott of South Africa. They declared that they would not perform at the South African resort Sun City, which had been luring American artists to play there, and sales of the recording went to antiapartheid causes. Van Zandt, a veteran of Bruce Springsteen's band, later went on to found the Rock and Roll Forever Foundation, providing educational material for students and teachers (TeachRock 2019a). The events of 1985 are part of a longer trajectory of rock musicians lending their energies for social and political causes (see figure 60).

See figure 60. Rock for a cause

PARENTS MUSIC RESOURCE CENTER

In the early 1980s the national parent-teacher organization (PTO) proposed that recordings that had lyrics with sexually explicit content should carry a label to warn parents. A group of politically connected Washington, DC, mothers, most notably Susan Baker (wife of treasury secretary James Baker III) and Tipper Gore (wife of Senator Al Gore), upset at lyrics in the music of Madonna and Prince (among others) that they heard via their young children, responded by founding the Parents Music Resource Center (PMRC) in May 1985. They began lobbying record labels to either print song lyrics on their album covers so that parents could see what they were buying or put warning labels on certain recordings. They also released a list of fifteen recordings, nicknamed the Filthy Fifteen, that they found particularly offensive, including artists and groups such as Prince, Judas Priest, AC/DC, Twisted Sister, Madonna, Black Sabbath, and Cyndi Lauper.

On September 19, 1985, a Senate hearing, chaired by Senator John Danforth, was held "not to promote any legislation . . . but to simply provide a forum for airing the issue itself . . . for bringing it out in the public domain" (Danforth, qtd. in U.S. Senate 1985: 1). Susan Baker indicated that the PMRC was organized by "mothers of young children who are very concerned by the growing trend in music toward lyrics that are sexually explicit, excessively violent, or glorify the use of drugs and alcohol. Our primary purpose is to educate and inform parents about this alarming trend as well as to ask the industry to exercise self-restraint" (Baker, qtd. in U.S. Senate 1985: 11).

Testifying against any kind of censorship were Dee Snider of Twisted Sister, Frank Zappa, and John Denver:

> My song "Rocky Mountain High" was banned from many radio stations as a drug-related song. This was obviously done by people who had never seen or been to the Rocky Mountains.... What assurance have I that any national panel to review my music would make any better judgment? ... The suppression of the people of a society begins in my mind with the censorship of the written or spoken word. It was so in Nazi Germany. It is so in many places today where those in power are afraid of the consequences of an informed and educated people. In a mature, incredibly diverse society such as ours, the access to all perspectives of an issue becomes more and more important. (Denver, qtd. in U.S. Senate 1985: 65)

In November, the Recording Industry Association of America (RIAA) asked its members to either print lyrics on album covers or affix a warning label. Most record companies chose the label. Walmart, which was a major outlet for record sales, along with some other outlets, declined to carry recordings that had warning labels. According to PMRC's figures, "of the approximately 7500 albums released between January 1986 and August 1989, only 121 contained questionable lyrics and 49 of those were already stickered" (Sanjek 1996: 669).[16]

Objections to lyrics in rock and R&B have a much longer history: "Music 'leerics' are touching new lows and if the fast-buck songsmiths and musicmakers are incapable of social responsibility and self-restraint then regulation-policing, if you will—will have to come from more responsible sources.... VARIETY urges a strong self-examination of the record business by its most responsible chief executive officers" (Abel 1955). Later that year (1955) the Houston chapter of the NAACP called for action to clean up the airwaves. As a result, Houston's juvenile delinquency and crime commission formed a "wash-out-the-air" committee, headed by a sociology

---

16 Chastagner (1999) and Schonfeld (2015) provide alternate takes on the PMRC. See Senate Commerce, Science and Transportation Committee (1985-v) for video of the hearing, including testimony from Zappa, Denver, and Snider.

professor at the historically black Texas Southern University. "First act of the group was to list 26 waxings mostly by indie labels, that had bothered Negro leaders as degrading or possibly contributory to juvenile delinquency. Most of the 26 were by Negro artists" (*Variety* 1955: 51). The artists included Ray Charles, B. B. King, Etta James, the Dominoes, and Elvis Presley ("Good Rockin' Tonight").

ALTERNATIVE, INDIE ROCK, AND HARDCORE

Throughout the 1980s local music scenes surfaced with punk-influenced bands playing original music, recording on independent labels, and playing to local crowds. For lack of a better term, they all became lumped into the marketing category *alternative* or *indie rock* (because they recorded on independent record labels). Especially productive locations included Minneapolis (Hüsker Dü, the Replacements); New York City (Sonic Youth); Boston (Pixies); Athens, Georgia (R.E.M., Indigo Girls); and the Pacific Northwest (the Melvins, Soundgarden, Mudhoney, Nirvana, Alice in Chains, and Pearl Jam) (see figure 61). Often late to catch on, the music industry awarded its first Alternative Music Performance Grammy in 1991, to Sinéad O'Connor. Subsequent winners from 1992–98 were R.E.M., Tom Waits, U2, Green Day, Nirvana, Beck, and Radiohead.

Few gained much commercial presence in the 1980s, other than R.E.M., and it was not until 1991 that the scene broke wide open with Nirvana's second album, *Nevermind* (1991, #1), which sold four million copies less than a year after its release (it sold ten million by 1999), with its single "Smells Like Teen Spirit" hitting #6 on the pop chart. The floodgates quickly opened for a remarkable concentration of like-minded Pacific Northwest bands: Alice in Chains (*Dirt*, 1992, #6); Pearl Jam (*Ten*, 1992, #2); and Soundgarden (*Superunknown*, 1994, #1).

The term *grunge* was in national print the year of Nirvana's debut album (*Bleach*, 1989), which did not chart, and Soundgarden's second album (*Louder than Love*, #108), which did: "Soundgarden are Seattle's heaviest contenders since Jimi Hendrix. Amidst the crop of grunge bands flourishing in the Pacific Northwest, they're the one that could become the metal band for people who hate metal" (Corcoran 1989: 41). A few months earlier the Boston-based Pixies had attracted the following formula in a *Spin* magazine feature: "*Practice + sonic grunge – sarcasm = cool rock songs*" (Macnie 1989: 16). Nirvana lead singer Kurt Cobain (1967–94) was thrust into the spotlight as a culture hero, solidified by Nirvana's 1993 appearance on *MTV*

Unplugged playing acoustic instruments; the resulting album *MTV Unplugged in New York* (1994) debuted at #1, selling five million copies within three years and winning a Grammy Award in the Alternative Music category. Cobain succumbed to addictions and depression, committing suicide in 1994. Nirvana drummer Dave Grohl went on to form Foo Fighters, releasing a string of Top 10 albums from the late 1990s onward.

Talking Heads front man David Byrne has suggested that the commercial success of Nirvana was the culmination of a lineage extending from punk in the mid-1970s:

> Radio and a lot of the media in the States finally caught on about three or four years ago with the Nirvana phenomenon. There was a small film that came out around then. It was a documentary of a tour of Sonic Youth and Nirvana and it was called *1990*, or something, *The Year Punk Broke*. And it was an accurate title because it's almost as if in the States, at least, more than ten years after the fact, finally the radio stations and the media and whatnot realized that something was going on. The original groups, Clash and Sex Pistols, and us and all, most of us had long since disappeared. But in a sense we'd finally succeeded through these other groups. (David Byrne, speaking in the mid-1990s, qtd. in Espar and Thomson 1995-v, episode 9)[17]

The Pixies have been cited by Kurt Cobain as an important and direct influence: "I connected with that band so heavily I should have been *in* that band" (qtd. in Fricke 1994: 36). David Bowie, also a fan of the Pixies, suggested that they changed the format for delivering harder rock in the 1980s, appreciating three aspects: sound dynamics: a quiet verse, erupting in a blaze of noise in the chorus (the model for Nirvana's "Smells Like Teen Spirit"); interesting juxtapositions that lyricist Charles "Black Francis" Thompson brought together, including sordid material, with a sense of imagination and humor; and colors and extraordinary texture that guitarist Santiago provided.[18]

New York City–based Sonic Youth picked up fifteen years after the Velvet Underground left off in the late 1960s, with guitarists-vocalists Thurston Moore and Lee Ranaldo exploring noise and drones. Their bass guitarist, Kim Gordon (2015), was part of an unusual lineage of women bass players, including Carol Kaye (1960s Wrecking

---

17 See Markey (1992-v) for *1991: The Year Punk Broke*.

18 Bowie's comments, sprinkled throughout Quinn's (2001-v) documentary, may be found edited together on YouTube ("Bowie on Pixies," posted August 11, 2009).

Crew studio band), Tina Weymouth (Talking Heads), Janice-Marie Johnson (A Taste of Honey), and Kim Deal (Pixies, the Breeders).

The closest British equivalent to an American alternative rock band may have been Manchester's the Smiths, with lead vocalist Morrissey and guitarist Johnny Marr. Bucking the trend of synthpop dance music, their transparent guitar-bass-drums plus lead vocalist format brought them to #1 or #2 on the UK album charts, right from their debut album (*The Smiths*, 1984) through the 1980s, barely registering on U.S. charts until their third album, *The Queen Is Dead* (1986, #70). Their contemporaries R.E.M. (from Athens, Georgia), with a similar trio plus vocalist lineup, remained in the Top 40 from their debut album, *Murmur* (1983, #36), until their fifth album, *R.E.M. #5: Document* (1987, #10), broke into the Top 10.

One legacy of 1970s punk's anticommercial stance led to what became known as *hardcore punk* or simply *hardcore*.

> Hardcore was born as a double-negative genre: a rebellion against a rebellion. The early punks were convinced that rock and roll had gone wrong and were resolved to put it right, deflating arena-rock pretension with crude songs and rude attitudes. . . . But when punk, too, came to seem lame, the hardcore kids arrived, eager to show up their elders. The idea was to out-punk the punks, thereby recapturing the wild promise of the genre, with its tantalizing suggestion that rock music should be something more than mere entertainment—that it should, somehow, pose a threat to mainstream culture. (Sanneh 2015: 82)

This threat to mainstream culture, captured in the title of Spheeris's (1981-v) documentary about the early scene in Los Angeles—*The Decline of Western Civilization*—ensured that none of these bands broke into the pop charts. Some of the more particularly vibrant scenes in the early 1980s include the following:

> Los Angeles: Black Flag (EP *Nervous Breakdown*, 1979; *Damaged* [with Henry Rollins], 1981); Circle Jerks (*Group Sex*, 1980); X (*Los Angeles*, 1980)
> San Francisco: Dead Kennedys [with Jello Biafra] (*Fresh Fruit for Rotting Vegetables*, 1980; EP *In God We Trust, Inc.*, 1981)
> Washington, DC: Minor Threat [with Ian MacKaye] (EP *Minor Threat*, 1981); Bad Brains (moved to New York City in 1981)
> New York City: Bad Brains (*Bad Brains*, 1982)

In the predominantly white genre of hardcore, the widely admired all-black group Bad Brains stood out, although they were not alone. Twenty years later the documentary *Afro-Punk* (Spooner 2003-v) examined the phenomenon of blacks drawn to punk, spawning annual Afro-Punk festivals in Brooklyn, Atlanta, London, Paris, and Johannesburg (Afropunk 2019). New York–based Living Colour (with guitarist Vernon Reid) defied categories, as an African American guitar-bass-drums plus lead vocalist band looking to reclaim the legacy of Jimi Hendrix, drawing on a spectrum of rock and funk styles (Mahon 2004). They did not register on R&B charts but rather hit the upper reaches of the pop charts (they recorded on the major label subsidiary Epic): their greatest success came with their debut album *Vivid* (1988, pop #6) and its single "Cult of Personality" (pop #13), which won a Grammy for Best Hard Rock Performance.[19]

See figure 61. Alternative, indie, and postpunk

ELECTRONIC DANCE MUSIC

Electronic dance music (EDM) is a general umbrella term that covers an unwieldy array of musical genres and subgenres that foreground synthesized or sampled sounds with a beat strong enough to sustain interest in a dance space. The term dates from the early 1980s, labeling a phenomenon that began to take shape in the mid-1970s, about five years after electronic synthesizers first came onto the commercial market. Two works were key: the German electronic quartet Kraftwerk's twenty-two-plus-minute "Autobahn" (March 1975, pop #25), on their album *Autobahn* (February 1975, pop #5); and the collaboration between producer partners Giorgio Moroder and Pete Belotte and vocalist Donna Summer, "I Feel Love" (August 1977, pop #6, R&B #9) on her fifth album *I Remember Yesterday* (June 1977, pop #18, R&B #11). These represent the experimental electronic and disco origins of the art form.[20] In the 1980s British synthpop, Chicago house, and Detroit techno laid the foundation for the mainstream incursion of EDM, beginning with Madonna's "Vogue" (1990, pop

---

19 For more on grunge and hardcore, see Waksman (2009), Blush (2010), Yarm (2011), Spheeris (1981-v, 1988a-v, 1998b-v), and Rachman (2006-v); for indie and alternative, see Azerrad (2001) and Caress (2015).

20 Wendy Carlos's synthesizer soundtrack to the 1971 film *A Clockwork Orange*, a futuristic depiction of British youth delinquency, offered inspiration for early British EDM bands.

#1), MTV's weekly show *Amp* (1996–2001), and the Prodigy's *The Fat of the Land* (1997, pop #1), released on Madonna's Maverick label, all of which in turn led to EDM deejay concert performers gaining superstar status in the early 2000s.

Kraftwerk drew one of the earliest print usages of the term *electronic dance music*, in 1981 from David Ball of the British band Soft Cell: "Kraftwerk should have got much higher in the charts. They're the innovators of this electronic dance music" (qtd. in Bohn 1981: 28).[21] The 1975 British television appearance and tour of Kraftwerk was an important milestone. Andy McCluskey of Orchestral Manouevres in the Dark saw them in Liverpool and "witnessed the first day of the rest of my life. '75 was all, you know, the era of long hair and flared trousers and guitar solos, and these guys all came out in suits and ties, two of them look like they were playing the electronic tea trays with wired up knitting needles. And I was just blown away" (qtd. in Whalley 2009-v).

Kraftwerk electronic percussionist Wolfgang Flür remembered the occasion: "[We had] on grey suits, short hair, you know, and we looked like the children of [aerospace scientist] Wernher von Braun or [electrical engineer] Werner von Siemens. We saw us, you know, [as] engineer musicians. . . . There was a knock at our backstage door. . . . [OMD leader Andy McCluskey] said, 'You know guys, you have shown us the future, this is it! We throw away our guitars tomorrow and buy all synthesizers!'" (qtd. in Whalley 2009-v).

Hip hop pioneer Afrika Bambaataa, whose 1982 "Planet Rock" drew heavily on Kraftwerk, was similarly impressed with

these funky white boys from Germany that had this futuristic sound. When I first heard "Trans-Europe Express" [released 1978], I mean, I just went crazy and started gettin' it jammed at every party that we played in the Bronx. . . . [That record] caught on like hellfire with the black and Latino community. And I thought this would be the music for the future. . . . I started diggin' up a lot of other Kraftwerk records like "Robots," "Autobahn." So I looked around and started sayin', "I don't see no black electronic groups." So when

---

21 The American duo Suicide drew earlier print references: "basic electronic dance patterns," about their 1977 self-titled debut album, and "This is electronic dance music but it's raw, ugly, vicious and totally uncompromising," about their 1980 second album, *Suicide: Alan Vega and Martin Rev* (Needs 1980).

Kraftwerk came out with "Numbers" [1981], I said, "Yeah, that's where that electro funk would come"[22] (qtd. in Espar and Thomson 1995-v, episode 10).

Kraftwerk was having a similar impact in Detroit: "'They were so stiff, they were funky,' [Detroit] techno pioneer Carl Craig has said of Kraftwerk. This paradox—which effectively translates as 'they were so white, they were black'—is as close as anyone has got to explaining the mystery of why Kraftwerk's music had such a massive impact on black American youth" (Reynolds 1998: 14).

Part of the attraction may have been an appreciation for hearing soul and funk beamed back from abroad in new clothing. Kraftwerk electronic percussionist Karl Bartos noted, "We were all fans of American music: soul, the whole Tamla/Motown thing, and of course James Brown. We always tried to make an American rhythm feel, with a European approach to harmony and melody" (qtd. in Sicko 2010: 10). Yellow Magic Orchestra's convincing cover of Archie Bell and the Drells' "Tighten Up" (1968), from their 1980 album, *X∞Multiplies*, and performed on *Soul Train*, shows a similar familiarity with, and playful control of, soul and funk styles (Dex Digital 2017).

Electronic dance music is a transnational conversation, one of the first times in which African American musicians have fully participated in extended overseas exchanges, more so than earlier jazz circulations. Giorgio Moroder, born and raised in northern Italy, settled in Munich in his late twenties, where he teamed up with English producer Pete Belotte. There, in 1975, they began working with Boston-native Donna Summer (who had been singing in Broadway shows in Germany), almost singlehandedly establishing a Eurodisco aesthetic. Reynolds (1998: 24–25) has credited Moroder with three innovations that would lay the foundation for 1980s Chicago house and, consequently, electronic dance music more generally: (1) the dramatically extended megamix, beginning with Donna Summer's 1975 "Love to Love You Baby," which Moroder edited from a four-minute single to a sixteen-minute remix; (2) the four-to-the-floor bass drum disco pulse rhythm; and (3) purely electronic (synthesizer-based) dance music, beginning with Donna Summer's 1977 "I Feel Love."[23]

---

22 "Trans-Europe Express" entered the U.S. charts in June 1978 (pop #67); "Numbers" entered the charts in November 1981 (R&B #22, pop #103).

23 Lawrence (2003: 173–75) and Fink (2005a: 42, 55–61) discuss the "Love to Love You Baby" remix.

Kraftwerk came from Düsseldorf, part of a German wave of synthesizer-oriented bands, including Tangerine Dream (West Berlin) and Harmonia (Forst). Tokyo-based electronic band Yellow Magic Orchestra released their self-titled debut album in Japan in 1978 and in the United States the following year (January 1980, pop #81, R&B #27). YMO band member Ryuichi Sakamoto released his synth-heavy solo debut album, *Thousand Knives*, in 1978; his "Technopolis" on YMO's second album (*Solid State Survivor*, 1979) may have spawned the term *technopop*, which appeared about 1979 to describe YMO and then the early wave of British synth bands.[24]

Those British bands began releasing albums in 1979–80, not yet breaching the U.S. pop charts, but enjoying some UK chart success: Human League and Cabaret Voltaire from Sheffield; Joy Division from Manchester; and Orchestral Manoeuvres in the Dark from Merseyside. Within a year or two other bands breached the U.S. charts: Depeche Mode (*Speak and Spell*, 1981, #192) from Basildon; ABC (*The Lexicon of Love*, 1982, #24) and Heaven 17 (*Heaven 17*, 1983, #68) from Sheffield; and New Order ("Blue Monday," 1983, dance #5) from Manchester.[25] By the middle of 1982 Human League had spearheaded the second British Invasion with a #1 hit ("Don't You Want Me"), immediately followed by Soft Cell ("Tainted Love," #8) (see figure 58). By the end of the year, *Billboard* magazine had taken note of a "New British Invasion," referring to them as "techno-pop" groups (Kozak 1982). The broader category of synthpop can be distinguished from EDM, in that former features songs with prominent solo vocals with narrative lyrics; vocals in EDM are usually less prominent.[26]

In 1982 the oldest of three black deejay-producers who met in high school in the predominantly white middle-class enclave of Belleville outside of Detroit began releasing singles.[27] Juan Atkins led a wave (along with the other two) that yielded the 1988 compilation that would name a style and have a major impact on the future of electronic dance music: *Techno! The New Dance Sound of Detroit* (Rushton and May

---

24 See Comerford (1979), Henke (1980), and Kozak (1982). The 2017 documentary *Ryuichi Sakamoto: Coda* covers some of the many Hollywood films for which he wrote music, including *Merry Christmas, Mr. Lawrence* (1983), starring David Bowie; *The Last Emperor* (1987); and *The Revenant* (2015).

25 Before ABC, band member Martin Fry notes, "We were a four piece synthesizer group playing what we saw as electronic dance music" (qtd. in Martin 1982: 25). After the death of band member Ian Curtis, Joy Division reformed to become New Order.

26 For more on the regional scenes in England at this time, see Reynolds (2006).

27 Sicko (2010) is the major resource for Detroit techno.

1988-d). The Belleville Three, Atkins (1962–) and Derrick May (1963–), both born in Detroit, and Kevin Saunderson (1964–), born in Brooklyn, all moved to Belleville when they were in their teens. Atkins and May deejayed in high school, navigating the distinct inner-city and preppy high school scenes unique to Detroit's socioeconomic history, which included eclectic appreciation for Motown, funk, new wave, Eurodisco, and German and British synth groups.

When Cybotron, the duo of Juan Atkins and Vietnam veteran Richard "Rik" Davis, released their debut singles "Alleys of Your Mind" and "Cosmic Cars" in 1982, a supportive Detroit radio deejay, Charles Johnson ("the Electrifying Mojo"), gave them airplay, and they gained a local following. The West Coast Fantasy label put out their debut album, *Enter* (1983), whose single "Clear" hit #52 on the R&B chart (called *black* at the time).[28] *Billboard* (1983) ran a short profile, in which Davis credited Jimi Hendrix, Pink Floyd, and Tangerine Dream as inspirations, referring to Cybotron's sound as "techno-wave." As a black Detroiter, Davis understood the racial dynamics and went by the name 3070, "to confuse those who would insist on ethnic designations" (*Billboard* 1983).[29] After "Techno City" (1984) Atkins went solo (using the name Model 500), releasing "No UFOs" (1985) on his Metroplex label. This was an underground do-it-yourself world, where the artists formed their own labels to put out their own music.

Derrick May (aka Mayday), deeply impressed by deejay Frankie Knuckles and the house scene in Chicago, began releasing records on his own Transmat label under the name Rhythim Is Rhythim in 1987, including "Nude Photo" and "Strings of Life," which contained samples from the Detroit Symphony Orchestra. His debut album, *Innovator: Soundtrack for the Tenth Planet*, was first issued in the United Kingdom in 1991.[30] Kevin Saunderson (aka Master Reece) formed the group Inner City with vocalist Paris Grey (from outside of Chicago), releasing the single "Big Fun" (November 1988, R&B #50) and album *Big Fun* (February 1990, pop #162, R&B #58) on his own KMS label. Four singles from the album hit #1 on *Billboard*'s Hot Dance Music chart between 1988 and 1989, including the title track and the crossover "Good Life" (March 1989, pop #73). Inner City would place five songs in the UK Top 20 during

---

28 Missy Elliot's 2005 hit "Lose Control" (pop #3) samples "Clear" prominently. *Enter* was renamed *Clear* in 1990. Davis's solo recording "Methane Sea" (1978) was a prototype of the style.

29 Davis later cited Carlos's synthesizer soundtrack for *2001: A Space Odyssey* and Ultravox's *Rage in Eden* (1981) as inspirations (Rubin 2016).

30 May performed some of his works with the Detroit Symphony Orchestra in 2015 (DK 2015).

this time and sell close to six million records in the 1980s, making them one of the biggest commercial successes of the underground Detroit techno scene.[31]

The UK connection came in 1988, when Birmingham (UK) record-label owner Neil Rushton collaborated with May on *Techno! The New Dance Sound of Detroit*, licensing tracks from the Belleville Three's labels. Atkins contributed "Techno Music," which named the genre once the compilation was released on Virgin subsidiary 10 Records, moving a relatively obscure Midwestern musical style onto the international market (Rushton and May 1988-d).[32] Detroit deejays performed in London clubs, although northern England (Birmingham, Sheffield, and Manchester) had greater interest in techno, making the association with its earlier northern soul legacy. Home to the Smiths and New Order, Manchester was particularly sympathetic to techno, as was Sheffield, where Warp Records began releasing their own version of techno. "The parallels between Detroit and Sheffield are numerous: struggles with an industrial base and near-fatal dependency on it, great musical traditions (Detroit's Motown and Sheffield's synth-pop), limited options for youth, and so on" (Sicko 2010: 76). Rushton's (1990-d) compilation, *Bio Rhythm*, featured techno artists from both Detroit and Sheffield.[33] Techno would take off in the United Kingdom, creating an unprecedented number of subgenres, the most well-known of which would be drum and bass, which absorbed parts of hip hop and Jamaican dub. Goldie's 1995 debut album, *Timeless*, is a classic in the style.

Chicago house was contemporaneous with Detroit techno in the 1980s, although its dynamics played out differently, thriving in clubs underground before commercial vinyl records were released in 1984. Comparing house and techno, Derrick May said, "It's a difference of respect. House still has its heart in '70s disco. We don't have any of that respect for the past. Its strictly future music. We have a much greater aptitude for experiment" (qtd. in Cosgrove 1988b). Godfather of house Frankie Knuckles acknowledged the connection, hitting on one reason why house may have been welcomed in England, where a decade earlier punk had stripped down the excesses of rock: "House was initially a reaction against the overproduction of disco, and that

---

31 For UK chart appearances, search "Inner City" in Official Charts (2019).

32 Atkins called the style *techno* in Cosgrove (1988a: 86). May found the term too limiting, preferring *electronic dance music* (Needs 1990).

33 Follow-up releases include *Equinox* (Booker 1991-d), which featured the next generation of Detroiters like Carl Craig, and *Tresor II* (1993-d), a compilation that paired Detroit and Berlin.

reaction was, quite rightly, to want to strip things down. So we got a lot of stripped-down beat tracks which was fine in the beginning" (qtd. in Owen 1987).

The summer and fall of 1986 was a watershed for house, when sudden national and international media attention broke, with a flurry of articles devoted to it in *Billboard*, *Melody Maker* and two other British magazines, and *Spin*.[34] A New Music Seminar in New York in July 1986, highlighting Chicago's DJ International label artists, was a catalyst (Chin 1986), and a compilation album released in the United Kingdom that year (*House Sound of Chicago* 1986-d) set off a wave of interest there.

Frankie Knuckles (1955–2014) birthed the style. Born in the Bronx, New York, Knuckles deejayed in his teens at the Continental Baths in New York City with his friend Larry Levan. Knuckles moved to Chicago to deejay at the Warehouse in 1977 and soon developed a following that was legendary. Knuckles had a special talent for moving a crowd, expertly mixing mainstream and underground tracks into each other for a nonstop all-night dance event. As a gay black deejay catering to a gay black crowd in one of America's largest black communities and trained in one of New York City's premier gay institutions, Knuckles created a welcoming place of respite, what many felt as a religious experience: "For most of the people that went to The Warehouse it was Church" (Knuckles, qtd. in Broughton 1995 [2010]: 234). Not serving alcoholic beverages, the Warehouse could legally stay open all night, and so the music would go from Saturday evening through Sunday morning or afternoon.

In the early 1980s Knuckles began making his own edits via tape: "I would rerecord, reedit, and extend existing records. I would take the break section and make a new intro with it. I would restructure the song in the middle, change the break around a little bit, and up the tempo via the pitch control" (qtd. in Lawrence 2003: 408; see also Broughton 1995). The owner of the Warehouse, Richard Williams, noted that "those edits drove the crowd wild: 'You'd be like, I [have] that album at home, and it doesn't sound like that. What the hell is going on?'" (qtd. in J. Arnold 2012). About this time the term *house* became shorthand for the kind of records that Knuckles would play at the Warehouse, connected to the record store Importes Etc., which collaborated with Knuckles by stocking the music he played there (J. Arnold 2016). The term had entered the youth lexicon as slang roughly equivalent to cool, hip, or the latest fashion. The peculiar style of dancing to house became known as *jacking*.

---

34 George (1986); Chin (1986); Owen (1986); Garratt (1986); Witter (1986); Walters (1986).

Knuckles left the Warehouse in 1983 to open up his own place, Power Plant (1983–86), then on to C.O.D.s (1986), Power House (1987), a residency at Delirium in London in September 1987, and then back to New York in 1988 (Lawrence 2005: 47). After Knuckles left the Warehouse it changed names to the Music Box, where Chicago native Ron Hardy would deejay. Knuckles and Hardy would provide the laboratory from 1983 onward for a creative cauldron, in which young aspiring producers would bring their works on tape to the club to be played that night to gauge crowd reaction. This laboratory was supported by a group of deejays known as the Hot Mix Five, who began playing extended mixes in 1981 of dance music on WBMX FM, establishing an audience for the music played in clubs as well as an eventual outlet for local producers.

About 1983 some deejays began bringing in drum machines to play along with their records. Knuckles got his first drum machine, a Roland TR 909, about 1984 from Derrick May.[35] Local radio and a rich club scene with deejays Knuckles, Hardy, Farley "Jackmaster Funk" Keith (1962–), and Steve "Silk" Hurley (1962–) created an atmosphere that soon encouraged local production.

Jamie Principle's "Your Love," produced by Knuckles, was the first house track, initially distributed on reel-to-reel tape; it was not released on vinyl until 1986. Jesse Saunders and Vince Lawrence's "On and On" was the first house track distributed on vinyl, in early 1984, using a drum machine, synthesized bass, sparse vocals, and some sound effects. "'We didn't think we could touch Jamie, but Jesse's bullshit sold, and we could visualize doing better than that,' says post office worker Marshall Jefferson, who was keeping half an eye on the unfolding scene. 'Jesse was responsible for the house music boom. Without Jesse Saunders, the non-musician would not be making music'" (Lawrence 2005: 16).

In 1985 two local independent record labels were established to release house music on vinyl: Trax and DJ International. Early house recordings mainly used drum machines and synthesizers. They occasionally registered on the national dance charts but rarely crossed over to the R&B or pop charts, and some found success on the British singles chart. Some key early recordings include the following:

JM Silk (producer Steve "Silk" Hurley and vocalist Keith Nunnally), "Music Is the Key" (September 1985, dance #9); sold eighty-five thousand twelve-inch

35 See Walters (1986: 62), Broughton (1995 [2010]: 236), and Lawrence (2005: 15).

singles, pointing up a new market; DJ International's first record and first house track to chart nationally.

Chip E., "Like This" (December 1985, dance #15); EP *Jack Trax*: "It's House," "Time to Jack" (1985).

Jesse Saunders and Farley Jackmaster Funk, "Love Can't Turn Around" (July 1986, dance #15; August 1986, UK #10), with vocalist Daryl Pandy; first house track to chart in United Kingdom; lyric rewrite of Isaac Hayes's "I Can't Turn Around" (1975).

JM Silk, "Jack Your Body" (July 1986, dance #25; January 1987, UK #1), at top of UK singles chart, inspired British group M/A/R/R/S' hit "Pump Up the Volume" (entered U.S. charts October 1987, pop #13, R&B #8, dance #1).

JM Silk, "I Can't Turn Around" (October 1986, dance #1); RCA label debut; cover of Isaac Hayes's "I Can't Turn Around" (1975).

Marshall Jefferson (aka Virgo), "Move Your Body (The House Music Anthem)" (1986); mixed by Ron Hardy, first house track to use a piano.

By the mid-1980s house demographics in Chicago opened up beyond its predominantly black gay origins, but house was not able to break into a national market. Picked up by the major label RCA, JM Silk's debut album *Hold on to Your Dream* did not chart (partly because the local language got lost in an attempt to go "urban contemporary"), and they were dropped from the label (Owen 1987). Marshall Jefferson produced and mixed "Acid Tracks" (1987) by the trio Phuture (with DJ Pierre), which would give rise to acid house, which had an important impact in England. "Acid Tracks" utilized the TB [transistor bass] 303, a failed project by the Japanese Roland Corporation initially intended to emulate a bass line to accompany guitarists. Roland discontinued it, only to see Chicago musicians repurposing it, setting off an international wave.[36] This kind of experimental stretching of technology for new purposes is typical of African American, indeed, African diasporic artistic practice: Jamaican dub in the 1970s is the paradigmatic example (Veal 2007).

House lyrics mainly concerned dancing and sex: "The entire lyric for 'Time to Jack' was 'Time to jack, jack your body,' because that was all that was important. . . . People

---

36 Roland has recently issued a digital version of the TB 303 (Hamill 2014). For a listing of acid house documentaries, see Kent-Smith (2018); for an album compilation of acid house, see *Can You Jack?* (S. Baker 2005-d).

didn't need to hear a story. 'Time to jack, jack your body'—that was the story right there" (Chip E., qtd. in Lawrence 2005: 43). That story gains significance, given the context of the mid-1980s (the acronym AIDS was coined in 1982, and by the end of 1985 over 3,500 AIDS deaths were reported by the CDC).[37] "For Chicago's black gays threatened by AIDS, jacking the night away at an after-hours club has become the most physically gratifying alternative to sex. . . . [Chip E.:] 'We gear our music for dancing, not for radio.' . . . House is about the loss of decorum and control. From sexual extravagance to dance-floor excess, everything about house is geared toward *losing it*" (Walters 1986: 62, 64).

In 1987 the city of Chicago passed a law requiring juice bars to keep the same hours as liquor bars, and the club scene soon declined. WBMX went off air the following year, and the doors opened for hip hop, which had not yet made much of a dent in the city. But by then Knuckles had paved the way for the future of the solo deejay superstar. "For a night's work Frankie often earns more than most of us make in a month, but he's worth it. Whereas most DJs play two-hour slots, Frankie won't desert the decks for eight to ten hours at a stretch, and what he does to records has to be heard to be believed" (Witter 1987: 17).

House lived on in Europe, as deejays were engaging larger and larger crowds in new club and rave cultures. Madonna's "Vogue" (entered charts April 1990, pop #1, dance #1, R&B #16), which sold two million copies within several months, drew on house, giving it a certain legitimacy that bypassed, however, most of its pioneers.[38] "The first time I actually realized that house had become a worldwide . . . phenomenon was with Madonna's 'Vogue.' I just looked at that record and what it had done here in the United States and I just thought, it's legit now" (Frankie Knuckles, qtd. in Espar and Thomson 1995-v, episode 10). By the early 2010s deejays were rivaling major rock bands in their performance fees, and *Forbes* magazine began compiling its "World's Highest Paid DJs List" in 2012 (Greenburg 2012).[39]

See figure 58. Second British Invasion groups: Artists and first pop Top 10 singles

---

37 By the end of 1991 the World Health Organization estimated that 8–12 million people were HIV-positive, including 1.5 million to have progressed to AIDS.

38 The piano in the chorus to "Vogue" evokes the sound of Marshall Jefferson's "Move Your Body" (1986) and Derrick May's "Strings of Life" (1987).

39 For documentaries on house, see Hindmarch (2001-v) and Sumner (2017-v).

INTO THE 1990s

Major developments in the early 1990s included the mainstream arrival of heavy metal, rap, and alternative (grunge) at the top of the pop charts, including Metallica's 1991 *Metallica* (#1) and albums by N.W.A., Ice Cube, Dr. Dre, Snoop Dogg, Nirvana, Pearl Jam, and Soundgarden (see figures 53, 54, and 61). By the mid-1990s a new generation of rap groups and solo stars had taken over the scene (see figures 62 and 63). The groups included Wu-Tang Clan, base for an extraordinary number of rappers who went solo (Method Man, GZA, Ol' Dirty Bastard, Raekwon, Ghostface Killah, and RZA, who produced for others); A Tribe Called Quest; the Roots; the Fugees; Arrested Development; and Outkast. The solo stars of this generation defined a state of the art that remains the standard: Tupac Shakur, Snoop Dogg, Jay-Z, Notorious B.I.G, and Nas. Women rappers came into their own just after this generation hit, including Lil' Kim and Missy Elliot in the second half of the decade.

By the mid-1990s white women singer-songwriters leading bands came back with a passion, including Sheryl Crow and Lisa Loeb in 1994; Alanis Morissette and Joan Osborne in 1995; Jewel in 1996; and Paula Cole, Shawn Colvin, Sarah McLachlan, and Fiona Apple in 1997 (see figure 64). Boy bands were all the rage by the second half of the decade, initially kicked off by New Kids on the Block (with Donnie Wahlberg) in the late 1980s and Boyz II Men in the early 1990s, and then picked up by Backstreet Boys and NSYNC (with Justin Timberlake).

The music industry changed dramatically in the early 2000s as sales of physical media such as CDs, cassettes, and vinyl dropped off due to digital downloading. With retail sales in the United States declining from $14.58 billion in 1999 to $8.48 billion by 2008, the industry was forced to rethink its model. Online streaming services and social media platforms such as YouTube emerged as waves of the future, altering recorded music–consumption patterns forever. Even so, singles and albums maintain their currency as the stock-in-trade of the music business, an extraordinary phenomenon given all that has transpired since the beginnings of rock and roll.

See figure 53. Rap groups and LPs moving into the mainstream, 1984–1990

See figure 54. Some key rap record labels

See figure 61. Alternative, indie, and postpunk

See figure 62. Rap groups entering the pop Top 10 (albums), 1992–1997

See figure 63. Solo emcees entering the pop Top 10 (albums), 1993–1997

See figure 64. Women rock singer-songwriters, 1994–1997

II

FIGURES

FIGURE 1. COPYRIGHT IN THE UNITED STATES

All of the text in this section is excerpted and edited from the following United States Copyright Office publications (www.copyright.gov/circs):
Copyright Basics (circular 1, rev. 2017)
United States Copyright Office: A Brief Introduction and History (circular 1a)
Compulsory License for Making and Distributing Phonorecords (circular 73, rev. 2018)
Music Licensing Reform, Statement of Marybeth Peters, The Register of Copyrights, before the
    Subcommittee on Intellectual Property, Committee on the Judiciary, United States Senate,
    July 12, 2005
More Information on Fair Use
(Some terms and lines are in boldface to signal their importance or in brackets to clarify.)

It is a principle of American law that an author of a work may reap the fruits of his or her intellectual creativity for a limited period of time. Copyright is a form of protection provided by the laws of the United States for original works of authorship, including literary, dramatic, musical, architectural, cartographic, choreographic, pantomimic, pictorial, graphic, sculptural, and audiovisual creations. "Copyright" literally means the right to copy. The term has come to mean that body of exclusive rights granted by law to authors for protection of their work. (circular 1a)

Copyright provides the owner of copyright with the exclusive right to:

1. Reproduce the work in copies or phonorecords [audio recordings];
2. Prepare derivative works [e.g., translation, abridgement, arrangement] based upon the work;
3. Distribute copies or phonorecords of the work to the public by sale or other transfer of ownership or by rental, lease, or lending;
4. Perform the work publicly if it is a literary, musical, dramatic, or choreographic work; a pantomime; or a motion picture or other audiovisual work;
5. Display the work publicly if it is a literary, musical, dramatic, or choreographic work; a pantomime; or a pictorial, graphic, or sculptural work. This right also applies to the individual images of a motion picture or other audiovisual work;
6. Perform the work publicly by means of a digital audio transmission if the work is a sound recording. (circular 1)

The owner of copyright has the exclusive right to license others to engage in the same acts under specific terms and conditions. Copyright protection **does not extend to any idea, procedure, process, slogan, principle, or discovery**. (circular 1a)

Compulsory License (section 115 of the Copyright Act)

Due to concerns about potential monopolistic behavior, Congress also created a **compulsory license** to allow anyone to make and distribute a **mechanical reproduction** of [their own version of] a nondramatic musical work without the consent of the copyright owner provided that the person adhered to the provisions of the license, most notably paying a statutorily established royalty to the copyright owner. (*Music Licensing Reform*)

Section 115 does not cover sound recordings. Rather, it covers the reproduction and distribution of nondramatic musical compositions. **A musical composition and a sound recording are two separate works for copyright purposes. The author of a musical composition is generally the composer and any lyricist.** A sound recording, on the other hand, is the fixation of a series of musical spoken, or other sounds, often of a musical composition. **The author of a sound recording is generally the performer(s)** whose performance is fixed **and the producer** who captures and processes the performance to make the final recording. Licenses generally must be obtained separately from the copyright owners of the sound recording and the underlying musical composition. **Copyright in a sound recording is not the same as, or a substitute for, copyright in the underlying musical composition.**

Anyone wishing to make and distribute phonorecords of a nondramatic musical work can negotiate directly with the copyright owner or his or her agent. But if the copyright owner is unwilling to negotiate, or if the copyright owner cannot be contacted, the person intending to record the work or make a DPD [digital phonorecord delivery] can use the compulsory license. (circular 73)

Fair Use

Fair use is a legal doctrine that promotes freedom of expression by permitting the unlicensed use of copyright-protected works in certain circumstances. Section 107 of the Copyright Act provides the statutory framework for determining whether something is a fair use and identifies certain types of uses—such as criticism, comment, news reporting, teaching, scholarship, and research—as examples of activities that may qualify as fair use. **Section 107 calls for consideration of the following four factors in evaluating a question of fair use:**

1. Purpose and character of the use, including whether the use is of a commercial nature or is for nonprofit educational purposes;
2. Nature of the copyrighted work;
3. Amount and substantiality of the portion used in relation to the copyrighted work as a whole;
4. Effect of the use upon the potential market for or value of the copyrighted work.

Courts evaluate fair use claims on a case-by-case basis, and the outcome of any given case depends on a fact-specific inquiry. This means that there is no formula to ensure that a predetermined percentage or amount of a work—or specific number of words, lines, pages, copies—may be used without permission. (*More Information on Fair Use*)

FIGURE 2. COPYRIGHT TIMELINE

1790: **First copyright law** enacted under the new U.S. Constitution. Term of 14 years with privilege of renewal for term of 14 years. Books, maps, and charts protected.

1831: **First general revision** of the copyright law. Music added to works protected against unauthorized printing and vending. First term of copyright extended to 28 years with privilege of renewal for term of 14 years.

1865: Photographs and photographic negatives added to protected works.

1870: **Second general revision** of the copyright law. Copyright activities, including deposit and registration, centralized in the Library of Congress. Works of art added to protected works.

1897: **Music protected against unauthorized public performance** (mainly applied to music theater).

1909: **Third general revision** of the copyright law. Term of protection measured from date of publication of the work. Renewal term extended from 14 to 28 years. Two major provisions added: compulsory license (2-cent royalty fee); and protection for public performance for profit.

1912: Motion pictures, previously registered as photographs, added to classes of protected works.

1914: Performing rights organization **American Society of Composers, Authors and Publishers (ASCAP)** formed by Tin Pan Alley songwriters to recover royalties from public performances.

1939: Performing rights organization **Broadcast Music, Inc. (BMI)** formed as an alternative to ASCAP. Catered to songwriters involved in jazz, blues, R&B, and eventually rock and roll.

1952: Universal Copyright Convention signed at Geneva, Switzerland (effective in USA in 1955).

1972: Act providing limited copyright protection to **sound recordings** fixed and first published on or after this date.

1976: **Fourth general revision** of the copyright law (effective 1978). Term of protection for works created on or after this date is the life of the author plus 50 years after the author's death.

1992: **Digital Audio Home Recording Act** required copy management systems in digital audio recorders and imposed royalties on sale of digital audio recording devices and media. Royalties are collected, invested, and distributed among the owners of sound recordings and musical compositions, certain performing artists and/or their representatives. Clarified legality of home taping of analog and digital sound recordings for private noncommercial use.

1997: **No Electronic Theft Act** set penalties for willfully infringing a copyright by reproducing or distributing, including by electronic means, phonorecords totaling more than one thousand dollars in retail value. Aimed at preventing file sharing over the internet.

1998: **Sonny Bono Copyright Term Extension Act** extended the term of copyright protection for most works to the life of the author plus 70 years after the author's death.

1998: **Digital Millennium Copyright Act** implemented WIPO (World Intellectual Property Organization) Copyright Treaty and the WIPO Performances and Phonograms Treaty; limited certain online infringement liability for Internet service providers.

2018: **Music Modernization Act** facilitated licensing of music by digital services (downloading, streaming), creating a single licensing database. **Compensating Legacy Artists for their Songs, Service, and Important Contributions to Society (CLASSICS) Act** insured royalties from digital services for sound recordings made before 1972. **Allocation for Music Producers Act** facilitated royalty payments from digital services to producers and engineers.

Sources: U.S. Copyright Office (2019b, 2019c).

1857: Édouard-Léon Scott de Martinville patented the phonautograph in France, capturing sound traces onto paper, making the first recordings of the human voice in 1860. The recordings were meant to be seen, not heard.

1877: **Thomas Edison** demonstrated tinfoil cylinder **phonograph**, envisioned as an office machine for speaking.

1878: **Edison Speaking Phonograph Company** formed.

1885: Charles Sumner Tainter and Chichester Bell invented **graphophone**, which cut grooves into a wax coated cardboard cylinder.

1887: **American Graphophone Company** formed. **Emile Berliner** patented **gramophone** (from whch comes **Grammy** Awards), which used flat discs that were louder than cylinders. Two machines were needed: one to cut grooves into the disc and one to play it back. The master disc could be electroplated, which could then stamp out and mass produce copies or **records**.

1880s (late): Jesse Lippincott consolidated Edison patents and sales rights to graphophone and formed **North American Phonograph Company**, with regional franchises.

1889: Manager of **Pacific Phonograph Company** (North American's West Coast licensee), added coin-activated mechanism and for a nickel listeners could hear an entertainment cylinder in Palais Royal Saloon in San Francisco.

1892: **Columbia Phonograph Company** (DC franchise of N. American) had issued about 100 different recordings of the Marine Band sold at two dollars per cylinder.

1894: "The organization of the **United States Gramophone Company** in Washington, DC, in 1894 [by Berliner] marked the true beginning of the enormous record industry" ("The Gramophone," LOC 2019b). Berliner's 7-inch records sold for sixty cents, and by 1897 were made of shellac, which remained the industry standard until the late 1940s. Advantages of discs: they could be mass-produced; were difficult to break; could be stored upright in a small space; and had a blank center where printed information could be placed.

1890s (mid): Columbia and Edison had introduced affordable phonographs. Columbia had over one thousand cylinder titles in its catalog.

1901: Berliner and Eldridge R. Johnson (machinist who manufactured gramophones) formed **Victor Talking Machine Company** with Johnson heading it.

1903: Dinwiddie Colored Quartet recording of "jubilee and camp meeting shouts" released by Victor.

1900s (early): **Victor, Edison, and Columbia** pooled patents and golden era of **acoustic recording** lasted until after World War I.

1909: More than 27 million phonograph records and cylinders were manufactured this year.
Victor Herbert and John Phillip Sousa led move for **Copyright Act of 1909** mandating a royalty for the composer of two cents for each cylinder, record, or piano roll manufactured (called mechanicals).

1910s: 10 inch, 78 rpm (revolutions per minute) disc became the standard format.

1914: First African American ensemble gained recording contract, with Victor because of association with dancers Vernon and Irene Castle: James Reese Europe's Syncopated Society Orchestra.

1920: Al Jolson's Columbia recording of George Gershwin's "Swanee" sold over 2 million records, shifting music consumption from Tin Pan Alley sheet music to recordings. Perry Bradford's "Crazy Blues," recorded by singer Mamie Smith on the Okeh label, was the first recorded blues sung by an African American, **initiating a decade of blues recordings.** Talent scout Ralph Peer dubbed them **race records** ("the race" was used in a positive sense in African American newspapers at the time). Prohibition began; nationwide ban on the production, importation, transportation, and sale of alcoholic beverages (repealed 1933).

1921: **Black Swan** label (black-owned, independent) started by W. C. Handy and Harry Pace.

1923: **Bessie Smith signed to Columbia.**

1924: **Paramount recorded the first country blues**, Papa Charlie Jackson. Acquired Black Swan label.

1925: Victor and Columbia began issuing **electrically recorded discs**.

1926: Columbia absorbed OKeh.

1927: Automatic Musical Instrument Company (AMI) introduced its Selective Phonograph (**jukebox**). Jimmie Rodgers and The Carter Family, two of country music's most influential artists, were first recorded.

1928: Jimmie Rodgers's "Blue Yodel No. 1 (T for Texas)" issued on Victor, would sell a million copies.

1929: Bessie Smith starred in *St. Louis Blues*. Race records peaked at about 500 new releases.

1929: David Sarnoff engineered **merger between RCA and Victor** and became president. Edison label ceased production.

1933: Prohibition repealed. Wurlitzer and Rockola entered the jukebox business.

1934: **American Decca** formed.

1936: **150,000 juke boxes** in operation in US, accounting for **40 percent of record trade**.

1938: CBS purchased Columbia Records.

1930s: *Billboard* and *Variety* began charting jukebox record hits. The major record labels were: Columbia, RCA Victor, and Decca.

Sources: First Sounds (2008), Sanjek (1996), Library of Congress (2019a, 2019b).

FIGURE 4. GROWTH OF RADIO IN THE UNITED STATES

1886-89: Heinrich Hertz demonstrated properties of radio waves.

1897: Guglielmo Marconi established the Wireless Telegraph and Signal Company in the UK.

1899: Marconi established American Marconi in the US.

1910: Live Enrico Caruso broadcast from Metropolitan Opera in NYC.

1919: Operations and assets of American Marconi were transferred to new entity, **Radio Corporation of America (RCA)**, as a holding company for the major radio patent holders in the US. RCA stock was divided among General Electric (GE), Westinghouse (radio equipment manufacturers), and American Telephone and Telegraph (AT&T) (transmitter manufacturers). RCA would market GE and Westinghouse products, and AT&T would control telephone services.

1920: Westinghouse's KDKA went on the air from its offices in Pittsburgh; its November presidential election returns broadcast was a milestone.

1921: US Department of Commerce began issuing licenses for radio broadcasting stations.

1922: Over 500 radio stations newly licensed this year to operate in the US.

1924: National Barn Dance program introduced by Sears Roebuck station WLS in Chicago.

1925: WSM Barn Dance in Memphis (later renamed the Grand Ole Opry) launched by George D. Hay.

1926: AT&T left broadcasting and sold flagship station WEAF (in NYC, later to become WNBC) to RCA. RCA formed subsidiary, **National Broadcasting Company (NBC)**, the first company founded solely to operate a national radio network. The 15-station Red network, fed by WEAF, aired sponsored programs with live orchestras. The 10-station Blue network (WJZ, became WABC) aired educational talks and cultural presentations.

1927: United Independent Broadcasters joined Columbia Phonograph Company (CPC) to form **Columbia Phonograph Broadcasting System**, the second national radio network. Federal Radio Commission formed (precursor to FCC).

1928: CPC pulled out and name was shortened to **Columbia Broadcasting System (CBS)**. CBS and NBC were the major competitors for coast-to-coast broadcasting.

1932: RCA, GE, and Westinghouse split up in government anti-trust suit.

1934: **Federal Communications Commission** (FCC) established.

1943: The NBC Blue network became the **American Broadcasting Company (ABC)** when the FCC dictated that RCA divorce the NBC Blue and Red networks.

1961: FCC authorized FM multiplexing, broadcasting two signals simultaneously on a single channel, allowing for stereo broadcasts.

1965: FCC required a station's AM and FM programming in cities larger than one hundred thousand to differ at least 50 percent of the time.

FIGURE 5. MUSIC ON TELEVISION, 1940s–1980s

FIGURE 5. MUSIC ON TELEVISION, 1940s–1980s

1948 49 **50** 51 52 53 54 55 56 57 58 59 **60** 61 62 63 64 65 66 67 68 69

Toast of the Town (CBS), renamed Ed Sullivan Show in 1955
Your Hit Parade (NBC)
Bandstand (WFIL, Phila., Bob Horn), added teens dancing in 1952
The Big Beat (ABC, Alan Freed)*
American Bandstand (ABC, Dick Clark)
Shindig! (ABC)
Hullabaloo (NBC)
Music Scene (ABC)

UNITED KINGDOM
Ready Steady Go!
Top of the Pops

1970 71 72 73 74 75 76 77 78 79 **80** 81 82 83 84 85 86 87 88 89

NETWORK
Soul Train (WCIU, Chicago, Don Cornelius)
Don Kirschner's Rock Concert
The Midnight Special (NBC)
Friday Night Videos (NBC)
Night Tracks (TBS)
Headbangers Ball (MTV)
Yo! MTV Raps (MTV)
Rap City (BET)
Country Music Television (CMTV)
The Nashville Network (TNN)

CABLE
MTV
BET
VH1

UNITED KINGDOM
The Old Grey Whistle Test

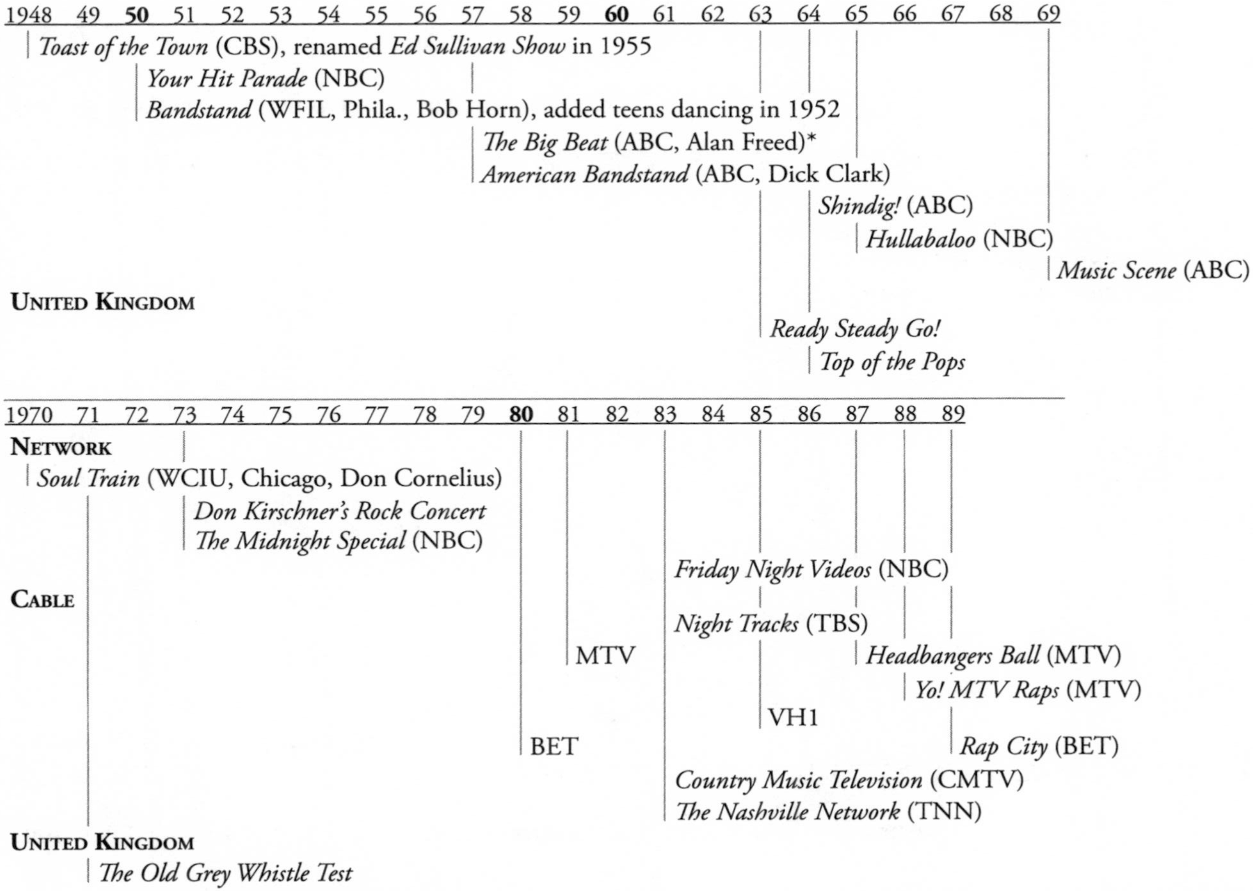

* National broadcast cancelled within months when Frankie Lymon danced with a white girl on air; show relaunched locally in NYC.

FIGURE 6. AFRICAN AMERICANS IN STARRING ROLES IN TELEVISION

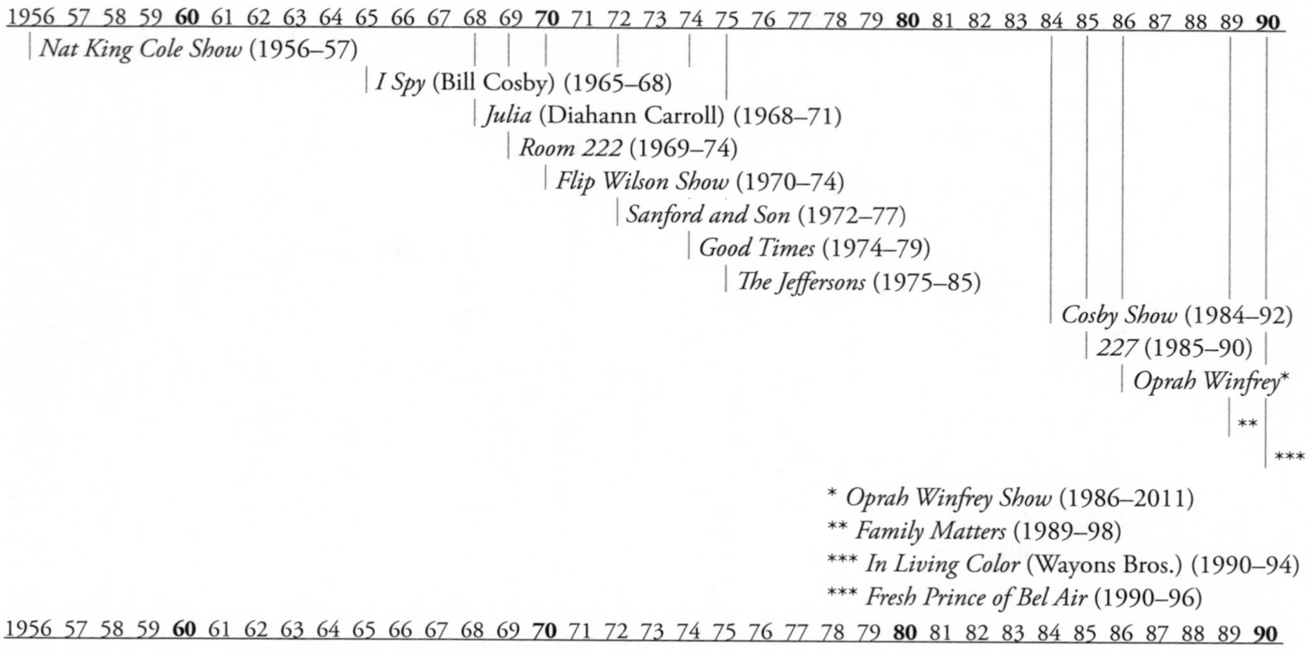

1956 57 58 59 **60** 61 62 63 64 65 66 67 68 69 **70** 71 72 73 74 75 76 77 78 79 **80** 81 82 83 84 85 86 87 88 89 **90**

| Nat King Cole Show (1956–57)

| I Spy (Bill Cosby) (1965–68)

| Julia (Diahann Carroll) (1968–71)

| Room 222 (1969–74)

| Flip Wilson Show (1970–74)

| Sanford and Son (1972–77)

| Good Times (1974–79)

| The Jeffersons (1975–85)

| Cosby Show (1984–92)

| 227 (1985–90)

| Oprah Winfrey*

1956 57 58 59 **60** 61 62 63 64 65 66 67 68 69 **70** 71 72 73 74 75 76 77 78 79 **80** 81 82 83 84 85 86 87 88 89 **90**

* Oprah Winfrey Show (1986–2011)
** Family Matters (1989–98)
*** In Living Color (Wayons Bros.) (1990–94)
*** Fresh Prince of Bel Air (1990–96)

Source: Fearn-Banks and Burford-Johnson (2014).

FIGURE 7. MAGAZINES

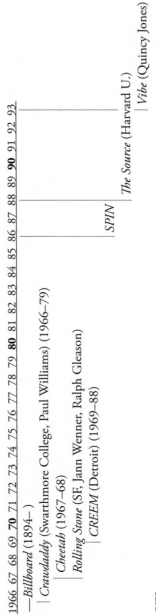

1966 67 68 69 70 71 72 73 74 75 76 77 78 79 **80** 81 82 83 84 85 86 87 88 89 **90** 91 92 93

—*Billboard* (1894–)
| *Crawdaddy* (Swarthmore College, Paul Williams) (1966–79)
| *Cheetah* (1967–68)
| *Rolling Stone* (SF, Jann Wenner, Ralph Gleason)
| *CREEM* (Detroit) (1969–88)
SPIN
| *The Source* (Harvard U.)
| *Vibe* (Quincy Jones)

UK

—*Melody Maker* (1926–2000; merged with *NME* 2001)
—*New Musical Express* (*NME*) (1952–)

1966 67 68 69 70 71 72 73 74 75 76 77 78 79 **80** 81 82 83 84 85 86 87 88 89 **90** 91 92 93

FIGURE 8. INDUSTRY POPULARITY CHARTS (*BILLBOARD*)

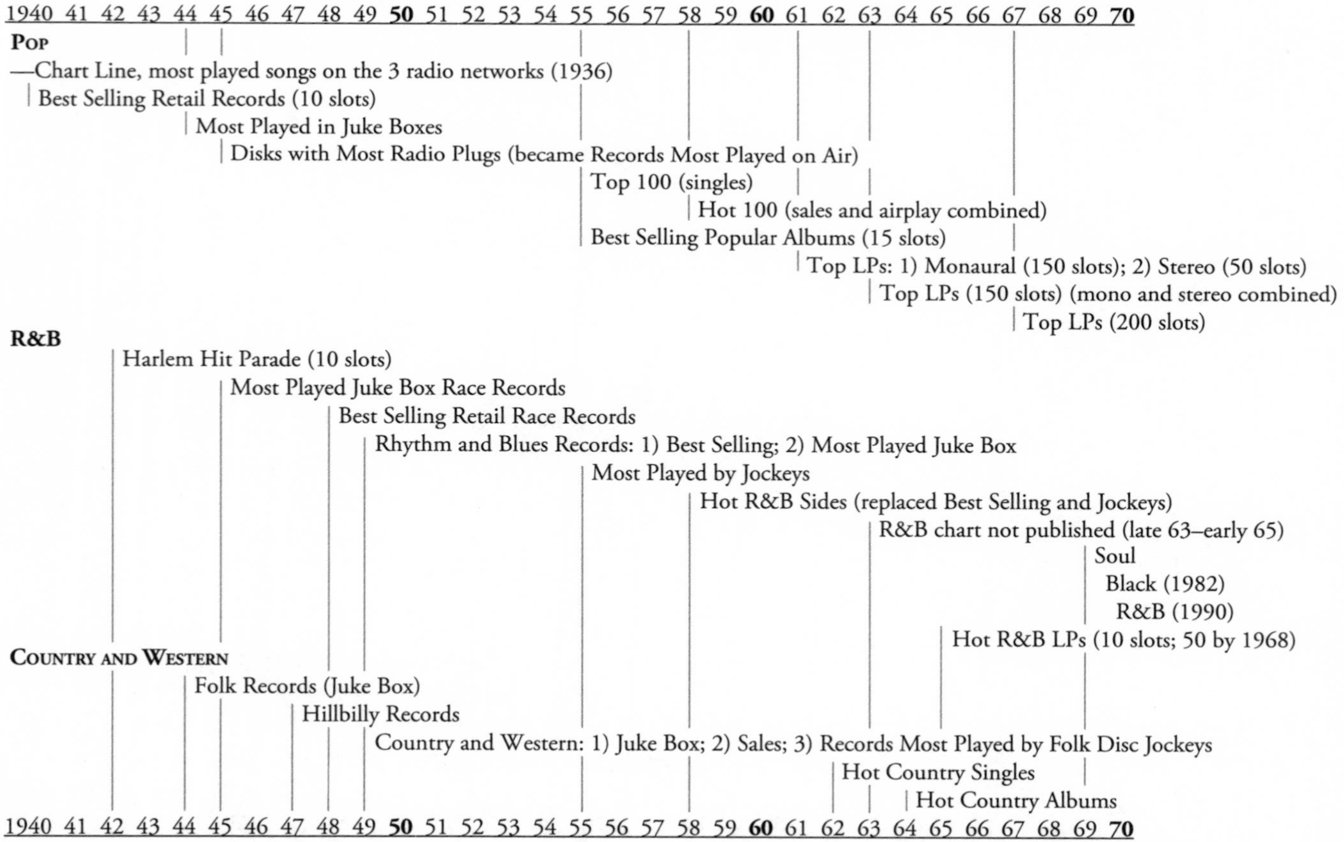

Pop

1940 41 42 43 44 45 46 47 48 49 **50** 51 52 53 54 55 56 57 58 59 **60** 61 62 63 64 65 66 67 68 69 **70**

—Chart Line, most played songs on the 3 radio networks (1936)
Best Selling Retail Records (10 slots)
Most Played in Juke Boxes
Disks with Most Radio Plugs (became Records Most Played on Air)
Top 100 (singles)
Hot 100 (sales and airplay combined)
Best Selling Popular Albums (15 slots)
Top LPs: 1) Monaural (150 slots); 2) Stereo (50 slots)
Top LPs (150 slots) (mono and stereo combined)
Top LPs (200 slots)

R&B

Harlem Hit Parade (10 slots)
Most Played Juke Box Race Records
Best Selling Retail Race Records
Rhythm and Blues Records: 1) Best Selling; 2) Most Played Juke Box
Most Played by Jockeys
Hot R&B Sides (replaced Best Selling and Jockeys)
R&B chart not published (late 63–early 65)
Soul
Black (1982)
R&B (1990)
Hot R&B LPs (10 slots; 50 by 1968)

Country and Western

Folk Records (Juke Box)
Hillbilly Records
Country and Western: 1) Juke Box; 2) Sales; 3) Records Most Played by Folk Disc Jockeys
Hot Country Singles
Hot Country Albums

1940 41 42 43 44 45 46 47 48 49 **50** 51 52 53 54 55 56 57 58 59 **60** 61 62 63 64 65 66 67 68 69 **70**

Hot Dance/Disco charts: Disco Action (1974); Disco Top 100 (1979); Hot Dance/Disco (1984); Hot Dance-Club Play (1987). *Billboard* began using Broadcast Data Systems in 1988 and Soundscan in 1991. Whitburn (1999–2013) compiles *Billboard* chart data.

FIGURE 9. GRAMMY CATEGORIES

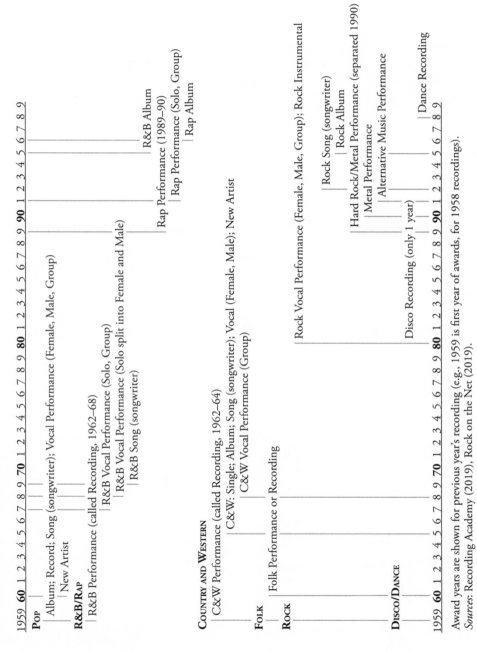

Award years are shown for previous year's recording (e.g., 1959 is first year of awards, for 1958 recordings).
Sources: Recording Academy (2019), Rock on the Net (2019).

FIGURE 10. INNOVATIONS IN SOUND AND MUSICAL INSTRUMENT TECHNOLOGY, 1948–2001

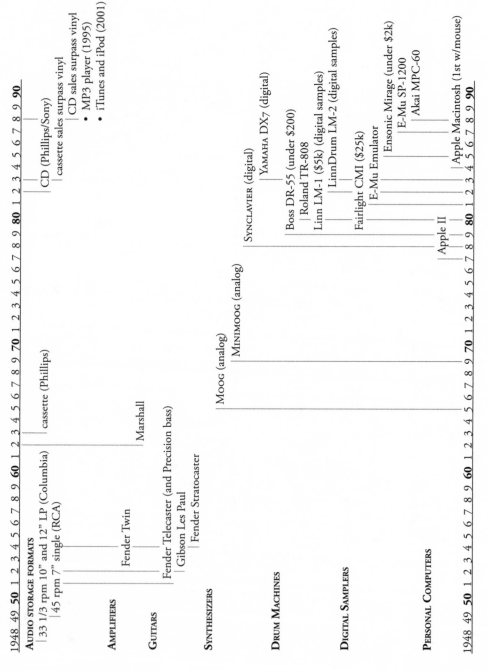

FIGURE 11. "HIGH WATER EVERYWHERE, PART 1," BY CHARLEY PATTON

Lyrics from Calt and Wardlow (1988: 200-202), with revisions by Eric Charry; beat count by Charry.

1.   The backwater done rose around Sumner now, drove me down the line. (2x)
    An' I tell that what the water, done to (Joe Lee's?) town.
    4 4 3.5 5 (beats per measure; 1st line, four measures)
    4 4 4   4   (2nd line, four measures)
    4 4 4   1.5 (3rd line, four measures)

2.   Lord the whole 'round country Lord! River has overflowed. (2x)
        "You know I can't stay here; I'm—I'll go where it's high boy!"
    I was goin' to the hilly country, 'fore they got me barred.
    4 4 3.5 5
    4 4 4   4 4
    4 4 4   1.5

3.   Lookey here [boys] around Leland [tell me], river was risin' high. (2x)
        "Boy it's risin' over there, y'hear?"
    I'm gonna move over to Greenville, 'fore I bid "Goodbye."
    4 4 3.5 5
    4 4 4   4 2
    4 4 4   1.5

4.   Lookey here water now Lordy . . . rose most [rowboats?] everywhere.
    The water at Greenville—and Leland! Know it done rose everywhere.
        "Boy, you can't never stay here!"
    I would go down to Rosedale, but they tell me water there.
    4 4 4.5 5
    4 4 4   4 2
    4 4 4   1.5

5.   Well [they tell me] the water now mama, done took short little town. (2x)
        "Boy I'm goin' to Vicksburg!"
    Well I'm goin' down Vicksburg, over that higher mound.
    4 4 3.5 5
    4 4 4   4 2
    4 4 4   1.5

6.   [Well] I am goin' [over the hill where] up that water, where it don't never flow. (2x)
        "Boy, Sharkey County an' everything was down in Stover."
    (Bolivar County?) was inchin', over that Tallahatchie skid.
        "Boy went in Tallahatchie to find it over there!"
    4 4 2.5 5
    4 4 4   4 6
    4 4 4   3.5

7.   Lord the water done rushed over, down old Jackson road. (2x)
        "Boy it starched my clothes!"
    I'm goin' back to the hilly country, won't be worried no more.
    4 4 3.5 5
    4 4 4   4 2
    4 4 4   4

FIGURE 12. EARLY BLUES SINGERS

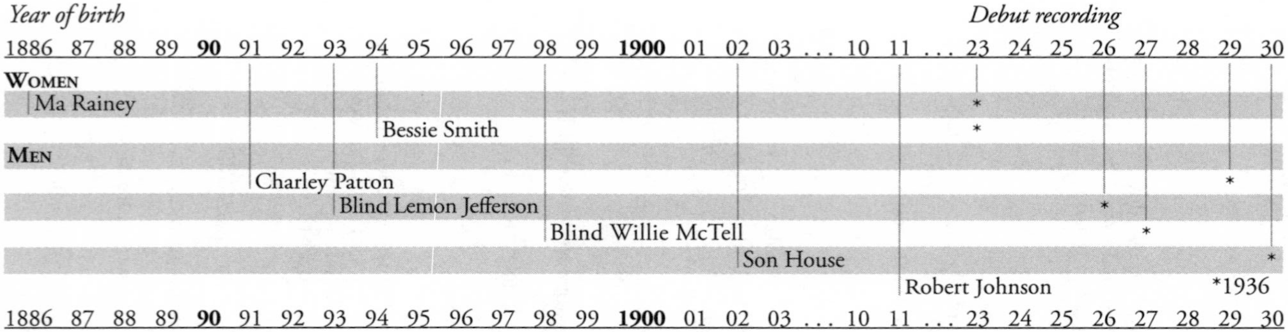

Women: Ma Rainey (b. Georgia, 1886–1939); Bessie Smith (b. Tennessee, 1894–1937).
Men: Charley Patton (b. Mississippi Delta, 1891?–1934); Blind Lemon Jefferson (b. Texas, 1893?–1929);
Blind Willie McTell (b. Georgia, 1898?–1959); Son House (b. Mississippi Delta, 1902–88); Robert Johnson (b. Mississippi, 1911–38).
Not shown: Muddy Waters (b. Mississippi Delta, 1913–83), debut recording 1941.
* First recording 1936.

FIGURE 13. TWELVE-BAR BLUES FORM

A skeletal 12-bar blues form can be diagrammed using Roman numerals indicating chords built on degrees of a scale. For example, the chords in a 12-bar blues in the key of *A* are *A* (I), *D* (IV), and *E* (V). In this diagram, each chord (symbolized by a Roman numeral) is played for four counts (beats) and represents one measure (or bar). It should be read from left to right, with each numbered box representing one bar of four beats. In this form, one line of lyrics takes up four bars, the same line is sung again over the next four bars (usually with the same melody and a different set of chords), and a responding line is sung over the last four bars. This lyric scheme can be diagrammed as *aab*. A 16-bar blues may double the length of the first four bars, as in "Hoochie Coochie Man."

Measure: Chord: Lyrics:	1. **I** 1st line of lyrics	2. **I** (or IV)	3. **I**	4. **I**
Measure: Chord: Lyrics:	5. **IV** 1st line repeated	6. **IV**	7. **I**	8. **I**
Measure: Chord: Lyrics:	9. **V** 2nd line	10. ***V**	11. **I**	12. **I**

* The IV chord can be substituted here.

FIGURE 14. SOME KEY INDEPENDENT RECORD LABELS, 1940S–1950S (DATE FOUNDED AND ARTIST'S DEBUT RECORDING)

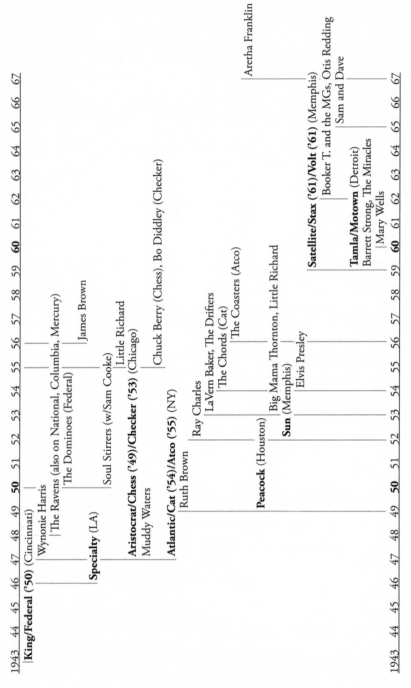

Major labels in the 1950s: Columbia; RCA-Victor; Decca; Capitol (LA); MGM (Hollywood); and Mercury (Chicago). Label founders: Syd Nathan (King); Art Rupe (Specialty); Phil and Leonard Chess (Chess); Ahmet Ertegun (Atlantic); Don Robey (Peacock); Sam Phillips (Sun); Jim Stewart and Estelle Axton (Stax); and Berry Gordy (Motown).

FIGURE 15. "CHOO CHOO CH-BOOGIE," BY LOUIS JORDAN

Instrumental Introduction (12-bar blues)

Verse (12-bar blues): "Heading for the station with a pack on my back"

Chorus (8 bars): "Choo Choo"

Piano solo (12-bar blues)

Verse (12-bar blues): "You reach your destination but alas and alack"

Chorus (8 bars): "Choo Choo"

Sax (alto) solo (12-bar blues)

Sax (alto) solo (8 bars): same chord pattern as the Chorus

Verse (12-bar blues): "Goin' to settle down by the railroad track"

Chorus (8 bars): "Choo Choo"

Brass ensemble (8 bars)

Coda (2 bars)

FIGURE 16. ELECTRIC BLUES GUITARISTS, 1950s–1960s (R&B TOP 10 SINGLE HITS AND POP LP DEBUTS)

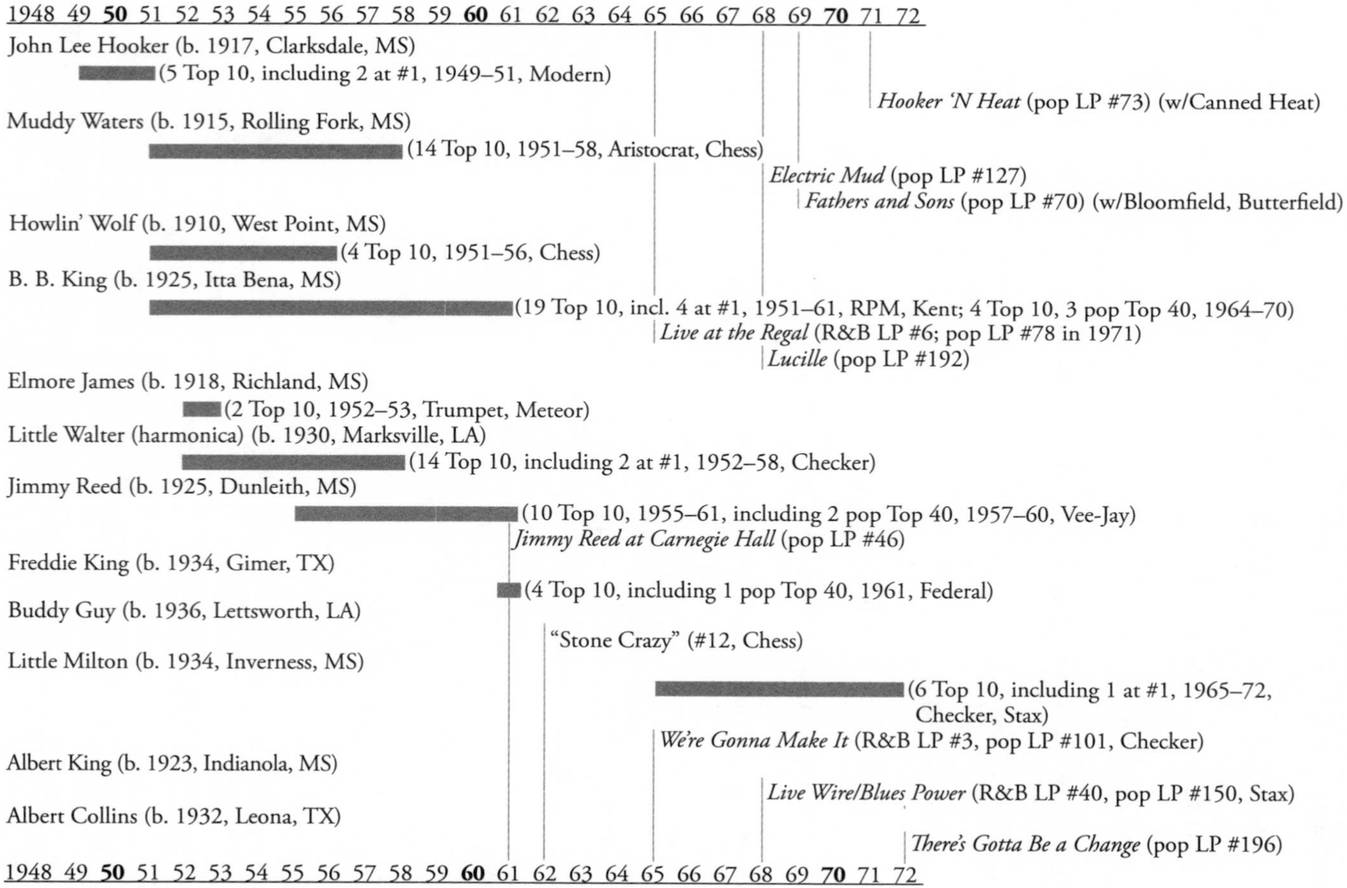

1948 49 **50** 51 52 53 54 55 56 57 58 59 **60** 61 62 63 64 65 66 67 68 69 **70** 71 72

John Lee Hooker (b. 1917, Clarksdale, MS)
(5 Top 10, including 2 at #1, 1949–51, Modern)
Hooker 'N Heat (pop LP #73) (w/Canned Heat)

Muddy Waters (b. 1915, Rolling Fork, MS)
(14 Top 10, 1951–58, Aristocrat, Chess)
Electric Mud (pop LP #127)
Fathers and Sons (pop LP #70) (w/Bloomfield, Butterfield)

Howlin' Wolf (b. 1910, West Point, MS)
(4 Top 10, 1951–56, Chess)

B. B. King (b. 1925, Itta Bena, MS)
(19 Top 10, incl. 4 at #1, 1951–61, RPM, Kent; 4 Top 10, 3 pop Top 40, 1964–70)
Live at the Regal (R&B LP #6; pop LP #78 in 1971)
Lucille (pop LP #192)

Elmore James (b. 1918, Richland, MS)
(2 Top 10, 1952–53, Trumpet, Meteor)

Little Walter (harmonica) (b. 1930, Marksville, LA)
(14 Top 10, including 2 at #1, 1952–58, Checker)

Jimmy Reed (b. 1925, Dunleith, MS)
(10 Top 10, 1955–61, including 2 pop Top 40, 1957–60, Vee-Jay)
Jimmy Reed at Carnegie Hall (pop LP #46)

Freddie King (b. 1934, Gimer, TX)
(4 Top 10, including 1 pop Top 40, 1961, Federal)

Buddy Guy (b. 1936, Lettsworth, LA)
"Stone Crazy" (#12, Chess)

Little Milton (b. 1934, Inverness, MS)
(6 Top 10, including 1 at #1, 1965–72, Checker, Stax)

Albert King (b. 1923, Indianola, MS)
We're Gonna Make It (R&B LP #3, pop LP #101, Checker)
Live Wire/Blues Power (R&B LP #40, pop LP #150, Stax)

Albert Collins (b. 1932, Leona, TX)
There's Gotta Be a Change (pop LP #196)

1948 49 **50** 51 52 53 54 55 56 57 58 59 **60** 61 62 63 64 65 66 67 68 69 **70** 71 72

Nor shown: T-Bone Walker (6 Top 10, 1947–49, Black and White, Comet).

FIGURE 17. WOMEN R&B SINGERS, 1940s–1950s (R&B TOP 10 SINGLE HITS AND CROSSOVERS TO POP TOP 40)

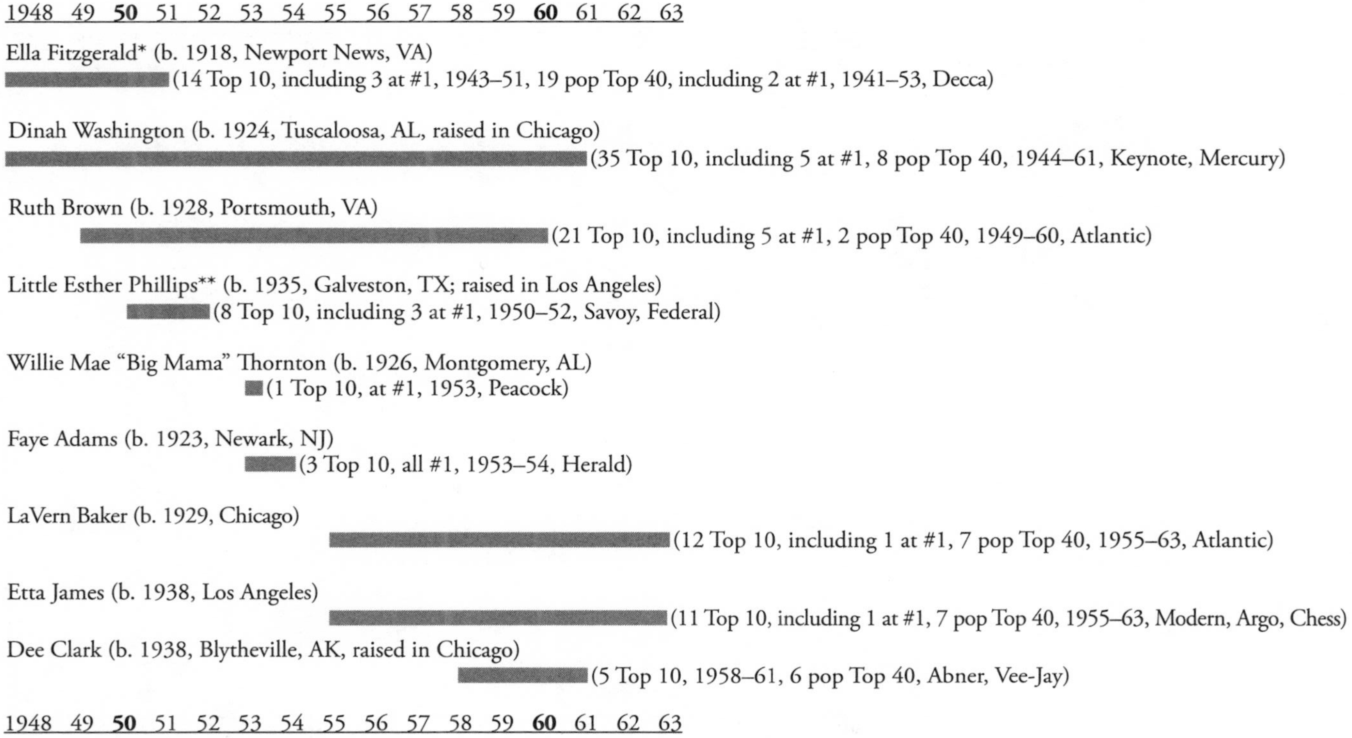

1948 49 **50** 51 52 53 54 55 56 57 58 59 **60** 61 62 63

Ella Fitzgerald* (b. 1918, Newport News, VA)
(14 Top 10, including 3 at #1, 1943–51, 19 pop Top 40, including 2 at #1, 1941–53, Decca)

Dinah Washington (b. 1924, Tuscaloosa, AL, raised in Chicago)
(35 Top 10, including 5 at #1, 8 pop Top 40, 1944–61, Keynote, Mercury)

Ruth Brown (b. 1928, Portsmouth, VA)
(21 Top 10, including 5 at #1, 2 pop Top 40, 1949–60, Atlantic)

Little Esther Phillips** (b. 1935, Galveston, TX; raised in Los Angeles)
(8 Top 10, including 3 at #1, 1950–52, Savoy, Federal)

Willie Mae "Big Mama" Thornton (b. 1926, Montgomery, AL)
(1 Top 10, at #1, 1953, Peacock)

Faye Adams (b. 1923, Newark, NJ)
(3 Top 10, all #1, 1953–54, Herald)

LaVern Baker (b. 1929, Chicago)
(12 Top 10, including 1 at #1, 7 pop Top 40, 1955–63, Atlantic)

Etta James (b. 1938, Los Angeles)
(11 Top 10, including 1 at #1, 7 pop Top 40, 1955–63, Modern, Argo, Chess)

Dee Clark (b. 1938, Blytheville, AK, raised in Chicago)
(5 Top 10, 1958–61, 6 pop Top 40, Abner, Vee-Jay)

1948 49 **50** 51 52 53 54 55 56 57 58 59 **60** 61 62 63

* Ella Fitzgerald, "Mac the Knife," R&B Top 10, pop Top 40 (1960)
** Little Esther Phillips, "Release Me," R&B #1, pop #8 (1962)

FIGURE 18. BIRTH YEARS OF EARLY ROCK AND ROLL, SOUL, AND FUNK LEADERS

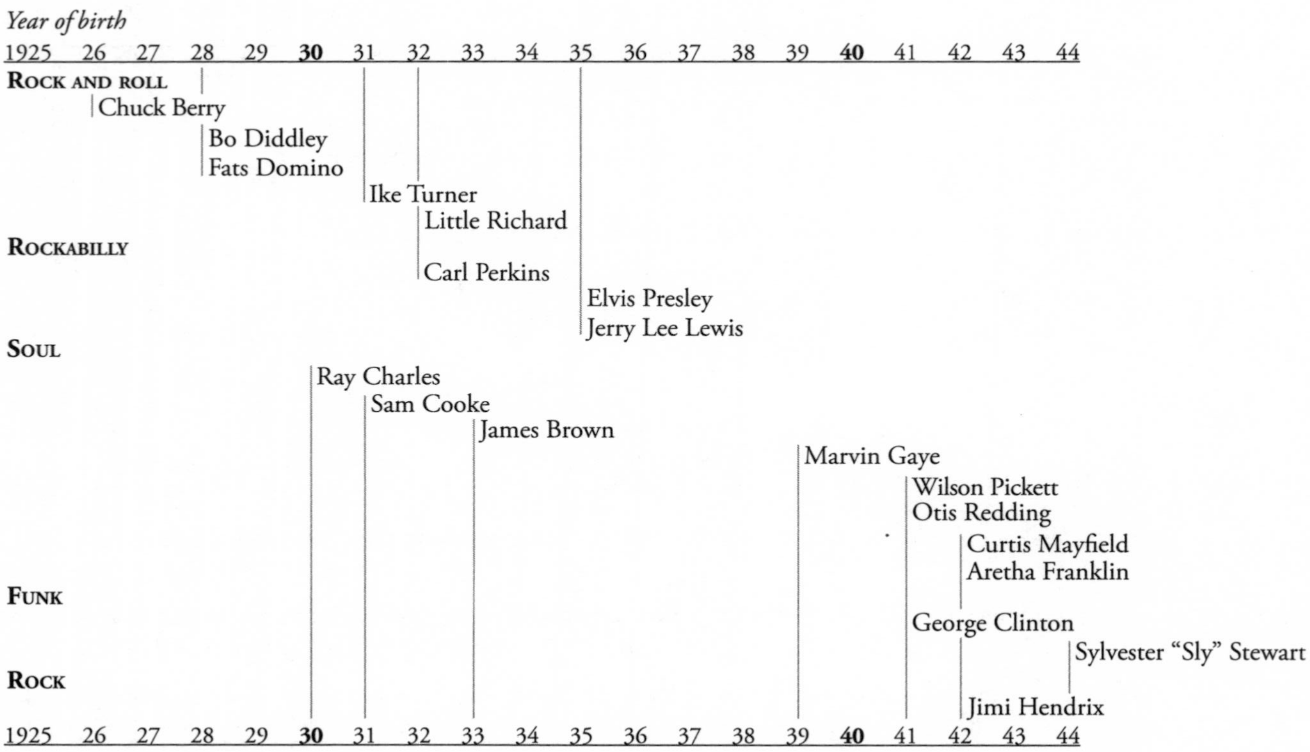

Year of birth

1925 26 27 28 29 **30** 31 32 33 34 35 36 37 38 39 **40** 41 42 43 44

ROCK AND ROLL
Chuck Berry
Bo Diddley
Fats Domino

ROCKABILLY
Ike Turner
Little Richard
Carl Perkins
Elvis Presley
Jerry Lee Lewis

SOUL
Ray Charles
Sam Cooke
James Brown
Marvin Gaye
Wilson Pickett
Otis Redding
Curtis Mayfield
Aretha Franklin

FUNK
George Clinton
Sylvester "Sly" Stewart
Jimi Hendrix

ROCK

1925 26 27 28 29 **30** 31 32 33 34 35 36 37 38 39 **40** 41 42 43 44

FIGURE 19. ELVIS PRESLEY TOP 10 HITS

Highest position (# of weeks at #1 or #2), title, date entered Top 40

<u>1956</u>
#1 (8 weeks), "Heartbreak Hotel," 3/10/56
#1 (1 week), "I Want You, I Need You, I Love You," 6/2/56
#1 (11 weeks), "Don't Be Cruel," 8/4/56 (*A* side)
#1 (11 weeks), "Hound Dog," 8/4/56 (*B* side)
#1 (5 weeks), "Love Me Tender," 10/20/56
#2 (2 weeks), "Love Me," 11/24/56

<u>1957</u>
#1 (3 weeks), "Too Much," 1/26/57
#1 (9 weeks), "All Shook Up," 4/6/57
#1 (7 weeks), "(Let Me Be Your) Teddy Bear," 6/24/57
#1 (7 weeks), "Jailhouse Rock," 10/14/57

<u>1958</u>
#1 (5 weeks), "Don't," 1/27/58
#8, "I Beg of You," 2/3/58
#2 (1 week), "Wear My Ring around Your Neck," 4/21/58
#1 (2 weeks), "Hard Headed Woman," 6/30/58
#4, "One Night," 11/10/58
#8, "I Got Stung," 11/10/58

<u>1959</u>
#2 (1 week), "(Now and Then There's) a Fool Such As I," 3/30/59
#4, "I Need Your Love Tonight," 3/30/59
#1 (2 weeks), "A Big Hunk O' Love," 7/13/59

<u>1960</u>
#1 (4 weeks), "Stuck on You," 4/11/60
#1 (5 weeks), "It's Now or Never," 7/25/60
#1 (6 weeks), "Are You Lonesome To-night," 11/14/60

<u>1961</u>
#1 (2 weeks), "Surrender," 2/20/61
#5, "I Feel So Bad," 5/22/61
#4, "(Marie's The Name) His Latest Flame," 9/4/61
#5, "Little Sister," 8/28/61
#2 (1 week), "Can't Help Falling in Love," 12/18/61

1962

#1 (2 weeks), "Good Luck Charm," 3/24/62
#5, "She's Not You," 8/11/62
#2 (5 weeks), "Return to Sender," 10/27/62

1963

#3, "(You're the) Devil in Disguise," 7/13/63
#8, "Bossa Nova Baby," 11/2/63

1965

#3, "Crying in the Chapel," 5/8/65

1969

#3, "In the Ghetto," 5/17/69
#1 (1 week), "Suspicious Minds," 9/20/69
#6, "Don't Cry Daddy," 12/13/69
    "Rubberneckin'," 12/13/69

1970

#9, "The Wonder of You," 5/23/70
    "Mama Liked the Roses," 5/23/70

1972

#2 (1 week), "Burning Love," 9/9/72

FIGURE 20. TOP 40 CROSSOVER POP HITS BY BLACK ROCK AND ROLL ARTISTS
Highest position, title, date entered Top 40

1955
Fats Domino, #10, "Ain't It a Shame," 7/16/55
Chuck Berry, #5, "Maybellene," 8/20/55

1956
Little Richard, #17, "Tutti Frutti," 1/28/56
Little Richard, #6, "Long Tall Sally," 4/7/56
Fats Domino, #35, "Bo Weevil," 4/7/56
Fats Domino, #3, "I'm in Love Again"; #19, "My Blue Heaven," 5/5/56
Little Richard, #33, "Slippin' and Slidin' [Peepin' and Hidin']," 6/30/56
Chuck Berry, #29, "Roll Over Beethoven," 6/30/56
Little Richard, #17, "Rip It Up," 7/14/56
Fats Domino, #14, "When My Dreamboat Comes Home," 7/28/56
Fats Domino, #2, "Blueberry Hill," 10/13/56

1957
Fats Domino, #5, "Blue Monday," 1/12/57
Fats Domino, #4, "I'm Walkin'," 3/9/57
Little Richard, #21, "Lucille," 4/6/57
Chuck Berry, #3, "School Day(s)," 4/20/57
Fats Domino, #8, "Valley of Tears," 5/27/57
Fats Domino, #6, "It's You I Love," 6/24/57
Little Richard, #10, "Jenny, Jenny," 6/24/57
Fats Domino, #29, "When I See You," 8/26/57
Little Richard, #8, "Keep a Knockin'," 10/7/57
Fats Domino, #23, "Wait and See," 10/21/57
Chuck Berry, #8, "Rock and Roll Music," 11/11/57
Fats Domino, #26, "The Big Beat," 12/23/57
Fats Domino, #32, "I Want to Know," 12/30/57

1958
Chuck Berry, #2, "Sweet Little Sixteen," 2/24/58
Little Richard, #10, "Good Golly, Miss Molly," 2/24/58
Chuck Berry, #8, "Johnny B. Goode," 5/5/58
Fats Domino, #22, "Sick and Tired," 5/5/58
Little Richard, #31, "Ooh! My Soul," 6/23/58
Chuck Berry, #18, "Carol," 9/15/58
Fats Domino, #6, "Whole Lotta Loving," 12/1/58

1959
Chuck Berry, #32, "Almost Grown," 4/20/59
Fats Domino, #16, "I'm Ready," 5/25/59
Chuck Berry, #37, "Back in the U.S.A.," 7/13/59
Fats Domino, #8, "I Want to Walk You Home"; #17, "I'm Gonna Be a Wheel Some Day," 8/10/59
Bo Diddley, #20, "Say Man," 10/5/59
Fats Domino, #8, "Be My Guest"; #33, "I've Been Around," 11/9/59

FIGURE 21. FIVE COVER COMPARISONS, 1954–1956

Pop: Best Seller in Stores (25–30 positions); Most Played in Juke Boxes (20 positions);
Most Played by Jockeys (20 positions).

1. "Shake, Rattle and Roll" (composed by Jesse Stone)
   a) Joe Turner, entered R&B charts **5/8/54** (highest R&B Best Seller position: #1; no pop
      charting).
   b) Bill Haley and His Comets, entered pop charts **8/21/54**: Best Seller #7; Juke Box #8;
      Jockey #9.

2. "Tweedlee Dee" (composed by Winfield Scott)
   a) LaVern Baker (Atlantic), entered both pop and R&B charts **1/15/55** (highest R&B Best
      Seller position: #4).
   b) Georgia Gibbs (Mercury), entered pop charts **1/29/55**.
   Pop Best Seller rankings week by week from January 15 through April 2, 1955
   a) Baker: 27, 25, 25, 29, 24, 26, **22**, 30, 26, 27, 24, –
   b) Gibbs: –, –, 22, 17, 12, 7, 5, 6, **3**, 4, 4, 3

3. "Ain't It/That a Shame" (composed by Fats Domino)
   a) Fats Domino: entered R&B charts **5/14/55** (#1 for 11 weeks); entered pop charts **7/16/55**.
   b) Pat Boone entered pop charts **7/9/55**.
   Pop Best Seller rankings week by week from July 9 through September 17, 1955
   a) Domino: –, 20, 23, 22, 19, 25, 18, **16**, –, 24, –
   b) Boone: 19, 16, 8, 5, 4, **2**, 2, 2, 2, 2, 2

4. "Tutti Frutti" (composed by Little Richard)
   Pop Best Seller rankings week by week from January 28 through March 17, 1956
   a) Richard: 24, 24, 21, **18**, 24, –, –, –
   b) Boone: –, –, 15, 10, 9?, 8, 7, **6**

5. "Long Tall Sally" (composed by Little Richard)
   Pop Best Seller rankings week by week from April 7 through June 2, 1956
   a) Richard: 23, 13, 12, 12, 13, **6**, 15, 13, 13
   b) Boone: –, –, –, –, –, **23**, 25, –, –

FIGURE 22. FIVE STYLES OF EARLY ROCK AND ROLL, 1954–1956

(from Gillett 1996: 23–35)

<u>Northern Band Rock 'n' Roll</u>
  Bill Haley and His Comets

<u>New Orleans Dance Blues</u>
  Fats Domino
   • Dave Bartholomew (big band leader, trumpeter, cowriter, recording supervisor, session
     band leader)
   • Tenor sax solos by Lee Allen or Herb Hardesty
  Little Richard (born and raised in Georgia)

<u>Memphis Rockabilly</u>
  Elvis Presley
  Johnny Cash
  Carl Perkins
  Jerry Lee Lewis

<u>Chicago Rhythm and Blues</u>
  Chuck Berry
  Bo Diddley

<u>Vocal Group Rock and Roll</u>
  The Chords ("Sh-Boom," 1954, NY)
  The Penguins ("Earth Angel," 1954, LA)
  The Platters ("Only You," 1955, LA)
  Frankie Lymon and the Teenagers ("Why Do Fools Fall in Love," 1956, NY)
  The Coasters ("Searchin'," 1957, LA)

FIGURE 23. ROCKABILLY ARTISTS AND THEIR DEBUT RECORDINGS

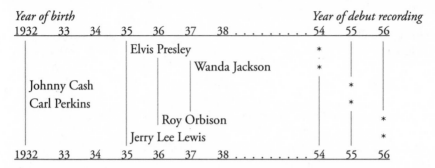

Elvis Presley (b. Tupelo, MS); Wanda Jackson (b. Maud, OK);
Johnny Cash (b. Kingsland AK); Carl Perkins (b. Tiptonville, TN);
Roy Orbison (b. Vernon, TX); Jerry Lee Lewis (b. Ferriday, LA).

All on Sun Records, except Wanda Jackson (Decca, Capitol).

FIGURE 24. "STAND BY ME" FORM AND ARRANGEMENT
(BEN E. KING, JERRY LEIBER, AND MIKE STOLLER)

Section	# Bars	Instruments
Intro	8	bass, conga, scraper, triangle
Verse	8	add keyboard, acoustic guitar
Verse	8	(same)
Chorus	8	add string section doubling the bass
Verse	8	add vocal background, strings long notes
Verse	8	(same, with strings in a higher range)
Chorus	8	add string section doubling the bass (in a higher range)
Verse (2x)	8 + 8	strings solo melody with string counterpoint and vocal background
Chorus	8	same as previous chorus
Chorus	8	fade out

FIGURE 25. BRILL BUILDING SONGWRITING TEAMS AND SELECT POP HITS

<u>Mike Stoller (composer)/Jerry Leiber (lyricist)</u>
"Hound Dog," Big Mama Thornton, R&B #1 (1953) (pre-Brill, in Los Angeles)
"Searchin'," The Coasters, #3 (1957)
"Jailhouse Rock," Elvis Presley, #1 (1957)
"Yakety Yak," The Coasters, #1 (1958)
"Charlie Brown," The Coasters, #2 (1959)
"Stand by Me," Ben E. King, #4 (1961) (written with King)
"On Broadway," The Drifters, #9 (1963) (written with Mann/Weil)

<u>Mort Shuman (composer)/Doc Pomus (lyricist)</u>
"A Teenager in Love," Dion and the Belmonts, #5 (1959)
"This Magic Moment," The Drifters, #16 (1960)
"Save the Last Dance for Me," The Drifters, #1 (1960)

<u>Carole King (composer)/Gerry Goffin (lyricist)</u>
"Will You Love Me Tomorrow," Shirelles, #1 (1960)
"The Loco-Motion," Little Eva, #1 (1962)
"Up on the Roof," The Drifters, #5 (1962)
"One Fine Day," The Chiffons, #5 (1963)
"Pleasant Valley Sunday," The Monkees, #3 (1967)

<u>Barry Mann (composer)/Cynthia Weil (lyricist)</u>
"Uptown," The Crystals, #13 (1962)
"On Broadway," The Drifters, #9 (1963) (written with Leiber/Stoller)
"You've Lost that Lovin' Feeling," The Righteous Brothers, #1 (1964) (written with Spector)
"Kicks," Paul Revere and the Raiders, #4 (1966)

<u>Ellie Greenwich (composer)/Jeff Barry (lyricist)</u>
"Da Doo Ron Ron," The Crystals, #3 (1963) (written with Spector)
"Be My Baby," The Ronettes, #2 (1963) (written with Spector)
"Chapel of Love," The Dixie Cups, #1 (1964) (written with Spector)
"Leader of the Pack," The Shangri-Las, #1 (1964) (written with Shadow Morton)

<u>Burt Bacharach (composer)/Hal David (lyricist)</u>
"Anyone Who Had a Heart," Dionne Warwick, #8 (1963)
"Walk on By," Dionne Warwick, #6 (1964)
"What the World Needs Now Is Love," Jackie DeShannon, #7 (1965)
"What's New Pussycat?," Tom Jones, #3 (1965)
"The Look of Love," Dusty Springfield, #22 (1967)
"I Say a Little Prayer," Dionne Warwick, #4 (1967)

FIGURE 26. TEEN IDOLS: LATE 1950s–1960s TOP 40 HITS

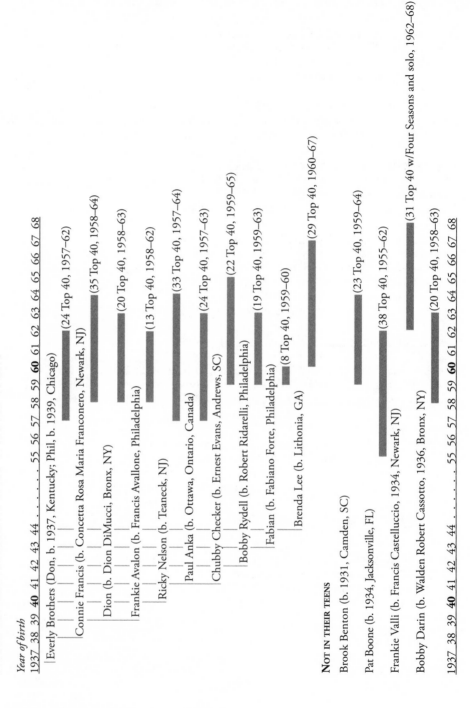

FIGURE 27. MOTOWN POP TOP 10 SINGLES, 1960–1970

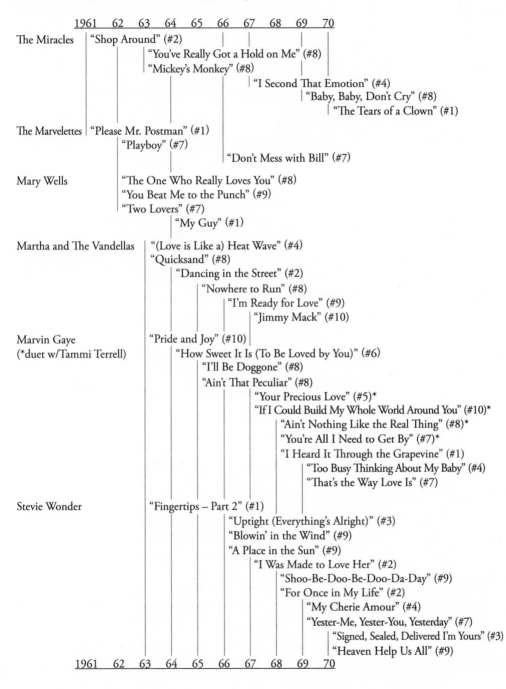

The Miracles — "Shop Around" (#2), "You've Really Got a Hold on Me" (#8), "Mickey's Monkey" (#8), "I Second That Emotion" (#4), "Baby, Baby, Don't Cry" (#8), "The Tears of a Clown" (#1)

The Marvelettes — "Please Mr. Postman" (#1), "Playboy" (#7), "Don't Mess with Bill" (#7)

Mary Wells — "The One Who Really Loves You" (#8), "You Beat Me to the Punch" (#9), "Two Lovers" (#7), "My Guy" (#1)

Martha and The Vandellas — "(Love is Like a) Heat Wave" (#4), "Quicksand" (#8), "Dancing in the Street" (#2), "Nowhere to Run" (#8), "I'm Ready for Love" (#9), "Jimmy Mack" (#10)

Marvin Gaye (*duet w/Tammi Terrell) — "Pride and Joy" (#10), "How Sweet It Is (To Be Loved by You)" (#6), "I'll Be Doggone" (#8), "Ain't That Peculiar" (#8), "Your Precious Love" (#5)*, "If I Could Build My Whole World Around You" (#10)*, "Ain't Nothing Like the Real Thing" (#8)*, "You're All I Need to Get By" (#7)*, "I Heard It Through the Grapevine" (#1), "Too Busy Thinking About My Baby" (#4), "That's the Way Love Is" (#7)

Stevie Wonder — "Fingertips – Part 2" (#1), "Uptight (Everything's Alright)" (#3), "Blowin' in the Wind" (#9), "A Place in the Sun" (#9), "I Was Made to Love Her" (#2), "Shoo-Be-Doo-Be-Doo-Da-Day" (#9), "For Once in My Life" (#2), "My Cherie Amour" (#4), "Yester-Me, Yester-You, Yesterday" (#7), "Signed, Sealed, Delivered I'm Yours" (#3), "Heaven Help Us All" (#9)

1961   62   63   64   65   66   67   68   69   70

1961　62　63　64　65　66　67　68　69　70

The Supremes
"Where Did Our Love Go" (#1)
"Baby Love" (#1)
"Come See About Me" (#1)
"Stop! In the Name of Love" (#1)
"Back in My Arms Again" (#1)
"I Hear a Symphony" (#1)
"My World Is Empty Without You" (#5)
"Love Is Like an Itching in My Heart" (#9)
"You Can't Hurry Love" (#1)
"You Keep Me Hangin' On" (#1)
"Love Is Here and Now You're Gone" (#1)
"The Happening" (#1)
"Reflections" (#2)
"In and Out of Love" (#9)
"Love Child" (#1)
"I'm Gonna Make You Love Me" (#2)
"I'm Livin' in Shame" (#10)
"Someday We'll Be Together" (#1)
"Up the Ladder to the Roof" (#10)
"Stoned Love" (#7)

The Temptations
"My Girl" (#1)
"Beauty Is Only Skin Deep" (#3)
"(I Know) I'm Losing You" (#8)
"All I Need" (#8)
"You're My Everything" (#6)
"I Wish It Would Rain" (#4)
"Cloud Nine" (#6)
"I'm Gonna Make You Love Me" (#2)
"Run Away Child, Running Wild" (#6)
"I Can't Get Next to You" (#1)
"Psychedelic Shack" (#7)
"Ball of Confusion" (#3)

The Four Tops
"I Can't Help Myself (Sugar Pie Honey Bunch)" (#1)
"It's the Same Old Song" (#5)
"Reach Out (I'll Be There)" (#1)
"Standing in the Shadows of Love" (#6)
"Bernadette" (#4)

Gladys Knight and the Pips
"I Heard It Through the Grapevine" (#2)
"If I Were Your Woman" (#9)

The Jackson Five
"I Want You Back" (#1)
"ABC" (#1)
"The Love You Save" (#1)/"(I Found That Girl)"
"I'll Be There" (#1)

1961　62　63　64　65　66　67　68　69　70

One or two pop Top 10 hits: The Contours; Jr. Walker and the All Stars; Isley Brothers; David Ruffin; Jimmy Ruffin; Edwin Starr; Diana Ross; and Rare Earth.

FIGURE 28. BIRTH YEARS OF SINGER-SONGWRITERS

Year of birth

Year first LP as soloist

WOMEN

1939 **40** 41 42 43 44 45 46 47 48 49 **50** 51 .... **60** 61 62 63 64 65 66 67 68 69 **70** 71 72 73

- Joan Baez* — Joan Baez
- Judy Collins*
- Aretha Franklin** — *A Maid of Constant Sorrow* / *Aretha: With the Ray Bryant Combo*
- Buffy Sainte-Marie — *It's My Way!*
- Janis Ian — Janis Ian
- Laura Nyro — *More Than a New Discovery*
- Joni Mitchell — *Song to a Seagull*
- Melanie — *Born to Be* (renamed *My First Album*)
- Roberta Flack* — *First Take*
- Carole King — *Writer*
- Carly Simon — Carly Simon
- Melissa Manchester — *Home to Myself*

MEN

1939 **40** 41 42 43 44 45 46 47 48 49 **50** 51 .... **60** 61 62 63 64 65 66 67 68 69 **70** 71 72 73

- Bob Dylan — Bob Dylan
- Tom Rush*** — *Tom Rush at the Unicorn*
- Paul Simon/Art Garfunkel — *Wednesday Morning, 3AM*
- Richie Havens — *Mixed Bag*
- Van Morrison — *Blowin' Your Mind!*
- David Bowie — David Bowie
- Cat Stevens — *Matthew and Son*
- Leonard Cohen (b. 1934) — *Songs of Leonard Cohen*
- Randy Newman — *Randy Newman*
- James Taylor — *James Taylor*
- Neil Young — *Neil Young*
- Jackson Browne — Jackson Browne
- Bruce Springsteen — *Greetings from ....*

* Not primarily a songwriter (Collins started recording her own songs in 1967; Baez started in 1970; Flack started in 1971).

** Recorded a gospel LP 1956, with Columbia 1961–66, then Atlantic, which featured her songwriting more.

*** *Circle Game* (6th LP, 1968) featured songs by Joni Mitchell, James Taylor, Jackson Browne, and Rush.

Not shown: Odetta (b. 1930, debut solo LP 1954, recorded her own songs starting 1962); Nina Simone (b. 1933, debut LP 1958); Billy Joel (b. 1949, debut LP 1971); Elton John (b. 1947, debut LP 1969).

FIGURE 29. BOB DYLAN TOP 40 POP SINGLES AND LPS IN THE 1960S

Date = when it first entered the Top 40 (or the LP chart)
Chart # = highest chart position

Date	Chart #	Song or Album	Recording artist or group
Singles			
7/13/63	2	"Blowin' in the Wind"	Peter, Paul, and Mary
9/28/63	9	"Don't Think Twice, It's Alright"	Peter, Paul, and Mary
5/15/65	39	"Subterranean Homesick Blues"	Dylan
6/5/65	1	"Mr. Tambourine Man"	The Byrds
8/7/65	15	"All I Really Want to Do"	Cher
8/14/65	2	"Like a Rolling Stone"	Dylan
8/21/65	8	"It Ain't Me Babe"	The Turtles
8/21/65	40	"All I Really Want to Do"	The Byrds
10/9/65	7	"Positively 4th Street"	Dylan
4/23/66	2	"Rainy Day Women #12 & 35"	Dylan
7/16/66	20	"I Want You"	Dylan
10/1/66	33	"Just Like a Woman"	Dylan
4/29/67	30	"My Back Pages"	The Byrds
8/2/69	7	"Lay Lady Lay"	Dylan
LPs			
1962		*Bob Dylan* (LP did not chart)	
1963	22	*The Freewheelin' Bob Dylan*	
1964	20	*The Times They Are A-Changin'*	
	43	*Another Side of Bob Dylan*	
1965	6	*Bringing It All Back Home*	
	3	*Highway 61 Revisited*	
1966	9	*Blond on Blonde*	
1967	10	*Bob Dylan's Greatest Hits*	
1968	2	*John Wesley Harding*	
1969	3	*Nashville Skyline*	
1970	4	*Self Portrait*	
	7	*New Morning*	
1971	14	*Bob Dylan's Greatest Hits, Vol. 2*	
1973	16	*Pat Garrett and Billy the Kid*	
1973	17	*Dylan*	
	1	*Planet Waves*	
	3	*Before the Flood*	
1975	1	*Blood on the Tracks*	
	7	*The Basement Tapes*	

FIGURE 30. BEACH BOYS, BEATLES, AND ROLLING STONES POP TOP 40 COMPARISONS, 1962–1971

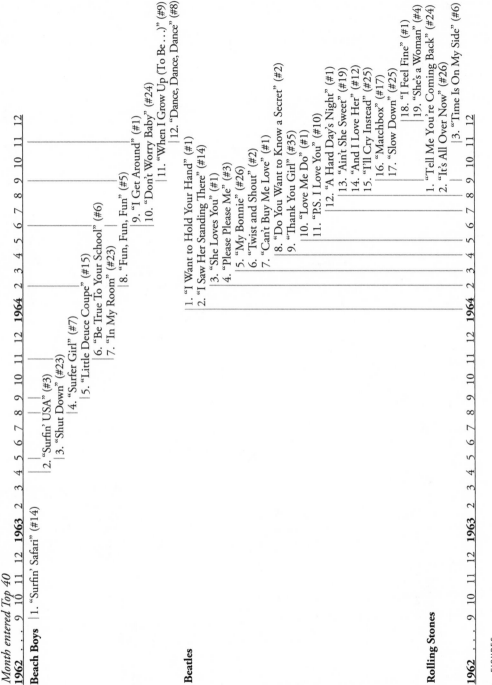

FIGURES

Beach Boys

1965 2 3 4 5 6 7 8 9 10 11 12 **1966** 2 3 4 5 6 7 8 9 10 11 12

13. "Do You Wanna Dance" (#12)
14. "Help Me, Rhonda" (#1)
15. "California Girls" (#3)
16. "The Little Girl I Once Knew" (#20)
17. "Barbara Ann" (#2)
18. "Sloop John B" (#3)
19. "Caroline, No" (#32)
20. "Wouldn't It Be Nice" (#8)
21. "God Only Knows" (#39)
22. "Good Vibrations" (#1)

Beatles

20. "Eight Days a Week" (#1)
21. "I Don't Want to Spoil the Party" (#39)
22. "Ticket to Ride" (#1)
23. "Help!" (#1)
24. "Yesterday" (#1)
25. "We Can Work It Out" (#1)
26. "Day Tripper" (#5)
27. "Nowhere Man" (#3)
28. "Paperback Writer" (#1)
29. "Rain" (#23)
30. "Yellow Submarine" (#2)
31. "Eleanor Rigby" (#11)

Rolling Stones

4. "Heart of Stone" (#19)
5. "The Last Time" (#9)
6. "(I Can't Get No) Satisfaction" (#1)
7. "Get Off of My Cloud" (#1)
8. "As Tears Go By" (#6)
9. "19th Nervous Breakdown" (#2)
10. "Paint It, Black" (#1)
11. "Mother's Little Helper" (#8)
12. "Lady Jane" (#24)
13. "Have You Seen Your Mother, Baby, Standing . . .?" (#9)

1965 2 3 4 5 6 7 8 9 10 11 12 **1966** 2 3 4 5 6 7 8 9 10 11 12

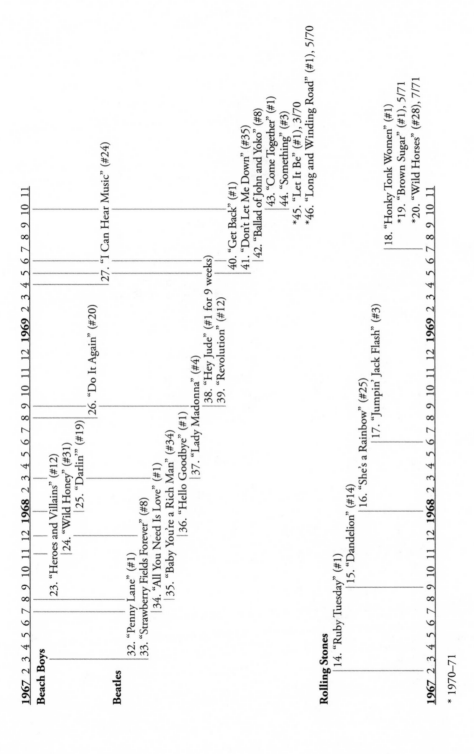

1967 2 3 4 5 6 7 8 9 10 11 12 **1968** 2 3 4 5 6 7 8 9 10 11 12 **1969** 2 3 4 5 6 7 8 9 10 11

Beach Boys

23. "Heroes and Villains" (#12)
24. "Wild Honey" (#31)
25. "Darlin'" (#19)
26. "Do It Again" (#20)
27. "I Can Hear Music" (#24)

Beatles

32. "Penny Lane" (#1)
33. "Strawberry Fields Forever" (#8)
34. "All You Need Is Love" (#1)
35. "Baby You're a Rich Man" (#34)
36. "Hello Goodbye" (#1)
37. "Lady Madonna" (#4)
38. "Hey Jude" (#1 for 9 weeks)
39. "Revolution" (#12)
40. "Get Back" (#1)
41. "Don't Let Me Down" (#35)
42. "Ballad of John and Yoko" (#8)
43. "Come Together" (#1)
44. "Something" (#3)
*45. "Let It Be" (#1), 3/70
*46. "Long and Winding Road" (#1), 5/70

Rolling Stones

1967 2 3 4 5 6 7 8 9 10 11 12 **1968** 2 3 4 5 6 7 8 9 10 11 12 **1969** 2 3 4 5 6 7 8 9 10 11

14. "Ruby Tuesday" (#1)
15. "Dandelion" (#14)
16. "She's a Rainbow" (#25)
17. "Jumpin' Jack Flash" (#3)
18. "Honky Tonk Women" (#1)
*19. "Brown Sugar" (#1), 5/71
*20. "Wild Horses" (#28), 7/71

* 1970–71

FIGURE 31. BEATLES U.S. ALBUMS: POP ALBUM CHART POSITIONS

( ) = *number of weeks at #1 or #2,* and *month/year entered chart*

1964 65 66 67 68 69 70

#1 (11 weeks): *Meet the Beatles!* (UK *With*, 11/63) (2/64)
#2 (9 weeks): *Introducing . . . The Beatles* (UK *Please Please Me,* 3/63) (2/64)
#1 (5 weeks): *The Beatles' Second Album* (4/64)
#1 (14 weeks): *A Hard Day's Night* (7/64)
#2 (9 weeks): *Something New* (8/64)
#1 (9 weeks): *Beatles '65* (UK *Beatles for Sale*) (1/65)
#1 (6 weeks): *Beatles VI* (6/65)
#1 (9 weeks): *Help!* (8/65)
#1 (6 weeks): *Rubber Soul* (12/65)
#1 (5 weeks): *Yesterday . . . and Today* (7/66)
#1 (6 weeks): *Revolver* (9/66)
#1 (15 weeks): *Sgt. Pepper's Lonely Hearts Club Band* (6/67)
#1 (8 weeks): *Magical Mystery Tour* (12/67)
#1 (9 weeks): *The Beatles [White Album]* (12/68)
#2 (2 weeks): *Yellow Submarine* (2/69)
#1 (11 weeks): *Abbey Road* (10/69)
#2 (4 weeks): *Hey Jude* (3/70)
#1 (4 weeks): *Let It Be* (5/70) [rec. early 69, before *Abbey Road*]
(post-production by Phil Spector)

1964 65 66 67 68 69 70

FIGURE 32. BRITISH INVASION GROUPS/ARTISTS AND DEBUTS IN U.S. POP SINGLES TOP 40

Group/artist *Month and year first single entered Top 40 (highest position)*

1964 2 3 4 5 6 7 8 9 10 11 12 **1965** 2 3 4 5 6...**1966**

Group/artist	Entry
The Beatles*	"I Want to Hold Your Hand"/"I Saw Her Standing There" (#1/#14)
Dusty Springfield	"I Only Want to Be With You" (#12)
Dave Clark Five**	"Glad All Over" (#6)
The Searchers*	"Needles and Pins" (#13)
Peter and Gordon**	"A World Without Love" (#1)
Gerry and the Pacemakers*	"Don't Let the Sun Catch You Crying" (#4)
Chad and Jeremy**	"Yesterday's Gone" (#21)
The Animals***	"House of the Rising Sun" (#1)
The Rolling Stones**	"Tell Me (You're Coming Back)" (#24)
Manfred Mann	"Do Wah Diddy Diddy" (#1)
The Kinks**	"You Really Got Me" (#7)
Herman's Hermits****	"I'm Into Something Good" (#13)
The Zombies	"She's Not There" (#2)
Marianne Faithfull	"As Tears Go By" (#22)
Petula Clark	"Downtown" (#1)
Freddie and the Dreamers****	"I'm Telling You Now" (#1)
Wayne Fontana and the Mindbenders****	"Game of Love" (#1)
Tom Jones	"It's Not Unusual" (#10)
Them (w/ Van Morrison)*****	"Here Comes the Night" (#24)
The Yardbirds	"For Your Love" (#6)
Donovan	"Catch the Wind" (#23)
The Hollies****	"Look Through Any Window" (#32)

1964 2 3 4 5 6 7 8 9 10 11 12 **1965** 2 3 4 5 6...**1966**

* from Liverpool (Merseybeat); ** from London; *** from Newcastle; **** from Manchester; ***** from Belfast, N. Ireland. April 4, 1964, the top five slots on the *Billboard* Hot 100 singles chart were all by the Beatles. May 21, 1965, seven UK and one Australian singles were in the U.S. Top 10.

FIGURE 33. BIRTH YEARS OF EARLY 1960s GROUPS

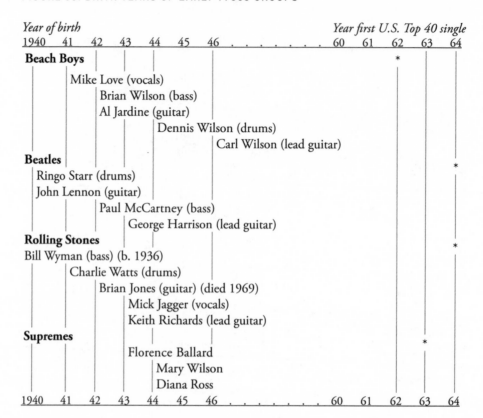

FIGURE 34. SOUL: NAMING A GENRE IN SONG AND ALBUM TITLES

1955 56 57 58 59 **60** 61 62 63 64 65 66 67 68 69

The Soul Stirrers (began releasing gospel singles 1951)

Ray Charles | "A Bit of Soul" (Atlantic, released 1964)

"Hornful Soul" (Atlantic)

Genius + Soul = Jazz (Impulse)

Milt Jackson   "Soul in 3/4" (Savoy)
(vibraphone)   *Plenty, Plenty Soul* (Atlantic)

Milt Jackson and   *Soul Brothers* (Atlantic)
Ray Charles   *Soul Meeting* (Atlantic, released 1961)

John Coltrane (tenor sax) | *Soultrane* (Prestige)

Coleman Hawkins (tenor sax) | *Soul* (Prestige)

Hank Crawford (tenor sax)   *More Soul* (Atlantic)

Stevie Wonder | *The Jazz Soul of Little Stevie* (Tamla/Motown)

Sam Cooke | *Mr. Soul* (RCA)

King Curtis   *Soul Serenade* (Capitol)

James Brown | *Grits and Soul* (Smash)

Handful of Soul (Smash)

Sings Raw Soul (King)

"Funky Soul #1"/
"The Soul of J.B."

Plays Nothing But Soul
(King)

"Soul Pride" (King)
"Soul Power" (1971)

Otis Redding   *Otis Blue/Sings Soul* (Volt/Atco)

Sings Soul Ballads (Volt/Atco)

The Soul Album (Volt/Atco)

Dictionary of Soul (Volt/Atco)

Aretha Franklin   *Soul Sister* (Columbia)

Lady Soul (Atlantic)

Soul '69 (Atlantic)

Wilson Pickett   "634-5789 (Soulsville U.S.A.)"

"Soul Dance #3" (Atlantic)

Sam and Dave   "Soul Man"

Soul Men (Stax)

1955 56 57 58 59 **60** 61 62 63 64 65 66 67 68 69

The August 18, 1960 issue of *Down Beat* had five full-page ads from the Prestige and Riverside labels proclaiming the arrival of *soul jazz*.

FIGURE 35. MID TO LATE 1960s U.S. ROCK (PSYCHEDELIC AND HARD)
(FIRST TOP 40 POP SINGLES AND ALBUMS / R&B CHART POSITION)

<u>1965   66   67   68   69   70   71</u>

NEW YORK CITY

Lovin' Spoonful (10 singles, 4 LPs in Top 40, 1965–67)

"Do You Believe in Magic" (#9); *Do You Believe in Magic* (#32)

"Summer in the City" (#1); *Hums of the Lovin' Spoonful* (#14)

Jimi Hendrix Experience (London; New York) (1 single in Top 40, all 4 LPs released during his life in Top 10, 1967–70)

Are You Experienced? (#5/R&B #10)

Axis: Bold as Love (#3/R&B #6)

"All Along the Watchtower" (#20); *Electric Ladyland* (#1/R&B #5)

Band of Gypsys (#5/R&B #14)

SOUTHERN CALIFORNIA

The Doors (Los Angeles) (8 singles, 9 LPs in Top 40, 1967–71)

"Light My Fire" (#1); *The Doors* (#2)

"Hello I Love You" (#1); *Waiting for the Sun* (#1)

"Riders on the Storm" (#14); *L.A. Woman* (#9)

Steppenwolf (Los Angeles) (6 singles, 8 LPs in Top 40, 1968–71)

"Born to Be Wild" (#2); *Steppenwolf* (#6)

"Magic Carpet Ride" (#3); *The Second* (#3)

Iron Butterfly (San Diego)

"In-A-Gadda-Da-Vida" (#30); *In-A-Gadda-Da-Vida* (#4)

SAN FRANCISCO

Jefferson Airplane* (Grace Slick) (2 singles, 9 LPs in Top 40, 1967–72)

"Somebody to Love" (#5); *Surrealistic Pillow* (2nd LP) (#3)

"White Rabbit" (#8); same as above LP

Big Brother and the Holding Company* (Janis Joplin)

"Piece of My Heart" (#12); *Cheap Thrills* (#1/R&B #7) (2nd LP)

The Grateful Dead** (No singles, 11 [out of 23] LPs in Top 40, 1967–87)

The Grateful Dead (#73)

Santana** (5 Top 40 singles, 4 Top 10 LPs, 1969–72)

Santana (#4/R&B #13); "Evil Ways" (#9) (released 1970)

Sly and the Family Stone (10 singles, 5 LPs in Top 40, 1968–74)

"Dance to the Music" (#8/R&B #9); *Dance to the Music* (#142/R&B #11)

"Everyday People" (#1/R&B #1); *Stand!* (#13/R&B #3)

"I Want To Take You Higher" (#38/R&B #24); on *Stand!* and *Greatest Hits* (#2/R&B #1)

There's a Riot Goin' On (#1/R&B #1)

Other SF area bands: Country Joe and the Fish, Quicksilver Messenger Service, Moby Grape, Blue Cheer, Steve Miller Band.

Credence Clearwater Revival (El Cerrito, CA) (16 singles, 7 LPs in Top 40, 1968–72)

"Suzie Q. (Part One)" (#11); *Creedence Clearwater Revival* (#52)

"Proud Mary" (#2); *Bayou Country* (#7/R&B #41)

<u>1965   66   67   68   69   70   71</u>

* woman lead vocalist
** jam band

FIGURE 36. FUNK: NAMING A GENRE IN SONG AND ALBUM TITLES

JAZZ
"Funky Start Boogie," 1944, Albert Ammons (piano)
"Funky Butt," 1947, Mezz Mezzrow (clarinet)
"Funky Blues," 1951, Flip Phillips (tenor sax)
"Opus de Funk," 1953, Horace Silver (piano) (Blue Note)
"Funk Junction," 1954, King Pleasure (vocals) with Quincy Jones Band (Prestige)
"Calling Dr. Funk," 1955, Vince Guaraldi (piano) (Fantasy)
"Barrel of Funk," 1956, Hank Mobley (tenor sax) with Donald Byrd/Lee Morgan (Blue Note)
"D's Funk," 1956, Lee Morgan (trumpet) (Blue Note)
"Funky," on *Funky,* 1957, Gene Ammons (tenor sax) (Prestige)
"Groove Funk Soul," on *Grove Funk Soul,* 1959, Joe Castro (piano) (Atlantic)
His Majesty King Funk, 1965, Grant Green (guitar) (Verve)

	1967	68	69	70	71	72	73	74	75	76

R&B

Dyke and the Blazers — "Funky Broadway," *The Funky Broadway* (Original Sound)

Wilson Pickett — "Funky Broadway" (Atlantic)
"Funky Way" (Atlantic)

Hank Ballard and the Midnighters — "Funky Soul Train" (King) (cowritten by James Brown)

James Brown — "Funky Soul #1" (King)
"Just Plain Funk" (King)
"Ain't It Funky Now (Parts 1 and 2)" (King)
Ain't It Funky (King)
"Funky Drummer (Parts 1 and 2)" (King)
Sho Is Funky Down Here (King)
"Make it Funky" (Polydor)
"Funky Side of Town" (Polydor)
"Funky President" (Polydor)

The Meters — "Funky Miracle" (Josie)
"Good Old Funky Music" (Josie)
"Gettin' Funkier All the Time" (Reprise)

Funkadelic — *Funkadelic* (Westbound)
"Funky Dollar Bill" (Westbound)

Parliament — "Funky Woman" (Invictus)
Mothership Connection (Casablanca)
(4 out of 7 titles):
"P. Funk (Wants to Get Funked Up)"
"Unfunky UFO"
"Supergroovalisticprosifunksication"
"Give up the Funk (Tear the Roof ...)"
The Clones of Dr. Funkenstein

1967	68	69	70	71	72	73	74	75	76

FIGURE 37. GROUPS WITH ORGAN, 1960s

1959	**60**	61	62	63	64	65	66	67	68	69	**70**

James Brown

Booker T. and the MGs ("Green Onions")

The Animals ("House of the Rising Sun")

Dave Clark 5

The Zombies

Paul Revere and the Raiders

The Monkees

Small Faces

Spencer Davis Group

Procol Harum

Doors

The Band

Crazy World of Arthur Brown

Deep Purple

Iron Butterfly

Steppenwolf

Allman Brothers

Santana

Yes

Jethro Tull

King Crimson

Genesis

Crosby, Stills, and Nash

Emerson, Lake, and Palmer

Isley Brothers

1959	**60**	61	62	63	64	65	66	67	68	69	**70**

FIGURE 38. INTEGRATED GROUPS, 1960s TO EARLY 1970s

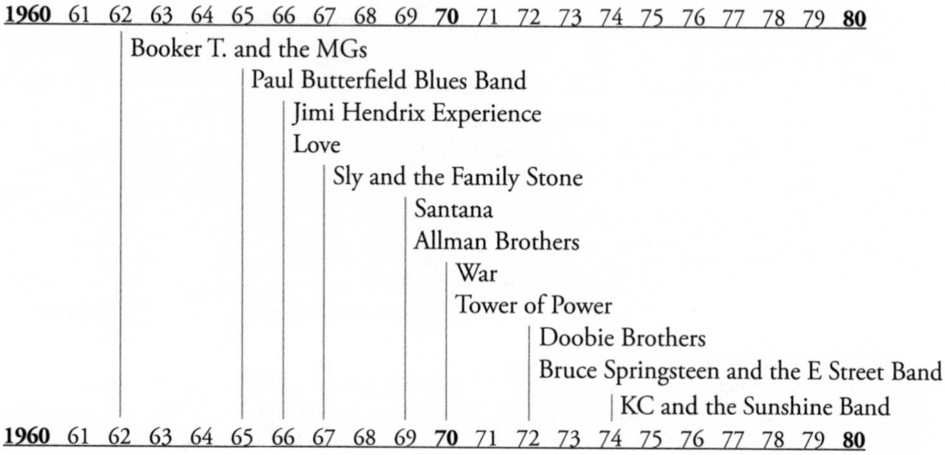

1960 61 62 63 64 65 66 67 68 69 **70** 71 72 73 74 75 76 77 78 79 **80**

Booker T. and the MGs
Paul Butterfield Blues Band
Jimi Hendrix Experience
Love
Sly and the Family Stone
Santana
Allman Brothers
War
Tower of Power
Doobie Brothers
Bruce Springsteen and the E Street Band
KC and the Sunshine Band

1960 61 62 63 64 65 66 67 68 69 **70** 71 72 73 74 75 76 77 78 79 **80**

FIGURE 39. GROUPS WITH LATIN PERCUSSION

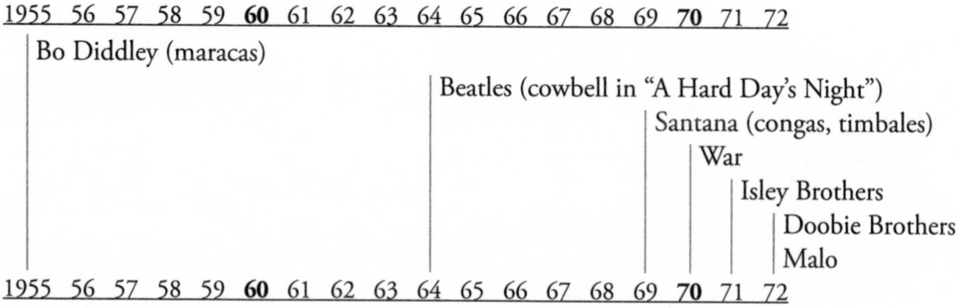

1955 56 57 58 59 **60** 61 62 63 64 65 66 67 68 69 **70** 71 72

Bo Diddley (maracas)
Beatles (cowbell in "A Hard Day's Night")
Santana (congas, timbales)
War
Isley Brothers
Doobie Brothers
Malo

1955 56 57 58 59 **60** 61 62 63 64 65 66 67 68 69 **70** 71 72

FIGURE 40. BIRTH AND DEATH YEARS OF 1960s MUSICIANS

Year of birth										*Year of death*							
1940	41	42	43	44	45	46	. . . .	65	66	67	68	69	70	71

```
Year of birth                                      Year of death
1940   41   42   43   44   45   46 . . . . . . . . 65   66   67   68   69   70   71
     │ Otis Redding                                          *         │          │
     │   │ Brian Jones (Rolling Stones)                            *   │          │
     │   │   │ Alan Wilson (Canned Heat)                                     *     │
     │   │ Jimi Hendrix                                                      *     │
     │   │   │ Janis Joplin                                                  *     │
     │   │   │ Jim Morrison                                                        *
     │   │   │   │ Duane Allman                                                    *
1940   41   42   43   44   45   46 . . . . . . . . 65   66   67   68   69   70   71
```

Otis Redding (September 9, 1941–December 10, 1967; airplane crash)
Brian Jones (Febuary 28, 1942–July 3, 1969; drowned in swimming pool, drug and alcohol abuse)
Alan Wilson (July 4, 1943–September 3, 1970; barbituate overdose, possibly releated to depression)
Jimi Hendrix (November 27, 1942–September 18, 1970; choked on vomit while asleep, drug related)
Janis Joplin (January 19, 1943–October 4, 1970; heroin related)
Jim Morrison (December 8, 1943–July 3, 1971; heart failure, possibly drug or alcohol related)
Duane Allman (November 20, 1946–October 29, 1971; motorcycle accident)

FIGURE 41. ALL-TIME TOP 40 HITS: SOLOISTS AND GROUPS (THROUGH 1999)

Soloists

40 or more
Elvis Presley, 113, 1956–77 (18 at #1)
Elton John, 59, 1970–99 (9 at #1)
Stevie Wonder, 46, 1963–87 (10 at #1)
Aretha Franklin, 34, 1967–76; 45 total 1961–98
James Brown, 43, 1960–74
Madonna, 40, 1983–99 (11 at #1)
Marvin Gaye, 39, 1963–77; 40 total 1963–82

30–39
Neil Diamond, 38, 1966–83
Fats Domino, 37, 1955–63
Paul McCartney (and Wings, and others), 37, 1971–89 (9 at #1)
Michael Jackson, 36, 1971–96 (13 at #1)
Ricky Nelson, 36, 1957–72
Rod Stewart, 34, 1971–98
Billy Joel, 33, 1974–93
Ray Charles, 32, 1957–71; 33 total 1957–89
Prince, 32, 1979–99 (5 at #1)
Dionne Warwick, 31, 1963–87
Janet Jackson, 31, 1986–99 (8 at #1)
Bobby Vinton, 31, 1962–75
Whitney Houston, 30, 1985–99 (11 at #1)

20–29
Sam Cooke, 29, 1957–65
Brenda Lee, 29, 1960–67
Olivia Newton John (solo and with others), 29, 1971–96
Nat King Cole, 28, 1954–64
Kenny Rogers (with First Edition, and solo), 27, 1968–84
Diana Ross (solo and duets), 27, 1970–85
Gladys Knight, 24, 1961–75; 27 total 1961–96
Barry Manilow, 25, 1974–83
Jackie Wilson, 24, 1958–68
George Michael (with Wham!, and solo), 23, 1984–96
Roy Orbison, 22, 1960–66
Linda Ronstadt, 21, 1967–90
Neal Sedaka, 21, 1958–80
Dion (with the Belmonts, and solo), 21, 1958–68
Donna Summer, 20, 1975–89 (4 at #1)

Groups

40 or more
Beatles, 47, 1964–70 (20 at #1)
Rolling Stones, 41, 1964–89 (8 at #1)

30–39
Temptations, 37, 1964–75 (4 at #1)
Beach Boys, 36, 1962–88 (4 at #1)
Chicago, 35, 1970–91
Supremes, 33, 1963–76 (12 at #1)

20–29
Hall and Oates, 29, 1976–90 (6 at #1)
Miracles, 29, 1960–75
Bee Gees, 28, 1967–83
Four Seasons, 27, 1962–68; 31 total 1962–94 (5 at #1)
Platters, 23, 1955–67 (4 at #1)
Kool and the Gang, 22, 1973–87
Four Tops, 22, 1964–73
Three Dog Night, 21, 1969–75

16–19
Huey Lewis and the News, 18, 1982–93
Journey, 18, 1979–96
Spinners, 17, 1961–80
Jackson Five, 17, 1969–75 (4 at #1); Jacksons, 7, 1976–84
Impressions, 17, 1958–74
Foreigner, 16, 1977–88
Simon and Garfunkel, 16, 1965–82
Styx, 16, 1975–91
Van Halen, 16, 1978–95
The Who, 16, 1967–82
Doobie Brothers, 16, 1972–89

FIGURE 42. BLAXPLOITATION FILMS AND THE NEXT GENERATION

```
1970  71  72  73  74  75 . . . . 1989  90  91  92  93
```

Cotton Comes to Harlem (writer: Chester Himes; director: Ossie Davis)
Sweet Sweetback's Baadasssss Song (music: Earth, Wind, and Fire; director: Melvin van Peebles)
Shaft (music: Isaac Hayes; director: Gordon Parks, Jr.)
Super Fly (music: Curtis Mayfield; director: Gordon Parks, Jr.)
Cleopatra Jones (music: J. J. Johnson; director: Jack Starrett)
The Mack (Richard Pryor; music: Willie Hutch; director: Michael Campus)
Coffy (Pam Grier; music: Roy Ayers; director: Jack Hill)
Foxy Brown (Pam Grier; music: Willie Hutch; director: Jack Hill)

. . . . . .

Do the Right Thing (Public Enemy's "Fight the Power"; music: Bill Lee; director: Spike Lee)
Boyz n the Hood (Ice Cube; music: Stanley Clarke; director: John Singleton)
Jungle Fever (music: Stevie Wonder; director: Spike Lee)
New Jack City (director: Mario van Peebles)
Juice (Tupac Shakur; music: Hank Shocklee and The Bomb Squad; director: Ernest R. Dickerson)
Malcolm X (music: Terence Blanchard; director: Spike Lee)
Menace II Society (music: QDIII; dirs.: Albert and Allen Hughes)
Poetic Justice (Tupac, Janet Jackson; music: Stanley Clarke; dir.: Singleton)

```
1970  71  72  73  74  75 . . . . 1989  90  91  92  93
```

FIGURE 43. FUNK BANDS: THEIR DEBUT LP YEAR AND THEIR FIRST POP TOP 10 SINGLE

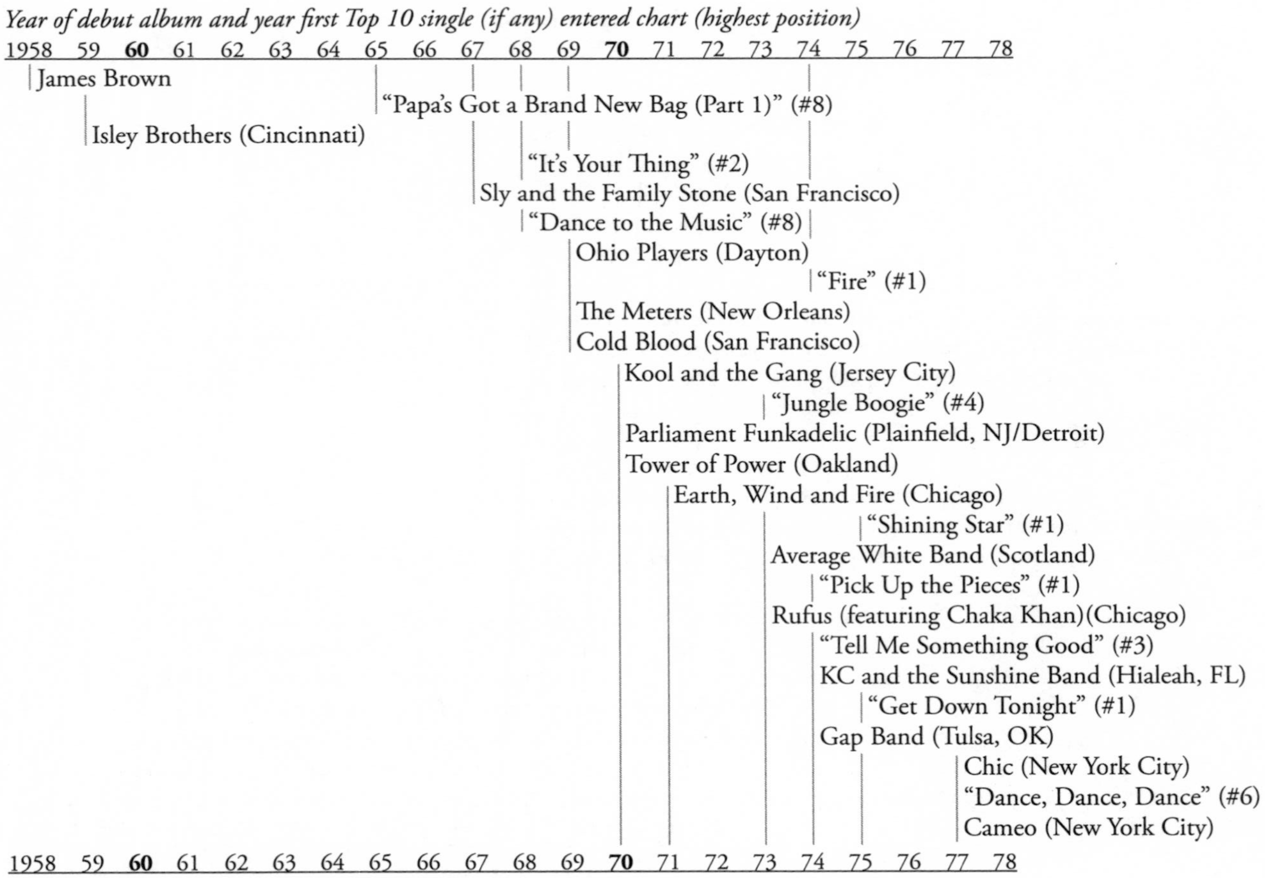

Year of debut album and year first Top 10 single (if any) entered chart (highest position)

FIGURE 44. PROGRESSIVE, ART, EXPERIMENTAL, AND GLAM ROCK

1966	67	68	69	70	71	72	73	74

UK (PROGRESSIVE/ART)

Moody Blues (Birmingham): *Days of Future Passed* (2nd LP)
Pink Floyd (London): *The Piper at the Gates of Dawn*
Procol Harum: *Procol Harum*
Soft Machine (Canterbury): *The Soft Machine*
King Crimson (London): *In the Court of the Crimson King*
The Who (London): *Tommy* (6th LP)
Yes (Birmingham): *Yes*
Jethro Tull (Blackpool): *Stand Up* (2nd LP); *Aqualung* (1971, 4th LP)
Emerson, Lake, and Palmer (Bournemouth, Dorset): *Emerson, Lake, and Palmer*
Genesis (Godalming): *Trespass* (2nd LP)
Roxy Music (London): *Roxy Music*
Robert Fripp (KC guitarist) and Brian Eno (RM keyboardist): *No Pussyfooting*
Brian Eno: *Here Come the Warm Jets*

UK (GLAM)

T. Rex (London): *Electric Warrior* (6th LP)
David Bowie (London): *The Rise and Fall of Ziggy Stardust and the Spiders from Mars* (5th LP)
Queen (London): *Sheer Heart Attack* (3rd LP)

U.S. (EXPERIMENTAL/UNDERGROUND)

Frank Zappa and the Mothers of Invention (Los Angeles): *Freak Out!*
The Velvet Underground (New York): *The Velvet Underground and Nico*
Captain Beefheart and His Magic Band (Glendale, CA): *Safe as Milk*
Kansas (Topeka): *Kansas*

U.S. (GLAM/GLITTER)

Lou Reed (produced by David Bowie): *Transformer* (2nd solo LP)
Alice Cooper (Detroit): *School's Out* (5th LP)
New York Dolls (NY): *New York Dolls*
Kiss (Queens, NY): *Kiss*

GERMANY (EXPERIMENTAL)

Can (Cologne): *Tago Mago* (3rd LP)
Kraftwerk (Düsseldorf): *Autobahn* (4th LP)
Harmonia (Forst): *Musik von Harmonia*

1966	67	68	69	70	71	72	73	74

Debut albums unless otherwise noted.

FIGURE 45. EARLY TO MID 1970s ROCK: TOP 40 SINGLES AND ALBUMS

1969	70	71	72	73	74	75	76

US

HARD ROCK

Grand Funk Railroad (Flint, MI) (8 of first 11 LPs reached Top 10, 1969–74)

Grand Funk (2nd LP, #11)

"Closer to Home" (#22); *Closer to Home* (3rd LP, #6)

"We're an American Band" (#1); *WAAB* (8th LP, #2)

James Gang (Cleveland, OH)

James Gang Rides Again (2nd LP, #20)

Aerosmith (Boston)

"Dream On" (#59; #6 in 1976); *Aerosmith* (1st LP, #21)

"Sweet Emotion" (#36); *Toys in the Attic* (3rd LP, #11)

"Last Child" (#21); *Rocks* (4th LP, #3)

"Walk This Way" (#10); *Toys in the Attic*

BOOGIE

Doobie Brothers (San Jose, CA) (8 of first 10 LPs reached Top 10, 1973–80)

"Listen to the Music" (#11)

"Long Train Runnin'" (#8)

"Black Water" (#1)

"Takin' it to the Streets" (#13, R&B #57)

SOUTHERN BOOGIE

Allman Brothers (Macon, GA)

Idlewild South (2nd LP, #38)

At Fillmore East (3rd LP, #13)

Eat a Peach (4th LP, #4)

"Ramblin Man" (#2); *Brothers and Sisters* (5th LP, #1)

ZZ Top (Houston, TX)

Tres Hombres (3rd LP, #8)

The Marshall Tucker Band (Spartanburg, SC)

The Marshall Tucker Band (1st LP, #29)

Lynyrd Skynyrd (Jacksonville, FL)

Lynyrd Skynyrd (1st LP, #27)

"Sweet Home Alabama" (#8); *Second Helping* (2nd LP, #12)

"Free Bird" (#19); *Lynyrd Skynyrd*

CANADA

Bachman-Turner Overdrive (Winnipeg)

"Let it Ride" (#23); *Bachman-Turner Overdrive II* (2nd LP, #4)

"Takin' Care of Business" (#12)

"You Ain't Seen Nothing Yet" (#1); *Not Fragile* (3rd LP, #1)

UK

Bad Company (London)

"Can't Get Enough" (#5); *Bad Company* (1st LP, #1)

"Movin' On" (#19)

1969	70	71	72	73	74	75	76

FIGURE 46. FOLK ROCK AND COUNTRY ROCK GROUPS

Musician	Byrds	GD	BS	Poco	D&C	FBB	CSNY	LR	Eagles	RT	Manassas
David Crosby (v, g)	1965						1969				
Roger McGuinn (v, lg)	1965										
Gene Clark (v)	1965				1968						
Chris Hillman (v, b)	1965				1968	1968					1972
Gram Parsons (v, g)	1968				1968	1968					
Clarence White (lg)	1968										
Jerry Garcia (lg, v)		1965					**			1972	
Bob Weir (v, g)		1965								1972	
Mickey Hart (d)		1967								1972	
Richie Furay (v, g)			1966	1968							
Stephen Stills (v, g, k)			1966				1969			1972	1972
Neil Young (v, g)			1966				1970				
Jim Messina (v, lg)			1967	1968							
Graham Nash* (v, g)							1969				
Byron Berline (f)					1969	1971					1972
Bernie Leadon (v, g)					1968	1969			1972		
Randy Meisner (v, b)				1968				1971	1972		
Don Henley (v, d)								1971	1972		
Glenn Frey (v, g, k)								1971	1972		

Key: v (vocals); g (guitar); lg (lead guitar); b (bass); k (keyboard); f (fiddle); d (drums).
GD: Grateful Dead; BS: Buffalo Springfield; D&C: Dillard and Clark; FBB: Flying Burrito Brothers;
CSNY: Crosby, Stills, and Nash—Young added spring 1970; LR: Linda Ronstadt; *RT: Rolling Thunder* (Mickey Hart's debut solo album).
* Nash was lead vocalist with the British group The Hollies.
** Garcia played pedal steel guitar on "Teach Your Children" on CSNY's second album (*Déjà Vu,* 1970).

FIGURE 47. DISCO SINGERS AND GROUPS AND THEIR DEBUT DISCO LPS

	1973	74	75	76	77
Hues Corporation	*Freedom for the Stallion* (RCA Victor), "Rock the Boat" (released 1974)				
Love Unlimited Orch. (Barry White)	*Rhapsody in White* (20th Century), "Love's Theme"				
Gloria Gaynor		*Never Can Say Goodbye* (MGM)			
Van McCoy		*Disco Baby* (4th LP, Avco), "The Hustle"			
Donna Summer		*Love to Love You Baby* (2nd LP, Oasis/Casablanca)			
Vicki Sue Robinson		*Never Gonna Let You Go* (RCA Victor), "Turn the Beat Around"			
Village People		*Village People* (Casablanca)			
Evelyn "Champagne" King		*Smooth Talk* (RCA Victor), "Shame"			
Bee Gees and other artists		*Saturday Night Fever Soundtrack* (RSO), "Stayin', Alive," "Night Fever"			
	1973	74	75	76	77

FIGURE 48. PUNK AND NEW WAVE GROUPS AND THEIR DEBUT LPS

| 1967 | 68 | 69 | **70** | 71 | 72 | 73 | 74 | 75 | 76 | 77 | 78 | 79 | **80** | 81 | 82 |

PROTOPUNK

| The Velvet Underground: *The Velvet Underground and Nico* (Lou Reed, John Cale) [New York]

| The Stooges: *The Stooges* (prod. John Cale) [Ann Arbor, Michigan]

| MC5: *Kick out the Jams* [Detroit]

NEW YORK

| Patti Smith Group: *Horses* (w/Lennie Kaye; prod. Cale)

Ramones: *Ramones*

The Modern Lovers (Jonathan Richman; prod. Cale; rec. 1971–72) [Boston]

Blondie*: *Blondie*

Television*: *Marquee Moon* (Tom Verlaine, Richard Lloyd)

Richard Hell and the Voidoids: *Blank Generation*

Talking Heads*: *77*

LONDON

The Damned: *Damned, Damned, Damned*

The Clash: *The Clash*

Elvis Costello*: *My Aim is True*

Sex Pistols: *Never Mind the Bollocks, Here's the Sex Pistols*

NEXT GENERATION
UK

| Public Image Ltd.: *First Image* (John Lydon)

| Gang of Four: *Entertainment*

| Psychedelic Furs: *Psychedelic Furs*

USA

| Pere Ubu: *The Modern Dance* [Cleveland]

Devo: *Q: Are We Not Men? A: We Are Devo!* [Cleveland]

HARDCORE PUNK

| X: *Los Angeles* [LA]

| Dead Kennedys: *Fresh Fruit for Rotting Vegetables* [SF]

| Black Flag: *Damaged* [LA]

| Bad Brains: *Bad Brains* [Washington, DC/NY]

| 1967 | 68 | 69 | **70** | 71 | 72 | 73 | 74 | 75 | 76 | 77 | 78 | 79 | **80** | 81 | 82 |

* new wave/postpunk

FIGURE 49. DISCO AND PUNK COMPARISONS

Feature	Disco	Punk
Sound	Smooth, lush, sensual	Hard-edged, loud, shouting
Music	R&B, jazz, and pop blend	Pared down rock chords, shed R&B influences
Tempo	Medium (bpm in lower 120s)	Fast
Dance	Highly choreographed, group coordination, controlled, partner-pairing	Chaotic, solo, uncontrolled
Lyrics	Dance-oriented, romantic, escapist, hedonist	Defiant, "anti"-aesthetic, alienated youth-oriented, nihilist
Arrangements	Dense, with full orchestra	Minimal, just guitar, bass, drums
Racial/Ethnic orientation	Black, Latina/o	White
Sexual orientation	Marked (male homosexual)	Unmarked (heterosexual)
Class orientation	Working class (focus on the weekend)	Middle class (romance of poverty); unemployed
Clothing	Dress up: polyester, formal, form-fitting	Dress down: ripped jeans and cotton T-shirts, leather, safety pins
Song durations	Long, to keep people on dancefloor	Short (2–3 minutes)
Radio	Initially shunned, then pervasive	Initially shunned, minimal acceptance
Technology	Sophisticated studio production	Do-it-yourself (DIY), raw
Primary actors	Producer, DJ, solo vocalist	Live musicians as a group
Critical reception	Trashed as formulaic, fluff	Praised for its rawness and political potential
Social impact	Inclusive: brought races, ethnicities, and sexualities together on dancefloor; offended some heterosexual whites	Exclusive: polarizing, shock symbols (Nazi regalia) sent out mixed political messages

FIGURE 50. WOMEN ROCK SINGERS FRONTING BANDS, 1970s (DEBUT AND SUCCEEDING ALBUMS)

	1970	71	72	73	74	75	76	77	78	79	1980	81
Fanny (June and Jean Millington)	*Fanny* (did not chart)				*Fanny Hill* (#135) (3rd LP)							
Joan Armatrading					*Whatever's for Us* (did not chart)			*Show Some Emotion* (#52) (4th LP)		*If You Knew Suzi* (#37) (5th LP)		
Suzi Quatro					*Suzi Quatro* (#142)							
Patti Smith						*Horses* (#47)	*Radio Ethiopia* (#122)		*Easter* (#20)	*Wave* (#18)		
Heart (Ann and Nancy Wilson)							*Dreamboat Annie* (#7)					
The Runaways (Joan Jett, Lita Ford)							*The Runaways* (#194)	*Queens of Noise* (#172)				
Deborah Harry							*Blondie* (did not chart)	*Plastic Letters* (#72)	*Parallel Lines* (#6)			
Pat Benatar									*In the Heat of the Night* (#12)	*Crimes of Passion* (#2)		
Rickie Lee Jones										*Rickie Lee Jones* (#3)		
Chrissie Hynde										*Pretenders* (#9)		
Joan Jett											*Bad Reputation* (#51)	*I Love Rock-n-Roll* (#2)
	1970	71	72	73	74	75	76	77	78	79	1980	81

Fanny and The Runaways were all-women bands. June Millington, Nancy Wilson, Jett, Ford, and Hynde played electric guitar. Quatro played bass.

FIGURE 51. GENDERED INSTRUMENTS

Piano (women)
Aretha Franklin, Nina Simone, Carole King, Roberta Flack, Joni Mitchell

Piano (men)
Little Richard, Jerry Lee Lewis, Elton John, Jackson Browne, Billy Joel

Acoustic guitar (women)
Memphis Minnie, Wanda Jackson, Joan Baez, Joni Mitchell

Acoustic guitar (men)
Elvis Presley, Bob Dylan, Crosby, Stills, Nash, and Young

Electric guitar (women)
Memphis Minnie, Sister Rosetta Tharpe, Peggy "Lady Bo" Jones and Norma-Jean "The Duchess" Wofford (Bo Diddley's band), Barbara Lynn, Joan Jett and Lita Ford (The Runaways), Carlita Dorhan (A Taste of Honey)

Drums (women)
Maureen Tucker (Velvet Underground), Karen Carpenter, Bobbye Hall (percussion)

Electric bass (women)
Carol Kaye (LA studio musician), Suzi Quatro, Tina Weymouth (Talking Heads), Janice-Marie Johnson (A Taste of Honey), Kim Gordon (Sonic Youth), Kim Deal (Pixies)

FIGURE 52. JAZZ AND JAZZ ROCK ALBUMS IN THE POP TOP 40

1955 56 57 58 59 **60** 61 62 63 64 65 66 67 68 69 **70** 71 72 73 74 75 76 77

Louis Armstrong (2 LPs in Top 40, 1955–56; *Hello Dolly!*, #1, 1964)
Ella Fitzgerald (6 LPs in Top 40, 1955–61, 1 of which in Top 10)
Dave Brubeck (11 LPs in Top 40, 1955–63, 5 of which in Top 10)
Sarah Vaughan (4 LPs in Top 40, 1956–57)
Duke Ellington (*At Newport*, #14, 1957)
Ahmad Jamal (3 LPs in Top 40, 1958–60, including *But Not for Me* at *the Pershing*, #3)
Stan Getz (4 LPs in Top 40, 1962–64, including *Jazz Samba*, #1, and *Getz/Gilberto*, #2)
Cannonball Adderley (3 LPs in Top 40, 1962–67)
Nancy Wilson (13 LPs in Top 40, 1962–67, 4 of which in Top 10)
Herb Alpert and the Tijuana Brass (13 LPs in Top 40, 1962–69, 6 of which at #1)
Herbie Mann (3 LPs in Top 40, 1962–75)
Lee Morgan (*The Sidewinder*, #25, 1964)
Wes Montgomery (2 LPs in Top 40, 1967–68)
Blood, Sweat and Tears

Chicago

Miles Davis

Donald Byrd

Mahavishnu Orchestra (John McLaughlin)

Carlos Santana and Mahavishnu John McLaughlin

Blood, Sweat and Tears (#1)
Blood, Sweat and Tears 3 (#1)
Next 3 LPs in Top 40 (1971–72)
Chicago Transit Authority (#17)
Chicago II (#4)
Chicago III (#2)
Chicago at Carnegie Hall (#3)
Chicago V–IX all #1 (1972–75)

Bitches Brew (#35, R&B #4)

Black Byrd (#36, R&B #2)
Street Lady (#33, R&B #6)
Birds of Fire (#15)
Love Devotion Surrender (#14)

1955 56 57 58 59 **60** 61 62 63 64 65 66 67 68 69 **70** 71 72 73 74 75 76 77

1955 56 57 58 59 **60** 61 62 63 64 65 66 67 68 69 **70** 71 72 73 74 75 76 77

Herbie Hancock — Head Hunters (#13, R&B #2)
Thrust (#13, R&B #2)
Man-Child (#21, R&B #6)

Return to Forever (Chick Corea) — Where Have I Known You Before (#32)
No Mystery (#39)
Romantic Warrior (#32, R&B #23)
Musicmagic (#38)

Weather Report — Tale Spinnin' (#31, R&B #12)
Heavy Weather (#30, R&B #33)

George Benson (6 more LPs in Top 40, 1977–83, 4 of which in Top 10) — Breezin' (#1, R&B #1)

Steely Dan — Aja (#3) (w/Wayne Shorter)

Maynard Ferguson — Conquistador (#22)

Chuck Mangione (3 more LPs in Top 40, 1978–80) — Feels So Good (#2)

1955 56 57 58 59 **60** 61 62 63 64 65 66 67 68 69 **70** 71 72 73 74 75 76 77

FIGURE 53. RAP GROUPS AND LPS MOVING INTO THE MAINSTREAM, 1984-1990

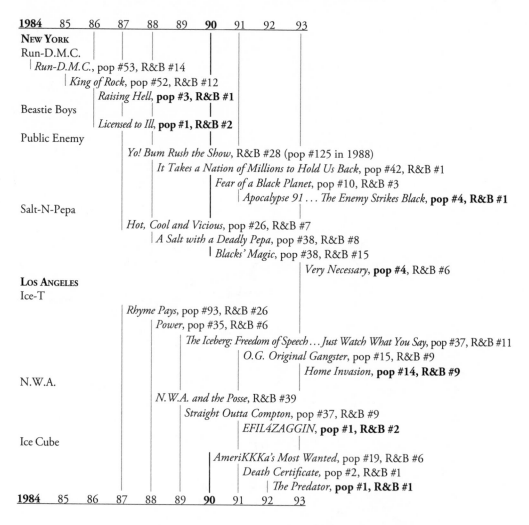

FIGURE 54. SOME KEY RAP RECORD LABELS

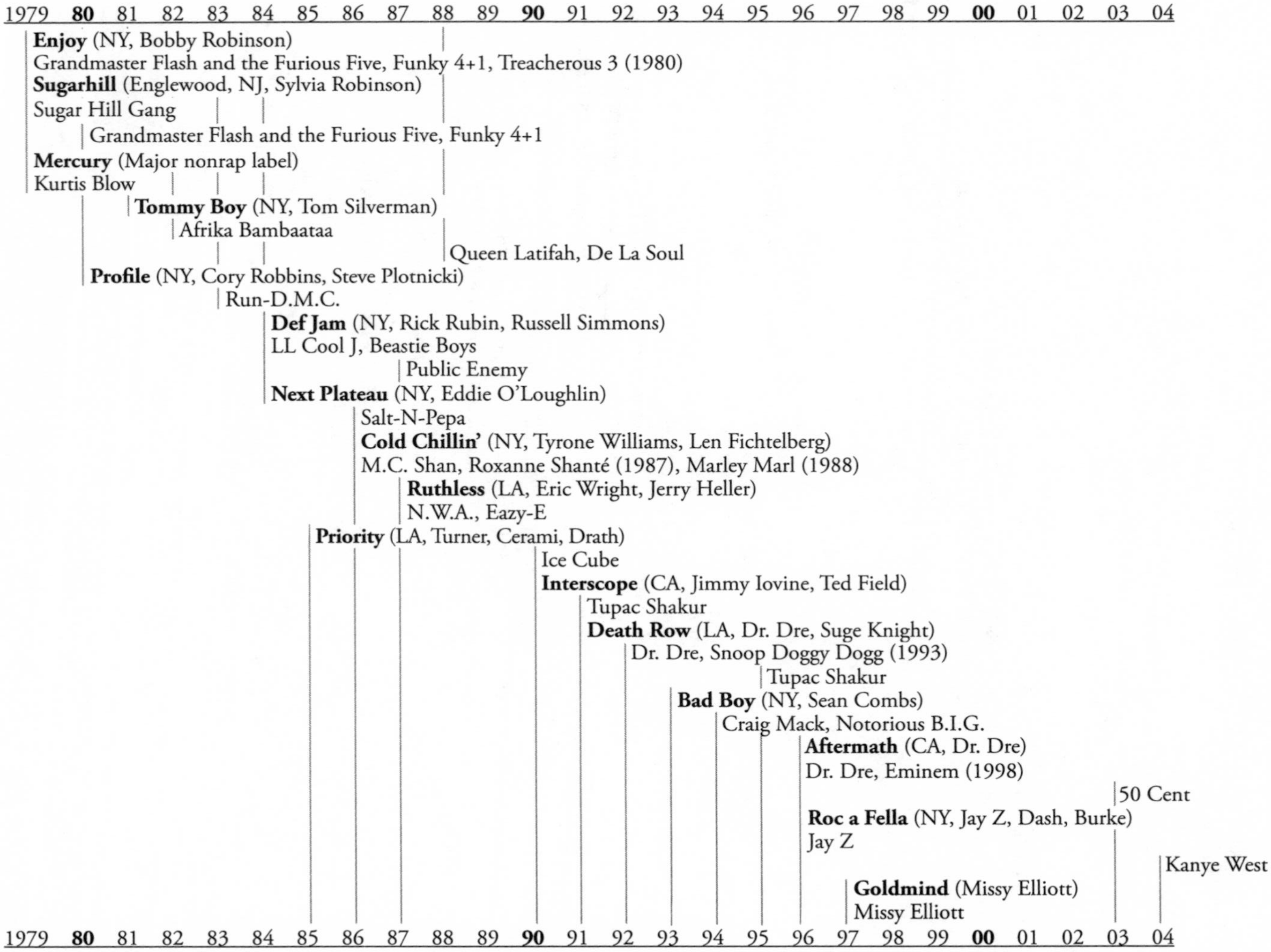

1979 **80** 81 82 83 84 85 86 87 88 89 **90** 91 92 93 94 95 96 97 98 99 **00** 01 02 03 04

Enjoy (NY, Bobby Robinson)
Grandmaster Flash and the Furious Five, Funky 4+1, Treacherous 3 (1980)
Sugarhill (Englewood, NJ, Sylvia Robinson)
Sugar Hill Gang
Grandmaster Flash and the Furious Five, Funky 4+1
Mercury (Major nonrap label)
Kurtis Blow
Tommy Boy (NY, Tom Silverman)
Afrika Bambaataa
Queen Latifah, De La Soul
Profile (NY, Cory Robbins, Steve Plotnicki)
Run-D.M.C.
Def Jam (NY, Rick Rubin, Russell Simmons)
LL Cool J, Beastie Boys
Public Enemy
Next Plateau (NY, Eddie O'Loughlin)
Salt-N-Pepa
Cold Chillin' (NY, Tyrone Williams, Len Fichtelberg)
M.C. Shan, Roxanne Shanté (1987), Marley Marl (1988)
Ruthless (LA, Eric Wright, Jerry Heller)
N.W.A., Eazy-E
Priority (LA, Turner, Cerami, Drath)
Ice Cube
Interscope (CA, Jimmy Iovine, Ted Field)
Tupac Shakur
Death Row (LA, Dr. Dre, Suge Knight)
Dr. Dre, Snoop Doggy Dogg (1993)
Tupac Shakur
Bad Boy (NY, Sean Combs)
Craig Mack, Notorious B.I.G.
Aftermath (CA, Dr. Dre)
Dr. Dre, Eminem (1998)
50 Cent
Roc a Fella (NY, Jay Z, Dash, Burke)
Jay Z
Goldmind (Missy Elliott)
Missy Elliott
Kanye West

1979 **80** 81 82 83 84 85 86 87 88 89 **90** 91 92 93 94 95 96 97 98 99 **00** 01 02 03 04

FIGURE 55. "FIGHT THE POWER" SAMPLE AND LYRIC SOURCES

Lyrics

Public Enemy	Source
"Brothers and sisters" (0:53)	Soul Children ft. Jesse Jackson, "I Don't Know…" (0:00)
"People people, got to get over" (1:44)	James Brown, "Funky President" (0:17)
"Fight the powers that be" (2:05)	Isley Brothers, "Fight the Power, Part 1 and 2" (0:36)
"Don't worry be happy" (3:23)	Bobby McFerrin, "Don't Worry Be Happy"

Samples

Public Enemy	Source
drum beat (0:23 onward)	James Brown, "Hot Pants Road" (0:06)
drum beat (0:23 onward)	James Brown, "Funky drummer" (5:22 or 5:34)*
James Brown grunt (0:24)	James Brown, "Say it Loud . . ." (0:00)
women's chorus (1:14, 1:19)	Bob Marley and the Wailers, "I Shot the Sheriff" (0:01)
"People people, got to get over" (1:48)	James Brown, "Funky President" (0:17)
"Oooo-oooo" (1:59)	Sly and the Family Stone, "Sing a Simple Song" (3:43)
guitar background (2:41)	Sly Johnson, "Different Strokes" (0:26)
"Yaaah" (3:34)	Afrika Bambaataa, "Planet Rock" (0:13)

Source: Who Sampled (2019)
"Fight the Power" timings keyed to 4:43 *Fear of a Black Planet* album version.
* Depending on the version.

FIGURE 56. EARLY METAL GROUPS, NEW WAVE OF BRITISH HEAVY METAL, AND AMERICAN METAL
(DEBUT LP AND FIRST APPEARANCE ON US POP LP CHART)

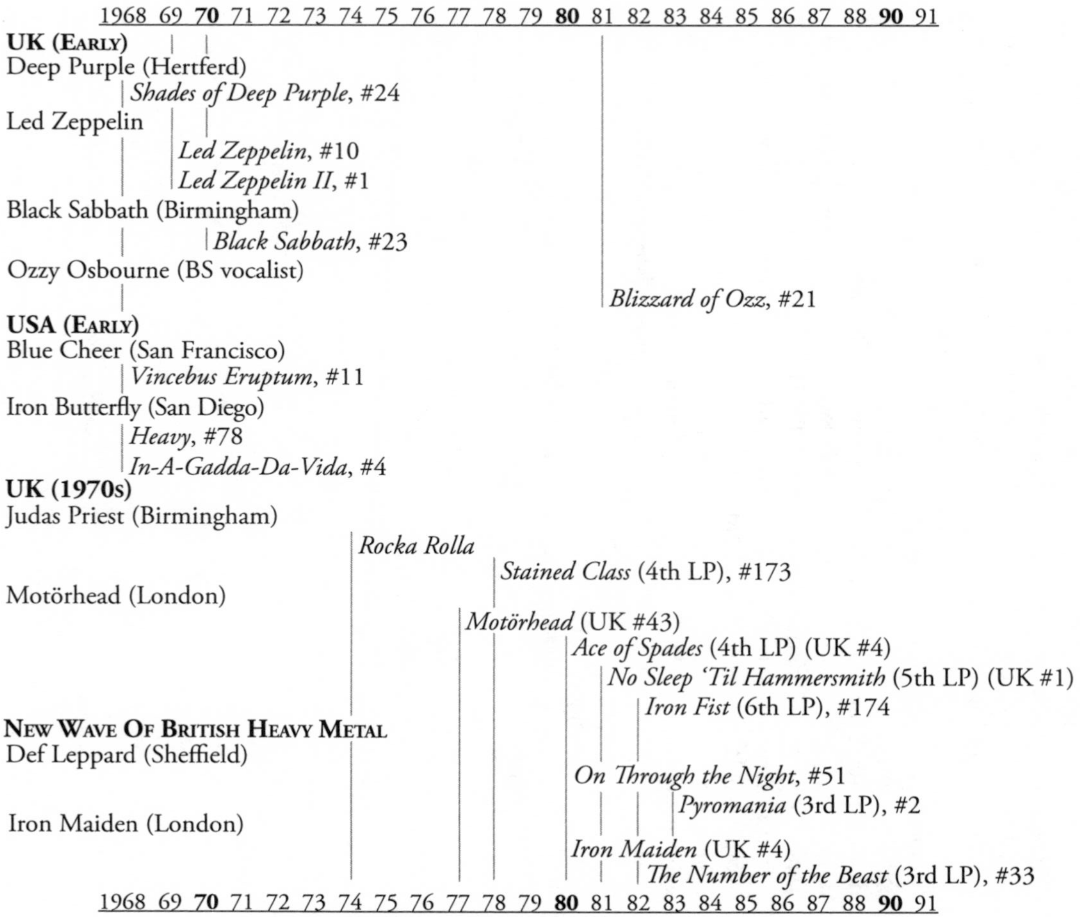

1968 69 **70** 71 72 73 74 75 76 77 78 79 **80** 81 82 83 84 85 86 87 88 **90** 91

UK (EARLY)
Deep Purple (Hertferd)
  Shades of Deep Purple, #24

Led Zeppelin
  Led Zeppelin, #10
  Led Zeppelin II, #1

Black Sabbath (Birmingham)
  Black Sabbath, #23

Ozzy Osbourne (BS vocalist)
  Blizzard of Ozz, #21

USA (EARLY)
Blue Cheer (San Francisco)
  Vincebus Eruptum, #11

Iron Butterfly (San Diego)
  Heavy, #78
  In-A-Gadda-Da-Vida, #4

UK (1970s)
Judas Priest (Birmingham)
  Rocka Rolla
  Stained Class (4th LP), #173

Motörhead (London)
  Motörhead (UK #43)
  Ace of Spades (4th LP) (UK #4)
  No Sleep 'Til Hammersmith (5th LP) (UK #1)
  Iron Fist (6th LP), #174

NEW WAVE OF BRITISH HEAVY METAL
Def Leppard (Sheffield)
  On Through the Night, #51
  Pyromania (3rd LP), #2

Iron Maiden (London)
  Iron Maiden (UK #4)
  The Number of the Beast (3rd LP), #33

1968 69 **70** 71 72 73 74 75 76 77 78 79 **80** 81 82 83 84 85 86 87 88 **90** 91

1968 69 **70** 71 72 73 74 75 76 77 78 79 **80** 81 82 83 84 85 86 87 88 **90** 91

USA (THRASH/SPEED)
Metallica (Los Angeles/SF Bay Area)

Kill 'Em All (charted after 1986 reissue)
Ride the Lightning, #100
Master of Puppets, #29
…And Justice for All, #6
Metallica, #1

Slayer (Huntington Beach, CA)

Show No Mercy
Reign in Blood (4th LP), #94

Anthrax (New York City)

Fistful of Metal
Spreading the Disease, #113

Megadeth (Los Angeles)

Killing is My Business…and Business is Good!
Peace Sells…But Who's Buying?, #76

USA (POP/LITE)
Van Halen (Pasadena, CA)

Van Halen, #19
Van Halen II, #6
Women and Children First, #6
(next six LPs in Top 5, 1981–91)

1968 69 **70** 71 72 73 74 75 76 77 78 79 **80** 81 82 83 84 85 86 87 88 **90** 91

FIGURE 57. HARD ROCK, METAL, AND PUNK COMPARISONS

Feature	Hard rock	Heavy metal	Punk
vocals	can be screaming, upper range	screaming, low range	loud
musical influences	blues, Rolling Stones	European classical technique (18th–19th century)	60s garage bands
band names	not marked	ominous	"The . . ."
album names	not marked	ominous	not marked
song lengths	radio friendly	epic	short
fanbase	male and female, mostly white	predominently male, mostly white	male and female, mostly white
keyboards	yes	rare	rare
aesthetic	hedonist; party	gothic; the past	anti; nihilist; topical
stance	highly commercial	outsider	anticommercial
instrumental ability	competent	ensemble virtuosity	do-it-yourself (DIY)

Group/artist   Month and year first pop Top 10 single entered Top 40 (highest position indicated)

1982 2 3 4 5 6 7 8 9 10 11 12 **1983** 2 3 4 5 6 7 8 9 10 11 12

Human League* — "Don't You Want Me" (#1)
Soft Cell** — "Tainted Love" (#8)
A Flock of Seagulls*** — "I Ran (So Far Away)" (#9)
Joe Jackson**** — "Steppin' Out" (#6)
Culture Club** — "Do You Really Want to Hurt Me" (#2)
Duran Duran***** — "Hungry Like a Wolf" (#3)
Thomas Dolby — "She Blinded Me with Science" (#5)
Eurythmics — "Sweet Dreams (Are Made of This)" (#1)
Spandau Ballet** — "True" (#4)

1982 2 3 4 5 6 7 8 9 10 11 12 **1983** 2 3 4 5 6 7 8 9 10 11 12

1984 2 3 4 5 6 7 8 9 10 11 12 **1985** 2 3 4 5 6 7 8 9 10 11 12 **1986** 2 3 4 5

Thompson Twins — "Hold Me Now" (#3)
Bananarama** — "Cruel Summer" (#9)
Wham! (Bushey, England) — "Wake Me Up Before You Go-Go" (#1)
Frankie Goes to Hollywood*** — "Relax" (#10)
The Power Station — "Some Like It Hot" (#6)
Simple Minds (Glasgow, Scotland) — "Don't You (Forget about Me)" (#1)
Sade** — "Smooth Operator" (#5)
Tears for Fears — "Everybody Wants to Rule the World" (#1)
Howard Jones (Southampton, Hampshire, England) — "Things Can Only Get Better" (#5)
Robert Palmer — "Addicted to Love" (#1)
Pet Shop Boys — "West End Girls" (#1)
Orchestral Manoeuvres in the Dark — "If You Leave" (#4)
Peter Gabriel** — "Sledgehammer" (#1)

1984 2 3 4 5 6 7 8 9 10 11 12 **1985** 2 3 4 5 6 7 8 9 10 11 12 **1986** 2 3 4 5

Not shown (earlier first Top 10): Gary Numan, "Cars" (3/80, #9); The Police, "De Do Do Do, De Da Da Da" (11/80, #10). Grammy Awards: The Police (5 Grammy Awards, 1980–83); Culture Club (Best New Artist, 1983); Sade (Best New Artist, 1985). * from Sheffield; ** from London; *** from Liverpool; **** from Staffordshire; ***** from Birmingham.

FIGURE 59. SUPERSTARS OF THE 1980s

1975 76 77 78 79 **80** 81 82 83 84 85 86 87 88 89 **90** 91

Bruce Springsteen (b. 1949)
| Born to Run (3rd LP, pop #3, Columbia)
| Darkness on the Edge of Town (pop #5, Columbia)
The River (pop #1, Columbia)
Nebraska (pop #3, Columbia)
Born in the U.S.A. (pop #1, Columbia)
Live 1975–85 (pop #1, Columbia)
Tunnel of Love (pop #1, Columbia)

Michael Jackson (b. 1958)
Off the Wall (5th solo LP, pop #3, R&B #1, 1st on Epic)
Thriller (pop #1, R&B #1, Epic)
Bad (pop #1, R&B #1, Epic)
Dangerous (pop #1, R&B #1, Epic)

Prince (b. 1958)
| Prince (2nd LP, R&B #3, Warner)
| Dirty Mind (pop #45, R&B #7, Warner)
| Controversy (pop #21, R&B #3, Warner)
| 1999 (pop #9, R&B #4, Warner)
Purple Rain (pop #1, R&B #1, Warner)
Around the World in a Day (pop #1, R&B #4, Warner)
Parade (pop #3, R&B #2, Warner)
Sign "O" the Times (pop #6, R&B #4, Warner)

Madonna (b. 1958)
| Madonna (1st LP, pop #8, R&B #20, Sire)
Like a Virgin (pop #1, R&B #10, Sire)
True Blue (pop #1, R&B #47, Sire)
Like a Prayer (6th LP, pop #1, R&B #55, Sire)
I'm Breathless (pop #2, Sire)
Immaculate Collection (pop #2, R&B #81, Sire) [no more R&B charting after this]

Whitney Houston (b. 1963)
Whitney Houston (1st LP, pop #1, R&B #1, Arista)
Whitney (pop #1, R&B #2, Arista)
I'm Your Baby Tonight (pop #3, R&B #1, Arista)

1975 76 77 78 79 **80** 81 82 83 84 85 86 87 88 89 **90** 91

FIGURE 60. ROCK FOR A CAUSE

<u>1971</u>
Concert for Bangladesh (Madison Square Garden), conceived by George Harrison and
Ravi Shankar; performers included Bob Dylan and Eric Clapton (August).

<u>1976–81</u>
Rock Against Racism (UK), series of concerts.

<u>1979</u>
No Nukes (Madison Square Garden and Battery Park City, New York City), Musicians United for
Safe Energy (September).

<u>1984</u>
Band Aid, "Do They Know It's Christmas" (UK) (November).

<u>1985</u>
USA for Africa, "We Are the World" (January), Quincy Jones (prod.), Michael Jackson and
Lionel Ritchie (composers).
Live Aid (JFK Stadium, Philadelphia, and Wembley Stadium, London) conceived by Bob Geldoff
(July).
Farm Aid organized by Willie Nelson and John Mellencamp (September).
Artists United Against Apartheid, "Sun City," organized by Steven Van Zandt (October).

<u>1988</u>
Human Rights Now! World Tour for Amnesty International (September-October), Peter Gabriel,
Bruce Springsteen, Sting, Tracy Chapman, Youssou N'Dour.

<u>2001</u>
Concert for New York City (October).

<u>2005</u>
Live 8, organized by Bob Geldoff and Bono (July).
Concert for Hurricane Relief (September).

<u>2010</u>
Hope for Haiti Now telethon (January), "We Are the World 25 Haiti."

FIGURE 61. ALTERNATIVE, INDIE, AND POSTPUNK (DEBUT LP, DEBUT POP LP CHARTING)

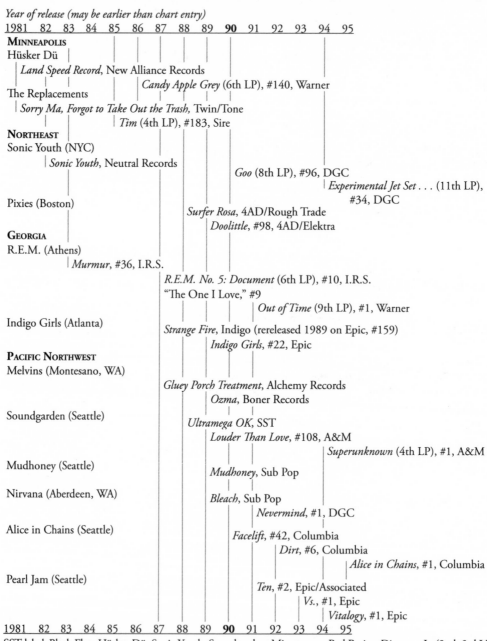

Year of release (may be earlier than chart entry)

1981 82 83 84 85 86 87 88 89 **90** 91 92 93 94 95

MINNEAPOLIS
Hüsker Dü
  Land Speed Record, New Alliance Records
The Replacements   Candy Apple Grey (6th LP), #140, Warner
  Sorry Ma, Forgot to Take Out the Trash, Twin/Tone
      Tim (4th LP), #183, Sire
NORTHEAST
Sonic Youth (NYC)
  Sonic Youth, Neutral Records
            Goo (8th LP), #96, DGC
              Experimental Jet Set . . . (11th LP),
                #34, DGC
Pixies (Boston)
        Surfer Rosa, 4AD/Rough Trade
        Doolittle, #98, 4AD/Elektra
GEORGIA
R.E.M. (Athens)
  Murmur, #36, I.R.S.
      R.E.M. No. 5: Document (6th LP), #10, I.R.S.
      "The One I Love," #9
              Out of Time (9th LP), #1, Warner
Indigo Girls (Atlanta)
      Strange Fire, Indigo (rereleased 1989 on Epic, #159)
          Indigo Girls, #22, Epic
PACIFIC NORTHWEST
Melvins (Montesano, WA)
      Gluey Porch Treatment, Alchemy Records
          Ozma, Boner Records
Soundgarden (Seattle)
        Ultramega OK, SST
        Louder Than Love, #108, A&M
                Superunknown (4th LP), #1, A&M
Mudhoney (Seattle)
        Mudhoney, Sub Pop
Nirvana (Aberdeen, WA)
        Bleach, Sub Pop
          Nevermind, #1, DGC
Alice in Chains (Seattle)
        Facelift, #42, Columbia
          Dirt, #6, Columbia
              Alice in Chains, #1, Columbia
Pearl Jam (Seattle)
        Ten, #2, Epic/Associated
            Vs., #1, Epic
            Vitalogy, #1, Epic

1981 82 83 84 85 86 87 88 89 **90** 91 92 93 94 95

SST label: Black Flag; Hüsker Dü; Sonic Youth; Soundgarden; Minutemen; Bad Brains; Dinosaur Jr. (2nd–3rd LPs).
Sub Pop label: Sonic Youth; Soundgarden; Nirvana; Mudhoney.

FIGURE 62. RAP GROUPS ENTERING THE POP TOP 10 (ALBUMS), 1992–1997

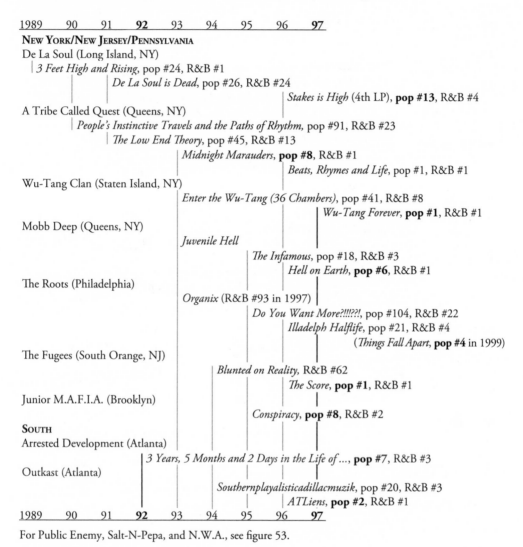

1989   90   91   **92**   93   94   95   96   **97**

NEW YORK/NEW JERSEY/PENNSYLVANIA

De La Soul (Long Island, NY)

  3 Feet High and Rising, pop #24, R&B #1

      De La Soul is Dead, pop #26, R&B #24

          Stakes is High (4th LP), **pop #13**, R&B #4

A Tribe Called Quest (Queens, NY)

  People's Instinctive Travels and the Paths of Rhythm, pop #91, R&B #23

  The Low End Theory, pop #45, R&B #13

      Midnight Marauders, **pop #8**, R&B #1

          Beats, Rhymes and Life, pop #1, R&B #1

Wu-Tang Clan (Staten Island, NY)

      Enter the Wu-Tang (36 Chambers), pop #41, R&B #8

          Wu-Tang Forever, **pop #1**, R&B #1

Mobb Deep (Queens, NY)

    Juvenile Hell

        The Infamous, pop #18, R&B #3

          Hell on Earth, **pop #6**, R&B #1

The Roots (Philadelphia)

    Organix (R&B #93 in 1997)

        Do You Want More?!!!??!, pop #104, R&B #22

          Illadelph Halflife, pop #21, R&B #4

              (*Things Fall Apart,* **pop #4** in 1999)

The Fugees (South Orange, NJ)

      Blunted on Reality, R&B #62

          The Score, **pop #1**, R&B #1

Junior M.A.F.I.A. (Brooklyn)

        Conspiracy, **pop #8**, R&B #2

SOUTH

Arrested Development (Atlanta)

    3 Years, 5 Months and 2 Days in the Life of ..., **pop #7**, R&B #3

Outkast (Atlanta)

        Southernplayalisticadillacmuzik, pop #20, R&B #3

          ATLiens, **pop #2**, R&B #1

1989   90   91   **92**   93   94   95   96   **97**

For Public Enemy, Salt-N-Pepa, and N.W.A., see figure 53.

FIGURE 63. SOLO EMCEES ENTERING THE POP TOP 10 (ALBUMS), 1993–1997

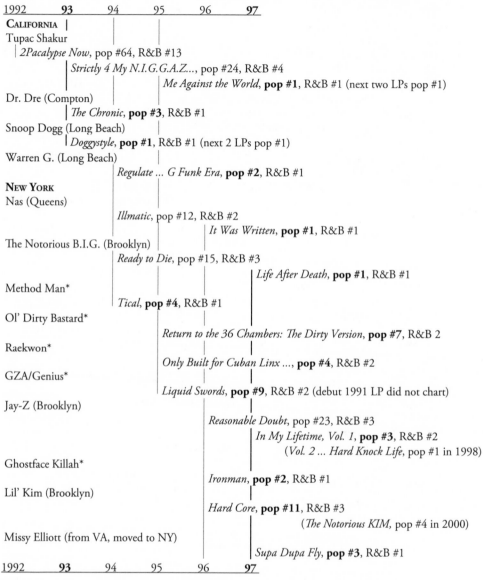

1992   **93**   94   95   96   **97**

CALIFORNIA

Tupac Shakur

  2Pacalypse Now, pop #64, R&B #13

    Strictly 4 My N.I.G.G.A.Z..., pop #24, R&B #4

      Me Against the World, **pop #1**, R&B #1 (next two LPs pop #1)

Dr. Dre (Compton)

  The Chronic, **pop #3**, R&B #1

Snoop Dogg (Long Beach)

  Doggystyle, **pop #1**, R&B #1 (next 2 LPs pop #1)

Warren G. (Long Beach)

    Regulate ... G Funk Era, **pop #2**, R&B #1

NEW YORK

Nas (Queens)

    Illmatic, pop #12, R&B #2

      It Was Written, **pop #1**, R&B #1

The Notorious B.I.G. (Brooklyn)

    Ready to Die, pop #15, R&B #3

      Life After Death, **pop #1**, R&B #1

Method Man*

    Tical, **pop #4**, R&B #1

Ol' Dirty Bastard*

      Return to the 36 Chambers: The Dirty Version, **pop #7**, R&B 2

Raekwon*

      Only Built for Cuban Linx ..., **pop #4**, R&B #2

GZA/Genius*

      Liquid Swords, **pop #9**, R&B #2 (debut 1991 LP did not chart)

Jay-Z (Brooklyn)

      Reasonable Doubt, pop #23, R&B #3

        In My Lifetime, Vol. 1, **pop #3**, R&B #2

          (*Vol. 2 ... Hard Knock Life*, pop #1 in 1998)

Ghostface Killah*

      Ironman, **pop #2**, R&B #1

Lil' Kim (Brooklyn)

      Hard Core, **pop #11**, R&B #3

        (*The Notorious KIM*, pop #4 in 2000)

Missy Elliott (from VA, moved to NY)

      Supa Dupa Fly, **pop #3**, R&B #1

1992   **93**   94   95   96   **97**

* Member of Staten Island-based Wu-Tang Clan.

Debut and succeeding albums, unless otherwise noted. For Ice Cube, see figure 53.

FIGURE 64. WOMEN ROCK SINGER-SONGWRITERS, 1994–1997 (DEBUT TOP 40 SINGLES)

	1994	1995	1996	1997
Lisa Loeb	"Stay (I Missed You)" (#1)			
Sheryl Crow	"All I Wanna Do" (#2)			
Alanis Morissette		"You Oughta Know" (#13)		
Joan Osborne		"One of Us" (#4)		
Jewel			"Who Will Save Your Soul" (#11)	
Paula Cole				"Where Have All the Cowboys Gone?" (#8)
Shawn Colvin				"Sunny Came Home" (#7)
Sarah McLachlan				"Building a Mystery" (#13)
Fiona Apple				"Criminal" (#21)

When we hear music, we try and place it within our own experiences to make sense of it. This can include identifying instruments and voices we hear, styles that they invoke, and sentiments being expressed. Depending on our experience, we may be able to make value judgments about its quality. Is it good, bad, original, imitative, virtuosic, innovative, thought provoking, sterile? Musical encounters may have an impact on us. Do they capture certain emotions, give comfort, incite to action, lull into complacency, provide an escape from daily life, lead to alternate realities, reinforce or shape our personal and group identities?

Our cultural and social backgrounds provide us with the tools and abilities to respond and be moved. The first three chapters in part 3 are designed to help us understand what goes into those backgrounds. Chapter 8 discusses some of the key identities that are part of the makeup of rock and R&B, and chapter 9 explores the historical background of the fundamental aesthetic sensibilities that have shaped rock and R&B. Chapter 10 provides an in-depth look at cross-cultural encounters, with two extended contrasting examples and four (more focused) case studies, which all lay the groundwork for the ensuing examination of the concept of appropriation. Chapter 11 looks at the academic study of rock and R&B, laying out some general themes of the book. I devote so much space to the first three chapters to provide a basis for more informed discussions of controversial topics at the heart (even if at the subconscious level) of rock and R&B.

Much of the discourse around rock and R&B produced by fans, journalists, academics, parents, and artists clusters around its cultural and social value or status. On the cultural side debates can arise about artistic merit, integrity, and authenticity, with art and commerce being two poles on a spectrum. Some artists or groups have a special aura about them because of their ability to reconcile the opposing tendencies of art and commerce. The Beatles, for example, continued to explore fresh innovative artistic ground while maintaining unprecedented popularity throughout their recording career (1962–70). Due to the nature of the music industry, which is driven by popularity and income streams (formerly record sales), accomplishments like what the Beatles have done are not that common.

On the social side debates can arise about rock's relation to society. Journalists sometimes use the word *anthem* to describe the importance of certain songs, meaning that they somehow capture the mood or lifestyle of a group of people or perhaps their desires (rather than their reality). Can rock affect behavior or cause social or personal change, and, if so, in what ways may it be positive or harmful or maintain the status quo?

Political progressives might embrace some of rock's messages, either in the lyrics or the sound, which might encourage listeners to alter their worldview and lifestyles. Aretha Franklin's version of "Respect" (1967), John Lennon's "All You Need Is Love" (1967), "Give Peace a Chance" (1969), and "Imagine" (1971), and Public Enemy's "Fight the Power" (1989), for example, may have provided inspiration to many.[1] Some of the lyrics and the sounds of 1970s punk expressed a disillusionment and alienation of youth and might be viewed as implicitly calling for some kind of positive change. Some of punk's shock tactics (including Nazi regalia), however, appealed to young extremists, who explicitly embraced violence and a white power agenda (Knopper 2018). In the face of charges that rock can incite indecent or harmful acts and proposals that warning labels should be put on certain albums (e.g., the Parents Music Resource Center in the 1980s), some might counter that rock does not cause but rather reflects or calls attention to a state of affairs or perhaps provides solace to those in distress.

Because of its popularity among youth, rock can be used to mobilize people for a variety of causes. This could lead to disconnects, for example, with Madonna singing the escape-themed "Holiday" ("It's time for the good times / Forget about the bad times. . . . / We need a holiday") at Live Aid in 1985, a global event intended to raise awareness and funds for relief from the devastating famine that had struck Ethiopia. Some musical styles that feature seemingly simple and innocuous lyrics, such as 1950s rock and roll or 1970s disco, have been credited with positive social change by bringing together diverse groups of people for concerts or for dancing.

Rap has generated debates, with some emcees (rappers) insisting that they rap about reality, and some commentators suggesting that it may be more entertainment and fantasy, which can sometimes promote negative stereotypes. A young Dr. Dre declared, "We only rap about stuff that we know about. Stuff that *can* happen or *did* happen. You know. Everything we say in our records is true" (MTV News Raw n.d.-v).[2] Some may voice opposing stances, depending on the context. In promoting his career, Tupac Shakur asserted, "What rap doesn't have is a real person. I'm 100% real." On the other hand, facing a trial that would ultimately send him to prison, he said,

---

1 Lynskey (2011) covers thirty-three songs with strong political content.

2 It was a common stance at the time. Twenty-two-year-old Snoop Dogg stated, "My raps are incidents where either I saw it happen to one of my close homies or I know about it from just being in the ghetto. . . . It's all everyday life, reality" (Touré 1993).

"This [trial] is all about my image. I'm selling records. This is what I do for a living. I'm selling records. Don't get it twisted; this is not my real life. This is not how my real life is supposed to be" (Perry 2004-v, episode 4).[3] Ice-T has voiced what is the most widespread claim for hip hop: "The key to hip hop is sing about your life, not my life, your life. There's people that live that life, and they'll buy your records" (episode 5).

Lyrics need not necessarily be taken literally but rather may offer a forum for highlighting or thinking about social situations. In rap the commitment in the delivery (one sign of authenticity) may be more significant than what the actual lyrics are saying. Without trivializing the reality of many rap lyrics, one can place this kind of authenticity within the larger field of rock and expressive art forms more generally. Discussing Bruce Springsteen's image as a working-class hero, Frith notes, "What's at stake here is not the authenticity of experience, but authenticity of feeling; what matters is not whether Springsteen has been through these things himself (boredom, aggression, ecstasy, despair) but that he knows how they work" (1988: 98). Responding to critiques about misogyny and negative portrayals of fellow Jews in the novels of Philip Roth, writer Lisa Halliday referenced a line Roth once quoted, from nineteenth-century novelist Gustave Flaubert, providing some perspective: "The task at hand is not to change it [humanity], but to know it."[4]

Moving beyond content to its form and affect (emotional impact), rock may provide a stimulus in the strength of delivery and commitment. Writing about her reaction to the Sex Pistols, rock critic Ellen Willis noted, "And there lay the paradox: Music that boldly and aggressively laid out what the singer wanted, loved, hated—as good rock and roll did—challenged me to do the same, and so, even when the content was anti-woman, anti-sexual, in a sense anti-human, the form encouraged my struggle for liberation. Similarly, timid music made me feel timid, whatever its ostensible politics" (1978: 22). Words can be powerful, though, as we have seen in the various critical viewpoints in the section on hip hop in chapter 7.

Highlight, help to think through, reflect, shape, reinforce, subvert . . . these are all things that rock and R&B can do. The following chapters provide a foundation for discussing how all this may play out.

---

3   The second quotation is excerpted in Touré (1994: 75). Ice Cube drew on a similar strategy in 1991 (as noted in the section on misogynist lyrics earlier).

4   Halliday tells the story in Remnick (2018); the Flaubert quote comes from a letter cited in Llosa (1986: 230).

Music is a primary field of action for exploring and asserting identity, whether on a personal level (how one perceives or wishes to project oneself) or at the level of a group of individuals having some common characteristics. Two crucial points about identity should be kept in mind: although much of our identity has some kind of biological basis (something we are born with), it is socially constructed; and that construction is based not only on how we perceive ourselves (that is, our subjectivity) but also on how others see us. The biological basis may be thought of as immutable or fixed, and the social construction process may be thought of as mutable, or open to possibilities, and forged by individuals and groups. However, this idea of anything being fixed or open to endless possibilities has its limits.

Two key terms have been umbrellas for thinking through the opposition of biological inheritance versus culture, sometimes posed as nature versus nurture, and they figure prominently in work on race and ethnicity as well as gender and sexuality: *essentialism* and *social construction* (Bohan 1993). Theorizing about race, ethnicity, gender, and sexuality all confront the notion of essentialism, that a person has a fixed inherited biological identity or essence. In recent decades sociologists have noted that "race and ethnicity, like gender, have come to be understood as something we do, not just something we have" and that "race is also—crucially—something others do to us" (Brubaker 2017). That is to say, individuals and groups actively construct identities, both their own and that of others. Many of us turn to music for just these purposes.

An insight from Kwame Anthony Appiah, who has done much important philosophical writing on identity and race in the past several decades, will help us to appreciate the broader significance and potential power of the music discussed here: "The large collective identities that call for recognition come with notions of how a proper person of that kind behaves: it is not that there is *one* way that gay people or blacks should behave, but that there are gay and black modes of behavior. These notions provide loose norms or models, which play a role in shaping the ground projects of those for whom these collective identities are central to their individual identities. Collective identities, again, provide what I have been calling scripts: narratives that people use in shaping their pursuits and in telling their life stories" (2005: 108). Appiah goes on to warn that these modes of behavior, norms, and models could become prescriptive, even tyrannical, in their expectations, with the potential to stifle autonomy and individuality. For many of us music is deeply involved in these scripts, narratives, and stories. It can help construct and reinforce them, to be sure, and, just as important, music can subvert, challenge, and rewrite them.

Identities can be conceptualized as embedded or coded within musical sounds and styles, with the codes being understood by acculturation, that is, being exposed to both the sounds and their cultural significance. The various codes, or sonic signifiers—sounds that have special meaning to a group of people—are not universal but rather are learned and created by specific communities; that is, they are socially constructed and not something inherent in the sounds themselves. (The problems that may occur when the codes are decontextualized—lifted from their cultural contexts—are discussed later, under appropriation.) Different communities around the world have developed their own *aesthetics*—standards of beauty or taste—which are the basis for the kinds of decisions that musicians make in shaping their art. While we are primarily concerned with sonic signifiers, many other signifiers are part of musical experiences, such as dress (fashion), body movements (dance), and visual artwork (e.g., album covers or posters).

YOUTH

Rock (and its tributaries, including rap) is the international language of youth. While different rock styles may have varying racial, gender, and class appeal, they are for the most part united in their youth orientation. This is part of its promise, that it can break down barriers constructed by older generations. It is also one of the few identities that we all either have had, currently have, or will have (or tragically never reach). Notwithstanding septuagenarian rock bands who have been at it for many decades, rock is at its heart youth music, which is one reason why middle-aged and senior citizens continue to listen to rock of earlier eras. Not only does it shape the present, but it is a unique and very effective way to go back in time and revisit the past. Part of the allure of Elvis Presley, who started releasing records when he was nineteen and charted nationally at age twenty, was his youth.

As a sociological phenomenon, youth entails the idea of being between childhood dependency and adult responsibility: "To be beyond dependency, but still dependent, and moving towards responsibility, but not responsible yet, releases the adolescent into a suspended state of social freedom that tends to become an end-in-itself. . . . Some adolescents seek to remain as children, whereas others seek to short-circuit freedom and become responsible immediately" (Weinstein 1983: 7). Youth may enjoy a privileged position to comment on society as outsiders looking at, or forward to, adulthood. That particular window has its own special status.

Cultures have typically been associated with ethnic groups or nationalities, tied up in language, cuisine, dress, music, and other aspects that mark their particularity. Post–World War II prosperity in the United States and United Kingdom gave many teens an unprecedented degree of leisure time and money that enabled them to create a highly visible culture of their own.[1] Youth became a major new and lucrative consumer market, able to purchase commodities and pursue leisure activities to shape new identities, and adults became concerned about new potentials for hedonist pursuit of pleasure and that they would become passive victims of market manipulation. The question of who was driving trends (youth or the culture industry) became all the more crucial.[2] The invention of the durable vinyl seven-inch 45 rpm single and twelve-inch 33⅓ rpm long-play (LP) album arrived just in time (late 1940s) to push recorded music as one of the primary teen consumer items, and music would soon become the center of teen culture.

Different rock styles may have associations with specific age groups, even splitting up these divisions. For instance, in 1972 Frith (1981) found significant differences between two-year cohorts among British school students. At the younger end (British fifth form, U.S. tenth and eleventh grades) they bought singles, watched *Top of the Pops*, went to youth clubs and discos (206–7). At the upper end (British sixth form, U.S. twelfth grade and college frosh), they bought albums, had more progressive tastes and went to folk clubs and concerts; they saw themselves, in the words of one sixth former, as individualists, "rebelling against unreasonable ideas and conventional ways of doing things" (206). Whatever their differences, "they still have more problems in common with each other than with the adults of their own class or sex" (217). British rave club culture of the early 1990s, primarily populated by fifteen- to nineteen-year-olds, followed by twenty-one- to twenty-four-year-olds, provides another example (Thornton 1996: 15–16). These boundaries could be tight: at the younger end regulated by being able to leave the house after eleven at night, having the requisite cash to spend, and being able to get into establishments with a loosely enforced drinking age of eighteen; at the older end regulated by moving out of the house and no longer needing to escape home or the family and by forming long-term partnerships or getting married (clubbers and ravers were predominantly single).

---

1 Parsons (1942) coined the phrase *youth culture* and was the first to investigate what it meant in the United States.
2 Frith (1981: 182–83), Bennett (2000: 34, 35), and Lipsitz (1994: 211) each address this issue.

Rock can express generation-specific sensibilities, as in teen anthems, such as Chuck Berry's "School Days" (1957), the Who's "My Generation" (1965), the Stooges' "No Fun" and "1969" (1969), and the Sex Pistols' "God Save the Queen" (1977). Ray Charles distinguished rhythm and blues from early rock and roll, noting that the former is more adult, from the perspective of both depth of emotion (or affect) and musical sophistication: "I never considered myself part of rock 'n' roll. . . . My stuff was more adult. It was more difficult for teenagers to relate to; so much of my music was sad or down. A tune like Little Richard's 'Tutti Frutti' was fun. Less serious. . . . Rock 'n' roll was also music that the teenagers were able to play themselves" (Charles and Ritz 1978: 177). This would change as rock audiences matured in the 1960s.

Serious studies of youth began in the 1920s and 1930s, by sociologists and criminologists based in Chicago who focused on juvenile delinquency.[3] Their work was marked by ethnographic engagement, illustrated by Whyte's University of Chicago doctoral dissertation, published as *Street Corner Society* (1943), based on his research among gang members in the Italian North End of Boston. Several landmark works were published in the 1970s. Labov's (1972) *Language in the Inner City*, based on research carried out among youth in New York City, helped establish the academic legitimacy of Black English Vernacular (also known as African American Vernacular English) as an English dialect. The same year Stanley Cohen's (1972) study of the 1964 English seaside clashes between two youth subcultures, the mods and rockers, put the phrase *moral panic* into general circulation; this refers to media portrayals of perceived threats from youth and reactions from authorities. Moral panics would arise again and again, for example, with punk rock in the 1970s, with the Parents Music Resource Center (PMRC) lobbying to put warning labels on certain albums in the 1980s, and with rap in the 1990s.[4]

The 1976 publication of the working papers of a cohort of researchers at the Centre for Contemporary Cultural Studies (CCCS) at the University of Birmingham in England was a major stimulus for the academic study of youth and music. *Resistance through Rituals: Youth Subcultures in Post-War Britain*, coedited by Stuart Hall, one of the founders of the field known as cultural studies, still generates debates about the viability of the term *subculture* to describe youth communities based on style (e.g.,

---

3 Bennett (2000) and Laughey (2006) provide histories of the study of youth culture.

4 Ingraham and Reeves have linked moral panic with recent practices of online shaming: "Citizens today have acquired an unprecedented capacity [through social media] to independently investigate, judge, and punish their peers for moral infractions" (2016: 456).

clothing, music) and how to interpret them (Hall and Jefferson 1976). Hebdige's (1979) *Subculture: The Meaning of Style* further applied the subculture concept toward the new music around him in 1970s England, primarily punk and reggae.

Many critiques of 1970s CCCS work (including Hebdige) deeply inform current perspectives.[5] These critiques include lacking ethnography (talking to youth); imposing Marxist class analysis (e.g., political resistance as opposed to the sheer pleasure) that may not have been relevant to the participants themselves (e.g., music can be a means of escaping rather than reinforcing or resisting one's class position); prioritizing theory over practice (the previous two critiques); focusing exclusively on outdoor male activity (i.e., young women and the domestic sphere were absent); posing a homologous relation among symbols and lifestyles of subcultures (e.g., that their fashion, consumer goods, and music all reflect a similar value system); suggesting that music expresses a bounded subculture (a condition) rather than shapes it (an ongoing process); banishing media and commerce from their definitions of authentic culture; and viewing subcultures as ahistorical, not paying attention to cultural or social change.[6] These last two critiques (media and change) come from Thornton (1996: 9), whose work involved participating in raves and speaking with ravers.

Hodkinson's work with goth provides an updated understanding of youth subcultures. David Bowie's 1970s "androgynous glamour and deep-voiced vocals ... provided an important precursor to goth, as did the somber, depressing angst of Joy Division toward the 1980s" (2002: 35). Two important touchstones were "Bela Lugosi's Dead" (1979) by Bauhaus, with its lyrics, eerie vocals and instrumental accompaniment, and androgynous visual appearance; and the somber direction of Siouxsie and the Banshees going into the 1980s (e.g., the 1981 album *Ju Ju*), which provided the mood, sound, and images. A number of British bands, including the Cure, formed a recognizable cohort, and in 1982 a London club, the Batcave, acted as an "initial melting pot" for bands and fans and a magnet for the music press, "keen in the wake of punk to find, report and, ultimately, construct any possible successors" (36). Hodkinson proposed four indicators of a subculture: *consistent distinctiveness* (a set of shared tastes, styles, and values); a clear and sustained subjective sense of group *identity* (likemindedness);

---

5   I draw on the following extended critiques: Thornton (1996), McRobbie (1976, 1980), Bennett (2000), Bennet and Kahn-Harris (2004), Hesmondhalgh (2005), and Laughey (2006). S. Hall (2006) addressed some of these critiques in the second edition of *Resistance through Rituals*.

6   McRobbie (1976, 1980) and Twersky (1981) address young women audiences for rock, novel for the time in academia.

commitment (concentrated and continuous practical involvement); and *autonomy* (independent record labels, DIY production, organization, and promotion of events outside of commercial mass media) (28–33).

Scene is occasionally used as an alternative to subculture, with the advantage that it recognizes networks of participants and places and shifting sensibilities. One of the clearest insider nonacademic definitions comes from David Byrne, lead singer with Talking Heads, discussing the punk club CBGB. Byrne credited owner Hilly Kristal with establishing an atmosphere that "made it possible for the whole scene to emerge, and, subsequently, to flow and flourish with a life all its own" (2012: 271). In the case of CBGB, the ingredients were (1) a sympathetic venue with low rent, where (2) artists could play their own material; (3) bands were paid fairly; (4) musicians could get in free once they played there and (5) there was space where it was possible to ignore the band; (6) a sense of alienation from the prevailing music scene; and (7) social transparency (no privacy for the musicians) (269–84).

One reason why CBGB thrived in the 1970s is that the legal drinking age in New York was eighteen.[7] Different musical styles and subcultures often have very clear and specific drug associations (H. Shapiro 2003), although the centrality of clubs serving alcohol seems to be a constant. Youth may feel a certain curiosity and invincibility (or recklessness) to pursue recreational (and harder) alcohol and drug use, noting the hypocrisy of antidrug rhetoric from adults who engage in legal drinking and prescription drug use. One classic contrast in preferences is the mind-altering marijuana and psychedelic culture of flower power–era mid-1960s San Francisco (Jefferson Airplane, Grateful Dead) versus the mood-altering amphetamine and heroin culture in the grittier downtown New York City scene (Velvet Underground, Andy Warhol entourage) of the same era (130–34). The Velvet Underground's May 1966 gig in San Francisco pointed up this contrast: "[We were] this terrible, terrible influence of the virus and disease of New York City into the beautiful new counterculture of the West Coast" (Lou Reed). "We just felt happy in being ostracized by both the West Coast and by the Woodstock generation" (John Cale). "The Velvets turned all their instruments on and left them near the speakers so they just created noise. And they all just walked away. God we were so mad. We wanted to get out of there. I hated San Francisco. I hated hippies" (dancer Mary Woronov).[8]

---

7 A national act raising the legal age to purchase alcohol to twenty-one was passed in 1984.

8 The Reed and Cale quotes are in Espar and Thomson (1995-v, episode 7). The Woronov quote is in Greenfield-Sanders (1998-v).

GENDER AND SEXUALITY

Music is a rich field of activity for exploring and understanding gender and sexuality, which in turn can add rich perspectives on how music works. The two terms *gender* and *sexuality*, often paired, have undergone radical examination since Simone de Beauvoir's 1949 declaration in *The Second Sex*: "One is not born, but rather becomes, a woman," a response to Sigmund Freud's "anatomy is destiny."[9] One way of thinking about this is that sex refers to the biological features of human females and males (chromosomes, sex organs, hormones, and other physical features), and gender refers to an identity that people construct in social interactions, using generally understood codes, such as styles of clothing and hair and ways of moving and talking (Mikkola 2017). Sexuality, then, is "the cultural way of living out our bodily pleasures and desires" (Weeks 2009: 47). Gender and sexuality are not aspects of human nature fixed at birth but rather practices (or performances) that we do to forge and live out our identities. Weeks (73) notes that "sexuality can be a terrain for the subversion and transgression of gender." *Queer* can refer to an "oppositional relation to the norm . . . *whatever* is at odds with the normal, the legitimate, the dominant . . . a positionality . . . available to anyone who is or who feels marginalized because of her or his sexual practices" (Halperin 1995: 62). The term *queer* can function both as an identity category and, paradoxically, as an oppositional stance to such categories.

The labeling of some 1970s music as soft rock (marked by acoustic guitars and pianos and introspective singer-songwriters, many of whom are women) and hard rock (a predominantly male genre marked by loud electric guitars and aggressive vocals) suggests that rock styles and musical instruments can take on gendered identities. A subgenre known as cock rock (Frith and McRobbie 1978–79), exemplified by groups like the Rolling Stones and Led Zeppelin (with Jimmy Page wearing his guitar low as a phallic symbol), with boastful lyrics portraying women as sex objects, has been the subject of inquiry of musicologist Susan Fast, who asks questions such as "Was/is Zeppelin's audience primarily male and what difference does this make? . . . Is there something inherently 'male' about the music itself (and how is 'male' defined)? Is it, in fact, misogynistic?" (1999: 246). She sent out surveys among Led Zeppelin fans and found that about one third of the respondents were women. One noted, "I attended the 7/27/73 MSG concert with two girlfriends. . . . I went to the concerts because I

---

9   See Butler (1986) for de Beauvoir's quotation and Moi (1999) for Freud's quotation. Butler (1990) has been an especially influential theorist in this area.

wanted to see the band. Period. I never had any boyfriends who shared my interest in Led Zep music. Not much has changed in that respect either: my husband *hates* Led Zep (and rock music in general)" (262). Regarding the song "Whole Lotta Love," Fast noted, "some women remarked at its overt sexuality and indicated that this was 'a turn-on' to them: as opposed to being fearful or ignorant of the raw sexuality depicted in this song, they identified with it completely; this also points to how easily women can relate to a song that is, supposedly, sung from a male point of view" (267).

Glam rock, which emerged in the early 1970s, gave an ironic entry for some gay men into rock, which was largely populated by heterosexual men. Glam sent mixed messages, in which Farber (2016) heard multiple sexualities: "brash riffs and blunt beats. . . . At the same time, glam's vocals had a fruity theatricality. . . . Glam was butch and femme at once: bisexuality in sound." Farber continues, "The identification that glam gave me wasn't to gay culture, then deep into disco, but to the throbbing new heart of rock 'n' roll. The result reflected a double con: A movement created overwhelmingly by straight people, out to stoke attention by 'acting gay,' had special meaning for gay youth who felt the need to pass for straight." Gill suggests that glam rock (specifically Bowie) changed attitudes: "I knew and know heterosexuals whose attitudes about sexual difference were radically altered by the atmosphere of glam rock, particularly by the field of ambiguity staked out by David Bowie. Many questioned their own attitudes to sexuality. . . . Others began to rethink their prejudices about sexual difference. Quite often this was brought about by the fact that their favourite music was being produced by a queer" (1995: 110). Farber (2016) personally testified to the power of Bowie and his music: "We weren't just Bowie fans. We felt we owed him our very identities."

For some male performers the 1970s were a liberating time. Bowie wore a dress on the cover of the UK release of *The Man Who Sold the World* (1970) and claimed that he was gay in *Melody Maker* magazine: "The expression of his sexual ambivalence establishes a fascinating game: is he, or isn't he?" his interviewer pondered in 1972. "In a period of conflicting sexual identity, he shrewdly exploits the confusion surrounding the male and female roles" (M. Watts 1972: 19). Lou Reed's "Walk on the Wild Side" (1972) paid tribute to his New York transgender and gay circle, and the Village People formed as an in-your-face camp representation of downtown New York gay lifestyles later in the decade. British rocker Tom Robinson released "Glad to Be Gay" in 1978, breaking into the UK Top 20.

Lesbian musical artists, though, had to be more cautious about their public personas. British vocalist Dusty Springfield, whose Top 40 run of ten hits went from 1964 to 1969, "responded to the pressure [of hiding her lesbian identity] . . . by presenting an extreme version of femininity, modelling herself on drag queens with her over-the-top gowns, bouffant hairdos and panda-eyed parody of French Vogue" (O'Brien 2002: 254). The aesthetic behind this kind of exaggerated presentation of gender or sexuality—*camp*—has been more typically associated with gay males, especially when used as an in-group subversion tactic.[10] The cover photo on Springfield's first British solo album, *A Girl Called Dusty* (1964), "provides a veritable catalog of subversive lesbian camp. . . . [She is] outfitted casually in denim jeans and a man's blue chambray work shirt. . . . Butch from the shoulders down, she is virtually a parodic femme from the neck up, displaying exaggeratedly back-brushed and suggestively mussed-up, peroxided hair; heavy, black kohl mascara; false eyelashes; and bright frosted-pink lipstick. This vampy overkill completely shatters any naturalistic illusion of femininity and creates a highly ironic lesbian resignification of the gay man in drag—in effect that of the *female* female impersonator" (P. J. Smith 1999: 107).

Springfield left the United Kingdom for the United States in 1970, battling rumors about her personal life, and by the late 1970s was openly supporting gay rights issues, well past her career peak (P. J. Smith 1999: 118; O'Brien 2002: 255). Jamaican-born Grace Jones, whose 1981 album *Nightclubbing* crossed over into the pop Top 40, pioneered an androgynous public persona in the early 1980s, before moving into feature films. Annie Lennox, with similarly close-cropped hair, took to wearing men's suits with her bandmate Dave Stewart in their early Eurythmics videos, including their #1 pop hit "Sweet Dreams (Are Made of This)" and, from the same album, "Love Is a Stranger," which featured remarkable gender play for its time.[11] Lennox employed "a camp sensibility—a code of appearance and behavior that mocks and ironizes gender norms—in order to undermine . . . gender assumptions. . . . It is not clear from viewing the video whether Lennox is a man in female drag (in the first part of the video) or a woman in male drag (in the second half). . . . This playfulness clearly posed some sort of perceived threat to an assumedly stable and proper relationship between biological sex and gender performance" (Piggford 1999: 284, 285).

---

10 For example, "David's [Bowie] present image is to come on like a swishy queen, a gorgeously effeminate boy. He's as camp as a row of tents, with his limp hand and trolling vocabulary" (M. Watts 1972: 19).

11 D. Hill (1986: 32) discusses the second video, which MTV banned until they could see Lennox's birth certificate showing that she was a female and not a male cross-dresser.

Both Jones and Lennox explored androgyny in the 1980s from the position of not having a lesbian identity to be exposed. Through the 1980s "many lesbians . . . felt that coming out in an industry predicated on heterosexual desire would be too risky. Rocking the institution of the family and the notion of female sexuality that pop clings to so tenaciously, a lesbian is an affront, someone to be labelled 'strange' or 'downright unsellable'" (O'Brien 2002: 264, 265).

k.d. lang coming out as a lesbian woman in 1992, in a cover story in *The Advocate* (Lemon 1992), was a first for a major pop artist (that year her second solo album, *Ingénue*, hit #18 on the pop chart). The following January Melissa Etheridge announced, "I'm proud to say I'm a lesbian," at a gay and lesbian inaugural ball for President Bill Clinton (J. Dunn 1995: 44). By that time Etheridge's first three albums had hit the pop Top 40; the next month she would win a Grammy Award for her single "Ain't It Heavy" in the category "Best Rock Vocal Performance, Female." Gay men coming out publicly was not much easier; they typically did so well past their initial career prime: Elton John in the late 1980s and Rob Halford of Judas Priest and George Michael of Wham! in the late 1990s.

Jimi Hendrix's use of his guitar at the 1967 Monterey Pop Festival can illustrate two extremes of how one can sexualize an instrument: in less than a half minute in "Hey Joe," he moves from a high-pitched screaming guitar solo, in which he brings the instrument to his mouth and plucks the strings with his teeth (or tongue), to returning it to his waist to accentuate the low steady bass line, holding it straight out like a phallic symbol, with pelvic thrusts. The sounds he extracts at these two extremes reinforce their meaning. His final acts in the final song in his set ("Wild Thing"), straddling his guitar laid on the ground, squirting lighter fluid onto it (is the guitar gendered female here?), lighting it afire, and then grabbing its neck and violently smashing it (is it a phallic symbol here?) is open to interpretation.[12] One thing is sure: his musical instrument, from which he elicits sounds that magnetically draw people to him, is not a neutral object in his hands. But, as with the other lenses we use here, additional perspectives are needed to tell a richer story. Hendrix's identity as an African American man surely informed what he projected onto his guitar (see Waksman 1999).

12 "Hey Joe" and "Wild Thing" are in *Jimi Plays Monterey* (Pennebaker and Hegedus 1986-v); "Wild Thing" is featured in *Monterey Pop* (Pennebaker 1968-v). Electric blues guitarists have famously named their guitars after women and later written songs about them, including B. B. King ("Lucille," 1968) and Albert King ("[I Love] Lucy," 1968).

Not only can instruments be gendered (given a gender identity), but so can the ebb and flow of a performance. Patti Smith, leader of an otherwise all-male band, noted, "'We're looking for something magic every night. We don't have a fixed set or formula. We're not like a male band either, in that the male process of ecstasy in performance is starting here,'—she starts jerking at the base of an imaginary giant phallus—'and building and building until the big spurt at the end. We're a feminine band, we'll go so far and peak and then we'll start again and peak, over and over. It's like [an] ocean'" (qtd. in Rambali 1978: 8).

Michael Jackson's relationship to rock in "Beat It" has been examined with an eye toward how he can upset gender norms, queering them, as Fast suggests. The video for "Beat It" "culminates in the full 'body wave,' a gesture that transforms the male bodies into sensuous, undulating curves, softening the usual hard masculinity of rock" (2012: 283). Jackson's portrayal throughout the video, Fast notes, challenges typically masculine images associated with rock: initially alone in the bedroom (a "private, domestic, feminized sphere"), striking "an old Hollywood movie diva" pose; dancing through a now-empty diner and pool hall; "queering it through his presence, before doing the same to its former inhabitants [gang members]," Jackson breaks up the fight and leads the choreography, "in effect teaching the others a new kind of physicality, a homosocial world comprised of bodies moving together" (283–84). His choice of guitar soloist in the recording, metal virtuoso Eddie Van Halen, was given a twist in his concert tours: virtuoso guitarist Jennifer Batten reinforced metal's racial coding as white, but "queers these expectations in terms of gender" (285). This was not a fluke; another woman virtuoso guitar player (Orianthi Panagaris) was set to go on tour with him before his death. Fast suggests that as an outsider to the "norms of rock (white, male, straight, aggressive masculinity), he [Jackson] used the genre to play, queerly, at and with convention" (288).

Jackson's interactions with Batten during her extended guitar solo on "Working Day and Night" (the 1992 live-in-Bucharest version broadcast on HBO) were similarly peculiar or "queer," in Fast's analysis. Batten follows him around the stage during her solo, and he gestures at her guitar, conjuring up sounds, seemingly directing and controlling her. Fast suggests that "this becomes a performance about controlling hegemonic white power. In this sense, the gendered power dynamics are normative, but the racial power dynamics are queer" (2012: 292). One never knows about intent, but Fast believes this to be an "overtly political act on Jackson's part" because he did not challenge "convention in black genres of music in the ways he did rock" (296).

In addition to interpretive work with gender and sexuality in performance (White-ley 2000; Whiteley and Rycenga 2006), other kinds of work focusing on the role of women musicians (Gaar 2002; O'Brien 2002; Carson, Lewis, and Shaw 2004) and critics (McDonnell and Powers 1995; Willis 2011) have been important concerns in rock literature. Some of the issues raised in this section came to the forefront in per-formance beginning in the 1970s and are taken up in the sections on glam and disco.

RACE AND ETHNICITY

Racial identities are at the very core of the whole history of rock and roll. While *black* and *white* can sometimes be an effective shorthand means of referring to musical styles and their audiences, these terms need to be handled with care and clarified. The music industry briefly endorsed the stylistic designation *black* when *Billboard* magazine renamed its soul charts (which had replaced rhythm and blues in the 1960s) to black music in the 1980s. (They moved back to R&B in the 1990s.) The unmarked or pop charts have always been understood to reflect national majority white population preferences. Country (formerly hillbilly and folk) charts largely reflect southern white preferences.

Since the 1920s, when a market for music made by African Americans targeted toward African Americans first opened up (called *race records*), the music industry explicitly recognized black and white markets. This segmentation came to be a driving force for those outside the pop market: how to break through or cross over into the much more lucrative pop market (by virtue of its sheer numbers and sales potential). Other music-industry categories and genres existed, but they would not figure into what would eventually become rock and R&B.[13] These categories had real world im-plications, in that they governed where a certain recording would be listed in print catalogs aimed at consumers and record store owners, where it could be found in a record store (or even the primary identity of a record store), and which radio stations would push it.

Conceptualizing and referring to U.S. markets, audiences, artists, and styles as

---

13 Classical and jazz are the two main other categories. American Folklife Center (1982) surveys early ethnic recordings, reproducing ads or catalogs from the Columbia, Okeh, and Victor labels between 1906 and 1934, using the categories Foreign, Hawaiian, Greek, Ukrainian, Romanian, Scandinavian, Turkish, German, Chinese, Italian, Irish, Jewish, Russian, Spanish-Mexican, Polish, and Portuguese.

black (or as "Negro" before the 1960s) and white was common currency. One of the founding pioneers of rock and roll, Chuck Berry, was quite explicit about his influences and how he used them:

> Over half of the songs I was singing at the Cosmo Club [about 1953] were directly from the recordings of [African Americans] Nat King Cole and Muddy Waters. Listening to my idol Nat Cole prompted me to sing sentimental songs with distinct diction. The songs of Muddy Waters impelled me to deliver the down-home blues in the language they came from, Negro dialect. When I played hillbilly songs, I stressed my diction so that it was harder and whiter. All in all it was my intention to hold both the black and the white clientele by voicing the different kinds of songs in their customary tongues." (1987: 90–91)

Berry had mastered these styles; he once had a gig cancelled in segregated Knoxville, Tennessee, when he showed up and the organizer then realized that he wasn't white (135–36).

Media, including the radio, was also commonly understood as catering to white or black audiences. For example, the year after Hank Ballard's composition and recording "The Twist" hit #16 on the R&B chart in spring 1959, he watched Chubby Checker's nearly identical cover version become a major pop hit and cultural phenomenon. Ballard later clearly articulated the racial dynamics of the industry: "When I first heard it by Chubby Checker, I thought it was me! . . . I heard this 'Twist' record blasting across white radio. I thought, 'Aw man, at last, I'm gonna get some white airplay; yeah, I'm gonna be a superstar.' And the disc jockey said, 'Chubby Checkerrrrr.'"[14]

There has long been an ebb and flow in the coming together and moving apart of musical styles associated with blacks and whites in the United States, as well as a long history of musical interaction. While the blues developed in southern rural African American communities, the repertory of blues artists typically included songs from outside that culture. The banjo moved from blacks to whites, and the fiddle moved in the opposite direction. The piano was picked up by African Americans who could

---

14 Ballard, qtd. in Peisch (1995-v, episode 2). Ballard's original eventually entered the pop chart in June 1960 (due to a Baltimore TV station playing it) before Checker's cover shot up that chart in August (quickly hitting #1) after he appeared on *American Bandstand*. Checker most likely pulled Ballard up to #28. Ballard received composer royalties from any cover versions. Both Ballard and Checker are African American.

afford access to it, and they created ragtime in the late nineteenth century, drawing on Euro-American military marching band music and the resources of the European tonal system.

Listener preferences in rock and roll also evince this ebb and flow, with white artists showing up on R&B charts, and black artists gaining definitive access to the white pop charts in the mid-1950s. Black artists would occasionally flood the upper reaches of those pop charts: 8 songs in the pop Top 10 in May 1972 were by black artists, and in October 2003 black artists held all 10 slots for the first time in its chart history. In the early years of rock and roll the number of Top 10 hits by white singers on the R&B charts ranged from 3 out of 64 (1955) to 45 out of 86 (1958) to 9 out of 98 (1961); the number of Top 10 hits by black singers on the pop charts ranged from 9 out of 51 (1955) to 37 out of 106 (1961) (Gillett 1996: 190). British musical invasions resulted in UK singles dominating the pop Top 10 in May 1965 (7 out of 10) and again in May 1985 (8 out of 10), squeezing black artists (except from Motown) off the upper reaches of the charts. In April 2001, on the other hand, there were no UK singles in the whole U.S. Top 100.

"The problem of the Twentieth Century is the problem of the color-line," wrote W. E. B. Du Bois (1903 [2007]: 3, 15, 32) in his classic *Souls of Black Folk* at the dawn of that century. Du Bois is widely considered as one of the most (if not the most) prolific, engaged, and influential thinkers on African American identity. His 1897 "The Conservation of Races," which he revised as the first chapter in *Souls* ("Of Our Spiritual Strivings"), has been the touchstone for much of the debates that followed. In it Du Bois wrestled with a definition of race, moving between biological (family, blood), cultural (language, traditions), and historical conceptions: "What, then, is a race? It is a vast family of human beings, generally of common blood and language, always of common history, traditions and impulses, who are both voluntarily and involuntarily striving together for the accomplishment of certain more or less vividly conceived ideals of life" (1897 [2007]: 181). Du Bois later added another possibility of racial belonging, the lived experience of racism, in this case, racial segregation: "The black man is a person who must ride 'Jim Crow' in Georgia" (1923 [1996]: 68). These four different conceptions (biological, cultural, historical, and existential) remain compelling and contested elements in African American identity to this day.[15]

---

15 Appiah (2014), Jeffers (2013), and Shelby (2005) provide richly detailed arguments for these issues.

Nowadays it is generally recognized that there is little biological basis for unique racial categories. People construct categories based on local perceptions of difference. So then what does race refer to, and what kind of positive value is in the concept of race for Americans? The short answer is that the term refers to socially constructed groups (based on some surface physical features), initially for the purpose of creating distinctions and hierarchies among groups of people, a "power dynamic separating people into dominant and subordinate groups" (Jeffers 2013: 409). The race concept continues to have meaning, which can serve to both keep people down and instill pride and group solidarity. Breaking up the human race into categories based on supposed biological features is at the root of racist ideologies about superiority and inferiority, which have a centuries-old basis in European thought and practice. Such ideologies have been used in the service of committing some of the worst human atrocities. The transatlantic slave trade was one such case, with Europeans trafficking some 12.5 million enslaved Africans to the Americas between 1500 and 1875, approximately 1.8 million of whom did not survive the voyage (Slave Voyages 2019). The vast majority of Africans ended up outside of British North America; by the period covered in this book (mid-twentieth century), descendants of enslaved Africans would make up roughly 10 percent of the population in the United States. Their impact on U.S. culture would far exceed their numbers.

Facing several centuries of attempts to enlist science to support racist ideologies, scientific and social scientific organizations finally issued public statements refuting such claims, denying the biological foundations of race. UNESCO issued four such statements between 1950 and 1967.

> "Scientists have reached general agreement in recognizing that mankind is one. . . . The scientific material available to us at present does not justify the conclusion that inherited genetic differences are a major factor in producing the differences between the cultures and cultural achievements of different peoples or groups" (1950). "National, religious, geographical, linguistic and cultural groups do not necessarily coincide with racial groups; and the cultural traits of such groups have no demonstrated genetic connexion with racial traits" (1951). "There is great genetic diversity within all human populations. Pure races—in the sense of genetically homogeneous populations—do not exist in the human species" (1964).[16]

---

16 Statements from 1950, 1951, and 1964 in UNESCO (1969: 30, 32, 39, 44).

In 1998 the American Anthropological Association (1998) weighed in with research in genetics: "Evidence from the analysis of genetics (e.g., DNA) indicates that most physical variation, about 94 percent, lies within so-called racial groups. Conventional geographic 'racial' groupings differ from one another only in about 6% of their genes. This means that there is greater variation within 'racial' groups than between them."

Ethnicity is a subset of race, although at times what they refer to can overlap. Ethnicity is based on several kinds of claims, which may be real or putative (commonly believed), including, "a claim to kinship, broadly defined; a claim to a common history of some sort; and a claim that certain symbols capture the core of the group's identity." Those symbols could include "geographical concentration, religious affiliation, language, and physical differences" (Cornell and Hartmann 2007: 19). For example, *white* typically refers to a race, which can encompass ethnicities such as Irish, Italian, Jewish, and Anglo-Saxon Protestant, among others. Similarly, *black* refers to a race, which can encompass ethnicities such as African American, Afro-Cuban, Afro-Brazilian, and Afro-Jamaican, among others. Many prefer to speak of racial identities, which has some basis in the way people live and think, as opposed to race, which has such a tortured past with boundaries impossible to define.

Blackness

Edward W. Blyden was one of the first to theorize what unites peoples of the African diaspora, a concept that has come to be termed *blackness*. Born in Saint Thomas in the Caribbean and educated in Liberia in West Africa, Blyden formulated the idea of an "African personality" in the 1890s, referring to a unique worldview based on communal life (the extended family), communion with nature, and communion with God (July 1967: 215–17). This idea had its analog in the Francophone world in the mid-twentieth-century literary style and cultural theory called Négritude, whose most famous proponent was Léopold Senghor, the first president of Senegal. Senghor summarizes it as follows: "Who would deny that Africans, too, have a certain way of conceiving life, and of living it? A certain way of speaking, singing, and dancing; of painting and sculpturing . . . [Negritude] is . . . *the sum of the cultural values of the black world*" (1970: 180).

Senghor responded to the racism of colonialism by valorizing precisely what Europeans devalued, claiming rhythm and emotion as defining traits of African culture. He had his African critics, who felt that he was proposing a narrow vision for African culture, even buying into European theories of racial hierarchy and romanticizing a mythological past that may not accurately reflect how Africans move in the modern world.

This valorizing of the body over the mind can still be a relevant strategy. In the episode on funk in a ten-part rock documentary, an African American senior vice president at CBS Records makes what at face value seems like an outrageous observation: "Most white people, when you listen to their music, they would rather turn up the treble. Whereas black people turn up the bass, for whatever reason, that's the way we are. That's where our music is rooted, in the rhythm section" (Larkin Arnold, qtd. in Espar and Thomson 1995-v, episode 8). Taken out of context, this statement characterizes African Americans (and European Americans, for that matter)—essentializes them—with a rather limited range of tastes and possibilities, rooted in rhythm as opposed to melody (implied by the word *treble*, at a higher end of the sound spectrum). *Bass* can stand in as a metaphor for the body (something you physically feel), leaving *treble* as a metaphor for the mind (melody), a split that goes back to Enlightenment-era thinking, which has come to devalue bodily expression.[17]

But, like Senghor, this example essentializes in a positive way (highlighting the value of bodily expression), a practice that has been called *strategic essentialism* by Gayatri Spivak (Danius and Jonsson 1993). After a quote from New York radio disc jockey Frankie Crocker, who continues in the same vein, explicitly connecting rhythm with bass—"The rhythm, the beat, the bass, from R&B, from rock and roll, came from the drum, the first musical instrument that was communicating from one drummer to a people carrying the message from his people, his community to the next"—CBS VP Arnold fills in the context, also connecting bass with drums: "And funk is when that bass line is just pumping in conjunction with the drums, and whatever else you want to put on top of it. But if you got the heavy bass line and the drum pounding, then you have some funk" (Espar and Thomson 1995-v, episode 8).

By applying this characterization to a specific genre (funk), which is rooted in a specific time (1970s) and place (urban United States), a whole group of people are no longer implicated in a timeless immutable assessment of their essence. Rather, here is one particular flowering, with one particular set of aesthetic sensibilities in action. Other genres, such as spirituals, the music of gospel choirs or soloists, city and country

---

17 Frith (1996: 123–44) has a wide-ranging discussion of the musical mind-body split with regard to rhythm.

blues, or much of what comes out of the jazz world, draw on other sensibilities and render the requirement of a heavy bass line and pounding drums irrelevant.

African diasporic cultures have been depicted with the metaphors of roots (common heritage) and routes (transplanted into diverse contexts). Aimé Césaire, a coarchitect of Négritude along with Senghor, used the images of vertical, referring to a common heritage in African civilization, and horizontal, referring to the common experiences of colonialism and racism manifesting different faces or cultures of that shared civilization (Diagne 2018). Amiri Baraka (1967b) referred to a "changing same" of black music, which can be thought of as routes (changing) and roots (same).[18]

Three pan-African arts festivals highlight the utility of the term *black*. The World Festival of Negro Arts, the first of its kind, was held in Senegal in 1966 under the sponsorship of Senegalese president Senghor, who used the term *Negro* (French: *Nègre*) to include people of the African diaspora and exclude North Africa, which has a strong Arab cultural presence. This was followed by the First Pan-African Cultural Festival in Algeria in 1969. *Pan-African* here was used to include all of Africa as well as those from the diaspora abroad. In 1977 Nigeria hosted the Second World Black and African Festival of Arts and Culture. Here, *Black* covers the diaspora and *African* covers the continent (including North Africa).

Since the 1960s the term *black* has gained wide currency to cover both the whole of the African diaspora and also national cultures, such as African American, Afro-Brazilian, and Afro-Cuban. Baraka's collection of essays, *Black Music* (1967a), was pioneering in its title, in synch with Stokely Carmichael's 1967 book *Black Power* and James Brown's 1968 "Say It Loud—I'm Black and I'm Proud." By the early 1970s black studies programs were firmly established on U.S. college campuses, all oriented toward understanding black (African and African diasporic) culture and history (Rogers 2012). This understanding encompassed both the positive forces of cultural achievement and the negative forces that have had to be overcome to produce those achievements, let alone survive and thrive as individuals and as a community.

Whiteness

Since the early 1990s the term *whiteness* has gained currency for interrogating the racial dynamics that structure European American lives. Like blackness, whiteness can refer to a worldview, a structural location within society, and cultural practices. It

18 Baraka published in the 1960s under his birth name, LeRoi Jones.

can be a deceptive term, though. Unlike blackness, whiteness is situated in a "location of structural advantage, of race privilege," and it is often not readily visible to those who live it (that is, it functions as an unmarked norm).[19] Furthermore, as music and cultural critic Kelefa Sanneh (2010: 70) notes, "a diagnosis of whiteness is often delivered, and received, as a kind of accusation . . . often accompanied by an implicit or explicit charge of racism." Historian Nell Irvin Painter (2015) observed in a *New York Times* editorial that the term is inadequate in its depiction of white identity, acting like a toggle switch between awfulness (white supremacy) and bland nothingness (a perceived lack of culture), with little ground in between.[20]

It is most valuable here as a conceptual tool, a critical perspective (Garner 2007: 174) for unmasking forces that seem normative (the way it's supposed to be, unquestioned), universal even, but are really the product of practices carried out by specific groups of people under specific historical conditions. Those forces include certain advantages, including better and more comfortable access for whites (particularly during the earlier eras discussed in this book) through the various gates of music-related industries, such as radio, television, major record labels, distribution networks, and performance venues, as well as license for a wider range of artistic and political stances.

In a North American context, whiteness refers to European cultures transplanted and transformed into a European American culture that has become an unmarked framework for all. Cultural achievements, rarely part of whiteness discourse, are more commonly discussed in specific national or ethnic contexts, as in Irish, English, German, Italian, or Jewish, or with the more general terms *European* or *Western*. The meeting of these cultures in North America, on a foundation of practices from British colonial times, has resulted in a uniquely American conglomerate culture, intimately wrapped up with African American and Native American cultures. From social, legal, and economic perspectives, however, with a basis in the history of enslavement and segregation of people of African descent, the European American component can effectively be captured by the umbrella term *white* for certain purposes of analysis. From a cultural perspective, I use *white* here interchangeably with *European American*.

---

19 Quoted from Frankenberg (1993: 1), who explains whiteness as a set of three linked dimensions: structural advantage, standpoint, and cultural practices.

20 Lander's (2019) self-deprecating *Stuff White People Like* (e.g., coffee, diversity, awareness, apologies, public radio, unpaid internships, sea salt) occupies some of the ground toward the bland end of the spectrum, reflecting just one (upper-middle-class) slice of white America.

Frankenberg's (1993: 196) ethnographic research among white women in the United States in the 1980s found that, for a significant number of them, "being white felt like being cultureless. . . . Whiteness as a cultural space is represented here as amorphous and indescribable, in contrast with a range of other identities marked by race, ethnicity, region, and class." But, as Frankenberg notes, "In the same way that both men's and women's lives are shaped by their gender . . . white people and people of color live racially structured lives. In other words, any system of differentiation shapes those on whom it bestows privilege as well as those it oppresses. White people are 'raced,' just as men are 'gendered.' . . . White people have too often viewed themselves as nonracial or racially neutral" (1).

Is there a cultural reality that all the diverse European American groups may share? As with peoples of the African diaspora sharing certain aesthetic preferences in music and dance, so it is with European Americans. But it is helpful to further dissect this broad grouping into ethnic realities that reflect the history of rock and R&B. This includes Scots Irish fiddle and English vocal traditions from the South; northern urban Jewish songwriters, independent record label and other industry personnel; northern urban Italian American singers in the 1960s; and more general Anglo-Protestant social and cultural norms, among others.

The concept of whiteness, which became the basis of an academic discipline in the 1990s, can shed light on some of the background structures and assumptions in rock and R&B.[21] One example is the early music-industry category *race records*, named in the 1920s (by white talent scout Ralph Peer) to refer to the new market of recordings made by African Americans for an African American audience. Race here refers to African Americans, with the implication that whites are not marked by race. (The term had a positive sense when used by blacks at the time and was replaced by rhythm and blues in the late 1940s.) Similarly, the counterpart to the unmarked predominantly white television show *American Bandstand* was the marked *Soul Train*.[22]

This notion that "white people frequently construct themselves as raceless individuals, unfettered by the kinds of collective identifications that they view other people

21 Roediger (1991), Frankenberg (1993), and Dyer (1997: 8) reflect the 1990s lineages of critical white studies in Marxist labor history, critiques of white feminism, and lesbian and gay studies; Garner (2007) provides a helpful introduction. African Americans since at least Du Bois have been writing about the phenomenon (anthologized in Roediger 1998).

22 *American Bandstand* producers tried to systematically exclude blacks from the audience (Delmont 2012: 180–94).

as having" (Garner 2007: 4) has ominous implications. This is akin to saying that "the white man has attained the position of being without properties, unmarked, universal, just human" (Dyer 1997: 38). bell hooks suggests that white students in her college classroom reacted strongly in discussions about whiteness, "because they believe that all ways of looking that highlight difference subvert the liberal belief in a universal subjectivity (we are all just people) that they think will make racism disappear. They have a deep emotional investment in the myth of 'sameness,' even as their actions reflect the primacy of whiteness as a sign informing who they are and how they think" (1992c: 167). This is a strong critique of a colorblind perspective that assumes not only a level playing field but also a level or universal worldview, including standards of measurement and evaluation. Those standards, however, are always going to be culturally marked; in the North American case, they are based on white, and especially Anglo-Saxon Protestant (WASP), culture. Recognizing the particularity of those standards can begin to address, and perhaps dismantle, the racial hierarchy that has been in place for centuries.

A very different kind of implication devalues the artistic sensibilities and capacities of whites: if they have no race, so neither would they have much culture of their own to express. An occasional theme in writing about rock, especially that dating to the charged atmosphere of the late 1960s and early 1970s, is of whites plundering black music, imitating, adding nothing of their own (or diluting it), yet reaping the benefits.[23] This claim demands a response, as it can be condescending and patronizing, no matter the very real history of the practice. Looking more closely at ethnicity, class, or region, whites have their own unique cultural traditions—even if some are newly constructed—and have similar human capacities for creativity, feeling, and empathy. Artistic assessments from African American peers, many of which are provided here, both recognize the insidious history of exploitation and express genuine appreciation and respect across the color line.

Noting the whiteness of certain rock styles need not be taken as a putdown (e.g., as a retreat from blackness) but rather as an analytical perspective for understanding how identities may be sonically shaped and may shift over time, especially in a heavily

---

23 Two representative examples are Jefferson's (1973) article "Ripping Off Black Music" and a comment from rock critic Dave Marsh (in Wharton 2002-v): "People say, well, you know, he [Elvis] stole everything from black people. I want to say, 'Why would that be controversial?' You know, I mean the music business is *built* on stealing from black people."

blues-based tradition. For instance, progressive rock musicians in England explored European classical music, with its longer forms, merging disparate sensibilities closer to home. Punk rock progenitor Iggy Pop (of the Stooges) noted that although he liked the blues,

> it didn't take me long to figure out that, you know, I wasn't middle-aged, I wasn't black, and I wasn't from Mississippi, but how about if I could take those ideas, but do that from the point of view of our life back in Michigan. . . . You'd go to the Ford plant; you'd watch the drill press, BANG, and that's such a great sound, BANG, and each one is another fender. . . . I thought, God, those are impressive sounds, big sounds, and they're so regular and simple. I thought those are sounds that even we could master. (Espar and Thomson 1995-v, episode 7)

The monochromatic hue of whiteness began to break up by the 1960s. The election of John F. Kennedy as the first non-Protestant president (1960), the Immigration and Nationality Act (1965) getting rid of national-origins quotas, and the gradual integration of the solidly Anglo-Protestant economic, political, and cultural elite expanded the cultural palette of whiteness (Kaufmann 2004: 2–3). The new kinds of public faces presented by rock and R&B surely contributed to this ongoing process.

Taking a more global perspective, whiteness is in part an ethnocentric phenomenon—treating the world as if one's own ethnicity is at the center—not limited to whites or even dominant majority groups. At an Afro-Cuban drum and dance gathering shown in the documentary *Routes of Rhythm* (Rosow and Dratch 1989-v), a Cuban national dish of rice and black beans, called *Moros y Cristianos* (Moors and Christians), is seen as a metaphor for Cuban culture. "It's a food of mixed cultures. It's a Creole food," remarks one woman. "White rice and black beans—that's Cuba," says another. One of the drummers says, "The white with the black. The Cuban with the Spaniard." This last comment centers those of African ancestry as "Cuban," while those of Spanish (European) ancestry are marked as foreigners—"Spaniard."

A bi- or multiracial presence in rock and R&B was rarely publicly identified until the 1990s, perhaps beginning with Mariah Carey (and including guitarist Slash, Lenny Kravitz, Alicia Keys, and Norah Jones). Probably the most visible early example was the 1960s vocal group the Ronettes. Their peers at the time were urban young black women groomed for mainstream U.S. acceptance, as in Motown's Marvelettes, Martha and the Vandellas, and the Supremes. Lead singer Ronnie Bennett and her sister Estelle (African American and Cherokee mother and Irish American father) and cousin Nedra (African American and Puerto Rican parents) had a more risqué image, perhaps under less societal pressure than Motown groups to present more wholesome images.

Latino, Chicano, and Native American

Although it is common nowadays to decry the racial binaries of black and white, these are indeed the two primary ethnic and racial forces that have shaped the history of rock and R&B.[24] They are not the only ones though; other streams have figured into this history, but on a less primal, formative level. Latino musicians have had an important impact on rock and R&B in two ways: through Mexican American or Chicano musicians, such as Ritchie Valens and Carlos Santana, bringing their culture into the rock world; and through musical elements of Cuban origin, including rhythmic patterns (clave, chachachá), chord progressions, and musical instruments (conga, timbales). Latino ethnic identities contrast with U.S. black-white binaries in their acknowledgment of hybridity, captured with the term *mestizaje* (racial and cultural mixture) in the case of Spanish and Native populations and creolization or syncretism in the case of Spanish (or French) and African populations.[25] This "willingness to acknowledge, explore, and celebrate it [hybridity] has been far more pronounced among Latin/o Americans than among non-Latinos," which helps to explain why in the United States, "where anxieties about racial and cultural mixing persist, bipolar racial imaginaries still generate much of the language used to describe popular music" (Pacini Hernandez 2010: 3, 6).

The composite category *Spanish/Hispanic/Latino*, used for the first time in the 2000 U.S. census, points up the complexity of ethnic labels.[26] *Latino*, an inhabitant of the United States from Latin America, implies a connection to that larger region.[27] *Hispanic*, a term stemming from the Nixon administration, connects Spanish speakers

---

24 Avant-Mier (2014: 9) proposes, however, "that in some contexts, Latin/o music, people, and culture have been central to the development of rock music."

25 *Mestizo* and *creole* refer to people. The U.S. equivalent would be *mulatto*, which has fallen out of use.

26 Morales (2002: 2–3) and Avant-Mier (2014: 1–2) provide informative discussions on these labels.

27 *Latinx* is a recent gender-neutral term replacing the forms of Latina (feminine) and Latino (masculine).

to Europe. *Spanish*, at least in the eastern United States, may be the preferred term for those of Spanish-speaking Caribbean origins (Cuba, Dominican Republic). These are not racial markers, and so, as the U.S. Census Bureau (2018) notes, "people who identify as Hispanic, Latino, or Spanish may be any race." *Chicano* initially had pejorative connotations but was reclaimed by Mexican American activists in the 1960s.

The designation *Latin music* has the advantage of capturing a broad "stylistic complex," including that of Cuba, Brazil, and others, but the disadvantage is that it "collapses the social and cultural differences among Latin Americans in a way that can perpetuate oppressive stereotypes, i.e., the notion that 'Latins' are 'all the same'" (Waxer 1994: 140). Similarly, "it is a big mistake to lump Latinos together," Morales notes, although, "there are important ways we feel like one people. They have to do with physicality (dancing, body language, suspension of reserve) and spirituality (that strange syncretism between Catholicism and African and indigenous religions that allows us to be sacred and profane at the same time)" (2004: 28).

Cuba received the fourth-largest number of enslaved Africans after Brazil, Jamaica, and Saint-Domingue (Haiti and the Dominican Republic). British North America and Mexico saw a much smaller African presence, and Mexico has the largest indigenous (Amerindian) population in Latin America, estimated from 7 to 13 percent, and over 60 percent mestizo (Spanish-Amerindian).[28] The ramifications of these figures are crucial: Afro-Cubans have retained and developed some of the most vibrant African-based percussion traditions outside Africa.

An audible Mexican American presence in rock emerged in the late 1950s with Ritchie Valens (1941–59). Born and raised in Pacoima, Los Angeles, Valens (born Valenzuela) burst into the Top 40 in early 1959, at age seventeen, with "La Bamba" (#22), based on a Mexican folk song. Valens's exuberant vocals, the catchiness of the tune, and the expertise of the studio musicians (drummer Earl Palmer and bassist-guitarist Carol Kaye) all contributed to a classic cultural translation.[29] The previous year the Champs hit #1 with the Latin-inflected "Tequila" (written by saxophonist Danny Flores). Although Valens died in 1959 (in the same plane crash as Buddy Holly), his legacy continued through the 1960s bands Cannibal and the Headhunters, from the Chicano neighborhood of East Los Angeles ("Land of a Thousand Dances,"

---

28 Slave Voyages (2019); U.S. Central Intelligence Agency (2019); Minority Rights Group International (2019).

29 The earliest recording of "La Bamba" (titled "El Jarocho"), a staple from Veracruz, Mexico, may be from 1939 by Alvaro Hernández Ortiz (Victor 76102); see Sheehy (2003).

1965, #30); Sam the Sham and the Pharaohs, from Texas ("Wooly Bully," 1965, #2); and ? [Question Mark] and the Mysterians, from Michigan ("96 Tears," 1966, #1). In 1987 Los Lobos, from East Los Angeles, hit #1 with a cover version of "La Bamba," released in conjunction with the biopic of the same title about Valens. It was the first time a Spanish-language song hit #1 on the *Billboard* pop singles chart.

Carlos Santana (1947–), who was born in Mexico and moved to San Francisco in his young teens, definitively brought in a sound to rock that was deeply rooted in Latin American styles. One obvious factor was instrumentation, including a conga (played by Puerto Rican Michael Carabello), a Cuban instrument that developed out of central African Kongo drumming traditions, and timbales (played by Nicaraguan Jose "Chepito" Areas), another Cuban drum that developed out of the European timpani. These two instruments alone represent a meeting of African-based (rumba drumming) and Spanish-based (indoor charanga ensemble) worlds on Cuban soil. Santana's guitar-playing style was drenched in minor-mode improvisations, which married blues to Iberian (Spain and Portugal) melodic sensibilities. The group Santana's cover of Puerto Rican Tito Puente's composition "Oye Como Va" (on their second album, *Abraxas*, 1970) was emblematic of their cross-cultural transformations, transferring the original flute and violin lines to the electric guitar and organ while maintaining the same chachachá (and mambo) feel and percussion base. This example "brings into focus a characteristic of U.S. Latino musical practices: Far from being defined by or limited to musical aesthetics associated with particular national groups, Latino music making has always entailed crossing musical, geographic, racial, and ethnic boundaries" (Pacini Hernandez 2010: 2).

The three largest Latino communities in the 1950s–80s were Chicanos in California and the Southwest, Puerto Ricans in New York City, and Cubans in Florida. The wave of cultural nationalism in the late 1960s and 1970s had differing impacts among them. In California Chicano rockers ethnically marked their music and "have been more willing to engage with rock than their New York Puerto Rican counterparts" (Pacini Hernandez 2010: 51).[30] New York's large Puerto Rican community invested in salsa, a cosmopolitan reshaping of Cuban dance music. The few breakthroughs into the pop charts illustrate the exceptions: Ray Barretto had one Top 40 entry, with the salsa and R&B mix (called boogaloo) "El Watusi" (1963); José Feliciano had many

---

30 Los Lobos marked their 1987 cover of "La Bamba" by playing an accordion and shifting to an
    acoustic mariachi ensemble toward the end of the song.

hits in the late 1960s and early 1970s, drawing on a less locally marked Latin American style; and Tony Orlando (and Dawn) had great success in the 1970s, rarely bringing in any local flavor. After them Puerto Ricans did not move into the Top 40 until the late 1990s with Ricky Martin and Jennifer Lopez (2010: 43). Salsa, one of the most vibrant musics that developed in the United States beginning in the 1960s, lived largely outside of U.S. mainstream pop and R&B (Flores 2016).[31]

The recent film *Rumble: The Indians Who Rocked the World* (Bainbridge and Maiorana 2017-v) has brought a broader awareness of a Native American presence in rock (TeachRock 2019b). Named after the song "Rumble" (which hit #16 in 1958) by guitarist Link Wray, of Shawnee origins, the film covers rock artists who had Native American ancestry as well as possible Native American sonic influences. The former category includes 1960s singer-songwriter Buffy Sainte-Marie, the Band guitarist Robbie Robertson, Jimi Hendrix, and the 1970s band Redbone. The latter includes speculations about the nature of close black and Native contacts impacting the development of the blues.

Some readers may be taken aback by frequent reference to the race or ethnicity of musical artists and their fans, perhaps assuming that the music industry is a colorblind meritocracy, rewarding talent justly. But the U.S. music industry has not worked like that, nor do we work like that as listeners. By paying attention to just how color aware we all are, especially by identifying unmarked practices as ethnically or racially marked, we may gain a deeper understanding and appreciation of the intersecting forces that go into producing an artwork and also its patterns of dissemination and reception. One overarching question to contemplate throughout the history of rock and R&B is, Why would one community of people bounded by race or ethnicity be interested in the musical expression of another community? The case studies in this book—often steeped in cross-cultural interaction, exchange, immersion, or what some might call theft—provide oftentimes optimistic responses, pointing to the joys of human curiosity and discovery.

---

31 For more on the Chicano and Latino presence in rock, see Marsh (1984), Guevara (1985), Loza (1993), Reyes and Waldman (1998), Roberts (1999), Sublette (2007), and Berríos-Miranda, Dudley, and Habell-Pallán (2018).

DEMOGRAPHICS

It will be helpful to understand the growth and relative size of two demographics in particular: youth, because they emerged in the post–World War II era as a new and powerful consumer group driving rock and roll; and African Americans, because their cultural expression had an impact on U.S. culture much greater than their numbers would suggest.

The population of the United States almost doubled between 1940 and 1990, going from 131.7 million to 248.7 million, rising between 19 million (from 1940–50) to 28.6 million (1950–60) people per decade. The African American population of the United States dropped from 19 percent in 1790, the year of the first U.S. census, steadily down to 10 percent in 1920, at which point it remained stable until 1960, when it reached 10.5 percent. It continued to grow at roughly 0.5 percent per decade, reaching 11.1 percent in 1970, 11.7 percent in 1980, and 12.1 percent in 1990. These figures are crucial for understanding the phenomenon of crossing over from the African American market (race records, R&B) to the pop market. African Americans alone did not have the numbers to register an R&B hit very deep into the pop market. Beginning with the 2000 census individuals could self-identify with more than one race, and so out of the total 2010 U.S. population of 308.7 million, the category Black or African American was registered as either 12.6 percent (alone) or 13.6 percent (including combinations with other races).[32]

The decade after World War II was marked by the appearance of teens as a new and powerful market of consumers. In 1944 the term *teenager* moved into general circulation (Savage 2007: 453). That year "a magazine was launched that pulled together the strands of democracy, national identity, peer culture, target marketing, and youth consumerism into an irresistible package. . . . Launched out of editor Helen Valentine's deep-seated conviction that high school girls needed a magazine of their own, *Seventeen* excluded adults and directly addressed its target market" (448). The first issue sold out its four hundred thousand copies in two days, and in 1946 circulation hit one million (Palladino 1996: 103).

The purchasing power of teenage boys increased more than three and a half times from 1946 to 1956: their average weekly income (allowance plus job) went from $2.41

---

32 The census figures in this paragraph are from Hobbs and Stoops (2002: 11, 77), U.S. Census Bureau (2011: 2–3), and Black Demographics (2019).

to $8.96 in this ten-year span (*Time* 1956). In 1959 *Life* magazine called U.S. teenage consumers "a new $10 billion power": eighteen million teens owned ten million phonographs and over a million TV sets. Teens spent $75 million on single records. Elvis Presley had sold twenty-five million copies of singles over the past four years (*Life* 1959: 78, 83). By 1964 there were twenty-two million teenagers in the United States, and they were increasing three times as fast as the overall population. They were spending $100 million a year on records (Palladino 1996: 195).[33]

College attendance was also on the rise: in 1940, 15 percent of the college-age group attended college; by 1954 that rate climbed by 30 percent, and by 1960 almost 68 percent of the college-age group were attending college (Alba 1985: 142). Teens had arrived as a major cultural force: "The postwar spread of American values would be spearheaded by the idea of the Teenager. This new type was the ultimate psychic match of the times: living in the now, pleasure-seeking, product-hungry, embodying the new global society where social inclusion was to be granted through purchasing power. The future would be Teenage" (Savage 2007: 465).

The percentage of the population of fifteen- to twenty-four-year-olds in the United States between 1950 and 1990 varied from a low of 13.4 percent (1960) to a high of 18.8 percent (1980). The percentages in each decade and their real numbers are as follows: 14.7 percent and 22 million in 1950; 13.4 percent and 24 million in 1960; 17.4 percent and 35.4 million in 1970; 18.8 percent and 42.5 million in 1980; and 14.8 percent and 36.8 million in 1990 (Hobbs and Stoops 2002: 56, A-7).[34] This was the cohort that largely drove trends in music.

33 See Gallup and Hill (1961) for a snapshot of American youth in 1961.
34 The percentage continued to decline during the next decade.

European American and African American musical traditions are deeply intertwined. Pulling apart their textures takes much hard work. It is a minefield, risking assigning racially charged sonic markers, claiming that they define a group of people. Instead, it is productive to think about identities as involving creative choices that combine endless sonic possibilities into concrete forms and styles of expression. Some of those choices have grown out of the musical practice of well-defined communities, and some sounds, forms, and styles may be attractive enough that they are widely embraced and then reshaped to fit new contexts.

It is helpful to distinguish between performance style—the way something is played or sung—and repertory—the pieces of music (or compositions) performed (K. Miller 2010: 14). Many black country blues musicians had a broad repertory, which reached far outside their immediate community. For instance, guitarist Johnny Shines, reported this about his traveling companion in the 1930s, the legendary Mississippi bluesman Robert Johnson: "The country singer—Jimmie Rodgers—me and Robert used to play a hell of a lot of his tunes, man. Ragtime, pop tunes, waltz numbers, polkas. . . . Hillbilly" (qtd. in Guralnick 1989: 22). "He [Johnson] did anything that he heard on the radio. . . . I mean ANYTHING—popular songs, ballads, blues, anything. It didn't make him no difference what it was. If he liked it, he did it" (qtd. in Welding 1975: 29). Whites have been recording blues since the first decade of blues recordings (the 1920s), including some of the biggest country music stars, like Jimmie Rodgers ("Blue Yodel" series, beginning in 1927); the Carter Family ("Worried Man Blues," 1930); and Hank Williams ("Move It on Over," 1942). In these cases musicians can personalize pieces coming from a variety of sources, imbuing them with individual and community marks.

Early contact between European and African cultures occurred on transatlantic slave-trade voyages and intensified on southern plantations, where white slaveholders occasionally forced black performances, and blacks were exposed to the music of whites. Some blacks took up the fiddle for the entertainment of whites and for themselves. The banjo, an invention of plantation-based blacks with prototypes documented as early as the seventeenth century in the Caribbean, was also used for entertainment.[1] Whites later picked it up, altered its construction, and developed their own playing styles. Contact among blacks and whites working alongside one

---

1 Epstein (1977) has provided exemplary documentation of early black music in the United States, and Thompson (2014) has more recently taken a closer look at interactions during this era.

another in the streets, ship decks, and wharves, especially between free blacks and working-class whites in the North in the early nineteenth century, led to further exchanging styles of performance and repertories (C. Smith 2013).

The Second Great Awakening (led by Baptist and Methodist preachers), which swept across the country with outdoor camp meetings in the early 1800s—such as the historic Cane Ridge, Kentucky camp meeting attracting up to twenty thousand blacks and whites in August 1801—facilitated cultural exchange. Here the term *exchange* seems appropriate: "Blacks and whites worshipped and sang together in an atmosphere highly charged with emotion at camp meetings during the first half of the nineteenth century. That the participants were mutually influenced seems inescapable. Songs, parts of songs, and ways of singing music have been exchanged, without the excited folk knowing or caring who started what" (Epstein 1977: 199).

Blackface minstrelsy, in which northern whites cruelly caricatured blacks, hit the national stage in New York City, with Thomas "Daddy" Rice in the early 1830s and the Virginia Minstrels in the early 1840s (Lott 1993).[2] Minstrelsy was America's first homegrown popular music, but not the only music widely heard. Singers from Europe, such as Jenny Lind, and opera were widely appreciated in the North: "It is hard to exaggerate the ubiquity of opera music in America in the nineteenth century" (Levine 1988: 97). Operagoers at that time were a rowdier bunch than today, almost treating the event like a rock concert, expressing their appreciation at will and freely moving around the venue.

After emancipation blacks would take up minstrelsy, caricaturing whites caricaturing them, forming larger and larger troupes. Around the same time spirituals, which developed spontaneously in the religious worship of enslaved African Americans, were arranged for the concert stage at the historically black Fisk University by their white music director George White assisted by his students. The Fisk Jubilee Singers toured the United States in 1871 (and Europe two years later), giving birth to the first black entertainment industry (Graham 2018), eventually merging with black minstrel troupes.

From the 1880s to the 1920s, before the recording industry moved in, there was some fluidity in shared repertories and probably even performance styles among black and whites. In the beginning, in the 1880s, "black and white performers regularly

---

2 Rice played a character he called "Jim Crow," which eventually lent its name to the legalized system of segregation in the South.

employed racialized sounds. By the end [the 1920s], most listeners expected artists to *embody* them. This change closed off significant swaths of music to both black and white performers" (K. Miller 2010: 4). That is to say, that black and white musical styles were still circulating among one another in the 1880s, but when the recording industry began marketing to separate communities through their categories of hillbilly (or folk) and race records, new barriers began to be solidified.

The distribution of northern commercial music throughout the South beginning in the late nineteenth century through sheet music and touring theatrical shows was an important catalyst for expanding southern musical traditions (K. Miller 2010: 25). Blues, which developed in southern black communities reflecting new postemancipation sensibilities, would soon move across the color line, probably sometime in the early twentieth century (Russell 1970). As noted earlier, musical sounds and styles can contain codes, or sonic signifiers, learned by acculturation, which can be shaped to create individual and group identities. The following sections lay out the historical contexts in which some of those codes developed.

EUROPEAN AND EUROPEAN AMERICAN MUSIC

The European legacy has shaped U.S. musical aesthetics on many levels: the tonal language; the use of music notation; repertories of religious and secular song and of dance music (hymns, ballads, fiddle tunes); vocal and instrumental performance styles; and a philosophical split between the mind and the body, which has informed how one participates in events that feature music.

Tonality, the musical system of combining tones to make melody and harmony (see the glossary), developed several centuries ago in royal courts and churches across Europe. Melodies and harmonies (chords) in this universe are based on establishing and then exploiting hierarchies in which some tones and chords have greater gravitational pulls than others, creating a feeling of forward motion in acculturated listeners. "In its power to form musical goals and regulate the progress of the music toward these moments of arrival, tonality has become the principal musical means in Western culture by which to manage expectation and structure desire" (Hyer 2002: 728). The modern tonal system took shape during the seventeenth century, from Claudio Monteverdi composing madrigals (pieces for several voices) at the court of Mantua (northern Italy) at the early end to violinist Arcangelo Corelli composing for small instrumental ensembles in Rome in the 1680s. In the early eighteenth century, Johann

Sebastian Bach, employed as an organist and music director in courts and churches in Germany, brought this new system to one of the great heights of European artistic expression, especially in his sacred choral works for four voices (soprano, alto, tenor, bass) and his keyboard works.[3]

This system, inflected with African American sensibilities, remains the foundational musical grammar of rock. The prestige of European classical music (a symbol of an imperial past), the Christian religious practice of psalm and hymn singing, and the modern youthful energy of rock have spread this tonal system around the world, but in many places it is just one among others. Although it is widespread (dispersed in the course of colonial conquests and missionary projects), it is not universal but rather has very specific origins and associations.

Music notation in Europe dates back to ninth-century monasteries, where the oral traditions of early Christian chanting began to be written onto parchment as a memory aid. It took many centuries for the modern system of notation and the notion of a composer (one who writes music down) to develop. Notation allowed music, something that exists in sound, to be fixed visually and performed in other places and times. This led to a conceptual split between a composer and a performer and enabled new outlooks: musical performances could be entirely and consistently planned from beginning to end; large-scale forces could be controlled by a conductor; and an authoritative original version of a piece could be established and attributed. Songs and instrumental dance music conceived in open-ended oral traditions could be notated, fixed, and preserved, serving as a repertory source for future generations. Repertories could then accumulate and get larger and larger.

Major notated collections of music that had circulated in oral traditions began to be published in the eighteenth century, including English and Scottish ballads and songs, Scottish dance music and fiddle tunes, and hundreds of Irish harp and fiddle dance tunes.[4] In the 1910s Cecil Sharp (1917) and his assistant Maud Karpeles traveled the Appalachians (in North Carolina, Virginia, Tennessee, Kentucky, and West Virginia) collecting and notating songs and ballads. This southern song and ballad tradition impacted the urban folk revival in the 1960s, which in turn would have a major impact on rock. Kentucky-born Greenwich Village folksinger Jean Ritchie

---

3   Taruskin (2005) is the standard music history for this era.

4   See Percy (1765); Gow and Gow (1986), which is compiled from publications from 1784 to 1822; Burns (1787–1803); Bunting (1796, 1840); Child (1882–98); and O'Neill (1903).

released her version of "Lord Randal," documented by Sharp and earlier by Child in England, on an album in 1961. Bob Dylan composed his masterpiece "A Hard Rain's A-Gonna Fall" based on the lyric structure of "Lord Randal" the following year. "Nottamun Town" was collected by Sharp in Kentucky in 1917 from Jean Ritchie's older sister, Una, and cousin Sabrina. Ritchie released her version of it on an album in 1954. Dylan's "Masters of War" put new lyrics on top of the same melody.[5]

British song and dance traditions, as well as religious psalm singing, initially dispersed in North America in clear regional patterns. Puritans, with their psalm singing, dominated New England. Scottish immigrants spread the fiddle along the Appalachian trail beginning in the seventeenth century and it would soon become the most popular dance instrument on both sides of the Atlantic (Ritchie and Orr 2014: 29). But, as a classic text on country music notes, "English, highland Scots, Scotch-Irish, Catholic Irish, and Welsh elements mixed on the southern frontier.... Cultural intermixing had occurred so frequently and for such a long period of time that white folk culture should most appropriately be called 'British'" (Malone and Neil 2010: 3–4).

Group singing of Christian texts, especially the hymns of English Congregational minister Isaac Watts, would have an enormous impact on both literate and nonliterate Americans. Three types of song are mentioned in the New Testament: psalms (from the Old Testament Book of Psalms), hymns (nonscriptural praise songs), and spiritual songs.[6] Psalm singing, prevalent in New England during the colonial era, would give way to the exceptionally popular religious poems by Watts, published as *Hymns and Spiritual Songs* in 1707. These, and Watts's (1719) psalm settings—all just texts without music—were distributed so widely by missionaries during the Great Awakenings of religious revival (1730s–40s, 1790s–1850s) that at the time, along with the Bible, they were "by far the most important Western literary influence on the culture of the African in America. Account after account stresses the role of these two" (Hamm 1983: 128).[7] Watts's poetic language was one of the most direct encounters that African Americans had with the expressive possibilities of the English language.

---

5 It is not clear if Ritchie's recordings (1954-d, 1956-d, 1961-d) were Dylan's initial source. The Byrds' guitarist, Roger McGuinn (1999), has published his correspondence with Jean Ritchie about "Nottamun Town."

6 For example, see Ephesians 5:19 and Colossians 3:16 (King James).

7 Cofounder of Methodism John Wesley (1737) published his *Collection of Psalms and Hymns* in Charleston, South Carolina, with half of the seventy pieces coming from Watts. An American edition of Watts's *Hymns* was published in 1739.

Watts's texts were typically rendered in a style called *lining out*, in which the leader sings one line at a time, cueing the participants for their rendition of each line. Lining out was first documented in the 1640s in England, as an aid for congregants who could not read music, and it has continuing legacies into the present in black and white communities in the United States. Watts's work was so pervasive that any hymn composed in his style was called "Dr. Watts" by African Americans, including "Amazing Grace," by Englishman John Newton (who grew up listening to Watts hymns), published in 1789. Part of the allure of Watts was his ability to evoke "metaphors of physical trouble and spiritual transcendence" (Heilbut 2002: xxii).

Lining out in the tradition of Watts hymns still exists in certain southern rural white communities, particularly among Old Regular Baptists (Indian Bottom Association 1997-d), highlighting an old class distinction in English worship practices. In the same seventeenth-century England in which lining out was sanctioned by the church and tonality was developing, a rift was developing between "a gentry increasingly committed to the high-culture musical ideals of continental Europe . . . [who] held that music was primarily a *learned* art—that is, a literate one . . . and the common people, with their Psalms and what they remembered of the old way of singing them" (Wicks 1989: 63). That learned literate art would yield professionally trained choirs that would sing sacred works by Henry Purcell, George Frideric Handel, and Bach in four-part harmony. The old way would continue on in backcountry churches in the United States and eventually filter into country music.

Researching Old Regular Baptist churches in Kentucky, Wicks located sonic markers on a micro level, proposing "that a small number of melodic principles governed the approach to, departure from, and general treatment" of certain scale tones in any given melody (1989: 70–72). These markers included approaching the third- and fifth-scale degrees with a slide from below, departing the third-scale degree with a flourish down to the tonic, and the use of turns and quick shakes before or after certain tones. Using a musical transcription, she illustrated how some of these markers were exemplified in the hymn "Farther Along," sung by country music stars Dolly Parton, Linda Ronstadt, and Emmylou Harris (on their album *Trio*, 1987-d), concluding that this trio performs these "old-way gestures in such abundance that the whole session is no less than a stunning *tour de force*, a contemporary monument to the old melodic art and its characteristic voice production styles" (84–85).[8] Their album won a Grammy for

---

8 For a comparison, listen to Sam Cooke and the Soul Stirrers' version of "Farther Along" (1956).

Best Country Duo or Group with Vocal, and was nominated for Album of the Year (going against Michael Jackson, U2, Prince, and Whitney Houston), suggesting that these sonic markers of a centuries-old tradition maintain relevance.

By studying lining out traditions in Kentucky, Wicks was hoping to broaden our "conception of what constitutes the more comprehensive stylistic matrix characteristic of much of American popular song . . . [and show] that, while American country sound is undoubtedly in debt to rock music . . . it is also certain that, considering melodic and kinesic carry-overs, and the traits of voice production, an equal influence runs in direction of rock from country, and by extension, from a far older musical style than we had heretofore imagined" (1989: 92).

The singing on "Farther Along" demonstrates a characteristic Anglo-American vocal quality, drawn on by women folksingers of the 1960s, although without the regional southern accent. The male version of this clarity of vocal timbre (its quality or sound) has been called "high lonesome," referring to Kentucky-born Bill Monroe, who pioneered bluegrass in the 1940s. A similar kind of clarity, but with different regional accents, can be heard in various styles of rock, including the Beach Boys and Crosby, Stills, Nash, and Young. Even their guitars (electric and acoustic) take on this aesthetic for a clear sound, eschewing distortion, except when making overt gestures toward rock's blues roots (e.g., "Woodstock" on CSNY's 1970 album *Déjà Vu*).

Musical transcriptions of the melodic principles that Wicks noted tell only part of the story and may not provide enough information. The rate of speed of a slide into a tone; the way in which a singer inflects certain tones, such as creating an ambiguity between a minor and major third (the so-called blue note); and exactly how a melisma (singing many tones on a single syllable) is treated can be just as important in defining sonic markers. We look more closely at this in the next section, with Aretha Franklin's rendition of "Amazing Grace."

Language dialect is an important sonic marker. Chuck Berry's verses in "Maybelline" draw on African American dialect (what Labov [1972] has meticulously documented): dropping the ending *r* sound, he rhymes *road* with *ford* (pronouncing it *fohd*) and *four* with *more* (pronouncing them *foh* and *moh*). In his choruses, though, when he sings *true* the second time, he slides up from the second degree, drawing from country, with a similar inflection as the trio singing "Farther Along," and rounds his *r* sound.

Guitar-strumming styles can sonically mark a group identity. John Lee Hooker's "Boogie Chillen'" (1948) has a distinctive African American guitar style that establishes a dynamic relationship between onbeats and offbeats (by accenting one or the other), phrasing them as triplets (long-short, long-short, etc.). (This abstract process is called *swing* in the jazz world; the specific rhythm is called *boogie*, as in the title.) The white Texas rock band ZZ Top's "La Grange" (1973) uses this same rhythm, which has come to be a characteristic sound of 1970s southern boogie, reorienting the group identity of the strumming style, although there is little question of its origins—it is a trademark of Hooker's and also of a more generalized African American performance aesthetic.[9]

A related guitar-strumming style, not congruent with black aesthetics, has clear associations with certain white-coded genres of rock. This rhythm consists of steadily and evenly strumming two strokes per beat, without the dynamic accents or the triplet feel. Examples from protometal hard rock, punk, new wave, and heavy metal include Black Sabbath's "Paranoid" (1970), especially between the verses; the Ramones' "Beat on the Brat" (1976) and the Sex Pistols' "Liar" (1977); the Cars' "My Best Friend's Girl" and "Just What I Needed" (1978); and Metallica's "Master of Puppets" (1986), Megadeth's "Peace Sells" (1986), and Judas Priest's "Painkiller" (1990). The Police use this rhythm but add dynamics with changing chords in "Be My Girl" (1978) and "Every Breath You Take" (1983), and Metallica provides perhaps the most out-front example in "Enter Sandman" (1991), also adding dynamic accents but keeping the even eighth-note pulse going.

The role of dance in rock and R&B has a clear relationship to European and African legacies. The Enlightenment-era privileging of the mind over the body, combined with the Christian theological distinction between the spirit and the flesh, has shaped the role of dance in Europe and European America. Dyer's analysis of his own (English) whiteness led him to question the source of his relationship to his body: "What has made Christianity compelling and fascinating is precisely the mystery that it posits, that somehow there is in the body something that is not of the body which may be variously termed spirit, mind, soul or God. . . . The Enlightenment's largely atheistic shift . . . [broke] with the sense of the divinity, but not the presence, of the spirit within. Christianity maintains a conception of a split between mind and body, regarding the latter as at the least inferior and often as evil" (1997: 16). Continuing on, he noted in Christian men a model of "a divided nature and internal struggle between mind

---

9   A lawsuit against ZZ Top (*La Cienega Music Co. v. ZZ Top*) failed on a technicality concerning registration of copyright (Music Copyright Infringement Resource 2019).

(God) and body (man) . . . a dynamic of aspiration, of striving to be, to transcend . . . registered in suffering, self-denial and self-control" (17). This all became personal when, in the early 1980s in New York City, hanging out with a multiracial gay crowd, he attempted to join in a *Soul Train*–style dance line: "I have never felt more white than when I danced down between those lines. . . . All I can say is that at that moment, the black guys all looked loose and I felt tight. The notion of whiteness having to do with tightness, with self-control, self-consciousness, mind over body . . . I felt it" (6).[10]

Dance in England and in Anglo-America has had a very different status than in Africa and African America. One can start with cultural critic H. L. Mencken's famous quote: "Puritanism—The haunting fear that someone, somewhere, may be happy" (1949: 624). During colonial times English and African attitudes toward dance clashed, particularly on Sundays: "In the seventeenth and eighteenth centuries, the dances of the Africans were usually confined to Sunday, their only day of rest, but the English clergy was bitterly opposed to this desecration of the Lord's Day and did its best to stop the dancing" (Epstein 2015: 36).

Epstein's (1977: 207–16) documentation of antebellum black music is filled with white slaveholders and clergy complaining about the incompatibility of dancing with Christian morals. Southern whites surely danced—the popularity of the fiddle was based in part on its rich repertories of dance music, especially Scottish reels.[11] But the role of dance in everyday life was limited; the role of dance in the sacred sphere was largely absent.[12]

Dance in Europe took on a greater role as a spectacle to be watched or a genteel art form for couples requiring formal instruction, with a profusion of manuals, rather than one in which everyone present *must* participate at all levels of society. Taruskin (2005, 4: 49) refers to ballet, which originated at the French court of Henry III in the late sixteenth century, as "spectacular professional dancing for theatrical display." But the

---

10 On the other hand, see the discussion of Kraftwerk in the section on electronic dance music, especially Detroit techno pioneer Carl Craig's comment: "They were so stiff, they were funky" (qtd. in Reynolds 1998: 14).

11 Ritchie and Orr (2014: 32, 146–48, 232–33) and Malone and Neil (2010: 17–18) discuss southern white dance traditions. For an extended description of one event in nineteenth-century Georgia, see Longstreet (1850: 12–22).

12 African American Sam Moore (of 1960s soul group Sam and Dave) states, "We weren't dancers. We were doing the holy dance. That's something I got out of church" (Espar and Thomson 1995-v, episode 4).

later waltz was something else: "Social life in Vienna during much of the nineteenth century centered around the ballroom and the waltz ... not only for the ruling classes ... but also for the emerging bourgeoisie, who packed the twenty or thirty dance halls sprinkled through Vienna's suburbs.... Success in society required being able to dance and, in particular, to dance the waltz" (Zbikowski 2017: 129, 130). There may be some parallels between the role of dance in parts of Europe and Africa, but there are some distinct differences. For one, individual dancers stepping out from a group to engage one on one with an ensemble or master lead instrumentalist (most often drummers), prevalent in much African dancing, has little parallel in Europe. These moments "that emphasize individual expression provide musicians with opportunities for more creative freedom. Individual dance allows for maximum improvisation and communication with the master drummer under established rules of etiquette.... There are instances when the dancer leads or there is a mutual exchange of initiative" (J. Malone 1996: 14).

A key difference between white and black dance traditions in the United States concerns formal instruction, in the form of ballroom dance studios popularized by Vernon and Irene Castle and Arthur and Kathryn Murray beginning in the 1910s (especially in northern urban contexts). Here the waltz was eclipsed by black vernacular dances (e.g., the fox trot) that were simplified and codified to make them acceptable to a white urban public (J. Malone 1996: 143). On the other hand, "black youth and adults generally don't take classes to learn to social dance—their academies are dance halls, house parties, social clubs, and the streets. In fact, formal dance studios are usually years behind the real source of America's major social dances: the black community." Malone continues, quoting dancer Charles "Honi" Coles: "In Philadelphia, the only form of recreation was dancing. Everyone I knew could dance. I [didn't] know anyone who went to school to learn show business or dancing. You learned it ... as you were exposed to it" (28).[13]

As for the dynamism of black dance forms and their impact, some white *American Bandstand* teen dancers were watching a predominantly African American Philadelphia television dance show, bringing those moves onto *Bandstand*. The host, Mitch Thomas, reported, "I called Dick Clark [the *AB* host] and told him my kids were a

---

13 Ramsey (2003: 4) had a similar recollection about his childhood in 1960s Chicago: "A variety of music ... accompanied virtually every family gathering. Soul food and, most important, dance were central to these events and charged each with an air of communal celebration in which everyone—the young and the not-so-young—eagerly participated."

little upset because they were hearing that the Stroll started on 'Bandstand.' . . . He went on the show that day and said, 'Hey man, I want you all to know The Stroll originated on the Mitch Thomas dance show" (Delmont 2012: 173).

One productive way to think this through is that dance has a restricted role in European American culture, with a history of repression by religious authorities and a reputation as either a genteel art form or a frivolous pursuit. Bodily expression, as opposed to goal-oriented competitive sports, is devalued, except as a spectacle to watch. This can explain part of the appeal of early rock and roll (and part of the objections of parents): it was liberating to white teens. And it can explain why dancers can be so essential for R&B, funk, and hip hop groups and so rare in rock bands, excepting those clearly indebted to African American traditions.

AFRICAN AND AFRICAN AMERICAN MUSIC

Within the broad and diverse spectrum of musical styles of the African diaspora one can identify a number of shared musical features, especially within African American idioms. These features point to an African diasporic aesthetic of music making, a shared sensibility invoked by the phrase *black music*: active participation; dialogue; offbeat phrasing; filling in of the sound spectrum; improvisation; and a privileging of dance.[14] A more specifically African American aesthetic can be heard in the way the European tonal system is inflected in performance.

Active participation by all present is expected in African and African American music cultures. This can take the form of hand clapping, dancing, singing, or otherwise vocally responding. Even in music performed in a concert hall for seated audiences, such as jazz, applause and vocal approval is appreciated in the course of a performance. Senegalese singer Youssou N'Dour, whose concerts typically draw audience members to jump the stage and dance with his drummers, has noted this in his travels around the world: "I am much more sure of people's reaction at the end of a concert in Africa than in Europe or the United States. . . . In Africa, if you manage to move an audience, people get up, cheer, shout or come up on the stage to dance, and there you know

---

14 Gayle (1971), Southern (1983, 1997), Floyd (1996), O. Wilson (2001), Keyes (2003), Maultsby (2015a, 2015b), Burnim and Maultsby (2015), and Maultsby and Burnim (2017) are important resources for African American music, and Mintz and Price (1992) and Levine (1977) have laid important groundwork. Charry (2000) examines musical aesthetics of one large West African group and reprints historical reporting of music and dance there.

you've got to them" (Ba 1994-v). Contrast this with mid-1960s Beatlemania, where the focal point of young women fans would be to touch the band members rather than dance, still the focal point during a 1978 Bruce Springsteen concert, where women jump onstage to hug and kiss, rather than dance with, the star.[15] A more austere contrast would be withholding one's applause and remaining silent until the end of a performance of a European classical music composition, to the point of holding back and respecting the silence between movements in a symphony or concerto. This is not unique to classical music concerts: when electric blues guitarist Albert King was questioned about different reactions he gets from black and white audiences, he understood different modes of engagement, without making value judgments:

G[arland]: I've seen you perform before white audiences and, in comparison to black audiences, there seems to be little overt reaction, little movement and they don't seem to let go as much.

K[ing]: Not while you're playin', but they show it after you finish. They give you that much respect. They sit there and listen.[16] (Garland 1969: 164)

Maultsby (2017: 48) points to James Brown's decision to record live at the Apollo Theater in 1962 as an example of "the value placed on the interactive dimension of performance in Black communities, where audience feedback is regarded as a vital contribution and an enhancement to the cultural and aesthetic experience." His record label head, Syd Nathan, was against the idea: "I am not going to be spending money on something where a lot of people are going to be screaming. Who wants a lot of noise over the song?" Brown's *Live at the Apollo*, his eighth album (since 1959), was his first to make any *Billboard* national chart, hitting #2 on the pop chart (the R&B charts were discontinued from 1963 to 1965). Audience interaction was a major part of the album. To gain that level of popularity, significant numbers of whites were

---

15 "Rosalita (Come Out Tonight)," July 8, 1978, Phoenix, AZ, in Springsteen (2001-v). Springsteen's invitation to a fan (Courteney Cox) to come up onstage and dance with him in the video for "Dancing in the Dark" further illustrates the point in its staging, as do YouTube clips of live performances of the song.

16 See Albert King (1970-v) for his performance at the rock mecca Fillmore East (September 23, 1970).

also appreciating the aesthetic, perhaps as a result of being enculturated into African American aesthetics since the rise of rock and roll in the mid-1950s.

Related to active participation is a widespread preference for dialogue, conversation, or response (sometimes referred to as call and response). This can be heard in many denominations of African American churches (including Baptist, Pentecostal, Sanctified, and Holiness), wherein congregants continuously respond to a preacher's every line, mutually exhorting one another.[17] The interaction among members of James Brown's band provides a classic model, wherein the horn section, guitars, bass, drums, and Brown have intricate conversations with one another. A solo performance can be imbued with this aesthetic, as in a blues guitarist providing running commentary on the guitar in response to his vocal lines.

Chuck Berry's vocal interjections with Julian Lennon (John's son) on "Johnny B. Goode" is especially fascinating, given Berry's fluency in appealing to white and black audiences, the predominantly white Saint Louis audience in attendance at his sixtieth birthday celebration, and his varied interjections in each part of the song, vividly captured in the documentary *Chuck Berry: Hail! Hail! Rock 'n' Roll* (Hackford 1987-v). After singing the first verse in harmony with Lennon, Berry responds to each line of Lennon's chorus ("I hear yah," "Sing the song," "Oh, yeah!"). For the second chorus Berry playfully points after each line to Rolling Stones guitarist Keith Richards to respond instrumentally to Lennon. Berry kicks off the last verse with "Sing the song, Julian!" and then responds to each line ("Yes he did," "Yes you will," "Yes they will," "Yes, he's good," "Oh, yeah"). Berry responds to each line of the final chorus, this time encouraging the audience to participate ("C'mon, help the boy," "Help him!"). It is a striking display of bringing this aesthetic into the heart of middle America.

Related to the idea of a dialogue is offbeat phrasing: clapping, dancing, or otherwise sounding on the offbeats (even numbered beats in a measure) or between the beats, a hallmark of African American musical expression. This is so prevalent on so many levels of performance that it may not even be noticeable until attention is called to it, for instance, in a standard rock drumbeat of the bass drum kicking on beats 1 and 3 and the snare drum struck on the off (or so-called weak) beats 2 and 4. The drummer can add layers of offbeat phrasing, for example, by moving the bass kick from beat

---

17 For example, listen to "Remarks by Reverend C. L. Franklin" on Aretha Franklin's 1972 album *Amazing Grace.*

3 to its offbeat (the "and" of 3) or adding more kicks or other drum strokes creating further rhythmic tension.[18] "Heat Wave" (1963) by Martha and the Vandellas and "Turn Me Loose" (1967) on Sly and the Family Stone's debut album (*A Whole New Thing*) both feature classic gospel-style hand claps on the offbeats (2 and 4) along with a tambourine, which further evokes a gospel feel. The singing on both (after the two-minute mark on "Heat Wave") illustrates the next feature, an oversaturated sound.

There is a remarkable preference for an oversaturated, full-throated, yet fully controlled sound, filling in the sound spectrum. This aesthetic embraces sounds sometimes considered extraneous, such as vocal rasps and electronic distortion. It is especially prominent with individual soloists, as in the shouts of gospel and soul singers, the electronic distortion of electric blues guitarists, and the bottleneck slide used by acoustic blues guitarists.[19] It also can be heard in the prominence of nonpitched percussion (e.g., snare drum) and a subsonic bass boom in hip hop. This may be an adaptation of an African aesthetic of musical sound in which buzzing devices are often attached to instruments. Contrast this with a Western classical orchestra in which each instrumentalist strives to eliminate any buzzing or other nonpitched sounds, considered unwanted noise, or an old-time country or bluegrass acoustic string band. These are contrasting aesthetic preferences, with no right or wrong, but rather culturally appropriate aesthetics. The term *noise* typically has negative associations, but it can be flipped to have positive associations, as in "Bring the Noise" (1987) by the rap group Public Enemy. Not all noise is alike: a different kind of noise and distortion, one that fully saturates through sheer loudness (rather than targeted vocal or guitar

---

18 For instance, Greg Errico's drum break (at 2:10) on Sly and the Family Stone's "Sing a Simple Song" (*Stand*, 1969) moves the bass kick on beat 3 ahead to its offbeat and adds a bass kick on the sixteenth note before beat 1. On "My Brain (Zig Zag)" (on *Stand*) he alternates between four, three, four, and two bass kicks in a four-bar pattern: bars 1 and 3 are the same, with four kicks (all on offbeats except the first): x••x | ••x• | •x•• | •••• | (x = kick; • = sixteenth rest); bar 2 leaves out the fourth kick, and bar 4 leaves out the third and fourth kicks. With the bass kicks and snare (and other) drum hits in mind, listen to Clyde Stubblefield's drum break (at 5:20 or 5:34, depending on the release) on James Brown's 1970 single "Funky Drummer (Part 1 and 2)" (not issued on an album until *In the Jungle Groove*, 1986), one of the most sampled drumbeats in hip hop, and Donald Simmons's extraordinary drum break (at 3:58) on Curtis Mayfield's "Move on Up" (*Curtis*, 1970).

19 "Love Sensation" (1980), from gospel-turned–soul singer Loleatta Holloway, is an extraordinary example of this kind of oversaturation effortlessly alternating with an equally powerful, less saturated, clearer tone.

solo punctuation), is an important aesthetic in heavy metal, and identity communities can congeal around these sounds.

Virtually all African American music genres involve some kind of improvisation, creative decisions made while the performance is in progress. This kind of spontaneity is highly valued. It is a legacy of African modes of music making, wherein music events require significant input from the performers and participants, and pieces are open-ended, to be expanded or contracted according to the immediate context. It is an aesthetic stemming in part from the oral nature of African expressive culture; the concept of something being fixed was irrelevant because the technology to fix sound (speech, music) either in writing or recording was not available until relatively recently. African, and later African American, cultures, therefore, exploited the potentials of improvisation, considering it an essential part of the performance process.

Dance is highly prized in African American culture and has a long and rich history, well documented by Jacqui Malone (1996). This a clear legacy from Africa, where dance is an integral part of life, widely appreciated as an expressive art form and for its role in creating and maintaining social cohesion. The Motown record label used in-house choreographer Cholly Atkins for its artists, and it is quite common for R&B and soul groups to embrace dance as part of their overall performance aesthetic. In the early 1970s dancers on the nationally syndicated weekly television show *Soul Train* set a standard that would be hard to overstate. The show's creator and host, Don Cornelius, grew up in Chicago's South Side, where "a person's degree of coolness was wrapped up in how well he could dance. Wherever there was a party, Don was the one who would throw down, so it made sense that he brought this unbridled cool factor to televisions everywhere" (Questlove 2013: 97). A *Soul Train* clip from about 1972 shows young black men and women dancing in pairs down a line for about fifteen seconds each (eight-plus bars) to the O'Jays' "Love Train." There is a joy, creative play, comfort level, looseness, and control here that is extraordinary for non- and semiprofessional dancers, who were initially recruited at a Los Angeles playground.[20] The varied types of audience bodily engagement shown in the films of the

---

20 See *Soul Train* (1972-v). Questlove (2013: 92–105) provides background information on the dancers; see also George (2014). For an extreme contrast illustrating Dyer's anxieties about his own body, see Ben E. King singing "Stand by Me" in the midst of white teens dancing on a mid-1960s television variety show (B. King 1965-v; Peisch 1995-v, episode 2). With minimal movement, King contrasts dramatically with his dancing audience, who have the look of trying too hard.

predominantly white Monterey Pop (Pennebaker 1968-v) and Woodstock (Wadleigh 1970-v) festivals compared with the predominantly black Wattstax (Stuart 1973-v) festival is instructive in this regard.

The meeting of African musical systems with European tonality on American soil has given shape to melodic inflections that are sometimes called blue notes, yielding a blues mode (like a scale, but each degree has its own characteristic treatment). This is especially prominent in blues and gospel music in the treatment of the third and seventh degrees of the scale. For example, Charley Patton, one of the pioneers of the Mississippi Delta blues style, emphatically leans into the third scale degree as the melodic focal point of his 1929 recording "High Water Everywhere, Part 1," inflecting it so that it sometimes approaches the major third and sometimes the minor third. Hitting it right on, as a major or minor third, would be out of character with the style. Aretha Franklin, decades later in a gospel context singing the hymn "Amazing Grace" in a major key coming out of the European tonal tradition, inflects the major third degree by sliding into it rather than hitting it straight on.[21] Her very first two vocal phrases, hummed, go right to the heart of this sensibility. The fixed tuning of the piano and organ and the necessity of the choir to sing in tune together enforce the European tuning system, yet from the very first words ("A-ma-*zing*, amazing gr-*ace*"), she leans into that third degree, eventually hitting it right on, but arriving and departing it with inflections that clearly signal their African American sonic identity. In a performance with no steady tempo or overt rhythm (that stereotypical marker of black music), other sonic markers kick in, most notably active participation (clapping) and constant dialogue from those present ("Can I get a witness here tonight?" "Sing it!").

The handling of certain scale degrees is just one facet among many sonic markers (e.g., phrasing, specific harmonies) signaling a community identity. Speculation about the origins of these markers range from specific African traditions (many of which have an uncanny similarity in sound) to field hollers and the more private religious ring shouts in pre–Civil War times. Black spirituals developed out of hymn singing in the eighteenth century, drawing directly from the works of Isaac Watts (1707, 1719), and his hymns came to stand in for a whole style of religious singing among blacks, marked by slow-paced cadences with room for vocal melismas (melodic moans, singing many

---

21 The album, also called *Amazing Grace* (1972), was recorded live in a church with a gospel choir; a film of the event was recently released (Pollock 2018-v).

tones on a single syllable).[22] The greatest of all gospel singers, Mahalia Jackson, grew up on Watts hymns. "Dr. Watts? Now you're talking about the *power*. These songs, *hmmmm*, they come out of conviction and suffering. The worst voices can get through singing them, cause they're telling their experiences" (qtd. in Heilbut 2002: 59).

Heilbut cites singing hymns, with their built-in improvisatory openness, "for their characteristic performing styles—the blue-noted keening and humming, known as 'moaning,' and the intricately convoluted melismatic patterns, compact of slurs, spoken interpolations, and absolute rhythmic freedom. . . . Dr. Watts's singing allows for liberties, for elaborate ornamentation, always, however, signaled by 'spirit feel,' an elusive mood that can make a hymn like 'Amazing Grace' or 'The Day Is Past and Gone' go on for anywhere from five minutes to half an hour" (1982: 102). Dargan suggests that the "archaic linkage running from the field hollers through long-meter [Watts] hymns to the blues provided a foundation of shared memory. . . . Less visible, more amorphous forms such as (secular) cries, calls, and hollers, or (sacred) moans . . . and hymn singing . . . that commingled black singing and black speech were the crucibles where black vocal styles developed before meeting with wider popular acceptance" (2006: 2–3).

The African American vocal style appropriate for interpreting and expressing Watts's vivid imagery set aesthetic standards that would filter into blues and gospel music. The secularization in the 1950s and 1960s of the deep roots of gospel music by Clyde McPhatter, Ray Charles, Sam Cooke, and Aretha Franklin, among many others, deeply informed rock and R&B.

While many music cultures around the world may exploit any of these features, it is the particular usage and balance that gives African diasporic musics their distinctive and recognizable flavor. This is a key point that can address criticisms of attaching musical practices to particular groups of people. Any single musical feature might exhibit broad circulation and variety, especially when discussed in the abstract. Specific varieties and ways of deploying them, in combination with other features, however, can most certainly reflect intentional group aesthetic preferences. Identifying certain aesthetic preferences need not be taken as a prescription, nor as marks of racial authenticity—that is, any individuals may draw on other nongroup aesthetic values without losing their sense of identity.

---

22 Resources on psalmody, hymns, and Isaac Watts include Hamm (1983) and Dargan (2006).

The large African presence in Cuba, along with the particular nature of Spanish Catholic colonial rule, gave Cuban music its distinctive flavor, as African percussion and vocal traditions were integrated with Spanish guitar and vocal traditions. Religious traditions intermingled too, as enslaved Africans fused deities from their homelands with Catholic saints, forging new forms of worship. Afro-Cuban religions draw on drumming, dancing, and singing to call on deities to possess initiates. The most well-known religion is Santería, which uses three bata drums (double-headed drums that sit on the lap). While sacred drumming is typically closed off to the public, other types of secular drumming, using congas, is for public entertainment. From the 1930s onward the secular Cuban styles son (called rhumba abroad), mambo, and chachachá enjoyed wide international distribution and appreciation, with mambo and chachachá enjoying great popularity in New York City dance venues, such as the Palladium, in the 1950s.

The pervasive presence of Cuban music in the 1950s led to three of its characteristic features entering into rock in various guises: specific rhythmic patterns; chord patterns; and musical instruments. Much Cuban music is marked by a recurring rhythmic pattern, called *clave* (key), that regulates the music. Usually it is sounded out loud, tapping two short sticks (called claves) together, although sometimes it is implied in the music and not actually sounded. In son the clave pattern is: 1 • • 2 • • 3 • • • 1 • 2 • • • (or vice versa: 2 + 3 counts instead of 3 + 2).[23] The beats to Bo Diddley's "Bo Diddley" and the Rolling Stones' cover of Buddy Holly's "Not Fade Away" are based on the clave pattern. Chachachá is a dance step (1 • 2 • cha cha chá •) that was in vogue in the mid-1950s.[24] A stick-tapping pattern marking out these steps can be heard out in front of the mix on Ritchie Valens's "La Bamba" and in the drums and tambourine beat throughout the Rolling Stones' "Satisfaction."[25]

The chord pattern I-IV-V-IV (C-F-G-F in the key of C), while not owned by Cuba, was well exploited there. Cuban René Touzet, who led the number-one Latin band in Los Angeles, recorded "El Loco Cha Cha" in late 1955 or 1956, which, with this chord pattern, would have an important impact on rock over the next decade. R&B

---

23 In a steady pulse stream, numbers indicate a tap and dots indicate a rest.

24 Chachachá is sometimes written as chacha or cha-cha.

25 "La Bamba" was first recorded as an instrumental track, as Valens had a cold the day of the session. He later went back and overdubbed the vocals (and the chachachá pattern was also overdubbed). Both takes are on Valens (1994-d).

vocalist Richard Berry performed the song in Los Angeles for Mexican audiences and based his 1956 composition "Louie Louie" on it. Several cover versions later it became an emblematic chord progression in rock through the Kingsmen in 1963, when it hit #2 on the pop chart. Ritchie Valens's "La Bamba" has the same chord progression, but played in a different rhythm. The number of 1960s rock songs using this progression in one form or another is countless, although the Rolling Stones' "Get Off of My Cloud" may be the most recognizable (Sublette 2007; Avant-Mier 2014: 99).

The conga and timbales define the sound of Santana and permeated much rock into the 1970s. The conga, also called tumbadora, was originally associated with the secular drumming and dance style called rumba (not the same as rhumba), which calls for three congas of different tones as well as claves. It is this style that has permeated salsa and also filtered into 1970s rock.

___

Sonic identity markers can help to explain how communities gel around artists. We often hear them on a subconscious level, although some may be so out front that they are immediately apprehended and explicit connections are made. See if listening on this kind of analytical level to the various styles discussed in this book can bring further insight into your own preferences.

10

Cross-cultural encounters are at the heart of rock and R&B, and so identifying their varied dynamics is fundamental. Is cross-cultural understanding possible? Yes, of course. Otherwise, artists have failed, for part of their work is to convey their experiences, thoughts, and feelings. Or the fault may be ours, as listeners, not being able to hear and recognize this. People can appreciate the cultural expression of others on many levels, from amusement and entertainment to eye-opening understanding, empathy, and even life-changing integration into one's own personal identity. Who are we, and how are we, as outside observers, to make judgments about how one person or group uses aspects of culture developed by another person or group? But what if we consider ourselves insiders and find outside understandings, interpretations, or usages objectionable? These are questions that demand much thought, especially with regard to the boundaries that distinguish insiders from outsiders, subtle degrees and shades of separation within these categories (e.g., what is our actual relationship to artistic production in our group), and whether economic gain or taking undue credit is involved.

MARIAN ANDERSON AND BOB DYLAN

Marian Anderson (1897–1993) was a gifted African American singer who grew up in a working-class South Philadelphia neighborhood in the early twentieth-century singing in her local church. Her repertory consisted of African American spirituals and European classical vocal works (particularly Handel, Schubert, and Brahms). While she grew up immersed in the language and culture of the spirituals, she had little access to that associated with eighteenth- and nineteenth-century European (specifically German and Austrian) aristocracy, courts, and churches. Anderson did not have a formal voice teacher until high school. When she went to a music college to inquire about studying there, a white receptionist told her that they don't take "colored people." Reflecting back in her autobiography, she wrote, "True enough, my skin was different, but not my feelings" (1956: 38). Her United Baptist Church congregation raised funds to further her formal music education, including lessons with an Italian American voice teacher. Anderson was accepted to Yale University's School of Music, but her outside funding did not materialize in time.

In her late teens and early twenties, Anderson began touring colleges, churches, and concert halls, and she recorded on the Victor label. She studied French and Italian to help with her diction and found management, which eventually brought her $750 per concert (in the 1920s). In the early 1930s she went to study in London and Berlin, returning to Europe in 1933 for two years, concertizing extensively. She signed on to the prestigious artist management of Sol Hurok, and after a concert in Salzburg (the birthplace of Mozart), renowned conductor Arturo Toscanini famously told her, "Yours is a voice such as one hears once in a hundred years" (Anderson 1956: 158).

Anderson's 1939 Easter Sunday concert in Washington, DC, was a major event in U.S. history. When Anderson was denied the use of Constitution Hall by the Daughters of the American Revolution (at the time an exclusionary lineage-based organization) on the basis of her race, First Lady Eleanor Roosevelt resigned her DAR membership, and the secretary of the interior offered Lincoln Memorial for a free outdoor concert. The event was radio broadcast to the nation, and seventy-five thousand people filled the space between the memorial and Washington Monument. She opened with "America" and sang Schubert's "Ave Maria" and three African American spirituals.

Later that year Anderson sang at the White House for the Roosevelts and the king and queen of England. The previous year she earned $238,000, extraordinary for a concert singer at the time (Keiler 2000: 175). In 1955 she became the first African American to perform as a regular member of the Metropolitan Opera in New York. She sang at the inaugurations of presidents Eisenhower (1957) and Kennedy (1961) as well as at the 1963 March on Washington, receiving the Presidential Medal of Freedom that year. In a 2017 televised Kennedy Center celebration of the new National Museum of African American History and Culture, Mary J. Blige paid tribute to Anderson, singing "America."

African American spirituals, a product of the religious experience of an enslaved people, were initially brought to the concert hall by the historically black Fisk University choir and their white choir director in the 1870s. Their concert style of singing and harmonies drew from European models, reflected in some of their earliest recordings in 1909–11 (Fisk Jubilee Singers 1997-d). Much later recordings from isolated black communities on the Georgia and Carolina sea islands provide a window into how some of these spirituals may have been sung before their merging with European aesthetics (Carawan 1967-d). Given the range of African American experience, both styles of performing spirituals should be considered as authentic expressions of that experience. After a trip to Israel, Anderson described the significance of spirituals to her: "I could see in Israel the geographic places that represented the reality [of biblical references], and they stirred me deeply. I kept thinking that my people had captured the essence of that reality and had gone beyond it to express in the spirituals the deepest necessities of their human predicament" (1956: 262).

Anderson heard a range of singing styles in her early church experiences, but her focus was on that of the European classical tradition (or rather several national traditions), with diction appropriate to the style, which she also applied to her interpretation of spirituals. The term *appropriation* here does not really capture her relationship to a culture much different than the one she was born into, although Anderson did indeed reach out and make concerted efforts to use European culture to her advantage. (Note how the language of appropriation here has such a sinister aura.) The terms *assimilation* or *acculturation* are more typically used to describe how a marginalized minority culture uses the culture of a dominant majority population. The European classics were part of her U.S. cultural environment, dramatically opening up what can be considered as the scope of African American culture. Surely, Anderson was able to achieve cross-cultural understanding, not just in the way she was accepted as an artist, but in her authoritative grasp and expansion of a tradition whose ancestral heritage she was not born into.

Bob Dylan, raised in a Jewish middle-class home in northern Minnesota, became enamored in his late teens with white Oklahoman Woody Guthrie, and he moved to New York City to visit the terminally ill Guthrie and soak up all that early 1960s Greenwich Village could offer. There Dylan became obsessed with a new reissue of the 1930s recordings of black Mississippi bluesman Robert Johnson (in his midtwenties when recorded), finding an intense connection and inspiration with Johnson's "code of language" (Dylan 2004: 287–88). By the time of his sixth album (*Highway 61 Revisited*, 1965), Dylan was a star and a major voice for his generation, particularly (but not only) white middle-class college-aged youth.

Given the differences in sound and sentiment between mid-1960s folk rock and soul music, one might not expect a direct connection between his music and the growing black nationalist movement, which accelerated with the establishment of the Black Panther Party in 1966. In a passage titled "Huey Digs Bob Dylan," party cofounder Bobby Seale (1970: 181–86) related a story about how in 1967 the other cofounder, Huey Newton, was constantly listening to Dylan's "Ballad of a Thin Man" (from *Highway 61 Revisited*) while they were putting together early issues of their party newspaper, providing an impassioned and inspiring interpretation of the relevance and insights of Dylan's lyrics to their own situations. Many in their circle were captivated by the song: "This song Bobby Dylan was singing became a very big part of the whole publishing operations of the Black Panther paper. . . . This record became so related to us, even to the brothers who had held down most of the security" (Seale 1970: 186). A photo of Newton in 1970 shows him holding up Dylan's album for the camera (Shames and Seale 2016: 187).

What can one make of this connection? Dylan's first album (*Bob Dylan*, 1962) contained four cover versions of songs by African American bluesmen. How can one understand the admiration of Newton, Seale, and their circle for Dylan's work? Did they hear and appreciate a familiar blues vision mirrored and reinterpreted for contemporary times in Dylan's songwriting? Why didn't they lay claims that Dylan was appropriating and profiting from their culture? (Two years earlier Dylan had seven songs in the pop Top 40, all originals, and two albums in the Top 10.) Clearly, it was not the mere act of reaching out to African American culture but rather what he did with it that mattered. Dylan, whose most direct early experience with African Americans was presumably through recordings, absorbed aspects of their cultural expression from those recordings. In that particular time and place, some young African American political and cultural leaders, including Jimi Hendrix, who was as drenched in the blues traditions of his African American roots as any electric guitarist of his generation, felt a great attraction to Dylan's artistic expression.

But they were a minority among a minority, for, unlike Elvis Presley, none of Dylan's recordings showed up on the rhythm and blues charts. Elvis's music in the 1950s, on the other hand, had significant appeal for young African Americans, judging from his presence on R&B charts at the time. There was an undercurrent, however, which gained steam after the 1950s, that Elvis was profiting off of R&B in ways unavailable to pioneering black artists. Nowadays many observers routinely call this *cultural appropriation*. But how to explain that mid-1950s African American youth were playing his music in their neighborhood jukeboxes, requesting that his songs be played on R&B radio stations, and buying his records in their neighborhood shops? The point here is to understand what people were thinking at the time rather than impose our contemporary, and possibly irrelevant or misguided, interpretations.

Our ears, six decades later, may not be sensitized to what listeners heard when Elvis's music first came out. Just think of your own listening experiences: you may be able to recognize hundreds of songs released in the past five years and be able to very explicitly trace subtleties in the development of individual artists and creative streams and responses feeding one another's work. This provides you with a degree of expertise and consequently authority with certain genres of music of your own time.

In this text we try to gain access to what kinds of expertise and authority listeners had with the music of their own times.

A SPECTRUM: FOUR EXAMPLES

Many African American artists have held generous assessments of select white artists who trafficked in African American styles or who drew from the well of African American culture. We read about examples regarding Elvis, producer-songwriters Leiber and Stoller, and the Righteous Brothers and read statements from Muddy Waters, Ray Charles, Otis Redding, Hank Shocklee (of Public Enemy), and others. The positive reception of the by-many-accounts obnoxious New York City white rap trio Beastie Boys by some of their peers in the rap industry presents a difficult problem to think through.[1] Their debut album *Licensed to Ill* (1986) surpassed their Def Jam label-mates Run-D.M.C., whose third album (*Raising Hell*, 1986) earlier in the year became the first rap album to break into the pop Top 10, reaching #3; *Licensed to Ill* hit #1. One might think that whites encroaching on a black genre, and gaining greater commercial success, would not sit well with many.

Chuck D of Public Enemy (also on Def Jam) suggested, "You really couldn't doubt their legitimacy 'cause they were down with Def Jam and Run-D.M.C., and the beats were right. And as long as they talked about white boys and beer and stuff like that, who could knock their topics?" Journalist Frere-Jones noted that "The Beasties were able to be down because they had an obvious affinity for black music, but presented themselves honestly as these middle-class Jewish kids. They weren't trying to be something they weren't" (qtd. in Light 1998: 149, 153). Drummer Questlove (of the Roots, who moved to Def Jam in 2006) claimed them to be "one of the biggest influences on The Roots. . . . We thought it [the acapella version of 'Hold It Now, Hit It'] was the most revolutionary thing ever. It was like, yo, these guys are so bad they don't need a drum machine! They just rhyme by themselves. And, that tore our world around" (2012-v).

They crossed a line, however, opening for Run-D.M.C. at Harlem's Apollo Theater

---

1   Piccarella (1986: 103) titled his review of the Beastie Boys' debut album "White Trash on Dope" and noted, "Not since the Rolling Stones have white boys so forcefully co-opted a black music"; Christgau (1986) referred to the album's "wisecracking arrogance" and noted, "three white jerkoffs and their crazed producer are set to go platinum-plus with 'black' music that's radically original, childishly simple."

in 1986. In the words of their deejay, future cohost of *Yo! MTV Raps*, André "Doctor Dré" Brown: "Everybody was like, 'Look, whatever you do, don't say "n-gger."' . . . Ad-Rock says, 'All you n-ggers, wave your hands in the air!' I've never seen so many blank stares! . . . And Ad-Rock's going, 'Come on y'all, come on y'all,' and nobody's waving back. They finished the song, dropped the mics, and ran off the stage" (qtd. in Light 1998: 153). Still, they returned a year or two later to cohost *Showtime at the Apollo*. Daryl "D.M.C." McDaniels recalled during their 1986 tour together, in the "black South": "We expected to hear boos. . . . From the dressing room, we'd hear 'Yeaaaaaah! Yeaaahhh!' It was the black audience, praising these dudes. The reason they were so good: It wasn't white punk rockers trying to be black emcees. They wasn't talking about gold chains or Cadillacs. They were white rappers rapping about what they did. Real recognize real" (qtd. in Barshad 2011: 58). Their sort of parody may have been possible only at that particular moment in commercial hip hop's early years.

George Gershwin (composer), Ira Gershwin (lyricist), and DuBose Heyward (libretto) drew on, or appropriated, African American dialect and subject matter in their 1935 folk opera *Porgy and Bess* (based on Heyward's novel *Porgy*), which, unusual for its time, used a virtually all-black cast. African American writer Langston Hughes called it "the single biggest bread basket for the Negro in the history of the American stage. . . . It has fed, over long periods of time in many cities and many countries, a great many Negro performers" (1966: 447). *Porgy and Bess* has received its share of both criticism (overuse of dialect, stereotyped characters) and acceptance from African Americans. The original novel received praise from Hughes: the author Heyward "did see, with his white eyes, wonderful, hectic human qualities in the inhabitants of Catfish Row that made them come alive in his book" (1960: 382). Whatever shortcomings one might expect and perceive in such an undertaking by two children of Jewish immigrants and a child of southern white aristocracy, songs from *Porgy and Bess* were deliberately chosen by African Americans as vehicles for what have become some of the most inspired performances in American music history: Billie Holiday's "Porgy" (1948), Nina Simone's "I Loves You Porgy" (1958), Miles Davis's album-length *Porgy and Bess* (1959), and John Coltrane's "Summertime" (1961). As with the actors in the stage and film presentations, these musical artists inhabited the songs created by the Gershwins, humanized their subjects, and gave them compelling meaning.

An anecdote from an original 1935 cast member, Helen Dowdy, reported in a book exploring the origins of soul music by journalist Phyl Garland, further complicates the picture (they are both African Americans). Garland noted that "Gershwin, who had soaked up black soul at its source by spending some time in South Carolina's Charleston area, where the work was set, had heard these penetrating and haunting cries there and had written them into his opus. However, on returning to New York, he found it next to impossible to locate a black singer who could duplicate them, because all the black singers he auditioned were professionals who had been trained in the European classical tradition of singing and had come to look down on black music." Dowdy was in line for the part of Strawberry Woman, and while she was practicing at home, her mother (from the South) told her it was all wrong and corrected her, teaching her the vernacular phrasing. When Dowdy sang for Gershwin the following day, "Gershwin flipped, shouted, 'That's it!'" and, in her [Dowdy's] words, "just about fell out of his chair" (Garland 1969: 55). One could read this as yet another white savior story—Gershwin teaching African Americans to be their true selves. Or as Gershwin essentializing African Americans, insisting that they sing in their own southern vernacular. But, then again, Dowdy's mother taught her to do just that. (On the other hand, imagine the critiques if Gershwin instead insisted on an operatic interpretation of the song of Charleston street sellers.) Of course, it does make a difference who is doing the essentializing and that Gershwin auditioned classically trained black singers, perhaps not understanding their conflicted relationships with southern black vernacular styles. And how would one explain the context in which Garland, a writer and editor for *Ebony* magazine, writing about soul in the late 1960s when black power was a rallying cry, would paint such a sympathetic picture of Gershwin? These questions demand *multidimensional* perspectives that yield a rich tapestry of the possibilities, motivations, and impacts of cross-cultural traffic.

Reorienting a genre (like the Beastie Boys), overt parody (like what Weird Al Yankovic does), or attempts to portray a culture (as in *Porgy and Bess*), all by outsiders, are different than imitation with little self-consciousness or irony. An online video of eighteen-year-old Justin Bieber performing "Show You Off" at the 2012 American Music Awards counts his crotch grabs, totaling twenty-four in a four-minute performance. Michael Jackson brought this move into mainstream choreography in 1983, initially with a subtle touch at the end of his "Beat It" music video and during his televised *Motown 25* "Billie Jean" performance. It became his signature move with his "Bad" (1987) video. Madonna appropriated it in "Express Yourself" (1989). The previous decade Richard Pryor had recorded a comedy routine about the practice.[2] It became a defining move in a highly visible strain of commercial hip hop. In 2011, for instance, Jay-Z and Kanye West totaled over fifteen crotch grabs in a two-and-a-half-minute segment in their video for "Otis."

Bieber was roasted several months after his AMA performance when he hosted *Saturday Night Live* during Black History Month (February 9, 2013). His opening monologue self-satirized his lack of consciousness of black history, and a skit about a new security team of body doubles had a punch line that pointedly addressed his imitations of blackness. Bieber's presence (as of early 2019) on the various R&B, rap, and hip hop *Billboard* singles charts are almost all collaborations (*Billboard* 2019b). He is not present on any of those album charts, which can provide some indication of the extent of engagement with these styles. His business relationship with mentor Usher and producer L. A. Reid may have contributed to whatever viability he might have among African Americans.

Eminem, on the other hand, presents the go-to case of a white artist thoroughly integrating a black style and being widely embraced. His final rap battle in *Eight Mile*, the film that loosely resembles his life, provides part of the explanation: he raps his African American opponent (who, in contrast to Eminem's character, has parents in a stable marriage and attended a private school) into silent submission by an original take on rap's primary tenet (represent yourself), drawing on some of its primary codes of authenticity (street cred, battle skills, surviving in the face of adversity), which combine to erase his racial inauthenticity and outsider status. The other part of the explanation is his business arrangement: he signed with Aftermath, the record label founded by former N.W.A. member Andre "Dr. Dre" Young, who produced Eminem's albums. All nine of those albums (between 1999 and 2018) hit #1 on the R&B/hip hop album chart (a tenth *Hits* album reached #2). They did the same on the unmarked (pop) album chart, with the exception of his Aftermath debut, which reached #2 (*Billboard* 2019a).

A sharp critique (in this case of Madonna) by author and academic bell hooks makes the key point about the nature, or depth, of drawing from the well: "White folks who do not see black pain never really understand the complexity of black pleasure. And it is no wonder then that when they attempt to imitate the joy in living which

2   "White and Black People," on *Wanted* (1978).

they see as the 'essence' of soul and blackness, their cultural productions may have an air of sham and falseness that may titillate and even move white audiences yet leave many black folks cold" (1992b: 158). Bieber's caricature body moves are ripe for this kind of critique. The provocative title of culture critic Greg Tate's 2003 edited collection says it all: *Everything but the Burden: What White People Are Taking from Black Culture.*

CULTURAL APPROPRIATION

In a recent *New York Times* article looking at appropriation in pop culture, Parul Sehgal wonders if "we might, someday, learn to keep our hands to ourselves where other people's cultures are concerned," a very bleak view of the way the world actually works. "But then that might do another kind of harm," she continues, "Pakistani novelist Kamila Shamsie called for more, not less, imaginative engagement with her country: 'The moment you say a male American writer can't write about a female Pakistani, you are saying, Don't tell those stories. Worse, you're saying: As an American male you can't understand a Pakistani woman. She is enigmatic, inscrutable, unknowable. She's other. Leave her and her nation to its Otherness. Write them out of your history.' Can some kinds of appropriation shatter stereotypes? This has been literature's implicit promise: that entering into another's consciousness enlarges our own" (2015: 15).

Brubaker (2017) lays out some of the other related issues, referring to "epistemological insiderism," which is

> the belief that identity qualifies or disqualifies one from writing with legitimacy and authority about a particular topic. Few would argue directly that who we are should govern what we study. But subtler forms of epistemological insiderism are at work in the practice of assessing scholarly arguments with central reference to the identity of the author. . . . Epistemological insiderism not only stakes out certain domains as belonging to persons with certain identities; it also risks boxing persons with those identities into specific domains. It risks conveying the patronizing and offensive expectation that members of racial and ethnic minorities will focus their scholarship on race and ethnicity.

Arguments about appropriation do not rest wholly on what outsiders should or should not do. Also important are the opportunities available for marginalized groups to represent themselves. The stakes are high here, not only in reaping the economic benefit of one's intellectual property, but also in how a group is represented.

Among all the various impacts of outsiders drawing on the culture of others, is the (sometimes inadvertent) opening up of new and expanded markets for voices that have previously been excluded. We have seen just such cases where bland cover versions of R&B artists in the mid-1950s led white youth to seek out the original sources. In early 1956, for example, Pat Boone's diluted cover of Little Richard's "Tutti Frutti" quickly surpassed the original in popularity. But just a few months later Little Richard's "Long Tall Sally" made Boone's weak cover attempt look downright embarrassing, both from an aesthetic and commercial point of view. It was an ear-opening year for rock and roll.

Cultural appropriation is one of the most misunderstood concepts in contemporary pop culture. There is no generally agreed-on definition. It is not usually used literally, at face value, meaning that anyone can engage in it, but rather to refer to a dominant majority culture's use of a marginalized minority's culture. When it is the other way around, it is called *assimilation*, as in the majority culture is pervasive and readily available to assimilate. There is good reason for this distinction. A majority culture could create or perpetuate pernicious stereotypes, misrepresent aesthetic values, violate sacred or private expression, or curtail economic opportunities (Young 2010: 107). While some of this could be offensive (we all should have that right), some of this might cross the border into actual harm. All these offenses could be done by a minority culture, but with significantly less (if any) harmful impact because of power differentials: the majority culture in the United States holds most of the cards (economic, social, political). A minority culture appropriating from another minority culture, less frequently discussed, can indeed also have an impact.

However, and here is the key point, the *potential* to cause harm is not the same as actually causing harm. People and cultures learn and grow from contact with one another. Policing who may or may not engage in such contact or prescribing how it should be done not only can be counterproductive, narrow minded, and patronizing but also does not recognize how the world moves. Outsider perspectives, including collaborations, have the potential for great insights—we can learn much from how others see us, for better or worse. Langston Hughes recognized this, giving advice to African American writers, that "to write well about Negroes, it might be wise, occasionally at least, to look at them with white eyes—then the better will you see how distinctive we are" (1960: 380).

Replacing *appropriation* with *disrespect* in many cases would encourage more honest conversations. Accusations of appropriation can have a chilling effect, as in "You are not allowed to touch my culture." Accusations of disrespect, however, may be more to the point and speak to specific grievances in the nature of the contact. Objections to cultural appropriation (or disrespecting a culture) fall into three main areas: aesthetic shortcomings because of lack of experience (e.g., one has to live the life); not having the proper individual or group identity (which some believe is necessary for the proper experience) and therefore lacking authenticity (e.g., not being true to oneself); and unfair economic gain (further limiting the economic opportunities of a minority culture), including getting undeserved credit.

An assessment of the work of white songwriters Jerry Leiber and Mike Stoller by Carl Gardner, member of the African American vocal group the Coasters, with reference to their 1957 #1 R&B hits "Young Blood" and "Searchin'," both of which crossed over to the pop Top 10, can address all three objections: "Leiber and Stoller were writing black music. Here were two Jewish kids, knew my culture better than I knew my culture. And I said, 'How did they do that? . . . How did they know what we do?' Cause every song they wrote was in our culture." On the other hand, recalling something they wrote for the Coasters called "Colored Folks," Leiber acknowledged, "If they thought we were going too far, they would stop us" (Espar and Thomson 1995-v, episode 2). That review process, involving give-and-take, can be crucial.

Another example comes from Eric Burdon, vocalist with the 1960s British group the Animals: "I heard [bluesman] John Lee Hooker singing things like 'I been working in a steel mill trucking steel like a slave all day,' you know, and, 'I woke up this morning and my baby's gone away,' you know, and I, I related to that directly because that was happening to people, to grown men, on my block" (Espar and Thomson 1995-v, episode 5). This might read like personal delusion or fantasy, but see what Otis Redding, one of the most important soul singers ever, had to say in a 1967 interview when asked, "What do you think of Eric Burdon?": "Now, Eric is one of the best friends I have. He's a great guy. . . . I've seen him work in a club in England. This boy came on stage with a blues song and he tore the house up. They called me up on stage after he finished and I wouldn't go up. I knew I couldn't do anything to top it. Eric can really sing blues" (qtd. in Delehant 1967: 57).[3]

The task of evaluating the difference between superficial and offensive imitation on

---

3 Compare Burdon's relationship to the blues (and Redding's assessment) with Iggy Pop's realization (noted earlier) that it just wasn't his calling in life.

the one hand and deeper assimilation and even integration of another's cultural expression into one's own persona on the other demands an open, informed, and critical mind. Knee-jerk reactions, often leveled with the blunt weapon "cultural appropriation," often ignore the perspectives of those directly involved. The generosity of artists who are most directly impacted, those in the daily game of the music business, can be one instructive and inspiring model. And, surely, it is our responsibility to understand the origins of a style and give proper credit, including all the just financial rewards.

The question that opened this chapter—Is cross-cultural understanding possible?—permeates this book. It can be posed more broadly: can we, as members of a singular human race, transcend our various frameworks of identification (how we see ourselves and how others see us), no matter how oppressive or privileged they may be, and appreciate, understand, empathize with, and even in some cases integrate in our personas and beings the cultural expression of others? This should not be misunderstood as a colorblind approach, but, to the contrary, one that takes in and values our varied life experiences, both as members of groups and as unique individuals. The music history presented here offers obvious and resounding positive responses.

11

Rock history has been taught in classrooms for several decades, taking its place alongside other venerable areas of historical and cultural inquiry. A rich body of literature, including many textbooks and readers (collecting diverse primary sources), and film documentaries has developed, making it an especially vibrant field of study. One must be aware of the danger, however, of turning a living, constantly breathing tradition into a dry, static, hierarchical canon of masterworks, an inevitable byproduct of fixing histories in print. Identifying overarching themes in the study of rock may help to contextualize and organize some of the microscopic details presented here, revealing connections among disparate musical styles. These connections may in turn shed light on the larger significance of the music discussed here, both in the realm of creative expression and within the social and cultural fabric of contemporary life.

SOURCES

Music-industry press, whether aimed at the professional trade (*Billboard, Variety*) or fans (*Rolling Stone, Spin, New Musical Express*), as well as general-interest daily and weekly press (*New York Times, Time, Life*) are important sources for reconstructing histories of rock and R&B. Most of these periodicals are available for electronic searching in subscription databases, enabling finely detailed historically informed discussions of the emergence of the musical styles discussed here. I have drawn on these sources extensively, as well as Rock's Backpages (2019), probably the largest collection of articles from a broad cross-section of rock magazines, to provide primary-source accounts of when styles first arose. One job of music-industry and fan press is to inform their readership of new trends, and so they can be very helpful in tracking the regional rise of a style to national prominence, such as the labels of folk rock, country rock, and techno.

In the 1970s academic journals devoted to the study of rock began to be published, offering scholarly rigor, which includes an initial peer-review process, from a variety of perspectives. These journals present fresh research on often highly specialized topics. The now-standard journals include *Popular Music and Society* (1971–), *Popular Music* (1981–), and *Journal of Popular Music Studies* (1988–). More specialized journals have arisen as outlets for a critical mass of scholars, including *Dancecult: Journal of Electronic Dance Music Culture* (2009–), *Punk and Post-Punk* (2012–), *Rock Music Studies* (2014–), *Metal Music Studies* (2014–), *Journal of Hip Hop Studies* (2014–), and *Journal of World Popular Music* (2014–).

Starting in the 1990s rock textbooks began to flourish, with some going through many editions up to the present. They include Palmer (1995), which accompanied a ten-part video documentary series (Espar and Thomson 1995-v); Garofalo and Waksman (2017); Schloss, Starr, and Waterman (2012); and Covach and Flory (2015). They were preceded by *The Rolling Stone Illustrated History of Rock and Roll* (DeCurtis and Henke 1992), first published in 1976. Readers collecting primary-source material include Brackett (2014) and Cateforis (2019).

Major rock documentary videos, each with ten episodes, were produced in the 1990s by the A&E TV network (G. Johnson 1991-v), WGBH/BBC (Espar and Thomson 1995-v), and Time-Life (Peisch 1995-v). Since then, there has been an explosion of more focused multiepisode documentary videos, covering American roots music (Jim Brown 2001-v); hip hop (Perry 2004-v; Wheeler, Dunn, and McFadyen 2016–18-v); heavy metal (Warren 2006-v); the art of music recording (Dupre and Chermayeff 2016-v); and the first recordings of the electrical recording era in the 1920s (MacMahon 2017-v).

The Public Broadcasting System's American Masters series has covered many relevant artists, including Atlantic Records (Steinberg 2007-v), Joan Baez (Wharton 2009-v), Ray Charles (Y. Smith 1992-v), Patsy Cline (B. Hall 2017-v), Fats Domino (Lauro 2016-v), Bob Dylan (Scorsese 2005-v), David Geffen (Lacy 2012-v), Woody Guthrie (Frumkin 2006-v), Jimi Hendrix (Smeaton 2013-v), Quincy Jones (Kantor 2001-v), Janis Joplin (Berg 2016-v), Carole King (Neville 2011-v; Scott 2016-v), Joni Mitchell (Lacy 2003-v), Les Paul (Paulson 2007-v), Lou Reed (Greenfield-Sanders 1998-v), Pete Seeger (Jim Brown 2007-v), James Taylor (Neville 2011-v), Muddy Waters (Gordon and Neville 2002-v), and Hank Williams (Neville 2004-v).

Performances on the Ed Sullivan TV show from the 1950s and 1960s issued on DVD provide an extraordinary window into the early years of rock (Solt and Vines 2011-v). Gilliland's (1969a) fifty-five-hour-long radio series *Pop Chronicles* provides an equally extraordinary window into how musicians in the 1960s reflected on their music. Bloomsbury (2003–) has a novel 33 1/3 series featuring books devoted to individual albums by rock artists, with about 150 published through early 2019. The subscription website Rock's Backpages (2019) provides invaluable source material, and the educational website TeachRock (2019a) provides extensive lesson plans for high school teachers.

THEMES

Many themes and methods run through this book, sometimes below the surface, other times right out front. These should be kept in mind as new musical genres and artists are introduced.[4]

The human capacity for creativity. Everyone has the capacity for creating and
appreciating artistic expression. Understanding the social and cultural forces
that circulate around us, which may nourish or block those capacities, is key.

Musical communities do not exist in a cultural vacuum. Musicians can soak up
cultural currents from seemingly unlikely places. We are all intertwined.

The contrast of styles congealing versus the expansiveness of rock and R&B. While
styles can tightly congeal with readily identifiable features, musical artists can
also demonstrate an expansiveness that goes way beyond categories and genre
labels. This is not so much a tension in rock, but rather its strength.

Music creates identity. Music (both producing and experiencing it) is a primary
means of exploring identity, both one's own and that of others.

Art versus commerce. There is a constant tension between rock as self or group
expression and rock as commerce.

Rock as youth music, rock as opposition. They do not necessarily go together.
Sometimes youth can pose an oppositional stance to authority; sometimes
this is not the case.

*Technological innovations can drive musical, legal, and commercial developments,
and musical artists can drive technological innovation.*

Places and times matter. A single recording studio (Sun in 1950s Memphis), a
single small independent record label (Chess in 1950s Chicago or Motown in
1960s Detroit), a single venue (CBGB in 1970s New York), or a set of youth
cultural practices in a residential neighborhood (hip hop in the Bronx in the
1970s) can be the staging ground for a musical style that moves from local
significance to national prominence.

The power of rock. Why are we drawn to it? Some possibilities include one-on-
one communication of emotion or experience; the ability to create a com-

---

4   For a sample of literature theorizing about rock, see Frith and Goodwin (1990), Frith (1996),
Negus (1996), and Bennett and Waksman (2015).

munity, from the most intimate to the largest imaginable proportions; the sheer volume of sound; the sheer spectacle on a grand scale; the ability to get people to dance; and celebrity worship.

Listening and dancing. They are not necessarily mutually exclusive nor do they necessarily go hand in hand. Rock and R&B can encourage either or both.

Sources of authority. How does one gauge an artist's importance and influence? Possibilities include charts (sales, airplay); industry awards (Grammys); tours and venues played; musician citations of influence; critical acclaim; and peer group citations.

History as an exercise in selection. Readers will note my selection process is one that tends toward accentuating the positive. One could just as easily do otherwise.

Frameworks for organizing cultural history. How can such an unwieldy mass of music be organized to establish the rich diversity of linkages and connections that cut across time and place? Possibilities include using five-year slices (e.g., Espar and Thomson's [1995-v] ten-part documentary) or decades (a standard approach) and tracing styles, genres, and subgenres through their paths.

Influential individuals and groups versus general stylistic currents. What is the place of an artist within a musical tradition (individual versus communal effort)? Exploring the relationship between the creative language of individual voices and the expressive language available to all is crucial for a holistic understanding of both.

MELODY, CHORD, HARMONY, TONALITY, AND OVERTONES

A **melody**, also called a tune, is a sequence of tones, also called pitches or notes, that forms a coherent whole. It is usually referred to as a line, as in a melodic line. A **chord** is two or more tones sounded together simultaneously. In the European-based tonal system, a chord usually has three or more tones, in which case it is named after the most important (tonic) tone. **Harmony** refers to a combination of tones sounded at the same moment. It is similar to a chord, but a more abstract generalized reference. **Tonality** is the name of the system in which melodies are created, accompanying chords are formed, and instruments are tuned: twelve equal half steps in the space of an octave (in which the upper note vibrates at twice the frequency of the lower one). Tones have letter names attached to them (A, B, C, D, E, F, or G), and they can be combined one by one to form a scale (an ordered collection). A scale with seven tones (or degrees) can be named by either its letter name (e.g. C, D, E, F, G, A, B, C) or its degree numbers (I, II, III, IV, V, VI, VII, I). When a string is plucked, it vibrates at not only its full length (called the fundamental tone) but also its halves, thirds, quarters, and so forth. These additional vibrational ratios are called its harmonics or **overtones**. The rise and fall of the various overtones are what give a musical instrument its characteristic sound, as well as the sound of its attack and decay (e.g., plucking a string versus blowing into a saxophone).

RHYTHM, BEAT, TEMPO, METER, MEASURE AND BAR, AND REPERTORY

Rhythm is a sequence or flow of events in time, ranging from large-scale abstract events, as in the rhythm of the seasons, to smaller-scale accented and unaccented (loud and soft) hand claps or drumbeats in a song. A **beat** is a regularly recurring pulse, which is usually reinforced by the instrumental background, especially the drums (but also hand claps or a guitar). **Tempo** refers to the speed of a beat (e.g., slow, medium, or fast), and it is usually measured in beats per minute (**bpm**). **Meter** is the organization of beats into a regular repeating sequence. The metric organization of most rock music is four beats that make up one unit, called a **measure** or **bar**. A **repertory** (French: *repertoire*) is a body or collection of pieces. This typically refers to the repertory of a musician—that is, the breadth and number of pieces they can perform.

VERSE AND CHORUS

A **verse** is one or more lines of text that form a distinct unit. A line of text usually corresponds to a single sentence (although in some cases it could be just a phrase). A **chorus**, also called a refrain, is the line (or lines) that repeats regularly throughout a song, functioning to stay in the listener's ear and act as the main way of identifying the song. In a verse-chorus song form, the verse contains new lyrics that move the story line ahead, and the chorus contains the lines that get repeated throughout the song (e.g., Louis Jordan's "Choo Choo Ch-Boogie"; Ben E. King's "Stand by Me").

In a traditional (early) blues song form, *verse* refers to all the lines sung within the twelve-bar cycle (usually one line that gets repeated, followed by a responding line, diagrammed as aab). In later blues forms (1940s–) that draw on the verse-chorus form, two possibilities are common: (1) one twelve- or sixteen-bar cycle can function as a verse, and the next cycle can function as a chorus (e.g., the Dominoes' "Have Mercy Baby"; Big Mama Thornton's "Hound Dog"; Ruth Brown's "Mama He Treats Your Daughter Mean"); and (2) within one twelve- or sixteen-bar cycle, one part (e.g., four or eight bars) can function as a verse, and the other part can function as a chorus (Hank Williams's "Move It on Over"; Muddy Waters's "Hoochie Coochie Man"; Chuck Berry's "Roll over Beethoven").

BIBLIOGRAPHY (PRINT, ONLINE ARTICLES AND WEBSITES, RADIO PROGRAMS)

RBP indicates the article is available on Rock's Backpages.

Abbott, Kingsley, ed. 2001. *Callin' Out around the World: A Motown Reader*. London: Helter Skelter.

Abel. 1955. "A Warning to the Music Business." *Variety* (February 23): 2.

Ackerman, Paul. 1947. "Network Program Reviews and Analyses: Philco Radio Time." *Billboard* (October 11): 15.

———. 1956. "Square Circles Peg Rock and Roll Idiom as a Beat to Stick: Carnegie Hall, Theaters, Movies, Radio, TV—All Are Getting Hip." *Billboard* (February 4): 1, 54.

Adelt, Ulrich. 2016. *Krautrock: German Music in the Seventies*. Ann Arbor: University of Michigan Press.

Adler, Bill, ed. 1964. *Love Letters to the Beatles*. New York: Putnam's Sons.

Afropunk. 2019. Accessed March 10. https://afropunk.com.

Alba, Richard D. 1985. "The Twilight of Ethnicity among Americans of European Descent: The Case of Italians." *Ethnic and Racial Studies* 8 (1): 134–58.

Alexander, Michelle. 2012. *The New Jim Crow: Mass Incarceration in the Age of Colorblindness*. Rev. ed. New York: New Press.

AllMusic. 2019. Accessed March 10. www.allmusic.com.

American Folklife Center. 1982. *Ethnic Recordings in America: A Neglected Heritage*. Washington, DC: Library of Congress.

Anderson, Marian. 1956. *My Lord, What a Morning: An Autobiography*. New York: Viking.

Appiah, Kwame Anthony. 2005. *The Ethics of Identity*. Princeton: Princeton University Press.

———. 2014. *Lines of Descent: W. E. B. Du Bois and the Emergence of Identity*. Cambridge, MA: Harvard University Press.

Arnold, Jacob. 2012. "The Warehouse: The Place House Music Got Its Name." *Resident Advisor* (May 16). www.residentadvisor.net.

———. 2016. "Importes, Etc.: The Chicago Record Store That Popularized House." *Red Bull Music Academy Daily* (November 14). http://daily.redbullmusicacademy.com.

Arnold, Paul. 2012. "Chuck D Explains Why Suing the Notorious B.I.G. Was 'Stupid' and Why Jay-Z and Kanye West's Bases Are 'Corrupt to Rap.'" *HipHopDX* (March 9). http://hiphopdx.com.

Aronowitz, Alfred G. 1963. "Pop Music: The Dumb Sound." *Saturday Evening Post* (October 5): 88, 91–95. (RBP)

———. 1964. "Yeah! Yeah! Yeah! Music's Gold Bugs: The Beatles." *Saturday Evening Post* (March 21): 30–35.

———. 1968. "Friends and Neighbors Just Call Us the Band." *Rolling Stone* (August 24): 1, 8.

ASCAP (American Society of Composers, Authors and Publishers). 2019. "ACE [ASCAP Clearance Express] Repertory." Accessed March 10. www.ascap.com/repertory.

Aubrunner, Thomas. 2019. "Clarence White." Accessed March 10. www.burritobrother .com.

Audacity. 2019. "Digital Audio Fundamentals." (February 26). https://manual.audacity team.org.

Auslander, Philip. 2006. *Performing Glam Rock: Gender and Theatricality in Popular Music*. Ann Arbor: University of Michigan Press.

Avant-Mier, Roberto. 2014. *Rock the Nation: Latin/o Identities and the Latin Rock Diaspora*. New York: Continuum.

Azerrad, Michael. 2001. *Our Band Could Be Your Life: Scenes from the American Indie Underground, 1981–1991*. Boston: Little, Brown.

Baez, Joan. 1968. *Daybreak*. New York: Dial.

Bangs, Lester. 1969. "*Kick Out the Jams*, MC-5." *Rolling Stone* (April 5): 16–17.

———. 1970. "Of Pop and Pies and Fun: A Program for Mass Liberation in the Form of a Stooges Review, or *Who's the Fool?*" Pts. 1–2. *Creem* (November): 35–37; (December): 36–39; reprinted in Bangs (1987: 31–52).

———. 1971. "James Taylor Marked for Death, or What We Need Is a Lot Less Jesus and a Whole Lot More Troggs." *Who Put the Bomp* (Fall–Winter): 59–84; reprinted in Bangs (1987: 53–81).

———. 1987. *Psychotic Reactions and Carburetor Dung: The Work of a Legendary Critic; Rock 'n' Roll as Literature and Literature as Rock 'n' Roll*. Edited by Greil Marcus. New York: Knopf.

Baraka, Amiri. 1963. *Blues People: Negro Music in White America*. New York: Morrow.

———. 1967a. *Black Music*. New York: Morrow.

———. 1967b. "The Changing Same (R&B and New Black Music)." In Baraka (1967a: 180–211).

Barlow, William. 1989. *"Looking Up at Down": The Emergence of Blues Culture*. Philadelphia: Temple University Press.

Barnes, Dee. 2015. "Here's What's Missing from *Straight Outta Compton*: Me and the Other Women Dr. Dre Beat Up." *Gawker* (August 18). http://gawker.com.

Barnouw, Erik. 1966–70. *A History of Broadcasting in the United States*. 3 vols. New York: Oxford University Press.

———. 1975. *Tube of Plenty: The Evolution of American Television*. New York: Oxford University Press.

Barshad, Amos. 2011. "Rude Boys: The Birth of the Beastie Boys; An Oral History on the 25th Anniversary of *Licensed to Ill*." *New York Magazine* (May 2): 55–60.

Beardsley, Roger, and Daniel Leech-Wilkinson. 2009. "A Brief History of Recording to ca. 1950." Centre for the History and Analysis of Recorded Music. www.charm.kcl.ac.uk.

Beatles. 1993. *The Beatles: Complete Scores*. Milwaukee, WI: Leonard.

———. 2000. *The Beatles Anthology*. San Francisco: Chronicle Books.

Bennett, Andy. 2000. *Popular Music and Youth Culture: Music, Identity and Place*. New York: Palgrave.

Bennett, Andy, and Keith Kahn-Harris, eds. 2004. *After Subculture: Critical Studies in Contemporary Youth Culture*. New York: Palgrave Macmillan.

Bennett, Andy, and Steve Waksman, eds. 2015. *The Sage Handbook of Popular Music*. Los Angeles: Sage.

Benson, Carol, and Allan Metz, eds. 1999. *The Madonna Companion: Two Decades of Commentary*. New York: Schirmer.

Berríos-Miranda, Marisol, Shannon Dudley, and Michelle Habell-Pallán. 2018. *American Sabor: Latinos y Latinas en la Música Popular Estadounidense/Latinos and Latinas in US Popular Music*. Translated by Angie Berríos-Miranda. Seattle: University of Washington Press.

Berry, Chuck. 1987. *Chuck Berry: The Autobiography*. New York: Harmony Books.

Betrock, Alan. 1982. *Girl Groups: The Story of a Sound*. New York: Delilah Books.

Billboard. 1950. "Supreme Loses Case for 400G against Decca." (May 13): 12.

———. 1954. "Freed Enjoined from Use of 'Moondog' Label." (December 4): 21–22.

———. 1955a. "Rock 'n' Roll: Freed Ball Takes 24G at St. Nick." (January 22): 13, 16.

———. 1955b. Advertisement for WINS radio. (January 29): 57.

———. 1955c. "There Ought to Be a Law: Lavern Baker Seeks Bill to Halt Arrangement 'Thefts.'" (March 5): 13, 18.

———. 1957. "R&R and Rockabilly in Pop Field Is Live Show Hurdle." (March 23): 22.

———. 1964a. "Large Folk Groups Make Bids on Coasts." (July 25): 6, 36.

———. 1964b. "New Vee Jay Post to Siegel." (July 25): 4.

———. 1978. "The New Wave Coming of Age: A *Billboard* Spotlight." (January 14): 47–67.

———. 1983. "New on the Charts: Cybotron." (September 24): 24.

———. 2019a. "Eminem Billboard." Accessed March 10. www.billboard.com.

———. 2019b. "Justin Bieber Billboard." Accessed March 10. www.billboard.com.

Black Demographics. 2019. "African American Population Growth." Accessed March 10. http://blackdemographics.com.

Blair, John. 2015. *Southern California Surf Music, 1960–1966*. Charleston, SC: Arcadia.

Block, Adam. 1982. "The Confessions of a Gay Rocker." *The Advocate* (April 15): 43–47; reprinted in Cateforis (2019: 199–206).

Bloomsbury. 2003–. *33⅓* [book series]. New York: Bloomsbury. www.bloomsbury.com and http://333sound.com.

Blush, Steven. 2010. *American Hardcore: A Tribal History*. 2nd ed. Los Angeles: Feral House.

BMI (Broadcast Music, Inc.). 2019. "BMI Repertoire." Accessed March 10. http://repertoire.bmi.com.

Bogazianos, Dimitri A. 2012. *Five Grams: Crack Cocaine, Rap Music, and the War on Drugs.* New York: New York University Press.

Bohan, Janis S. 1993. "Regarding Gender: Essentialism, Constructionism, and Feminist Psychology." *Psychology of Women Quarterly* 17 (1): 5–21.

Bohn, Chris. 1981. "Sleeping Partners: Chris Bohn Investigates Some Strange Happenings with Soft Cell and Top of the Pops." *New Musical Express* (September 12): 28–29.

Bowman, Rob. 1997. *Soulsville U.S.A.: The Story of Stax Records.* New York: Schirmer.

Boyer, Horace. 1995. *How Sweet the Sound: The Golden Age of Gospel.* Photography by Lloyd Yearwood. Washington, DC: Elliott and Clark.

Brackett, David. 1994. "The Politics and Practice of 'Crossover' in American Popular Music, 1963 to 1965." *Musical Quarterly* 78 (4): 774–97.

———. 1995. "James Brown's 'Superbad' and the Double-Voiced Utterance." In *Interpreting Popular Music*, 108–56. Cambridge: Cambridge University Press.

———, ed. 2014. *The Pop, Rock, and Soul Reader: Histories and Debates.* 3rd ed. New York: Oxford University Press.

Bradley, Adam. 2009. *Book of Rhymes: The Poetics of Hip Hop.* New York: Basic Civitas.

Braunstein, Peter. 1998. "The Last Days of Gay Disco" *Village Voice* (June 30): 54–55, 58.

Brewster, Bill, and Frank Broughton. 2006. *Last Night a DJ Saved My Life: The History of the Disc Jockey.* Rev. ed. New York: Grove.

———. 2010. *The Record Players: DJ Revolutionaries.* New York: Black Cat.

Broackes, Victoria, and Geoffrey Marsh. 2013. *David Bowie Is.* London: Victoria and Albert Museum.

Bromell, Nick. 2000. *Tomorrow Never Knows: Rock and Psychedelics in the 1960s.* Chicago: University of Chicago Press.

Broughton, Frank. 1995 (2010). "Frankie Knuckles Interviewed in NYC." *djhistory.com* (February 27). In Brewster and Broughton (2010: 233–41). (RBP)

Brown, Andy R. 2015. "Explaining the Naming of Heavy Metal from Rock's 'Back Pages': A Dialogue with Deena Weinstein." *Metal Music Studies* 1 (2): 233–61.

Brown, James. 1986. *James Brown: The Godfather of Soul.* With Bruce Tucker. New York: Macmillan.

Brown, Mick. 2008. *Tearing Down the Wall of Sound: The Rise and Fall of Phil Spector.* New York: Vintage.

Brown, Ruth. 1996. *Miss Rhythm: The Autobiography of Ruth Brown, the Rhythm and Blues Legend.* With Andrew Yule. New York: Fine.

Brubaker, Rogers. 2017. "The Uproar over 'Transracialism.'" *New York Times* (Online) (May 18). www.nytimes.com.

Bruford, Bill. 2013. *The Autobiography: Yes, King Crimson, Earthworks and More.* Rev. ed. London: Foruli.

Bundy, June. 1956. "B'dway-Hollyw'd Show Tunes Dog-Day Sales Panacea." *Billboard* (June 16): 17–18.

Bunting, Edward. 1796. *A General Collection of the Ancient Irish Music, Containing a Variety of Admired Airs Never before Published*. London: Preston.

———. 1840. *The Ancient Music of Ireland, Arranged for the Piano Forte*. Dublin: Hodges and Smith.

Bunzel, Peter. 1960. "Music Biz Goes Round and Round: It Comes out Clarkola." *Life* (May 16): 118–20, 122, 125.

Burdon, Eric. 1966. "An 'Animal' Views America: Young British Rhythm-and-Blueser Talks on Music and Race." *Ebony* (December): 160–62, 164, 166, 168, 170.

Burnim, Mellonee V., and Portia K. Maultsby. 2015. *African American Music: An Introduction*. 2nd ed. New York: Routledge.

Burns, Robert. 1787–1803. *The Scots Musical Museum*. 6 vols. Edinburgh: Johnson.

Butler, Judith. 1986. "Sex and Gender in Simone de Beauvoir's *Second Sex*." *Yale French Studies* 72: 35–49.

———. 1990. *Gender Trouble: Feminism and the Subversion of Identity*. New York: Routledge.

Byrne, David. 2012. *How Music Works*. San Francisco: McSweeney's.

Cale, John, and Victor Bockris. 2000. *What's Welsh for Zen: The Autobiography of John Cale*. New York: Bloomsbury.

Callwood, Brett. 2010. *MC5: Sonically Speaking, A Tale of Revolution and Rock 'n' Roll*. Detroit: Wayne State University Press.

Caress, Adam. 2015. *The Day Alternative Music Died: Dylan, Zeppelin, Punk, Glam, Alt, Majors, Indies, and the Struggle between Art and Money for the Soul of Rock*. Montreat, NC: New Troy Books.

Carson, Mina, Tisa Lewis, and Susan M. Shaw. 2004. *Girls Rock! Fifty Years of Women Making Music*. Lexington: University Press of Kentucky.

Cateforis, Theo. 2000. "Are We Not New Wave? Nostalgia, Technology and Exoticism in Popular Music at the Turn of the 1980s." PhD diss., State University of New York, Stony Brook.

———. 2011. *Are We Not New Wave? Modern Pop at the Turn of the 1980s*. Ann Arbor: University of Michigan Press.

———, ed. 2019. *The Rock History Reader*. 3rd ed. New York: Routledge.

Caulfield, Keith. 2018. "U.S. Vinyl Album Sales Hit Nielsen Music-Era Record High in 2017." *Billboard* (Online) (January 3). www.billboard.com.

CBGB. 1975. "CBGB Rock Festival: Top 40 New York Unrecorded Rock Talent [advertisements]." *Village Voice* (July 21): 82; (July 28): 85; (August 4): 76.

Chairman Mao. 1998. "Behind the Boards: Louder than a Bomb." *Ego Trip* 4 (1): 112–15.

Chang, Jeff. 2005. *Can't Stop Won't Stop: A History of the Hip Hop Generation*. New York: St. Martin's Press.

Chapple, Steve, and Reebee Garofalo. 1977. *Rock 'n' Roll Is Here to Pay: The History and Politics of the Music Industry*. Chicago: Nelson-Hall.

Charles, Ray, and David Ritz. 1978. *Brother Ray: Ray Charles' Own Story*. New York: Dial.

Charry, Eric. 2000. *Mande Music: Traditional and Modern Music of the Maninka and Mandinka of Western Africa*. Chicago: University of Chicago Press.

Chastagner, Claude. 1999. "The Parents' Music Resource Center: From Information to Censorship." *Popular Music* 18 (2): 179–92.

Child, Francis James, ed. 1882–98. *The English and Scottish Popular Ballads*. 5 vols. Boston: Houghton Mifflin.

Chin, Brian. 1986. "Dance Trax." *Billboard* (August 2): 37.

Christensen, Thomas, ed. 2002. *The Cambridge History of Western Music Theory*. New York: Cambridge University Press.

Christgau, Robert. 1973. *Any Old Way You Chose It: Rock and Other Pop Music, 1967–1973*. New York: Penguin.

———. 1986. "Christgau's Consumer Guide." *Village Voice* (December 30): 87.

Christman, Ed. 1999. "Retail Track: In an Internet World, Not All the Predicted Changes Are Here Yet." *Billboard* (December 25): 58, 60.

———. 2007. "Retail Track: Vinyl Solution?" *Billboard* (April 28): 11.

Clinton, George. 2014. *Brothas Be, Yo George, Ain't That Funkin' Kind of Hard on You?* With Ben Greenman. New York: Atria.

CNN. 1999. "Eagles Hits Album Named Best-Selling of the Century." (December 8). http://archives.cnn.com.

Cohen, Ronald D. 2002. *Rainbow Quest: The Folk Music Revival and American Society, 1940–1970*. Amherst: University of Massachusetts Press.

Cohen, Stanley. 1972. *Folk Devils and Moral Panics: The Creation of the Mods and Rockers*. London: MacGibbon and Key.

Cohn, Nik. 1976. "Tribal Rites of the New Saturday Night." *New York Magazine* (June 7): 31–43.

Collier, Barnard L. 1969. "300,000 at Folk-Rock Fair Camp Out in a Sea of Mud." *New York Times* (August 17): 1, 80.

Comerford, Catherine. 1979. "Reviews: Venue, Yellow Magic Orchestra." *Stage and Television Today* (October 25): 14.

Conners, Peter H. 2017. *Cornell '77: The Music, the Myth, and the Magnificence of the Grateful Dead's Concert at Barton Hall*. Ithaca: Cornell University Press.

Considine, J. D. 1992. "Fear of a Rap Planet." *Musician* (February): 34–43, 92.

Conway, Cecilia. 1995. *African Banjo Echoes in Appalachia: A Study of Folk Traditions*. Knoxville: University of Tennessee Press.

Corcoran, Michael. 1989. "Northwest of Hell." *Spin* (December): 41–43.

Cornell, Stephen, and Douglas Harmann. 2007. *Ethnicity and Race: Making Identities in a Changing World*. 2nd ed. Thousand Oaks, CA: Pine Forge.

Cosgrove, Stuart. 1988a. "Seventh City Techno." *The Face* (May): 86–89. http://test pressing.org.

——. 1988b. *Techno! The New Dance Sound of Detroit*. Notes. Compiled by Neil Rushton and Derrick May. 10 Records DIXG 75.

Covach, John. 1997. "Progressive Rock, 'Close to the Edge,' and the Boundaries of Style." In *Understanding Rock: Essays in Musical Analysis*, edited by John Covach and Graeme M. Boone, 3–31. New York: Oxford University Press.

Covach, John, and Andrew Flory. 2015. *What's That Sound? An Introduction to Rock and Its History*. 4th ed. New York: Norton. First published in 2006.

Crenshaw, Kimberlé. 1991. "Beyond Racism and Misogyny: Black Feminism and 2 Live Crew." *Boston Review* (December 6): 30–33. http://bostonreview.net.

Crichton, Kyle. 1938. "Thar's Gold in Them Hillbillies." *Collier's* (April 30): 24, 27.

Cromelin, Richard. 1976. "Brian Wilson." Pts. 1–2. *Sounds* (July 31): 24–26; (August 7): 14–15. (RBP)

Crowe, Cameron. 1973. "The Allman Brothers Story." *Rolling Stone* (December 6): 46–50, 52, 54.

Crowley, Kent. 2011. *Surf Beat: Rock 'n' Roll's Forgotten Revolution*. New York: Backbeat Books.

Csida, Joe. 1947. "'Full-Blown' Musical on Wax Blazes Trail; Could Be Legit-Film Testube." *Billboard* (May 10): 4, 22.

Currie, Cherie. 2010. *Neon Angel: A Memoir of a Runaway*. With Tony O'Neill. New York: It Books.

Danius, Sara, and Stefan Jonsson. 1993. "An Interview with Gayatri Chakravorty Spivak." *boundary 2* 20 (2): 24–50.

Dargan, William T. 2006. *Lining Out the Word: Dr. Watts Hymn Singing in the Music of Black Americans*. Berkeley: University of California Press; Chicago: Center for Black Music Research.

Davis, Angela Y. 1998. *Blues Legacies and Black Feminism: Gertrude "Ma" Rainey, Bessie Smith, and Billie Holiday*. New York: Pantheon.

DeCurtis, Anthony. 2017. *Lou Reed: A Life*. New York: Little, Brown.

DeCurtis, Anthony, and James Henke, eds. 1992. *The Rolling Stone Illustrated History of Rock and Roll*. 3rd ed. New York: Random House.

Delehant, Jim. 1967. "Otis Redding: 'Soul Survivor.'" *Hit Parader* (August): 56–57. (RBP)

Delmont, Matthew F. 2012. *The Nicest Kids in Town: American Bandstand, Rock 'n' Roll, and the Struggle for Civil Rights in 1950s Philadelphia*. Berkeley: University of California Press.

Denisoff, R. Serge. 1986. *Tarnished Gold: The Record Industry Revisited*. New Brunswick, NJ: Transaction.

Dex Digital. 2017. "Japanese Gentlemen Come to Soul Train: The Japan-Soul Train Connection, Part 2 (with a Hip-Hop Bonus)." *Those People You Know Us* (April 27). www.thsppl.com.

Diagne, Souleymane Bachir. 2018. "Négritude." *Stanford Encyclopedia of Philosophy* (Summer), edited by Edward N. Zalta. http://plato.stanford.edu.

Dixon, Robert M. W., and John Godrich. 1970. *Recording the Blues*. New York: Stein and Day.

DK. 2015. "Derrick May Performs with the Detroit Symphony Orchestra." *6am* (August 16). www.6am-group.com.

Doggett, Peter. 2000. *Are You Ready for the Country: Elvis, Dylan, Parsons and the Roots of Country Rock*. London: Viking.

Donahue, Tom. 1967. "AM Radio: 'Stinking Up the Airwaves.'" *Rolling Stone* (November 23): 14–15.

Douglas, Susan J. 1987. *Inventing American Broadcasting, 1899–1922*. Baltimore: Johns Hopkins University Press.

———. 1999. *Listening In: Radio and the American Imagination, from Amos 'n' Andy and Edward R. Murrow to Wolfman Jack and Howard Stern*. New York: Times Books.

Dreier, Peter. 2011. "Reagan's Real Legacy." *The Nation* (Online) (February 4): www.thenation.com.

Du Bois, W. E. B. 1897 (2007). *The Conservation of Races*. Occasional Papers 2. Washington, DC: American Negro Academy; reprinted in Du Bois (2007: 179–88).

———. 1903 (2007). *The Souls of Black Folk: Essays and Sketches*. Chicago: McClurgh; reprinted in Du Bois (2007).

———. 1923 (1996). "The Superior Race." *Smart Set* (April): 55–60; reprinted in Du Bois (1996).

———. 1996. *The Oxford W.E.B. Du Bois Reader*. Edited by Eric J. Sundquist. Oxford: Oxford University Press.

———. 2007. *The Souls of Black Folk*. New edition. Edited by Brent Hayes Edwards. New York: Oxford University Press.

Dubspot. 2014. "Marley Marl Classic Recipes Roundup: Recreating Classic Hip Hop Songs Using Ableton Live." (May 12). http://blog.dubspot.com.

Dunn, Jancee. 1995. "Melissa Etheridge Takes the Long Hard Road from the Heartland to Hollywood." *Rolling Stone* (June 1): 38–41, 44–45.

Dyer, Richard. 1979. "In Defence of Disco." *Gay Left* (Summer): 20–23; reprinted in Frith and Goodwin (1990: 410–18).

———. 1997. *White*. New York: Routledge.

Dylan, Bob. 2004. *Chronicles*. Vol. 1. New York: Simon and Schuster.

Early, Gerald. 2004. *One Nation under a Groove: Motown and American Culture*. Rev. ed. Ann Arbor: University of Michigan Press.

Echols, Alice. 1999. *Scars of Sweet Paradise: The Life and Times of Janis Joplin*. New York: Metropolitan Books.

Edgers, Geoff. 2017. "Why My Guitar Gently Weeps: The Slow, Secret Death of the Six-String Electric. And Why You Should Care." *Washington Post* (Online) (June 22). www.washingtonpost.com.

Ehrenreich, Barbara, Elizabeth Hess, and Gloria Jacobs. 1986. "Beatlemania: Girls Just Want to Have Fun." In *Re-making Love: The Feminization of Sex*, edited by Barbara Ehrenreich, Elizabeth Hess, and Gloria Jacobs, 10–38. Garden City, NY: Anchor Press/Doubleday.

Einarson, John. 2001. *Desperados: The Roots of Country Rock*. New York: Cooper Square.

Elliott, Paul. 2007. "Ker-rang! The Rise and Fall of the New Wave of British Heavy Metal: Never Mind the Bollocks." *MOJO* (February): 48–56.

Emerson, Ken. 2005. *Always Magic in the Air: The Bomp and Brilliance of the Brill Building Era*. New York: Viking.

E-MU Systems. 2019. "Product History." Accessed March 10. www.creative.com /emu.

Ennis, Philip H. 1992. *The Seventh Stream: The Emergence of Rocknroll in American Popular Music*. Hanover, NH: Wesleyan University Press.

Epstein, Dena J. 1977. *Sinful Tunes and Spirituals: Black Folk Music to the Civil War*. Urbana: University of Illinois Press.

———. 2015. "Secular Folk Music." With Rosita M. Sands. In Burnim and Maultsby (2015: 34–49).

Evans, Mike. 2005. *Ray Charles: The Birth of Soul*. London: Omnibus.

Everett, Walter. 1999. *The Beatles as Musicians: Revolver through the Anthology*. New York: Oxford University Press.

———. 2001. *The Beatles as Musicians: The Quarry Men through Rubber Soul*. New York: Oxford University Press.

Farber, Jim. 2016. "Growing Up Glam and Gay." *New York Times* (November 4): D5.

———. 2017. "Classic Rock 'n' Roll and Its Gay Architects." *New York Times* (October 19): D1.

Farm Aid. 2019. Accessed March 10. www.farmaid.org.

Fast, Susan. 1999. "Rethinking Issues of Gender and Sexuality in Led Zeppelin: A Woman's View of Pleasure and Power in Hard Rock." *American Music* 17 (3): 245–99.

———. 2012. "Michael Jackson's Queer Musical Belongings." *Popular Music and Society* 35 (2): 281–300.

Fearn-Banks, Kathleen, and Anne Burford-Johnson. 2014. *Historical Dictionary of African American Television*. 2nd ed. Lanham, MD: Rowman and Littlefield.

Fink, Robert. 2005a. *Repeating Ourselves: American Minimal Music as Cultural Practice*. Berkeley: University of California Press.

———. 2005b. "The Story of ORCH5, or, the Classical Ghost in the Hip-Hop Machine." *Popular Music* 24 (3): 339–56.

Fintoni, Laurent. 2016. "Fifteen Samplers That Shaped Modern Music—and the Musicians Who Use Them." *Fact* (September 15). www.factmag.com.

First Sounds. 2008. "3/27/08: The World's Oldest Sound Recordings Played for the First Time." www.firstsounds.org.

Fitzgerald, Jon. 1995. "Motown Crossover Hits, 1963–1966, and the Creative Process." *Popular Music* 14 (1): 1–11.

———. 2007. "Black Pop Songwriting, 1963–1966: An Analysis of U.S. Top Forty Hits by Cooke, Mayfield, Stevenson, Robinson, and Holland-Dozier-Holland." *Black Music Research Journal* 27 (2): 97–140.

Fletcher, Tony. 1992. "Just Say Techno." *Spin* (September): 46–47.

———. 2009. *All Hopped Up and Ready to Go: Music from the Streets of New York 1927–77.* New York: Norton.

Flores, Juan. 2016. *Salsa Rising: New York Latin Music of the Sixties Generation.* New York: Oxford University Press.

Floyd, Samuel A., Jr. 1996. *The Power of Black Music: Interpreting Its History from Africa to the United States.* New York: Oxford University Press.

Fong-Torres, Ben. 1994. *The Rice Room: Growing Up Chinese-American from Number Two Son to Rock 'n' Roll.* New York: Hyperion.

———. 1998. *The Hits Just Keep on Coming: The History of Top 40 Radio.* San Francisco: Miller Freeman Books.

Ford, Lita. 2016. *Living Like a Runaway: A Memoir.* New York: Dey St.

Fox, Ted. 1986. *In the Groove: The People behind the Music.* New York: St. Martin's Press.

Frankenberg, Ruth. 1993. *White Women, Race Matters: The Social Construction of Whiteness.* Minneapolis: University of Minnesota Press.

Fricke, David. 1994. "Kurt Cobain, the Rolling Stone Interview." *Rolling Stone* (January 27): 34–38, 56.

Friedrich, Otto, Peter Stoler, Michael Moritz, and J. Madeline Nash. 1983. "The Computer Moves In." *Time* (January 3): cover, 14–18, 21–24.

Frith, Simon. 1981. *Sound Effects: Youth, Leisure, and the Politics of Rock 'n' Roll.* New York: Pantheon.

———. 1988. *Music for Pleasure: Essays in the Sociology of Pop.* New York: Routledge.

———. 1996. *Performing Rites: On the Value of Popular Music.* Cambridge, MA: Harvard University Press.

Frith, Simon, and Andrew Goodwin, eds. 1990. *On Record: Rock, Pop, and the Written Word.* New York: Pantheon.

Frith, Simon, and Angela McRobbie. 1978–79. "Rock and Sexuality." *Screen Education* (Winter) 29: 3–19; reprinted in Frith and Goodwin (1990: 371–89).

Fryer, Roland G., Jr., Paul S. Heaton, Steven D. Levitt, and Kevin M. Murphy. 2013. "Measuring Crack Cocaine and Its Impact." *Economic Inquiry* 51 (3): 1651–81.

Furia, Philip, and Laurie J. Patterson. 2016. *The American Song Book: The Tin Pan Alley Era.* New York: Oxford University Press.

Gaar, Gillian G. 2002. *She's a Rebel: The History of Women in Rock and Roll.* 2nd ed. New York: Seal.

Gallup, George, and Evan Hill. 1961. "Youth: The Cool Generation." *Saturday Evening Post* (December 23): 63–80.

Garcia, Luis-Manuel. 2014. "Richard Dyer, 'In Defence of Disco.'" *History of Emotions—Insights into Research* (November). www.history-of-emotions.mpg.de/en.

Garland, Phyl. 1967. "Aretha Franklin: 'Sister Soul.'" *Ebony* (October): 47–48, 50–52.

———. 1969. *The Sound of Soul*. Chicago: Regnery.

Garner, Steve. 2007. *Whiteness: An Introduction*. New York: Routledge.

Garofalo, Reebee, and Steve Waksman. 2017. *Rockin' Out: Popular Music in the USA*. 6th ed. New York: Pearson. First published in 1997.

Garratt, Sheryl. 1986. "Chicago House: Sample and Hold." Photography by John Stoddart. *The Face* (September): 18–23. (RBP)

Gary, Kays. 1956. "It's a Money-Maker: Elvis Defends Low-Down Style." *Charlotte Observer* (June 27): 1B.

Gates, Henry Louis, Jr. 1990. "2 Live Crew, Decoded." *New York Times* (June 19): A23.

Gayle, Addison, Jr., ed. 1971. *The Black Aesthetic*. Garden City, NY: Doubleday.

Gehr, Richard. 1988. "Metallica: Monsters of Metal." *Music and Sound Output* (September): 42–48, 72. (RBP)

Gendron, Bernard. 2002. *Between Montmartre and the Mudd Club: Popular Music and the Avant-Garde*. Chicago: University of Chicago Press.

George, Nelson. 1986. "House Music: Will It Join Rap and Go-Go? Chicago Dance Sound Mixes Local, European Styles." *Billboard* (June 21): 27.

———. 1988. *The Death of Rhythm and Blues*. New York: Pantheon.

———. 2014. *The Hippest Trip in America: Soul Train and the Evolution of Culture and Style*. New York: Morrow.

Giddens, Gary. 1976. "Just How Much Did Elvis Learn from Otis Blackwell?" *Village Voice* (October 25): 46–48.

Gilbert, David. 2015. *The Product of Our Souls: Ragtime, Race, and the Birth of the Manhattan Musical Marketplace*. Chapel Hill: University of North Carolina Press.

Gill, John. 1995. *Queer Noises: Male and Female Homosexuality in Twentieth-Century Music*. Minneapolis: University of Minnesota Press.

Gillett, Charlie. 1996. *The Sound of the City: The Rise of Rock and Roll*. 2nd ed. New York: Da Capo.

Gilliland, John. 1969a. *Pop Chronicles*. Fifty-five shows. Pasadena, CA: KRLA. https://digital.library.unt.edu.

———. 1969b. *Pop Chronicles: Show 15—The Soul Reformation; More on the Evolution of Rhythm and Blues*. Pt. 1. Track 3. In Gilliland 1969a.

Gleason, Holly, ed. 2017. *Woman Walk the Line: How the Women in Country Music Changed Our Lives*. Austin: University of Texas Press.

Gleason, Ralph. 1970. "Aquarius Wept." *Esquire* (August): 48, 50, 84–92.

Goldstein, Richard. 1970. *Goldstein's Greatest Hits: A Book Mostly about Rock 'n' Roll*. Englewood Cliffs, NJ: Prentice-Hall.

Goodman, Fred. 1997. *The Mansion on the Hill: Dylan, Young, Geffen, Springsteen, and the Head-On Collision of Rock and Commerce*. New York: Vintage.

Gordon, Kim. 2015. *Girl in a Band: A Memoir*. New York: Dey Street Books.

Gordon, Robert. 2013. *Respect Yourself: Stax Records and the Soul Explosion*. New York: Bloomsbury.

Gordy, Berry. 1994. *To Be Loved: The Music, the Magic, the Memories of Motown*. New York: Warner Books.

Gottlieb, Jack. 2004. *Funny, It Doesn't Sound Jewish: How Yiddish Songs and Synagogue Melodies Influenced Tin Pan Alley, Broadway, and Hollywood*. Albany: State University of New York Press.

Gould, Jonathan. 2017. *Otis Redding: An Unfinished Life*. New York: Crown Archetype.

Gow, Niel, and Nathaniel Gow. 1986. *The Gow Collection of Scottish Dance Music*. Compiled and edited by Richard Carlin. New York: Oak.

Graceland. 2019. "Quotes about Elvis." Accessed March 10. www.graceland.com.

Graham, Sandra Jean. 2018. *Spirituals and the Birth of a Black Entertainment Industry*. Urbana: University of Illinois Press.

Grateful Dead Internet Archive Project. 2019. "Grateful Dead Collection." Accessed March 10. https://archive.org/details/GratefulDead.

Green, Archie. 1965. "Hillbilly Music: Source and Symbol." *Journal of American Folklore* (July–September): 204–28.

Greenburg, Zack O'Malley. 2012. "The World's Highest Paid DJs, 2012." *Forbes* (Online) (August 2).

Guccione, Bob, Jr. 1986. "Bob Geldof's Response to Spin's Live Aid Article." *Spin* (August): 79.

Guevara, Ruben. 1985. "The View from the Sixth Street Bridge: The History of Chicano Rock." In Marsh and the editors of Rock and Roll Confidential (1985: 113–23, 125–26).

Guralnick, Peter. 1971. *Feel Like Going Home: Portraits in Blues and Rock 'n' Roll*. New York: Outerbridge and Dienstfrey.

———. 1986. *Sweet Soul Music: Rhythm and Blues and the Southern Dream of Freedom*. New York: Harper and Row.

———. 1989. *Searching for Robert Johnson*. New York: Obelisk Books/Dutton.

———. 1994. *Last Train to Memphis: The Rise of Elvis Presley*. Boston: Little, Brown.

———. 1999. *Careless Love: The Unmaking of Elvis Presley*. Boston: Little, Brown.

———. 2005. *Dream Boogie: The Triumph of Sam Cooke*. New York: Little, Brown.

———. 2015. *Sam Phillips: The Man Who Invented Rock 'n' Roll*. New York: Little, Brown.

Hager, Steven. 1982. "Afrika Bambaataa's Hip Hop." *Village Voice* (September 21): 69, 72–73.

Hall, Claude. 1965. "R&B Stations Open Airplay Gates to 'Blue-Eyed' Soulists." *Billboard* (October 9): 1, 49.

Hall, Stuart. 2006. "Once More around Resistance through Rituals." In *Resistance through*

Rituals: Youth Subcultures in Post-war Britain, edited by Hall and Tony Jefferson, vii–xxxii. 2nd ed. New York: Routledge.

Hall, Stuart, and Tony Jefferson, eds. 1976. *Resistance through Rituals: Youth Subcultures in Post-war Britain*. London: Hutchinson.

Halperin, David M. 1995. *Saint Foucault: Towards a Gay Hagiography*. New York: Oxford University Press.

Hamill, Jasper. 2014. "The World's Most Famous Electronic Instrument Is Back: Will Anyone Buy the Reissued TB-303?" *Forbes* (Online) (March 25). www.forbes.com.

Hamilton, Jack. 2016. *Just around Midnight: Rock and Roll and the Racial Imagination*. Cambridge, MA: Harvard University Press.

Hamm, Charles. 1979. *Yesterdays: Popular Song in America*. New York: Norton.

———. 1983. *Music in the New World*. New York: Norton.

Handy, W. C. 1941. *Father of the Blues*. New York: Macmilllan.

Hartman, Ken. 2012. *The Wrecking Crew: The Inside Story of Rock and Roll's Best-Kept Secret*. New York: Dunne Books.

Hauser, Thomas. 1991. *Muhammad Ali: His Life and Times*. New York: Simon and Schuster.

Hawkins, Stan, and Sarah Niblock. 2011. *Prince: The Making of a Pop Music Phenomenon*. Burlington, VT: Ashgate.

Hebdige, Dick. 1979. *Subculture: The Meaning of Style*. London: Methuen.

Heilbut, Anthony. 1982. "The Secularization of Black Gospel Music." In *Folk Music and Modern Sound*, edited by William Ferris and Mary L. Hart, 101–15. Jackson: University of Mississippi Press.

———. 2002. *The Gospel Sound: Good News and Bad Times*. 6th ed. New York: Limelight.

Henderson, David. 1981. *'Scuse Me While I Kiss the Sky: The Life of Jimi Hendrix*. New York: Bantam.

Hendrix, Janie L. 2008. "The Blood of Entertainers: The Life and Times of Jimi Hendrix's Paternal Grandparents." *Black Past* (March 11). www.blackpast.org.

Henke, James. 1980. "Yellow Magic Orchestra: Japanese Technopop Poised to Invade America." *Rolling Stone* (June 12): 14. https://www.rollingstone.com/music/music-news/yellow-magic-orchestra-188812/

Henke, James, and Parke Puterbaugh, eds. 1997. *I Want to Take You Higher: The Psychedelic Era, 1965–1969*. San Francisco: Chronicle Books.

Hermes, Will. 2011. *Love Goes to Buildings on Fire: Five Years in New York That Changed Music Forever*. New York: Faber and Faber.

Hesmondhalgh, David. 2005. "Subcultures, Scenes or Tribes? None of the Above." *Journal of Youth Studies* 8 (1): 21–40.

Heylin, Clinton. 2005. *From the Velvets to the Voidoids: The Birth of American Punk Rock*. Chicago: Chicago Review.

Hicks, Michael. 1999. *Sixties Rock: Garage, Psychedelic, and Other Satisfactions*. Urbana: University of Illinois Press.

Hill, Dave. 1986. *Designer Boys and Material Girls: Manufacturing the '80s Pop Dream*. Poole, UK: Blandford.

Hill, Sarah. 2016. *San Francisco and the Long Sixties*. New York: Bloomsbury Academic.

Hobbs, Frank, and Nicole Stoops. 2002. *Demographic Trends in the 20th Century*. U.S. Census Bureau. Census 2000 Special Reports. Series CENSR-4. Washington, DC: U.S. Government Printing Office.

Hodkinson, Paul. 2002. *Goth: Identity, Style and Subculture*. New York: Berg.

Holman, Michael. 1982. "An Interview with DJ Africa Bambaataa of the Zulu Nation." *East Village Eye* (January): 22, 29.

Holm-Hudson, Kevin, ed. 2002. *Progressive Rock Reconsidered*. New York: Routledge.

Holmstrom, John. 1976. "Editorial." *Punk* (January): 1. www.punkmagazine.com; reprinted in Holmstrom and Hurd (2012: 14).

———, ed. 2019. *Punk*. Accessed March 10. http://punkmagazine.com.

Holmstrom, John, and Bridget Hurd, eds. 2012. *Punk: The Best of Punk Magazine*. New York: HarperCollins.

hooks, bell. 1992a. *Black Looks: Race and Representation*. Boston: South End.

———. 1992b. "Madonna: Plantation Mistress or Soul Sister?" In hooks (1992a: 157–64).

———. 1992c. "Representing Whiteness in the Black Imagination." In hooks (1992a: 165–78).

Horning, Susan Schmidt. 2013. *Chasing Sound: Technology, Culture, and the Art of Studio Recording from Edison to the LP*. Baltimore: Johns Hopkins University Press.

Hoskyns, Barney. 1998. *Glam! Bowie, Bolan and the Glitter Rock Revolution*. London: Faber and Faber.

———. 2009. *Waiting for the Sun: A Rock 'n' Roll History of Los Angeles*. New ed. New York: Backbeat Books.

———. 2016. *Small Town Talk: Bob Dylan, the Band, Van Morrison, Janis Joplin, Jimi Hendrix and Friends in the Wild Years of Woodstock*. New York: Da Capo.

Hubbs, Nadine. 2014. *Rednecks, Queers, and Country Music*. Berkeley: University of California Press.

Hughes, Charles L. 2015. *Country Soul: Making Music and Making Race in the American South*. Chapel Hill: University of North Carolina Press.

Hughes, Langston. 1955. "Highway Robbery across the Color Line in Rhythm and Blues." *Chicago Defender* (July 2): 9.

———. 1960. "Writers: Black and White." In Hughes (2002: 380–83).

———. 1966. "The Negro and American Entertainment." In Hughes (2002: 430–54).

———. 2002. *Collected Works of Langston Hughes: Essays on Art, Race, Politics, and World Affairs*. Vol. 9. Edited by Christopher C. De Santis. Columbia: University of Missouri Press.

Hunter, Dave. 2005. *Guitar Rigs: Classic Guitar and Amp Combinations*. San Francisco: Backbeat.

Hutchinson, Tom, Amy Macy, and Paul Allen. 2010. *Record Label Marketing*. 2nd ed. Oxford, UK: Focal.

Hyer, Brian. 2002. "Tonality." In Christensen (2002: 726–52).

Ice Cube and Angela Y. Davis. 1992. "Nappy Happy: A Conversation with Ice Cube and Angela Y. Davis." *Transition* 58: 174–92.

Inglis, Ian. 2003. "'Some Kind of Wonderful': The Creative Legacy of the Brill Building." *American Music* 21 (2): 214–35.

Ingraham, Chris, and Joshua Reeves. 2016. "New Media, New Panics." *Critical Studies in Media Communication* 33 (5): 455–67.

Jackson, John A. 1997. *American Bandstand: Dick Clark and the Making of a Rock 'n' Roll Empire*. New York: Oxford University Press.

Jeffers, Chike. 2013. "The Cultural Theory of Race: Yet Another Look at Du Bois's 'The Conservation of Races.'" *Ethics* 123 (3): 403–26.

Jefferson, Margo. 1973. "Ripping Off Black Music: From Thomas 'Daddy' Rice to Jimi Hendrix." *Harper's* (January): 40, 42–45.

Jenkins, Mark. 2007. *Analog Synthesizers: Understanding, Performing, Buying*. Burlington, MA: Focal Press.

Johnson, Robert. 1956. "Million Dollar Quartet"; "TV News and Views." Photography by George Pierce. *Memphis Press-Scimitar* (December 5): 23, 37.

July, Robert W. 1967. *The Origins of Modern African Thought*. New York: Praeger.

Katz, Mark. 2010. *Capturing Sound: How Technology Has Changed Music*. Rev. ed. Berkeley: University of California Press.

———. 2012. *Groove Music: The Art and Culture of the Hip-Hop DJ*. New York: Oxford University Press.

Kaufmann, Eric P. 2004. *The Rise and Fall of Anglo-America*. Cambridge, MA: Harvard University Press.

Kaye, Lenny. 1970. "*Live Dead*: The Grateful Dead." *Rolling Stone* (February 7): 44.

———. 1972. *Nuggets: Original Artyfacts from the First Psychedelic Era, 1965–1968*. Notes. 2 LPs. Compiled by Lenny Kaye. Elektra 7E-2006.

Keating, Robert. 1986a. "Live Aid: The Terrible Truth." *Spin* (July): 74–80.

———. 1986b. "Sympathy for the Devil." *Spin* (September): 64–68, 72.

Keiler, Allan. 2000. *Marian Anderson: A Singer's Journey*. New York: Scribner.

Kent-Smith, Jasmine. 2018. "Six of the Best Documentaries Exploring the Highs and Lows of Acid House Culture." *Mixmag* (May 11). https://mixmag.net.

Kershaw, Matthew. 1996. "Breaker's Revenge: Interview with Arthur Baker." *Jazid*. (October). Captured July 26, 2007, at http://web.archive.org (www.arthurbaker.net/content /interview1.htm).

Keyboard. 2009. "Michael Jackson: Keyboard Sounds of His Signature Songs, Then and Now." With Michael Boddicker, Bruce Swedien, and Dave Polich. (September): 22–26, 28–30. www.keyboardmag.com.

Keyes, Cheryl. 2003. "The Aesthetic Significance of African American Sound Culture and Its Impact on American Popular Music Style and Industry." *World of Music* 45 (3): 105–29.

Kienzle, Rich. 2007. "Buck Owens and His Buckaroos: 'A Bunch of Twangy Guitars.'" *Vintage Guitar* (May): 44–46, 124, 126, 128, 130, 132.

Knopper, Steve. 2018. "Nazi Punks F**k Off: How Black Flag, Bad Brains, and More Took Back Their Scene from White Supremacists." *GQ* (Online) (January 16). www.gq.com.

Kopkind, Andrew. 1979. "The Dialectic of Disco: Gay Music Goes Straight." *Village Voice* (February 12): 1, 11–14, 16, 25.

Kozak, Roman. 1982. "New British Invasion: Techno-Pop Groups Make Chart Inroads." *Billboard* (December 25): 3, 18.

Kugelberg, Johan, and Jon Savage. 2012a. "An Etymology of Punk." In Kugelberg and Savage (2012b: 348–51).

———. 2012b. *Punk: An Aesthetic*. New York: Rizzoli International.

Labov, William. 1972. *Language in the Inner City: Studies in the Black English Vernacular*. Philadelphia: University of Pennsylvania Press.

Lander, Christian. 2019. *Stuff White People Like*. Accessed March 10. https://stuffwhitepeoplelike.com.

Lang, Michael. 2009. *The Road to Woodstock*. With Holly George-Warren. New York: Ecco.

Laughey, Dan. 2006. *Music and Youth Culture*. Edinburgh: Edinburgh University Press.

Lawrence, Tim. 2003. *Love Saves the Day: A History of American Dance Music Culture, 1970–1979*. Durham: Duke University Press.

———. 2005. *Can You Jack? Chicago Acid and Experimental House, 1985–1995*. Notes. Soul Jazz SJR CD111. www.timlawrence.info.

———. 2008. "Disco Madness: Walter Gibbons and the Legacy of Turntablism and Re-mixology." *Journal of Popular Studies* 20 (3): 276–329.

———. 2011. "Disco and the Queering of the Dance Floor." *Cultural Studies* 25 (2): 230–43.

———. 2019. "Tim Lawrence: Articles." Accessed March 10. www.timlawrence.info.

LeDuff, Charlie. 1996. "Saturday Night Fever: The Life." *New York Times* (June 9): CY1, 14–15.

Leiber, Jerry, and Mike Stoller. 2009. *Hound Dog: The Leiber and Stoller Autobiography*. With David Ritz. New York: Simon and Schuster.

Lemon, Brenda. 1992. "k. d. lang: Virgin Territory." *The Advocate* (June 16): 34–36, 38, 40, 42, 44, 46.

Levine, Lawrence. 1977. *Black Culture and Black Consciousness: Afro-American Folk Thought from Slavery to Freedom*. New York: Oxford University Press.

————. 1988. *Highbrow Lowbrow: The Emergence of Cultural Hierarchy in America*. Cambridge, MA: Harvard University Press.

Library of Congress. 2019a. "Emile Berliner and the Birth of the Recording Industry: Articles and Essays." Accessed March 10. www.loc.gov.

————. 2019b. "History of the Cylinder Phonograph." *Inventing Entertainment: The Early Motion Pictures and Sound Recordings of the Edison Companies*. Accessed March 10. www.loc.gov.

Licks, Dr. 1989. *Standing in the Shadows of Motown: The Life and Music of Legendary Bassist James Jamerson*. Book and 2 CDs. Milwaukee, WI: Leonard.

Life. 1955. "Rock 'n Roll: A Frenzied Teen-Age Music Craze Kicks Up a Big Fuss." (April 18): 166–68.

————. 1959. "A New, $10 Billion Power: The U.S. Teen-Age Consumer." Photography by Yale Joel. (August 31): 78–85.

Light, Alan. 1998. "The Story of Yo: The Oral History of the Beastie Boys." *Spin* (September): 146–49, 151–54, 156, 158, 160–61.

Linn, Roger. 2019. "Past Products Museum." *Roger Linn Design*. Accessed March 10. www.rogerlinndesign.com.

Lipsitz, George. 1994. "Who'll Stop the Rain? Youth Culture, Rock 'n' Roll, and Social Crises." In *The Sixties: From Memory to History*, edited by David Farber, 206–34. Chapel Hill: University of North Carolina Press.

Llosa, Mario Vargas. 1986. *The Perpetual Orgy: Flaubert and Madame Bovary*. Translated by Helen Lane. New York: Farrar, Straus and Giroux.

Lloyd, Richard. 2018. *Everything Is Combustible: Television, CBGB's and Five Decades of Rock and Roll; The Memoirs of an Alchemical Guitarist*. Mount Desert, ME: Beech Hill.

Lomax, Alan. 1993. *The Land Where the Blues Began*. New York: Pantheon.

Longstreet, Augustus Baldwin. 1850. *Georgia Scenes*. 2nd ed. New York: Harper.

Lott, Eric. 1993. *Love and Theft: Blackface Minstrelsy and the American Working Class*. New York: Oxford University Press.

Love, Darlene. 2013. *My Name Is Love: The Darlene Love Story*. With Rob Hoerburger. 2nd ed. New York: Morrow.

Love, Dennis, and Stacy Brown. 2002. *Blind Faith: The Miraculous Journey of Lula Hardaway, Stevie Wonder's Mother*. New York: Simon and Schuster.

Loza, Steven. 1993. *Barrio Rhythm: Mexican American Music in Los Angeles*. Urbana: University of Illinois Press.

Lynskey, Dorian. 2011. *33 Revolutions per Minute: A History of Protest Songs, from Billie Holiday to Green Day*. New York: Ecco

Macan, Edward. 1997. *Rocking the Classics: English Progressive Rock and the Counterculture*. New York: Oxford University Press.

MacLeod, Sean. 2015. *Leaders of the Pack: Girl Groups of the 1960s and Their Influence on Popular Culture in Britain and America*. Lanham, MD: Rowman and Littlefield.

Macnie, Jim. 1989. "The Pixies: Feedback and Applesauce." *Musician* (October 1): 16, 18, 26.

Mahon, Maureen. 2004. *Right to Rock: The Black Rock Coalition and the Cultural Politics of Race*. Durham, NC: Duke University Press.

———. 2011. "Listening for Willie Mae 'Big Mama' Thornton's Voice: The Sound of Race and Gender Transgressions in Rock and Roll." *Women and Music* 15: 1–17.

Majewski, Lori, and Jonathan Bernstein. 2014. *Mad World: An Oral History of New Wave Artists and Songs That Defined the 1980s*. New York: Abrams.

Malone, Bill C., and Jocelyn R. Neal. 2010. *Country Music, U.S.A.* 3rd ed. Austin: University of Texas Press.

Malone, Chris. 2017. "A Brief History of Little Richard Grappling with His Sexuality and Religion." *Billboard* (Online) (October 9). www.billboard.com.

Malone, Jacqui. 1996. *Steppin' on the Blues: The Visible Rhythms of African American Dance*. Urbana: University of Illinois Press.

Marcus, Greil, ed. 1969. *Rock and Roll Will Stand*. Boston: Beacon.

———. 1975. *Mystery Train: Images of America in Rock 'n' Roll Music*. New York: Dutton.

———. 1985. "Number One with a Bullet." *Artforum* (May): 99.

Margotin, Philippe, and Jean-Michel Guesdon. 2016. *The Rolling Stones: All the Songs, the Story behind Every Track*. New York: Black Dog and Leventhal.

Marsh, Dave. 1971. "Looney Tunes." *Creem* (May): 42–43.

———. 1984. "Rock and Roll's Latin Tinge." *Boston Phoenix* (January 17): sec. 3, 6, 16; reprinted in Marsh (1985: 83–88).

———. 1985. *Fortunate Son: The Best of Dave Marsh*. New York: Random House.

Marsh, Dave, and the editors of Rock and Roll Confidential, eds. 1985. *The First Rock and Roll Confidential Report*. New York: Pantheon.

Marshall, Wayne. 2006. "Giving Up Hip-Hop's Firstborn: A Quest for the Real after the Death of Sampling." *Callaloo* 29 (3): 868–92.

Martin, Gavin. 1982. "ABC: Romancing Tongue in Chic." *New Musical Express* (March 6): 24–25, 28. (RBP)

Mason, Nick. 2019. "A History of Music and Technology." 9 episodes. *BBC: Music Extra* and *Open University*. www.bbc.co.uk.

Mather, Olivia Carter. 2013. "Taking it Easy in the Sunbelt: The Eagles and Country Rock's Regionalism." *American Music* 31 (1): 26–49.

Mathieu, Jane. 2017. "Midtown, 1906: The Case for an Alternative Tin Pan Alley." *American Music* 35 (2): 197–236.

Maultsby, Portia K. 2015a. "African American Music Timeline." In Burnim and Maultsby (2015: xvi).

———. 2015b. "The Translated African Cultural and Musical Past." In Burnim and Maultsby (2015: 3–22).

———. 2017. "The Politics of Race Erasure in Defining Black Popular Music Origins." In Maultsby and Burnim (2017: 47–65).

Maultsby, Portia, and Mellonee V. Burnim, eds. 2017. *Issues in African American Music: Power, Gender, Race, Representation*. New York: Routledge.

McDonnell, Evelyn, and Ann Powers, eds. 1995. *Rock She Wrote: Women Write about Rock, Pop, and Rap*. New York: Delta.

McGuinn, Roger. 1999. "Fair Nottamun Town." *Folk Den: Roger McGuinn in the Folk Tradition* (October 1). www.ibiblio.org.

McKeen, William. 2017. *Everybody Had an Ocean: Music and Mayhem in 1960s Los Angeles*. Chicago: Chicago Review.

McNeil, Legs, and Gillian McCain. 1996. *Please Kill Me: The Uncensored Oral History of Punk*. Rev. ed. New York: Grove.

McRobbie, Angela. 1976. "Girls and Subcultures: An Exploration." With Jenny Garber. In Hall and Jefferson (1976: 209–22); reprinted in McRobbie (2000: 12–25).

———. 1980. "Settling Accounts with Subcultures: A Feminist Critique." *Screen Education* 34: 37–49; reprinted in McRobbie (2000: 26–43).

———. 2000. *Feminism and Youth Culture*. 2nd ed. New York: Routledge.

Medium. 2014. "History of the Record Industry. Part 1, 1877–1920s; part 2, 1920–1950s." (June 7, –8). https://medium.com.

Meltzer, Richard. 1970. *The Aesthetics of Rock*. New York: Something Else.

Mencken, H. L. 1949. *A Mencken Chrestomathy*. New York: Knopf.

Mikkola, Mari. 2017. "Feminist Perspectives on Sex and Gender." *Stanford Encyclopedia of Philosophy* (Winter), edited by Edward N. Zalta. https://plato.stanford.edu.

Miles, Barry. 2009. *The British Invasion: The Music, the Times, the Era*. New York: Sterling.

Miller, Jim. 1974. "Records: Up against the Wah-Wah; The Heavy Metal Hall of Fame." *Rolling Stone* (July 4): 72–73.

———, ed. 1976. *The Rolling Stone Illustrated History of Rock and Roll*. New York: Rolling Stone.

———. 1999. *Flowers in the Dustbin: The Rise of Rock and Roll, 1947–1977*. New York: Simon and Schuster.

Miller, Karl Hagstrom. 2010. *Segregating Sound: Inventing Folk and Pop Music in the Age of Jim Crow*. Durham: Duke University Press.

Milner, Greg. 2009. *Perfecting Sound Forever: An Aural History of Recorded Music*. New York: Faber and Faber.

Minority Rights Group International. 2019. "Mexico: Indigenous Peoples." Accessed March 10. https://minorityrights.org.

Mintz, Sidney W., and Richard Price. 1992. *The Birth of African-American Culture: An Anthropological Perspective*. Boston: Beacon. First published 1976 as *An Anthropological Approach to the Afro-American Past*.

Moi, Toril. 1999. "Is Anatomy Destiny? Freud and Biological Determinism." In *What Is a Woman? And Other Essays*, 369–93. New York: Oxford University Press.

Molanphy, Chris. 2014. "I Know You Got Soul: The Trouble with *Billboard's* R&B/Hip-Hop Chart." *Pitchfork* (April 14). https://pitchfork.com.

Morales, Ed. 2002. *Living in Spanglish: The Search for Latino Identity in America*. New York: St. Martin's Press.

Morgan, Joan. 1999. *When Chickenheads Come Home to Roost: My Life as a Hip-Hop Feminist*. New York: Simon and Schuster.

Motown Museum. 2019. "Motown: The Sound That Changed America." Accessed March 10. www.motownmuseum.org.

Moulton, Tom. 1974. "Disco Action." *Billboard* (October 26): 22.

Muhammad, Ali Shaheed, and Frannie Kelley. 2013. "Microphone Check: Marley Marl on the Bridge Wars, LL Cool J and Discovering Sampling." NPR (September 12). www.npr.org.

Murray, Charles Shaar. 1977. "Muddy Waters: The Blues Had a Baby . . . and They Called It Rock 'n' Roll." *New Musical Express* (April 30): 25–27, 30. (RBP)

Music Copyright Infringement Resource. 2019. George Washington University Law School and Columbia University Law School. Accessed March 10. https://blogs.law.gwu.edu/mcir.

Needs, Kris. 1980. "Albums: Suicide." *Zigzag* (April): 56. (RBP)

———. 1990. "Monster Rhythm." *Echoes* (September 22): 18. (RBP, as "Derrick May: What Is Techno?")

Negus, Keith. 1996. *Popular Music in Theory: An Introduction*. Hanover, NH: Wesleyan University Press.

New York Age. 1959. "Mr. Clark and Colored Payola." (December 5): 6; reprinted in Brackett (2014: 128).

New York Times. 2002. "Otis Blackwell, 70; Wrote Hits for Presley and Others." (May 9): C15.

Noakes, Tim. 2006. "Roger Linn: Dr. Beat." *Dazed and Confused* (April): 212–15.

———. 2014. "Roger Linn: Dr. Beat." *Dazed* (August 23). Enhanced online version of Noakes (2006). www.dazeddigital.com.

NPR (National Public Radio). 2017. "The 150 Greatest Albums Made by Women." (July 24). www.npr.org.

Oberdorfer, Don. 1956. "The Critics Stayed Home, and Elvis Was the Greatest." *Charlotte Observer* (June 27): 1B, 4B.

O'Brien, Lucy. 2002. *She Bop II: The Definitive History of Women in Rock, Pop and Soul*. London: Continuum.

OED (*Oxford English Dictionary*) Online. 2019a. "funk, n. 2; funky, adj. 3." (March) Oxford University Press. www.oed.com.

———. 2019b. "punk, n. 1 and adj. 2; punk, v. 1." (March) Oxford University Press. www.oed.com.

———. 2019c. "race, n. 6, Compounds, C2: race man, race woman." (March) Oxford University Press. www.oed.com.

Official Charts. 2019. Accessed March 10. www.officialcharts.com.

O'Neill, Francis, ed. 1903. *O'Neill's Music of Ireland: Eighteen Hundred and Fifty Melodies*. Chicago: Lyon and Healy.

Osborne, Richard. 2012. *Vinyl: A History of the Analogue Record*. Burlington, VT: Ashgate.

Owen, Frank. 1986 "Chicago: Last Night a DJ Saved My Life." Pt. 1. *Melody Maker* (August 16): 32–33. (RBP)

———. 1987. "Groovemaster No. 1: Frankie Knuckles." *Melody Maker* (June 20): 36. (RBP)

Pacini Hernandez, Deborah. 2010. *Oye Como Va! Hybridity and Identity in Latino Popular Music*. Philadelphia: Temple University Press.

Paglia, Camille. 1990. "Madonna: Finally, a Real Feminist." *New York Times* (December 14): A39.

Painter, Nell Irvin. 2015. "What Is Whiteness?" *New York Times* (June 21): SR8.

Palladino. Grace. 1996. *Teenagers: An American History*. New York: Basic Books.

Palmer, Robert. 1981. *Deep Blues*. New York: Viking Penguin.

———. 1995. *Rock and Roll: An Unruly History*. New York: Harmony Books.

Parsons, Talcott. 1942. "Age and Sex in the Social Structure of the United States." *American Sociological Review* 7 (5): 604–16.

PBS. 2001. "American Roots Music, Oral Histories: B. B. King." Ginger Group. pbs.org.

Pecknold, Diane, ed. 2013. *Hidden in the Mix: The African American Presence in Country Music*. Durham: Duke University Press.

Pegg, Nicolas. 2016. *The Complete David Bowie*. 7th ed. London: Titan.

Percy, Thomas. 1765. *Reliques of Ancient English Poetry*. 3 vols. London: Dodsley/Pall Mall.

Perone, James E. 2009. *Mods, Rockers, and the Music of the British Invasion*. Westport, CT: Praeger.

Peterson, Richard A. 1990. "Why 1955? Explaining the Advent of Rock Music." *Popular Music* 9 (1): 97–116.

———. 1997. *Creating Country Music: Fabricating Authenticity*. Chicago: University of Chicago Press.

Piccarella, John. 1986. "Beastie Boys: White Trash on Dope." *Village Voice* (December 23): 103, 105.

Piggford, George. 1999. "'Who's That Girl?' Annie Lennox, Woolf's *Orlando*, and Female Camp Androgyny." In *Camp: Queer Aesthetics and the Performing Subject*, edited by Fabio Cleto, 283–99. Ann Arbor: University of Michigan Press.

Pinch, Trevor, and Frank Trocco. 2002. *Analog Days: The Invention and Impact of the Moog Synthesizer*. Cambridge, MA: Harvard University Press.

Plasketes, George. 1992. "Romancing the Record: The Vinyl De-evolution and Subcultural Evolution." *Journal of Popular Culture* 26 (1): 109–22.

Prinzing, Scott. 2016. "Brothers of the Blade, Three Native Axmen: Robbie Robertson, Link Wray, and Jesse Ed Davis." In *Indigenous Pop: Native Americans from Jazz to Hip Hop*, edited by Jeff Berglund, Jan Johnson, and Kimberli Lee, 75–91. Tucson: University of Arizona Press.

Pruter, Robert. 1991. *Chicago Soul*. Urbana: University of Illinois Press.

Questlove (Ahmir Thompson). 2013. *Soul Train: The Music, Dance, and Style of a Generation*. New York: Harper Design.

Questlove (Ahmir Thompson) and Ben Greenman. 2013. *Mo' Meta Blues: The World According to Questlove*. New York: Grand Central.

Rambali, Paul. 1978. "Patti Smith: Breaking the Shackles of Original Sin." *New Musical Express* (September 16): 7–8. (RBP)

Ramsey, Guthrie P., Jr. 2003. *Race Music: Black Cultures from Bebop to Hip-Hop*. Berkeley: University of California Press.

Rasmussen, Christopher. 2008. "Lonely Sounds: Popular Recorded Music and American Society, 1949–1979." PhD diss., University of Nebraska–Lincoln.

RCA Victor. 1949. Advertisement. *Billboard* (February 19): 23.

Reagon, Bernice Johnson, ed. 1992. *We'll Understand It Better By and By: Pioneering African American Gospel Composers*. Washington, DC: Smithsonian Institution Press.

Recording Academy. 2019. "Grammy Awards: Awards and Winners." Accessed March 10. www.grammy.com/grammys/awards.

Reid, Gordon. 2004–5. "The History of Roland." 5 pts. *Sound on Sound* (November 2004–March 2005). www.soundonsound.com.

Remnick, David. 2018. "Philip Roth's American Portraits and American Prophecy." *New Yorker Radio Hour* (July 20). *New Yorker* and WNYC. www.wnycstudios.org.

Renoff, Greg. 2015. *Van Halen Rising: How a Southern California Backyard Party Band Saved Heavy Metal*. Toronto: ECW.

Repino, Robert, and Tim Allen. 2013. "Blaxploitation, from Shaft to Django." *OUPblog* (June 3). http://blog.oup.com.

Reyes, David, and Tom Waldman. 1998. *Land of a Thousand Dances: Chicano Rock 'n' Roll from Southern California*. Albuquerque: University of New Mexico Press.

Reynolds, Simon. 1998. *Generation Ecstasy: Into the World of Techno and Rave Culture*. Toronto: Little, Brown.

———. 2006. *Rip It Up and Start Again: Postpunk, 1978–1984*. New York: Penguin.

Rhodes, Lisa L. 2005. *Electric Ladyland: Women and Rock Culture*. Philadelphia: University of Pennsylvania Press.

Rhythm and Blues Foundation. 2019. Accessed March 10. http://rhythmblues.org.

RIAA (Recording Industry Association of America). 2019a. "Gold and Platinum." Accessed March 10. www.riaa.com.

———. 2019b. "U.S. Sales Database." Accessed March 10. www.riaa.com.

Ribowsky, Mark. 2010. *Signed, Sealed, and Delivered: The Soulful Journey of Stevie Wonder*. Hoboken, NJ: Wiley.

Ritchie, Fiona, and Doug Orr. 2016. *Wayfaring Strangers: The Musical Voyage from Scotland and Ulster to Appalachia*. Chapel Hill: University of North Carolina Press.

Ritz, David. 2014. *Respect: The Life of Aretha Franklin*. New York: Little, Brown.

Robbins, Ira. 2000. "Ladies and Gentlemen of the Jury . . . There Stands before You a Murderer—The Band That Killed Rock 'n' Roll." *Salon* (April 10). www.salon.com.

Roberts, John Storm. 1999. *The Latin Tinge*. 2nd ed. New York: Oxford University Press.

Robins, Wayne. 1976. "Punk Rock: Its Day Will Come." *Newsday* (January 25): pt. 2, 4–5. (RBP)

Robinson, J. P. 2018. "The Rotten Etymology of Punk: The Strange Story of How Punk Became Punk"; "Sources for 'The Rotten Etymology of Punk.'" *Medium* (August 20). medium.com.

Robinson, Lisa. 2015. "It Happened in Laurel Canyon." *Vanity Fair* (March): 258, 260, 262, 264, 266, 268, 270–71.

Robinson, Louie. 1957. "The Truth about That Elvis Presley Rumor." *Jet* (August 1): 58–61.

Rock and Roll Hall of Fame. 2019. "Inductee Explorer." Accessed March 10. www.rockhall.com/inductees.

Rock on the Net. 2019. "History of the Grammy Awards." Accessed March 10. www.rockonthenet.com/grammy.

Rock's Backpages (RBP). 2019. Accessed March 10. www.rocksbackpages.com (subscription only).

Roediger, David R. 1991. *The Wages of Whiteness: Race and the Making of the American Working Class*. New York: Verso.

———, ed. 1998. *Black on White: Black Writers on What It Means to Be White*. New York: Schocken Books.

Rogers, Ibram H. 2012. "The Black Campus Movement and the Institutionalization of Black Studies, 1965–1970." *Journal of African American Studies* 16 (1): 21–40.

Rohlfing, Mary E. 1996. "'Don't Say Nothin' Bad about My Baby': A Re-evaluation of Women's Roles in the Brill Building Era of Early Rock 'n' Roll." *Critical Studies in Mass Communication* 13 (2): 93–114.

Rolling Stone. 1970. "The Rolling Stones Disaster at Altamont: Let It Bleed." (January 21): 1, 3, 18–20, 22–28, 30–32, 34, 36.

———. 2012. "500 Greatest Albums of All Time." (May 31). www.rollingstone.com.

Ronstadt, Linda. 2013. *Simple Dreams: A Musical Memoir*. New York: Simon and Schuster.

Rose, Tricia. 1994. *Black Noise: Rap Music and Black Culture in Contemporary America*. Middletown, CT: Wesleyan University Press.

Roth, Jack. 1960. "Alan Freed and 7 Others Arrested in Payola Here." *New York Times* (May 20): 1, 62.

Roxon, Lilian. 1969. *Lilian Roxon's Rock Encyclopedia*. New York: Grossett and Dunlap.

Rubin, Mike. 2016. "Rik Davis: Alleys of His Mind." *Red Bull Music Academy Daily* (May 24). https://daily.redbullmusicacademy.com.

Russ, Martin. 2008. *Sound Synthesis and Sampling*. 3rd ed. Burlington, MA: Focal Press.

Russell, Tony. 1970. *Blacks, Whites, and Blues*. New York: Stein and Day.

———. 2010. *Country Music Originals: The Legends and the Lost*. New York: Oxford University Press.

Salon Staff. 2000. "Letters to the Editor: 'Ladies and Gentlemen of the Jury' by Ira Robbins." *Salon* (April 13). www.salon.com.

Sander, Ellen. 1968. "Pop in Perspective: A Profile." *Saturday Review* (October 26): 80–83.

———. 1973. *Trips: Rock Life in the Sixties*. New York: Scribner.

———. 2019. "Ellen Sander." *Unz Review: An Alternate Media Selection*. Accessed March 10. www.unz.com.

Sanders, Daryl. 2011. "Looking Back on Bob Dylan's *Blonde on Blonde*, the Record That Changed Nashville." *Nashville Scene* (May 5). www.nashvillescene.com.

Sanjek, Russell. 1988. *American Popular Music and Its Business: The First Four Hundred Years*. 3 vols. New York: Oxford University Press.

———. 1996. *Pennies from Heaven: The American Popular Music Business in the Twentieth Century*. Updated by David Sanjek. New York: Da Capo.

Sanneh, Kelefa. 2010. "Beyond the Pale: Is White the New Black?" *New Yorker* (April 12): 69–74.

———. 2015. "United Blood: How Hardcore Conquered New York." *New Yorker* (March 9): 82–86, 88–89.

Santana, Carlos. 2014. *The Universal Tone: Bringing My Story to Light*. With Ashley Kahn and Hal Miller. New York: Little, Brown.

Santelli, Robert. 1993. *The Big Book of Blues*. New York: Penguin.

Savage, Jon. 2007. *Teenage: The Creation of a Youth Culture*. New York: Viking.

Sawyer, Wendy, and Peter Wagner. 2019. "Mass Incarceration: The Whole Pie 2019." *Prison Policy Initiative* (March 19). www.prisonpolicy.org.

Scaduto, Anthony. 1971. *Bob Dylan: An Intimate Biography*. New York: Grosset and Dunlap.

Scherman, Tony. 1999. *Backbeat: Earl Palmer's Story*. Washington, DC: Smithsonian Institution Press.

Schloss, Joseph G. 2014. *Making Beats: The Art of Sample-Based Hip-Hop*. With a new afterword. Middletown, CT: Wesleyan University Press.

Schloss, Joseph, Larry Starr, and Christopher Waterman. 2012. *Rock: Music, Culture, Business*. New York: Oxford University Press. First edition 2006.

Schoenherr, Steven E. 2005. "Dr. Steven Schoenherr's 'Recording Technology History.'" *AES [Audio Engineering Society] Historical Committee* (July 6). www.aes.org/aeshc.

Schonfeld, Zach. 2015. "Parental Advisory Forever: An Oral History of the PMRC's War on Dirty Lyrics." *Newsweek* (October 9). www.newsweek.com.

Schu, Peter. 2017. "Video: Marty Stuart on Clarence White's Original StringBender Tele." *Reverb* (April 19). https://reverb.com.

Schwerin, Jules Victor. 1992. *Got to Tell It: Mahalia Jackson, Queen of Gospel*. New York: Oxford University Press.

Scoppa, Bud. 1973. "GP." *Rolling Stone* (March 1): 69.

Seale, Bobby. 1970. *Seize the Time: The Story of the Black Panther Party and Huey P. Newton*. New York: Random House.

Sehgal, Parul. 2015. "First Words: Takeover." *New York Times Magazine* (October 4): 13–15.

Selvin, Joel. 2016. *Altamont: The Rolling Stones, the Hells Angels and the Inside Story of Rock's Darkest Day*. New York: Dey St.

Senghor, Léopold Sédar. 1970. "Négritude: A Humanism of the Twentieth Century." In *The Africa Reader*, Vol. 2, *Independent Africa*, edited by Wilfrid Cartey and Martin Kilson, 179–92. New York: Random House.

Sepia. 1957. "How Negroes Feel about Elvis." (April): 19–20, 25.

Sewell, Amanda. 2014. "*Paul's Boutique* and *Fear of a Black Planet*: Digital Sampling and Musical Style in Hip Hop." *Journal of the Society for American Music* 8 (1): 28–48.

Shanahan, Tim. 2016. *Running with the Champ: My Forty-Year Friendship with Muhammad Ali*. New York: Simon and Schuster.

Shapiro, Harry. 2003. *Waiting for the Man: The Story of Drugs and Popular Music*. London: Helter Skelter.

Shapiro, Peter. 2014. "Saturday Mass: Larry Levan and the Paradise Garage." *Red Bull Music Academy* (April 22). http://daily.redbullmusicacademy.com.

Sharp, Cecil James, and Olive Dame Campbell. 1917. *English Folk Songs from the Southern Appalachians*. New York: Putnam's Sons.

Shaw, Arnold. 1978. *Honkers and Shouters: The Golden Years of Rhythm and Blues*. New York: Macmillan.

Shaw, Greg. 1973. "Punk Rock: The Arrogant Underbelly of Sixties Pop." *Rolling Stone* (January 4): 68.

Sheehy, Daniel. 2003. *La Bamba: Sones Jarochos from Veracruz*. Notes. Smithsonian Folkways, SFW40505.

Shelby, Tommie. 2005. *We Who Are Dark: The Philosophical Foundations of Black Solidarity*. Cambridge, MA: Belknap.

Shelton, Robert. 1986. *No Direction Home: The Life and Music of Bob Dylan*. New York: Beech Tree.

Shumway, David R. 2016. "The Emergence of the Singer-Songwriter." In Williams and Williams (2016: 11–20).

Sicko, Dan. 2010. *Techno Rebels: The Renegades of Electronic Funk*. 2nd ed. Detroit: Wayne State University Press.

Silber, Irwin. 1964. "An Open Letter to Bob Dylan." *Sing Out!* (November): 22–23.

Simon, Bill. 1956. "Rhythm and Blues Notes." *Billboard* (June 23): 59.

Slave Voyages. 2019. "Estimates." Accessed March 10. www.slavevoyages.org.

Smith, Christopher J. 2013. *The Creolization of American Culture: William Sidney Mount and the Roots of Blackface Minstrelsy*. Urbana: University of Illinois Press.

Smith, Patricia Juliana. 1999. "'You Don't Have to Say You Love Me': The Camp Masquerades of Dusty Springfield." In *The Queer Sixties*, edited by Patricia Juliana Smith, 105–26. New York: Routledge.

Smith, Patti. 2010. *Just Kids*. New York: HarperCollins.

Smith, Suzanne E. 1999. *Dancing in the Street: Motown and the Cultural Politics of Detroit*. Cambridge, MA: University of Harvard Press.

Smitherman, Gina. 1995. "'If I'm Lyin, I'm Flyin': An Introduction to the Art of the Snap." In *Double Snaps*, edited by James Percelay, Stephan Dweck, and Monteria Ivey, 14–33. New York: Morrow.

Smulyan, Susan. 1994. *Selling Radio: The Commercialization of American Broadcasting, 1920–1934*. Washington, DC: Smithsonian Institution Press.

Sontag, Susan. 1964. "Notes on Camp." *Partisan Review* 31 (4): 515–30.

Southern, Eileen, ed. 1983. *Readings in Black American Music*. 2nd ed. New York: Norton.

———. 1997. *The Music of Black Americans: A History*. 3rd ed. New York: Norton.

Spector, Ronnie. 1990. *Be My Baby: How I Survived Mascara, Minkskirts, and Madness, or My Life as a Fabulous Ronette*. With Vince Waldron. New York: Harmony Books.

Spellman, A. B. 1966. *Four Lives in the Bebop Business*. New York: Pantheon.

Springsteen, Bruce. 1998. *Songs*. New York: Avon.

———. 2016. *Born to Run*. New York: Simon and Schuster.

Sternfield, Aaron. 1965. "Rock + Folk + Protest = an Erupting New Sound." *Billboard* (August 21): 1, 14.

Stimeling, Travis, ed. 2014. *The Country Music Reader*. New York: Oxford University Press.

Stratton, Jon. 2009. *Jews, Race and Popular Music*. Burlington, VT: Ashgate.

Stubbs, David. 2015. *Future Days: Krautrock and the Birth of a Revolutionary New Music*. Brooklyn: Melville House.

Stumpel, Bob. 2014. "I've Got a Woman." *Ray Charles Video Museum* (November 3). http://raycharlesvideomuseum.blogspot.com.

Sublette, Ned. 2004. *Cuba and Its Music: From the First Drums to the Mambo*. Chicago: Chicago Review.

———. 2007. "The Kingsmen and the Cha-Cha-Chá." In *Listen Again: A Momentary History of Pop Music*, edited by Eric Weisbard, 69–94. Durham: Duke University Press.

Tannenbaum, Rob, and Craig Marks. 2012. *I Want My MTV: The Uncensored Story of the Music Video Revolution*. Rev. ed. New York: Plume.

Taruskin, Richard. 2005. *The Oxford History of Western Music*. 6 vols. New York: Oxford University Press.

TeachRock. 2019a. Accessed March 10. http://teachrock.org.

———. 2019b. "Rumble: The Indians Who Rocked the World." Accessed March 10. http://teachrock.org/rumble/.

Terkourafi, Marina, ed. 2010. *The Languages of Global Hip Hop*. New York: Continuum.

Terry, Penny, Pip, Brandy, and Tee. 1965a. "The Low Down." *Chicago Defender* (April 24): 16.

———. 1965b. "The Low Down." *Chicago Defender* (June 12): 30.

———. 1965c. "The Low Down." *Chicago Defender* (August 14): 40 (as Pip, Brandi, Penni, Terry Joe and Tee).

———. 1965d. "The Low Down." *Chicago Defender* (October 16): 28 (as Pip, Brandi, Penni, Terry Joe).

Thompson, Dave. 2009. *Your Pretty Face Is Going to Hell: The Dangerous Glitter of David Bowie, Iggy Pop, and Lou Reed*. New York: Backbeat Books.

Thompson, Katrina Dyonne. 2014. *Ring Shout, Wheel About: The Racial Politics of Music and Dance in North American Slavery*. Urbana: University of Illinois Press.

Thornton, Sarah. 1996. *Club Cultures: Music, Media and Subcultural Capital*. Hanover, NH: Wesleyan University Press.

Tiegel, Elliot. 1965a. "Folkswinging Wave On—Courtesy of Rock Groups." *Billboard* (June 12): 1, 10.

———. 1965b. "West Coast Clamors for Dylan Tunes." *Billboard* (September 4): 12, 47.

Time. 1956. "Bobby-Soxers' Gallup." (August 13): 74.

———. 1962. "Folk Singing: Sibyl with Guitar." (November 23): 54–56, 59–60.

———. 1983. "A Letter from the Publisher." (January 3): 5.

Titon, Jeff Todd. 1977. *Early Downhome Blues: A Musical and Cultural Analysis*. Urbana: University of Illinois Press.

Tolinski, Brad, and Alan di Perna. 2016. *Play It Loud: An Epic History of the Style, Sound, and Revolution of the Electric Guitar*. New York: Doubleday.

Touré. 1993. "Snoop Dogg's Gentle Hip-Hop Growl." *New York Times* (November 21): H32.

———. 1994. "The Professional: Tupac Shakur Gives the Performance of His Life." *Village Voice* (December 13): 75, 85.

Troubadour. 2019. "History." Accessed March 10. www.troubadour.com/history.

Troutman, John. 2016. *Kīkā Kila: How the Hawaiian Steel Guitar Changed the Sound of Modern Music*. Chapel Hill: University of North Carolina Press.

Trynka, Paul. 2007. *Iggy Pop: Open Up and Bleed*. New York: Broadway Books.

Twells, John. 2016. "The Fourteen Most Important Synths in Electronic Music History— and the Musicians Who Use Them." *Fact* (September 15). www.factmag.com.

Twersky, Lori. 1981. "Devils or Angels? The Female Teenage Audience Examined." *Trouser Press* (April): 27–29; reprinted in McDonnell and Powers (1995: 177–83).

UCSB Cylinder Archive. 2019. "Cylinder Recordings: A Primer." Accessed March 10. http://cylinders.library.ucsb.edu.

UNESCO (United Nations Educational, Scientific and Cultural Organization). 1969. *Four Statements on the Race Question*. Paris: UNESCO. https://unesdoc.unesco.org.

Unterberger, Richie. 2002. *Turn! Turn! Turn! The '60s Folk-Rock Revolution*. Milwaukee, WI: Backbeat Books.

———. 2003. *Eight Miles High: Folk-Rock's Flight from Haight-Ashbury to Woodstock*. San Francisco: Backbeat Books.

———. 2009. *White Light/White Heat: The Velvet Underground Day-by-Day*. London: Jawbone.

U.S. Census Bureau. 2011. "The Black Population: 2010." *2010 Census Briefs* (September). www.census.gov.

———. 2018. "Hispanic Origin: About." (March 7). www.census.gov.

U.S. Central Intelligence Agency. 2019. "Mexico." *World Factbook* (May 21). www.cia.gov.

U.S. Copyright Office. 2015. *Copyright and the Music Marketplace: A Report of the Register of Copyrights*. Library of Congress. (February). 2nd printing (May 2016). www.copy right.gov.

———. 2019a. "Circulars." Accessed March 10. www.copyright.gov/circs.

———. 2019b. "Orrin G. Hatch: Bob Goodlatte Music Modernization Act." Accessed March 10. www.copyright.gov.

———. 2019c. "Timeline: A Brief History of Copyright in the United States." Accessed March 10. www.copyright.gov/timeline.

U.S. Senate. 1985. *Record Labeling: Hearing before the Committee on Commerce, Science, and Transportation, United States Senate, Ninety-Ninth Congress, First Session, on Contents of Music and the Lyrics of Records, September 19, 1985*. Washington, DC: U.S. Government Printing Office. http://babel.hathitrust.org.

U.S. Sentencing Commission. 1995. *1995 Report to the Congress: Cocaine and Federal Sentencing Policy*. (February). www.ussc.gov.

Vaidhyanathan, Said. 2001. *Copyrights and Copywrongs: The Rise of Intellectual Property and How It Threatens Creativity*. New York: New York University Press.

Variety. 1953. "Negro Jocks Come into Their Own: Play Key Role in Music Biz." (February 25): 39, 46.

———. 1955. "Houston's 'Wash-Out-the-Air Comm.' Knocks 26 R&B Tunes Out of Box." (August 24): 51, 55.

Veal, Michael E. 2007. *Dub: Soundscapes and Shattered Songs in Jamaican Reggae*. Middletown, CT: Wesleyan University Press.

Vogel, Joseph. 2011. *Man in the Music: The Creative Life and Work of Michael Jackson*. New York: Sterling.

Waksman, Steve. 1999. *Instruments of Desire: The Electric Guitar and the Shaping of Musical Experience*. Cambridge, MA: Harvard University Press.

———. 2009. *This Ain't the Summer of Love: Conflict and Crossover in Heavy Metal and Punk*. Berkeley: University of California Press.

Wald, Elijah. 2015. *Dylan Goes Electric! Newport, Seeger, Dylan, and the Night That Split the Sixties*. New York: Dey St.

Wald, Gayle. 2007. *Shout, Sister, Shout: The Untold Story of Rock-and-Roll Trailblazer Sister Rosetta Tharpe*. Boston: Beacon.

Walker, Michael. 2006. *Laurel Canyon: The Inside Story of Rock-and-Roll's Legendary Neighborhood*. New York: Faber and Faber.

Walser, Rob. 1993. *Running with the Devil: Power, Gender, and Madness in Heavy Metal Music*. Middletown, CT: Wesleyan University Press.

Walters, Barry. 1986. "Burning Down the House." Photography by Gene Schwartz. *Spin* (November): 60–62, 64.

Ward, Brian. 1998. *Just My Soul Responding: Rhythm and Blues, Black Consciousness, and Race Relations*. Berkeley: University of California Press.

Warwick, Jacqueline. 2007. *Girl Groups, Girl Culture: Popular Music and Identity in the 1960s*. New York: Routledge.

Watts, Isaac. 1707. *Hymns and Spiritual Songs: In Three Books*. London: Humfreys. 1st American ed. 1739, Boston: Draper.

———. 1719. *The Psalms of David: Imitated in the Language of the New Testament*. London: Clark, Ford, and Cruttenden.

Watts, Michael. 1972. "Oh You Pretty Thing: David Bowie Talks to Michael Watts." *Melody Maker* (January 22): 1, 19, 42.

Waxer, Lise. 1994. "Of Mambo Kings and Songs of Love: Dance Music in Havana and New York from the 1930s to the 1950s." *Latin American Music Review* 15 (2): 139–76.

Weeks, Jeffrey. 2009. *Sexuality*. 3rd ed. New York: Routledge.

Weigel, David. 2017. *The Show That Never Ends: The Rise and Fall of Prog Rock*. New York: Norton.

Weinstein, Deena. 1983. "Rock: Youth and Its Music." *Popular Music and Society* 9 (3): 2–15.

———. 2000. *Heavy Metal: The Music and Its Culture*. Rev. ed. New York: Da Capo. First published 1991 as *Heavy Metal: A Cultural Sociology*.

———. 2014. "Just So Stories: How Heavy Metal Got Its Name: A Cautionary Tale." *Rock Music Studies* 1 (1): 36–51.

Welding, Pete. 1975. "Ramblin' Johnny Shines." *Living Blues* (July–August): 23–25, 27–32.

Weller, Sheila. 2008. *Girls Like Us: Carole King, Joni Mitchell, Carly Simon—and the Journey of a Generation*. New York: Washington Square.

Werner, Craig. 2004. *Higher Ground; Stevie Wonder, Aretha Franklin, Curtis Mayfield and the Rise and Fall of American Soul*. New York: Crown.

Wesley, John. 1737. *A Collection of Psalms and Hymns*. Charleston: Timothy.

Whitburn, Joel. 1990. *Joel Whitburn Presents the Hot 100 Charts: The Sixties*. Menomonee Falls, WI: Record Research.

———. 1999. *Joel Whitburn's Top R&B Albums, 1965–1998*. Menomonee Falls, WI: Record Research.

———. 2004. *Joel Whitburn's Hot Dance/Disco, 1974–2003*. Menomonee Falls, WI: Record Research.

———. 2008. *Joel Whitburn Presents Hot Country Albums, 1964–2007*. Menomonee Falls, WI: Record Research.

———. 2010a. *Joel Whitburn Presents Hot R&B Songs, 1942–2010*. 6th ed. Menomonee Falls, WI: Record Research.

———. 2010b. *Joel Whitburn Presents Top Pop Albums, 1955–2009*. 7th ed. Menomonee Falls, WI: Record Research.

———. 2013a. *Joel Whitburn's Hot Country Songs, 1944–2012*. 8th ed. Menomonee Falls, WI: Record Research.

———. 2013b. *Joel Whitburn's Top Pop Singles, 1955–2012*. 14th ed. Menomonee Falls, WI: Record Research.

White, Adam. 1990. *The Billboard Book of Gold and Platinum Records*. New York: Billboard Books.

White, Charles. 1984. *The Life and Times of Little Richard: The Quasar of Rock*. New York: Harmony Books.

Whiteley, Sheila. 2000. *Women and Popular Music: Sexuality, Identity, and Subjectivity*. New York: Routledge.

Whiteley, Sheila, and Jennifer Rycenga, eds. 2006. *Queering the Popular Pitch*. New York: Routledge.

Who Sampled. 2019. Accessed March 10. www.whosampled.com.

Whyte, William Foote. 1943. *Street Corner Society: The Social Structure of an Italian Slum*. University of Chicago Press.

Wicks, Sammie Ann. 1989. "A Belated Salute to the 'Old Way' of 'Snaking' the Voice on Its (ca) 345th Birthday." *Popular Music* 8 (1): 59–96.

Wiederhorn, Jon, and Katherine Turman. 2013. *Louder Than Hell: The Definitive Oral History of Metal*. New York: It Books.

Williams, Chris. 2013. "The 40th Anniversary of the Stevie Wonder Classic, *Innervisions*." *Wax Poetics* (August 7). www.waxpoetics.com.

Williams, Katherine, and Justin A. Williams, eds. 2016. *The Cambridge Companion to the Singer-Songwriter*. Cambridge: Cambridge University Press.

Williams, Paul, ed. 2002. *The Crawdaddy! Book: Writings (and Images) from the Magazine of Rock*. Milwaukee, WI: Leonard.

Willis, Ellen. 1968. "Dylan." *Cheetah* (March): 35–37, 66–71; reprinted in Willis (2011: 1–20).

———. 1969. "Rock, Etc.: *Changes*." *New Yorker* (March 15): 173.

———. 1972. "Rock, Etc.: *My Grand Funk Problem—and Ours*." *New Yorker* (February 26): 78–81; reprinted in Willis (2011: 111–14).

———. 1976. "Janis Joplin." In J. Miller (1976: 258–61); reprinted in Willis (1981: 61–67).

———. 1978. "Beginning to See the Light: On Rock and Roll, Feminism, and Night Blindness." *Village Voice* (March 27): 21–22; reprinted in Willis (2011: 148–57).

———. 1981. *Beginning to See the Light: Pieces of a Decade*. New York: Knopf.

———. 2011. *Out of the Vinyl Deeps: Ellen Willis on Rock Music*. Edited by Nona Willis Aronowitz. Minneapolis: University of Minnesota Press.

Wilson, Brian. 2016. *I Am Brian Wilson: A Memoir*. With Ben Greenman. Boston: Da Capo.

Wilson, Ollie. 2001. "'It Don't Mean a Thing If It Ain't Got That Swing': The Relationship Between African and African American Music." In *African Roots/American Cultures: Africa in the Creation of the Americas*, edited by Sheila Walker, 153–68. Lanham, MD: Rowman and Littlefield.

Wilson, Scott. 2016. "The Fourteen Drum Machines That Shaped Modern Music." *Fact* (September 22). www.factmag.com.

Witter, Simon. 1986. "Time to Jack: The House Sound of Chicago." *i-D* (September): 76–79. (RBP)

———. 1987. "Back to Jack." *New Musical Express* (August 15): 16–17. (RBP)

Worley, Matthew. 2017. *No Future: Punk, Politics and British Youth Culture, 1976–1984*. Cambridge: Cambridge University Press.

Yagoda, Ben. 2015. *The B Side: The Death of Tin Pan Alley and the Rebirth of the Great American Song*. New York: Riverhead Books.

Yarm, Mark. 2011. *Everybody Loves Our Town: An Oral History of Grunge*. New York: Crown Archetype.

Young, James O. 2010. *Cultural Appropriation and the Arts*. Malden, MA: Wiley-Blackwell.

Zak, Albin J. 2001. *The Poetics of Rock: Cutting Tracks, Making Records*. Berkeley: University of California Press.

Zappa, Frank. 1989. *The Real Frank Zappa Book*. With Peter Occhiogrosso. New York: Poseidon.

Zbikowski, Lawrence M. 2017. *Foundations of Musical Grammar*. New York: Oxford University Press.

Zimmerman, Nadya. 2008. *Counterculture Kaleidoscope: Musical and Cultural Perspectives on Late Sixties San Francisco*. Ann Arbor: University of Michigan Press.

DISCOGRAPHY

Dates in the text with -d appended to them (for discography) are listed here.

Baker, Stuart, compiler. 2005. *Can You Jack? Chicago Acid and Experimental House, 1985–95*. Notes by Tim Lawrence. Soul Jazz SJR CD 111.

Booker, Damon, comp. 1991. *Equinox/the Beginning/Night and DA: A Retrospective Compilation*. Buzz BZZLP 106102.

Carawan, Guy, prod. 1967. *Been in the Storm So Long: Spirituals and Shouts, Children's Game Songs and Folktales*. Folkways FS 3842.

Fisk Jubilee Singers. 1997. *Fisk Jubilee Singers, in Chronological Order*. Vol. 1, *1909–1911*. Document Records DOCD 5533.

The House Sound of Chicago. 1986. DJ International/London Records LON LP22.

Indian Bottom Association. 1997. *Songs of the Old Regular Baptists: Lined-Out Hymnody from Southeastern Kentucky*. Recordings and notes by Jeff Titon. Smithsonian Folkways SFCD 40106.

J Dilla. 2014. *The King of Beats: Ma Dukes Collector's Edition Box Set*. Yancey Media Group. http://jdillathekingofbeats.com.

Parton, Dolly, Linda Ronstadt, and Emmylou Harris. 1987. *Trio*. Warner Bros. 25491-1.

Ritchie, Jean. 1954. *Kentucky Mountain Songs*. Elektra EKL-25.

——. 1956. "Nottamun Town." *Elektra Folk Sampler*. Elektra SMP-2.

——. 1961. *British Traditional Ballads in the Southern Mountains*. Vol. 2. Folkways FA-2302.

Rushton, Neil, compiler. 1990. *Bio Rhythm: "Dance Music with Bleeps."* Network Records BIO CD1.

Rushton, Neil, and Derrick May (Mayday), compilers. 1988. *Techno! The New Dance Sound of Detroit*. Notes by Stuart Cosgrove. 10 Records DIXG 75.

Smith, Bessie. 1991. *The Complete Recordings*. Vol. 2. Columbia/Legacy C2K 47471.

Son House. 2013. *Field Recordings*. Vol. 17, *Son House: Library of Congress Recordings, 1941–1942*. Recorded by Alan Lomax. Document Records DOCD-5689.

Tresor II: Berlin-Detroit, a Techno Alliance. 1993. NovaMute NoMu 14.

Valens, Ritchie. 1994. *The Ritchie Valens Story*. Del Fi Records R2 71414.

Waters, Muddy. 1993. *The Complete Plantation Recordings: The Historic 1941–42 Library of Congress Field Recordings*. Recorded by Alan Lomax and John Work. Chess CHD-9344.

FILMOGRAPHY/VIDEOGRAPHY

Dates in the text with -v appended to them (for videography) are listed here.

Ahearn, Charlie, dir. 1982. *Wild Style*. Wild Style Productions.

Archer, Wesley, dir. 1996. "Homerpalooza." *The Simpsons*. Season 7, episode 24. (May 19.) Gracie Films/Twentieth Century Fox.

Arkush, Alan, dir. 1979. *Rock 'n' Roll High School*. New World.

Ba, Ndiouga Moctar, dir. 1994. *You, Africa: Youssou N'Dour and Super Etoile, the African Tour*. Kus Productions/California Newsreel.

Badham, John, dir. 1977. *Saturday Night Fever*. Paramount/RSO.

Bainbridge, Catherine, and Alfonso Maiorana, dirs. 2017. *Rumble: The Indians Who Rocked the World*. Rezolution Pictures.

Bar-Lev, Ami, dir. 2017. *Long Strange Trip: The Untold Story of the Grateful Dead*. Amazon Studios and others.

Berg, Amy J., dir. 2016. *Janis: Little Girl Blue*. Thirteen/WNET and others. American Masters. pbs.org.

Binder, Steve. 1964. *The T.A.M.I. Show*. Electronovision Productions.

Boyd, Joe, John Head, and Gary Weis, prods. 1973. [*A Film about*] *Jimi Hendrix*. Warner Bros.

Brown, Jim, dir. 2001. *American Roots Music*. 4 episodes. Ginger Group.

——, dir. 2007. *Pete Seeger: The Power of Song*. Thirteen/WNET and others. American Masters. pbs.org.

Budman, Richard, and John Bortolotti, prods. 2008. *The Story of Rapper's Delight by Nile Rodgers*. Popboxtv.

Camalier, Greg "Freddy," dir. 2013. *Muscle Shoals: The Incredible True Story of a Small Town with a Big Sound*. Ear Goggles.

Carluccio, John, dir. 2012. *Marley Marl Classic Recipes: Eric B. and Rakim "Eric B. Is President."* dubspot.com. Posted November 28. www.youtube.com.

Crouch, William Forest, dir. 1945. *Caldonia*. Featuring Louis Jordan and his Tympany Five. Astor Pictures.

Csaky, Mick, dir. 2011. *The Godmother of Rock and Roll: Sister Rosetta Tharpe*. BBC.

Dall, Christine, dir. 1989. *Wild Women Don't Have the Blues*. Calliope Film Resources.

Demme, Jonathan, dir. 1984. *Stop Making Sense*. Cinecom Pictures.

Dubin, Charles, dir. 1957. *Mister Rock and Roll*. Aurora.

Dunn, Alexander, dir. 2015. *808: The Heart of the Beat That Changed Music*. You Know Films/Atlantic Films.

Dupre, Jeff, and Maro Chermayeff, dirs. 2016. *Soundbreaking: Stories from the Cutting Edge of Recorded Music*. 8 episodes. Higher Ground/Show of Force/PBS.

Dylan, Bob, dir. 1972. *Eat the Document*. Unreleased documentary of 1966 UK tour.

——, dir. 1978. *Renaldo and Clara*. Lombard Street Films.

Ellwood, Alison. 2013. *History of the Eagles: The Story of an American Band*. Monhegan Films.

Espar, David, and Hugh Thomson, prods. 1995. *Rock and Roll*. 10 episodes. WGBH/BBC.

Fields, Jim, and Michael Gramaglia, dirs. 2003. *End of the Century: The Story of the Ramones*. Magnolia Pictures.

Franzen, Benjamin, dir. 2009. *Copyright Criminals*. Changing Images.

Frumkin, Peter, dir. 2006. *Woody Guthrie: Ain't Got No Home*. Thirteen/WNET and others. American Masters. pbs.org.

Gordon, Robert, and Morgan Neville, dirs. 2002. *Muddy Waters: Can't Be Satisfied*. Thirteen/WNET and others. American Masters. pbs.org.

Greenfield-Sanders, Timothy, dir. 1998. *Lou Reed: Rock and Roll Heart*. Thirteen/WNET and others. American Masters. pbs.org.

Hackford, Taylor, dir. 1987. *Chuck Berry: Hail! Hail! Rock 'n' Roll*. Delilah Films. Four-DVD box set issued 2006.

Hall, Barbara J., dir. 2017. *Patsy Cline*. TH Entertainment. American Masters. pbs.org.

Hanly, Francis, dir. 2017. *Sgt. Pepper's Musical Revolution with Howard Goodall*. Huge Films.

Heyn, John, dir. 1986. *Heavy Metal Parking Lot*. Pirate Video.

Hindmarch, Carl, dir. 2001. *Pump Up the Volume*. 3 pts. Flame/Channel 4.

Hurt, Byron, dir. 2006. *Hip-Hop: Beyond Beats and Rhymes*. God Bless the Child Productions/Independent Television Service.

Johnson, Grant, dir. 1991. *Golden Age of Rock 'n' Roll*. 10 episodes. Jon Bauman Productions/A&E TV.

Johnstone, Rob, exec. prod. 2008. *Aural Amphetamine: Metallica and the Dawn of Thrash*. Prism Films/Chrome Dreams/MVD Entertainment Group.

Justman, Paul, dir. 2002. *Standing in the Shadows of Motown*. Elliott Scott Productions.

Kantor, Michael, dir. 2001. *Quincy Jones: In the Pocket*. Thirteen/WNET and others. American Masters. pbs.org.

———, dir. 2004. *Broadway: The American Musical*. 6 episodes. Thirteen/WNET.

Keshishian, Alek, dir. 1991. *Madonna: Truth or Dare*. Propaganda Films/Boy Toy.

King, Albert. 1970. "Albert King—Full Concert—09/23/70—Fillmore East." Posted November 11, 2014. www.youtube.com.

King, B. B., and others. 1993. "B. B. King, Jeff Beck, Eric Clapton, Albert Collins and Buddy Guy in Apollo Theater 1993 Part 2." Posted November 24, 2010. www.youtube.com.

King, Ben E. 1965. "Stand by Me." *Lloyd Thaxton Show* (November 1). Posted April 12, 2015. www.youtube.com.

Kohn, Joseph, dir. 1955. *Rock and Roll Revue*. Featuring Duke Ellington, Dinah Washington, Ruth Brown, Nat King Cole, and Big Joe Turner. Studio Films.

Kral, Ivan, and Amos Poe, dirs. 1976. *The Blank Generation*.

Lacy, Susan, dir. 2003. *Joni Mitchell: Woman of Heart and Mind*. Thirteen/WNET and others. American Masters. pbs.org.

———, dir. 2012. *Inventing David Geffen*. Thirteen/WNET and others. American Masters. pbs.org.

Lauro, Joe, dir. 2016. *The Big Beat: Fats Domino and the Birth of Rock 'n' Roll*. Historic Music Library. American Masters. pbs.org.

Lerner, Murray, dir. 2007. *The Other Side of the Mirror: Bob Dylan Live at the Newport Folk Festival 1963–1965*. Sony/BMG.

Lester, Richard, dir. 1964. *A Hard Day's Night*. Walter Shenson/Proscenium.

———, dir. 1965. *Help!* Walter Shenson.

Lindsay-Hogg, Michael, dir. 1970. *Let It Be*. Apple Films.

Livingston, Jennie, dir. 1990. *Paris Is Burning*. Off White Productions.

Lommel, Ulli, dir. 1979. *Blank Generation*. Featuring Richard Hell and the Voidoids. Anchor Bay Entertainment.

Lowe, Richard, and Martin Torgoff, dirs. 2011. *Planet Rock: The Story of Hip Hop and the Crack Generation*. Prodigious Media/VH1 Rock Docs.

MacMahon, Bernard, dir. 2017. *American Epic*. 3 episodes. Lo-Max Film/Thirteen Productions. pbs.org.

Magnoli, Albert, dir. 1984. *Purple Rain*. Purple Films/Warner Bros.

Markey, Dave, dir. 1992. *1991: The Year Punk Broke*. Geffen Pictures/Sonic Life/We Got Power Films.

Maysles, David, Albert Maysles, and Charlotte Zwerin, dirs. 1970. *Gimme Shelter*. Maysles Films.

McDaniels, Ralph, host. 1993. "Video Music Box Special: Censorship? Rap under Attack." *Video Music Box* (June 30), WNYC-TV.

Meeske, Brent, dir. 2001. *The End of the Road: The Final Tour '95, a Tribute*. Joint Productions/Slow Loris Films.

Miller, Jesse James, dir. 2019. *Punk*. 4 episodes. Network Entertainment/Epix. www.epix.com.

Mischer, Don, dir. 1983. *Motown 25: Yesterday, Today, Forever*. StarVista Entertainment.

MTV News Raw. n.d. *Dr. Dre*. With Kurt Loder. Posted February 22, 2011 as "Dr. Dre Rare Interviews (NWA and Death Row days)." www.youtube.com.

Murphy, Dudley, dir. 1929. *St. Louis Blues*. RKO.

NBC TV. 1993. "Report on Gangsta Rap." With Elizabeth Vargas. *Now with Tom Brokaw and Katie Couric* (December 1).

Neville, Morgan, dir. 2004. *Hank Williams: Honky Tonk Blues*. Thirteen/WNET. American Masters. pbs.org.

———, dir. 2011. *Troubadors: Carole King/James Taylor and the Rise of the Singer-Songwriter*. Thirteen/WNET and others. American Masters. pbs.org.

Paulson, John, dir. 2007. *Les Paul: Chasing Sound*. Thirteen/WNET and others. American Masters. pbs.org.

Peisch, Jeffrey, prod. 1995. *The History of Rock 'n' Roll*. 1995. 10 episodes. Time-Life/Andrew Solt/QDE.

Pennebaker, D. A., dir. 1967. *Dont Look Back*. Leacock Pennebaker.

———, dir. 1968. *Monterey Pop*. Leacock Pennebaker.

———, dir. 1973. *Ziggy Stardust and the Spiders from Mars: The Motion Picture*. Mainman/Pennebaker.

Pennebaker, D. A., and Chris Hegedus, dirs. 1986. *Jimi Plays Monterey*. Are you Experienced?/Pennebaker Associates.

Pennebaker, D. A., Chris Hegedus, and David Dawkins, dirs. 1986. *Shake! Otis at Monterey*. Pennebaker Associates.

———, dirs. 2002. *The Complete Monterey Pop Festival*. 3 DVDs. Leacock Pennebaker.

Perry, Dana Heinz, dir. 2004. *And You Don't Stop: 30 Years of Hip Hop*. 5 episodes. Perry Films/VH1.

Pollock, Sydney, dir. 2018. *Amazing Grace*. Al's Records and Tapes.

Price, Will, dir. 1956. *Rock, Rock, Rock!* Vanguard.

Questlove (Ahmir Thompson). 2012. "Questlove Toasts the Beastie Boys Induction." *Rolling Stone* (April 17). www.youtube.com.

Quinn, Matt. 2001. *Gouge*. TalkBack Production/Channel 4 (U.K.).

Rachman, Paul, dir. 2006. *American Hardcore: The History of American Punk Rock, 1980–1986*. AHC.

Ramos, Josell, dir. 2003. *Maestro*. ARTrution.

Raymond, Alan, and Susan Raymond, dirs. 1987. *Elvis '56*. Lightyear Entertainment.

Rosow, Eugene, and Howard Dratch, dirs. 1989. *Routes of Rhythm*. 3 parts. Cultural Research/Communications/KCET TV.

Scorsese, Martin, dir. 1978. *The Last Waltz*. United Artists.

———, dir. 2005. *No Direction Home: Bob Dylan*. Thirteen/WNET and others. American Masters. pbs.org.

Scott, George, dir. 2016. *Carole King: Natural Woman*. 1515 Productions. American Masters. pbs.org.

Sears, Fred F., dir. 1956. *Rock around the Clock*. Clover Productions.

———, dir. 1957. *Don't Knock the Rock*. Clover Productions.

Senate Commerce, Science and Transportation Committee. 1985. "Rock Lyrics Record Labelling." (September 19). www.c-span.org.

Smeaton, Bob, dir. 2013. *Jimi Hendrix: Hear My Train A Comin'*. Thirteen/WNET and others. American Masters. pbs.org.

Smeaton, Bob, and Geoff Wonfor, dirs. 1996. *The Beatles Anthology*. 8 episodes. Apple Corps.

Smith, Yvonne, dir. 1992. *Ray Charles: Genius of Soul*. Thirteen/WNET and others. American Masters. pbs.org.

Solt, Andrew, and Greg Vines, prods. 2011. *Ed Sullivan's Rock 'n' Roll Classics*. 12 DVDs. SOFA Entertainment. www.edsullivan.com.

Soul Train. 1972. "Love Train O'Jays Soul Train Dance Contest." Posted November 17, 2011. www.youtube.com.

Spheeris, Penelope, dir. 1981. *The Decline of Western Civilization*. Spheeris Films.

———, dir. 1988a. *The Decline of Western Civilization*. Part 2, *The Metal Years*. I.R.S. World Media.

———, dir. 1998b. *The Decline of Western Civilization*. Part 3. Spheeris Films.

Splunteren, Bram van, dir. 1986. *Big Fun in the Big Town*. Five Day Weekend.

Spooner, James, dir. 2003. *Afro-Punk*. Afro-Punk Films.

Springsteen, Bruce. 2001. *Bruce Springsteen: Video Anthology, 1978–2000*. Thrill Hill Productions/Columbia Music Video.

Stein, Mandy, dir. 2009. *Burning Down the House: The Story of CBGB*. Plain Jane Productions.

Steinberg, Susan, dir. 2007. *Atlantic Records: The House That Ahmet Built*. Thirteen/ WNET and others. American Masters. pbs.org.

Stuart, Mel. 1973. *Wattstax*. Stax Films/Wolper Pictures.

Sumner, Jake, dir. 2017. *I Was There When House Took over the World*. 2 episodes. Pi Studios/Channel 4.

Talking Heads. 2011. *Talking Heads: Chronology*. Deluxe ed. Eagle Vision.

Tedesco, Danny, dir. 2008. *The Wrecking Crew*. Lunch Box Entertainment.

Temple, Julien, dir. 1980. *The Great Rock 'n' Roll Swindle*. Boyd's Company/Virgin Films.

——, dir. 2000. *The Filth and the Fury*. Jersey Shore/Nitrate Film.

Thorpe, David, dir. 2014. *Do I Sound Gay?* ThinkThorpe/Little Punk.

Wadleigh, Michael, dir. 1970. *Woodstock: Three Days of Peace and Music*. Wadleigh-Maurice.

Warren, Michael John, dir. 2006. *Heavy: The Story of Metal*. 4 episodes. 441/VH1.

Whalley, Ben, dir. 2009. *Synth Britannia*. BBC4.

Wharton, Mary, prod. 2002. *Elvis Lives*. NBC TV and others.

——, dir. 2009. *Joan Baez: How Sweet the Sound*. Thirteen/WNET. American Masters. pbs.org.

Wheeler, Darby, Sam Dunn, and Scot McFadyen, dirs. 2016–18. *Hip-Hop Evolution*. 8 episodes. Banger Films.

Zappa, Frank. 1987. "Interview." *The Cutting Edge, MTV* (June 28).

Zimmy, Thom, dir. 2018. *Elvis Presley: The Searcher*. 2 pts. HBO/Sony.

Page numbers in *italics* refer to figures.

Asylum Records, 122

A Taste of Honey, 170

"A Teenager in Love," 66, *211*

At Fillmore East, 124, *234*

Atkins, Cholly, 68, 303

Atkins, Juan, 174–75. *See also* Belleville Three, The; Cybotron

Atlantic Records: recording history, 16, 16n16, 32, 79–81, *200*, 321; songwriting, 60, 64

A Tribe Called Quest, 181, *253*

AT&T. *See* American Telephone and Telegraph (AT&T)

"At the Hop," 65

audion, 10–11. *See also* radio

audio-storage formats, 181, *196*; commercial recordings, 16, 44; early forms of, 6–8

Austin City Limits (television program), 125

Autobahn: album, 171, *233*; song, 171, 172

Autry, Gene, 38–39

Avalon, Frankie, 65, 73, *212*

"Ave Maria," 309

Average White Band, *232*

awards, 14–15, 323. *See* American Music Awards; Grammy Awards; Rock and Roll Hall of Fame

Axis: Bold as Love, 98, *224*

Axton, Hoyt, 90

B. T. Express, 129

B-52s, The, 139, 140–41

"Baby Love," 68, *214*

Bach, J. S., 18, 157, 291–92, 294

Bacharach, Burt, 4, 64, 65, *211*. *See also* Brill Building, The

Bachman-Turner Overdrive, *234*

"Backstabbers," 127

Backstreet Boys, 181

Bad: album, 161, *250*; music video, 314

Bad Boy (record label), *244*

Bad Brains, 170, *237, 252n*

Bad Company, *234*

"Bad Girls," 131, 134

Baez, Joan, 63, 69, 71, 89, 94, 113–14, *215*

Baker, Arthur, 20, 145, 146, 166

Baker, Ginger, 98. *See also* Cream

Baker, LaVern, 32, 42, 47–48, *200, 203, 208*

Baker, Susan. *See* Parents Music Resource Center (PMRC)

Bakersfield (California), 121. *See also* country and western

Ball, David, 172. *See also* Soft Cell

"Ballad of a Thin Man," 310

Ballard, Florence, *222*

Ballard, Hank, *225*, 273

Ballion, Susan "Siouxsie Sioux," 141. *See also* Siouxsie and the Banshees

Bambaataa, Afrika, 19, 20, 108, 145–47, 172–73, *244–45*

Bananarama, *249*

Band, The, 88, 90, *226*; country rock, 118, 120, 122

Band Aid, 164–65, *251*

Band of Gypsys, 224

Bangs, Lester, 102, 108, 136, 156

banjo, 37, 117, 289

Baraka, Amiri, 25, 102, 278. See also *Blues People*

Barbour, J. Berni, 41

Barnes, Dee, 153

Barretto, Ray, 285

Barry, Jeff, 65, 67, *211*. *See also* Brill Building, The

Bartos, Karl, 173. *See also* Kraftwerk

Bascomb, Manhattan Paul, 41

Basement Tapes, The, 120, *216*

bass guitar, 106, 277–78, 301; women players, 169–70, *239n*, 240

Batten, Jennifer, 271

"Black Magic Woman," 87

Blackmore, Ritchie, 157

black music (African music aesthetic), 299. *See also* African American music

Black Music (book), 278

Black Panther Party, 83, 310–11

Black Power: book, 278; phrase, 83, 314

black (racial term): African diaspora, 278; "blackness," 276–78, 312–13, 315–16. *See also* African Americans

Black Reign, 149

Black Sabbath, 156–58, 165–66, *246,* 296

Blackstar, 110

Blackwell, Otis, 54. *See also* Presley, Elvis

Blaine, Hal, 64. *See* Wrecking Crew, The

Blank Generation, 135, *237*

Blaxploitation (film term), 105, *231*

Bleach, 168, *252*

Blige, Mary J., 309

Blind Faith, 98

Blonde on Blonde, 120, *216*

Blondie: album, 139, 141, *237, 239;* band, 135, 137, 139, 141, 143, *237*

Blood, Sweat, and Tears, 142, *241*

Blood on the Tracks, 116, *216*

Bloomfield, Mike, 86

Blossoms, The, 67

Blow, Kurtis, 146, 147, *244*

Blow (film), 154

"Blowin' in the Wind," 69, 71, 81, 88, 126, *213, 216*

Blue, 114, 115

Blue Cheer, *246*

bluegrass, 39, 295. *See also* country and western

"Blue Moon of Kentucky," 39, 52

blue note (musical quality), 304

Blue Öyster Cult, 156, 158

blues, 25–29, *202,* 291, 305; Chicago, 31; country, 26, 28; influence on British rock bands, 85–86; jump, 30–31; lyrics, 29; musical form, 28; white singers, 289, 318; women singers, 27–28

Blues Breakers with Eric Clapton, 87

Blues Jam at Chess/Fleetwood Mac in Chicago, 87

Blues Legacies and Black Feminism (book), 29–30. *See also* Davis, Angela

Blues People (book), 25, 29

"Blue Suede Shoes," 42, 57

"Blue Yodel," *189,* 289

Blyden, Edward W., 276

BMI. *See* Broadcast Music, Inc.

Bob B. Soxx and the Blue Jeans, 67

Bobbettes, The, 66

Bob Dylan, 215, 216, 311

Bo Diddley: album, 59; song, 59, 306. *See also* Diddley, Bo

"Bohemian Rhapsody," 112

Bolan, Marc, 109. *See also* T. Rex

Bomb Squad, The, 148, *231*

Bono, *251. See also* U2

boogaloo, 285

"Boogie Chillen," 29, 295

Boogie Down Productions, 148

"Boogie on Reggae Woman," 106

"Boogie Wonderland," 134

boogie woogie, 29–31, 51, 59, 296. *See also* blues

"Boogie Woogie Stomp," 31

Booker T. and the MGs, 79, 86, 102, *200, 226, 227*

Boomtown Rats, The, 164

Boone, Pat, 48–49, *208, 212,* 317

"Borderline," 163

"Born in the USA," 21

"Born to Be Wild," 156, *224*

Born to Run (album and song), 116–17, *250*

Boston (band), 113, 139

"Both Sides Now," 114

Fame (recording studio), 69, 79–80, 88, 99
Fanny, *239*
Farley "Jackmaster Funk" Keith 178, 179
Farm Aid, 166, *251*
"Farther Along," 294, 295
Fathers and Sons, 86, *202*
"Fat Man, The," 50–51
Fat of the Land, The, 172
FCC. *See* Federal Communications
    Commission
Fear of a Black Planet, 148, *243, 245*
Federal Communications Commission
    (FCC), 12, 43, *190*
Feliciano, José, 285–86
feminism, 114, 163
Fender guitars and amps, 17–18, 121,
    121n21, 122, *196*
Ferguson, Maynard, *242*
Ferry, Brian, 111. *See* Roxy Music
festivals, 100–101, 108, 124, 135, 171, 278
fiddle, 37, 117, 289, 293
"Fight the Power," 55, 105, 148, *231, 245,*
    258
Fillmore, 86–87, 95, 121, 124
Filthy Fifteen, 166
"Fingertips Part 2," 126, *213*
"Fire and Rain," 115
Firebird Suite, The, 20
Fisk Jubilee Singers, The, 290, 309
Fitzgerald, Ella, *203, 241*
Flack, Roberta, *215*
"Flashlight," 106
Flatt, Lester, 39
Fleetwood Mac, 87
Flock of Seagulls, A, *249*
Flores, Danny, 284
"Flower Punk," 93, 136
Flür, Wolfgang, 172. *See also* Kraftwerk
Flying Burrito Brothers, The, 118n13, 119,
    120, 122, *235*

folk: early country music, 38; urban revival,
    69–72. *See also* folk rock; hillbilly
folk rock, 84, 89–91, 117, *235*; naming in
    Billboard, 90
Folkways (record label), 70
Fontana, D. J., 52
Foo Fighters, 169
Forbes (magazine), 180
Ford, Lita, 141. *See also* Runaways, The
Foreigner, 113, 139, *230*
"Forever Young," 90
"For Your Love," 98, *221*
Foster, Stephen, 6
Four Seasons, The, 66, *230*
Four Tops, The, *214, 230*
Francis, Connie, 65, *212*
Frankie Goes to Hollywood, *249*
Franklin, Aretha, 63, 80, *200, 204, 215,*
    229, 240, 295; covers, 88, 120; gospel,
    35, 37, 304–5; soul, 78–81, 84, 94,
    223
Freak Out!, 84, 92, *233*
Freddie and the Dreamers, *221*
Freed, Alan, 15, 42, 44–46, 48, 58; payola,
    60–61
Freewheelin' Bob Dylan, The, 71, 89, *216*
frequency modulation, 19. *See also*
    synthesizer
Fresh, Doug E., 148
Fresh Cream, 98, 156
Frey, Glenn, 115–16, 122, *235. See also*
    Eagles, The
Fripp, Robert, 107, *233. See also* King
    Crimson
"Fuck tha Police," 150
Fugees, The, 181, *253*
Fugs, The, 108
Fulfillingness' First Finale, 126
"Fun, Fun, Fun," 4, *217*
funk, 13–14, 96–97, 104, *225, 232;*

influence on hip hop, 106–7; sound, 277; style, 105–7

Funkadelic. *See* Parliament Funkadelic

Funk Brothers, The, 68

Funkentelechy vs. the Placebo Syndrome, 106

"Funky Drummer," 97, *225, 245,* 302n18

Furay, Richie, 118, 119, *235. See also* Poco

Furious Five, The, 146–47, *244*

Gabriel, Peter, 160, *249, 251. See also* Genesis

Gallery, The, 130

Gamble, Kenneth, 127

Gang of Four, *237*

gangs, 154–55. *See also* rap

Gap Band, *232*

garage band, 137. *See also* punk

Garcia, Jerry, 122, 124, *235. See also* Grateful Dead, The

Gardner, Carl, 318. *See also* Coasters, The

Garfunkel, Art, 117, *215. See* Simon and Garfunkel

Garland, Phyl, 102, 313–14

Gates, Henry Louis, Jr., 152

gay, 77, 111, 130-34, 177, 180, *238,* 261, 268–70

Gaye, Marvin, 19, 63, 69, 80, *204, 213, 229*

Gaynor, Gloria, 129, 131, 134, *236*

"Gee," 46–47

Geffen, David, 122

Geldoff, Bob, 164, *251. See also* Boomtown Rats, The

General Electric (GE), 11

Genesis, 107, 160, 164, *226, 233*

Germany, 24, 74, 108, 172, 173, *233,* 291–92

Gerry and the Pacemakers, *221*

Gershwin, George, 24, *188,* 313–14

Gershwin, Ira, 24, 313–14

"Get Off of My Cloud," *217,* 307

Getz, Stan, *241*

Ghostface Killah, 181, *254. See also* Wu-Tang Clan

Gibbons, Walter, 128–29

Gibbs, Georgia, 47–48, *208*

Gibson, Bob, 71

Gibson Guitar Corporation, 16–17, *196*

Gilbert, W. S., 24

Gilded Palace of Sin, 119

Gilliland, Henry C., 38

Gimme Shelter (documentary), 101

Ginsberg, Allen, 90

girl groups, 63, 66–67, 94, 140–41

"Girl You Need a Change of Mind," 128

"Give Peace a Chance," 258

"Glad to Be Gay," 268

glam rock, 109–12; queer identity, 109, 268

Gleason, Ralph J., 101. *See Rolling Stone* (magazine)

"God Save the Queen," 135, 264

Goffin, Gerry, 65, 67, *211. See also* Brill Building, The

Go-Gos, The, 140–41

Goldie, 176

Goldmind (record label), *244*

"Goodnight Irene," 70

"Good Rockin' Tonight," 30, 41, 52, 168

"Good Times," 105, 142–43, 146

"Good Vibrations," 73, 92, *217*

Gordon, Kim, 169. *See also* Sonic Youth

Gordy, Jr., Berry, 67–69, *200. See also* Motown Records

Gore, Tipper. *See* Parents Music Resource Center (PMRC)

gospel, 34–37, 305; composers, 35–36; influence on soul, 78–79, 81

Gospel Singers Convention, 36

goth, 265

Gottehrer, Richard, 137. *See also* Sire Records

Gotti, Irv, 4

"Working Day and Night," 271
Workingman's Dead, 124
World War II, 9, 45
Woronov, Mary, 266
Worrell, Bernie, 105, 106, 143. *See also* Parliament Funkadelic
"Worried Man Blues," 289
"Wouldn't It Be Nice," 73, *217*
Wray, Link, 72, 286
Wrecking Crew, The, 64, 169–70. *See also* Spector, Phil
Wu-Tang Clan, 21, 181, *253, 254*
Wyman, Bill, 77, 85, *222. See also* Rolling Stones, The

X (band), 170, *237*

"Yakety Yak," 60, *211*
Yankovic, Weird Al, 314
Yardbirds, The, 49, 76, 77, 98, 156, 157, *221*
Yellow Magic Orchestra, 19, 173, 174
Yellow Submarine, 75, *220*
Yes, 18, 107, 108, *226, 233*
"Y.M.C.A," 133

Yo! MTV Raps (television program), 150, *191*, 313
"You Better Not Do That," 121
"You Can't Hurry Love," 68, *214*
Young, Neil, 115, 116, 122, 166, *215, 235. See also* Crosby, Stills, Nash, and Young
Young, Rusty, 119, 122, 125. *See also* Poco
"Young Blood," 60, 318
"Your Cheatin' Heart," 39
"You're So Vain," 114
"Your Love," 178
"You Send Me," 81
"You Showed Me," 149
youth, 262–66, 322; consumer market, 263, 287–88; scholarship on, 264–65; youth culture, 263n1. *See also* teenagers
"You've Got a Friend," 115
"You've Lost That Lovin' Feeling," 65, 82, *211*

Zappa, Frank (and the Mothers of Invention), 84, 92, 93, 108, 136, 167, *233*
Ziggy Stardust. See Rise and Fall of Ziggy Stardust and the Spiders from Mars, The
Zombies, The, 102, *221, 226*
ZZ Top, *234,* 296

ERIC CHARRY is professor of music at Wesleyan University. He is the author of *Mande Music* and editor of *Hip Hop Africa*.